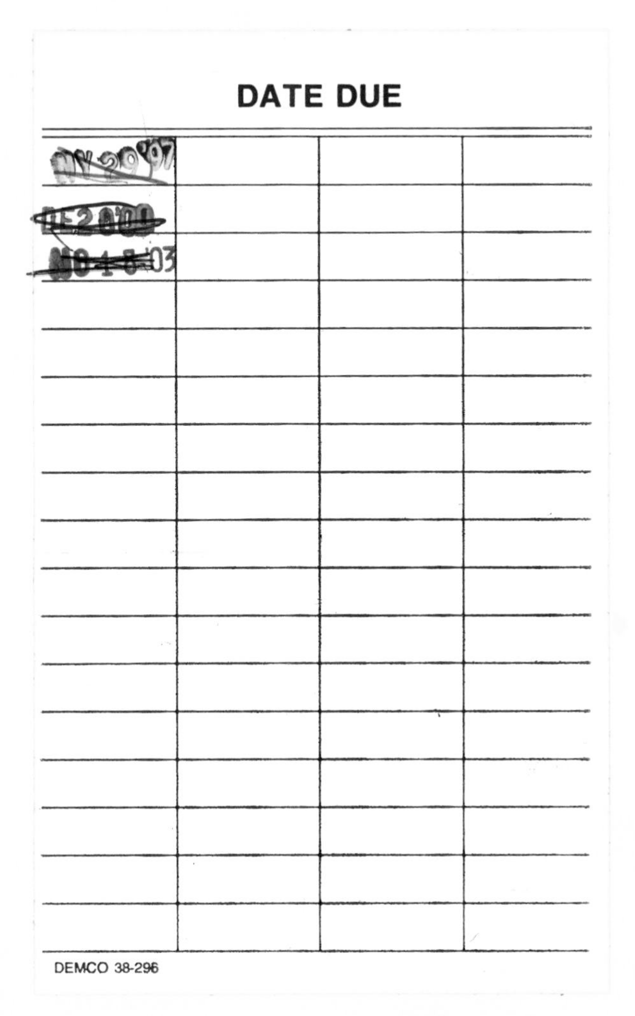
DATE DUE
DEMCO 38-296

THE POLITICS OF DIVERSITY

The POLITICS *of* DIVERSITY

Immigration, Resistance, and Change in Monterey Park, California

JOHN HORTON
with the assistance of
Jose Calderon, Mary Pardo, Leland Saito,
Linda Shaw, and Yen-Fen Tseng

TEMPLE UNIVERSITY PRESS  *Philadelphia*

Temple University Press, Philadelphia 19122

Published 1995
Printed in the United States of America

♾ The paper used in this book meets the requirements of the American National Standard for Information Sciences—Permanence of Paper for Printed Library Materials, ANSI Z39.48-1984

Text design by Arlene Putterman

Library of Congress Cataloging-in-Publication Data
Horton, John, 1932–
The politics of diversity : immigration, resistance, and change in Montery Park, California / John Horton ; with the assistance of Jose Calderon . . . [et al.].
p. cm.
Includes bibliographical references and index.
ISBN 1-56639-327-2 (alk. paper). — ISBN 1-56639-328-0 (pbk. : alk. paper)
1. Monterey Park (Calif.)—Social conditions. 2. Chinese Americans—California—Monterey Park—Social conditions. 3. Immigrants—California—Monterey Park—Ethnic identity. 4. Pluralism (Social science)—California—Monterey Park. I. Calderon, Jose. II. Title.
HN80.M66H67 1995
306′.09794′76—dc20 94-23618

Contents

Maps, Tables, and Photographs *vii*

Acknowledgments *ix*

Introduction
MULTIETHNIC L.A. *3*

1
FROM MONTEREY PARK TO LITTLE TAIPEI *10*

2
BUILDING COMMUNITY AT THE GRASSROOTS *35*

3
POLITICAL BREAKS AND TRANSITIONS *59*

4
THE BACKLASH: SLOW GROWTH AND ENGLISH ONLY *79*

5
THE STRUGGLE FOR MINORITY AND IMMIGRANT RIGHTS *101*

6
FROM NATIVISM TO ETHNIC AND INTERETHNIC POLITICS *123*

7
THE DILEMMAS OF DIVERSITY *149*

8
CRISIS OF AMERICAN, ETHNIC, AND IMMIGRANT IDENTITIES *185*

9
NEGOTIATING A CULTURE OF DIVERSITY *215*

10
THE PRACTICE AND POLITICS OF DIVERSITY *226*

Notes *239*

Index *261*

Maps, Tables, and Photographs

MAPS
1 Monterey Park Surrounded by Los Angeles Freeways *2*
2 Settlement Pattern of Earlier Immigrants Who Arrived Before 1980 as Percentage of Total Population by Census Tract in Central Los Angeles County, 1990 *16*
3 Settlement Pattern of Recent Immigrants Who Arrived Between 1980 and 1990 as Percentage of Total Population by Census Tract in Central Los Angeles County, 1990 *17*

TABLES
1 Ethnic Change in Monterey Park, 1960–1990 *12*
2 The Changing Asian Population of Monterey Park, 1970–1990 *12*
3 Ethnic Newcomers and Established Residents in Monterey Park, Rosemead, and South San Gabriel *19*
4 Taiwanese Immigration to Selected U.S. ZIP Code Regions, Fiscal Years 1983–1990 *23*
5 Selected Social Characteristics of U.S.- and Foreign-Born Residents of Monterey Park, Rosemead, and South San Gabriel *25*
6 Selected Social Characteristics of Chinese Immigrants by Place of Birth and Time of Immigration in Monterey Park, Rosemead, and South San Gabriel *26*
7 Ethnicity and Status in the Monterey Park Sports Club, 1988–1989 Basketball Season *44*
8 Candidate Preference and Voter Profile by Ethnicity, Monterey Park Municipal Elections, April 12, 1988 *115*
9 Patterns of Ethnic Empowerment, Monterey Park Municipal Elections, April 10, 1990 *140*
10 Candidate Preference and Voter Profile by Ethnicity, Monterey Park Municipal Elections, April 10, 1990 *143*
11 Comparison of Anglo Supporters of Hatch and Kiang in Monterey Park Municipal Elections, April 10, 1990 *146*

12 Ethnic Composition of Registered Voters in 1993 and Turnout in the Monterey Park Municipal Elections, April 14, 1992 *170*
13 Political Profile of Chinese American Voters by Nativity and Length of Residence, Monterey Park Municipal Elections, April 10, 1990 *172*

PHOTOGRAPHS *by Martin A. Sugarman follow page 126*

Acknowledgments

THIS PROJECT could not have come about without the efforts of the core research team: Jose Calderon, Mary Pardo, Leland Saito, Linda Shaw, and Yen-Fen Tseng. Although I wrote the text and am ultimately responsible for the analysis, much of the research and many of the ideas embedded in the analysis emerged from our day-to-day interactions and discussions.

Many other people participated at one time or another in the project. Lucie Cheng was involved at the early stages and freely offered advice and encouragement. Liangwen Kuo, Yen Espiritu, Jerry Kimery, and Cathrine Lee contributed to the fieldwork, along with a group of UCLA graduate students and undergraduates who carried out two exit polls. Ping-Chung Hsiung, Eun-Jin Lee, and Philip Yang contributed to the analysis of electoral and census data. Manuel Moreno-Evans was always there as a friend and colleague to provide intellectual and technical guidance regarding research on immigration. Michelle di Miscio, Connie To, and Lyndon Torres gave technical assistance and became part of our extended research family. Felix Lin and Terri Yachen Peng translated documents written in Chinese. With the skills of a sociologist and documentary photographer, Martin A. Sugarman showed me Monterey Park through the lens of his camera.

Wendy Dishman, William James Gibson, Patrick McCloskey, Carol Mithers, Nancy Stein, and Margaret Zamudio read the manuscript at various stages of disorder and struggled to give it order and clarity.

Special thanks are owed to the work of Charles Choy Wong, who was among the first to understand the historical significance of Monterey Park, so different from the Chinatowns of old. I also had the advantage of reading Timothy P. Fong's dissertation and book on Monterey Park, and benefited much from his understanding of the chronology of local events and critical evaluation of theories of immigrant incorporation and ethnic formation.

Parts of the text originally appeared in John Horton, "The Politics of Diversity in Monterey Park, California," in *Structuring Diversity: Ethnographic Perspectives on the New Immigration,* edited by Louise Lamphere (Chicago: University of Chicago Press, 1992); and in John Horton, "The Politics of Ethnic Change: Grass-Roots Responses to Economic

Restructuring in Monterey Park, California," *Urban Geography* 10 (1989).

Generous financial assistance was provided by the National Changing Relations Project of the Ford Foundation and by the Academic Senate, the Institute of American Cultures, and the Asian American Studies Center of the University of California at Los Angeles. I especially want to thank the Center for providing us with a base at UCLA, a place to work, secretarial assistance, and a socially committed and scholarly environment. Also, I am indebted to the Board of the National Changing Relations Project, particularly Robert Bach, Karen Ito, and Louise Lamphere, for helping me to understand immigrant incorporation as a process of interaction between newcomers and established residents.

This book is about interaction and is the result of five years of interaction with the people we met in Monterey Park—community activists; residents met casually in the streets, stores, and parks; the cooperative staff of City Hall. I give them very special collective thanks, for their deeds and names are too numerous to list. Remarkably patient with our persistent presence, residents even invited us to their meetings and homes, offering trust, insight, and proof that what the signs say is true: Monterey Park is "a city with a heart." Given the variety and force of local viewpoints, including my own, I hope that some residents will see their own lives honestly portrayed and feel a bit of the pride that I felt. This positive story needs to be told in a world that must learn to profit and prosper from immigration and ethnic diversity.

My editor, Michael Ames, deserves a special award for his patience, encouragement, and advice, as does Jane Barry for her careful and sensitive editing. Finally, I have to thank my life companion and friends—my personal, unfailing network of support—for putting up with all my stress and complaining during the birth process and for assuring me that one day this book would come forth.

THE POLITICS OF DIVERSITY

Map 1 *Monterey Park Surrounded by Los Angeles Freeways*

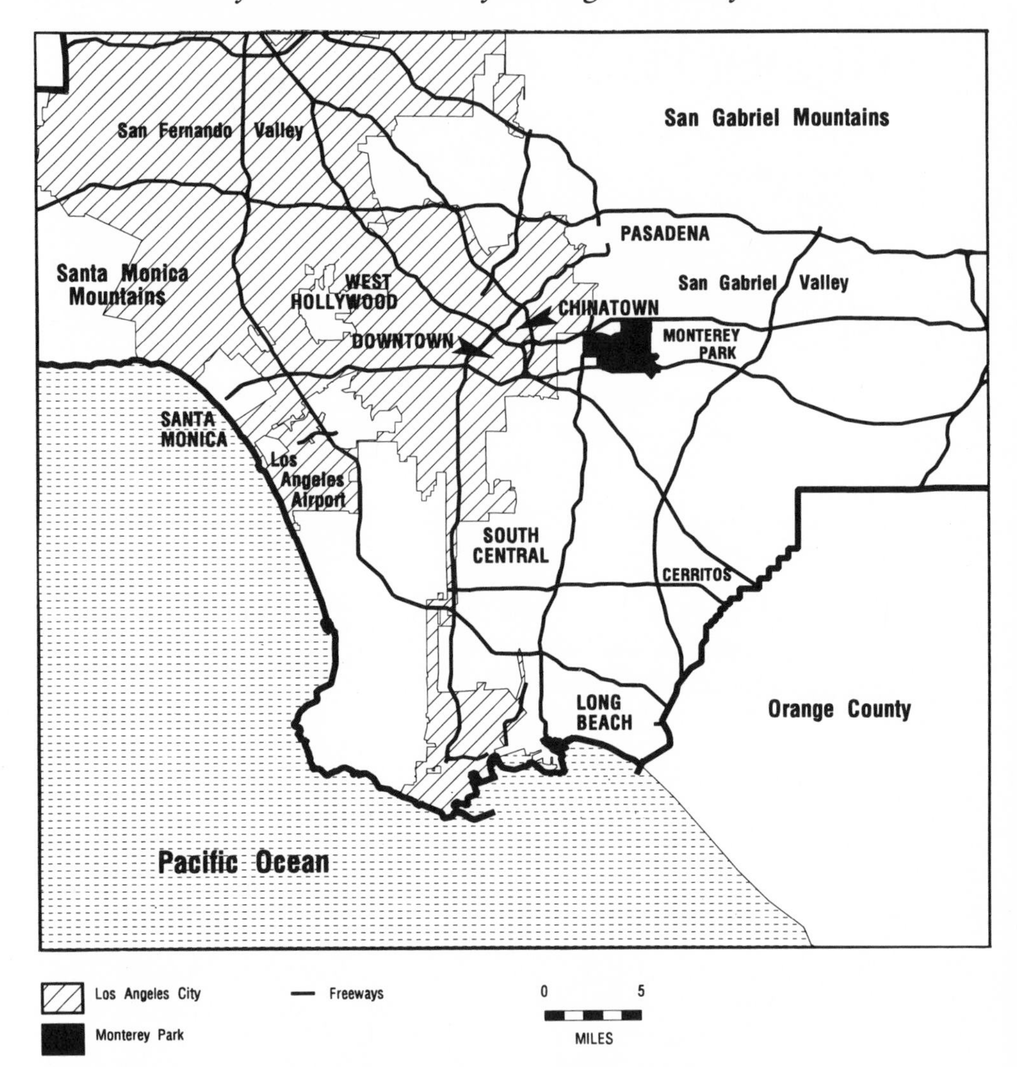

Source: Prepared by the Urban Research Section of Los Angeles County.

Introduction

MULTIETHNIC L.A.

Can we get along?
—Rodney King

LOS ANGELES is the stuff of dreams and nightmares, a production of film frames, media bytes, and marketable mythologies. In the 1980s, there was the tourist-enticing image of L.A. as a model of economic growth and the live-and-let-live multiculturalism of a vibrant city internationalized by immigrants from Asia, Africa, Mexico, Central America, and the Middle East. Then, in the 1990s, there were the riots, economic depression, and the "discovery" that immigrants were poisoning the wells of paradise.[1] The boosters of sunny diversity grew silent before the doomsayers proclaiming L.A. to be America's capital of ethnic conflict and nativist hostility toward newcomers who cost too much, take away jobs, and threaten the sanctity of the English language and Anglo culture.

Shifting rapidly from optimism to pessimism about immigration and diversity, the image-makers gloss over the variety and complexity of relations between ethnic groups and between newcomers and natives in local settings, the everyday microcosms of global transitions. This book is about one of those microcosms in Los Angeles County—Monterey Park, a multiethnic suburb transformed by immigration into the mainland's first majority-Asian city.

The inhabitants, thrust together by world demographic and economic forces, are mostly middle-class Chinese newcomers and native-born Anglo, Mexican American, and Asian American old-timers. Our story is about their interactions in neighborhoods, clubs, and political arenas. The unfinished story begins in the mid-1980s with tension between newcomers and established residents and continues to the recent subsidence of nativism into the shifting class and ethnic alignments that make up the evolving politics of diversity. One theme is immigrant incorporation, in this case a two-way street that changed both newcomers and old-timers. Another theme is the reconstruction of what it means to be immigrant, ethnic, and American in an increasingly multiethnic United

States. Monterey Park and the surrounding region of Asian immigration are interesting precisely because they are historically new and vital contexts for the negotiation and formation of Pacific Rim politics and identities.

I first visited Monterey Park on July 4, 1987, to see what being American meant in a bedroom community that was becoming a Pacific Rim city. At first glance, the "traditional" celebration in Barnes Park looked like a nostalgic reenactment of the "good old days" of small-town Middle America—picnickers stretched out on the sloping green, kids playing baseball, a band pumping out a Sousa march. But behind the scenes there had been a battle over the meaning of tradition. On one side, white conservatives, fearing the Balkanization and destruction of their town, had revived a moribund Fourth of July celebration in 1986 as a lesson in Americanism. On the other side, a mix of Asians and Latinos, no less patriotic and American than the whites, were determined to put their stamp on the event, including the food. "Should we have hot dogs only? What about egg rolls and tacos?" In 1987 the entertainment was multiethnic, but hot dogs were enjoying a temporary victory in an ongoing battle, conducted on many fronts, to determine the meaning of American identity under the new conditions of immigration and ethnic diversity.

All fronts converged on City Hall, the ultimate arena for struggles over representation, revenues, land use, and tradition. The arrival of newcomers and their businesses had undermined the old white power structure and unleashed new political actors who were taking stands for and against change: at one pole, angry resisters of immigration and the rapid, uncontrolled pace of economic development; at the other pole, women, minorities, and newcomers challenging traditional white male political dominance and pressing for inclusion and change. In the mid-1980s, the resisters were gaining the upper hand through popular slow-growth and Official English movements and putting immigrants and their supporters among established residents on the defensive.

The media were fascinated by the tensions and conflict. Residents, ever suspicious of the interpretations of outsiders, were dealing with the reality of change in their own ways. They had a more complex and, in many ways, a more promising message, and it contained lessons for other communities on the road to change. One lesson was about the possibilities of coalition and cooperation rather than confrontation and conflict under the stressful conditions of great racial, ethnic, and linguistic diversity. A second lesson, closely related to the first, was about the negotiated and fluctuating meaning of all these terms that we tend to take for granted.

Fortunately, we had opportunity to observe and listen to local residents. In 1988 and 1989, a multiethnic, multilingual team of six UCLA sociologists (two professors and four graduate students, now themselves professors) came together to investigate political and social relations between newcomers and established residents in Monterey Park.[2] We embodied some of the diversity we were trying to understand.

Yen-Fen Tseng, a Taiwanese immigrant, because of her language and cultural background had special access to recent immigrants and their organizations. She monitored the Chinese media, conducted interviews with immigrants, and observed them in civic organizations and other settings involving established residents. John Horton, being a white senior, had greater access to established Anglo residents in spite of his civil rights activism. As the "professor" and principal investigator, he led discussions of research findings in civic organizations and political clubs, and during the city-sponsored "Harmony Week." Mary Pardo focused on the experience and political participation of women, particularly Latinas, in electoral and neighborhood politics. Leland Saito followed local struggles to control development and explored how the Chinese immigration was both a problem and a resource for the development of Asian American politics. Jose Calderon, a resident of Monterey Park and a community organizer, was involved in the city at many levels, and had both a practical and a theoretical interest in Latino and interethnic politics. He was responsible for getting us interested in Monterey Park in the first place. Linda Shaw, our primary field trainer, had to contend with all of our observations. She deepened our understanding and practice of ethnography.

As a team, we worked well together and were changed by our collective experience. Each of us subsequently followed a particular strand of the original study that committed us to understanding and fostering the cultural and political connections made between people seemingly divided by ethnicity and immigrant or native status.[3] The project came very close to what we thought sociological research should be: collective and participatory, directed to the big issues of demographic, economic, and political change, yet firmly grounded in the complexities of local life.

The most intense years of team fieldwork were 1988 to 1990, and the core of our data comes from that period. During those years, we hung out a lot with residents, talking, driving, shopping, eating at Chinese restaurants, and watching the flow of daily events. Some of us got involved in community projects: working for the establishment of a day care center, preparing for a festival, or joining local organizations, like the West San Gabriel Valley Asian Pacific Democratic Club, the United Democratic Club, the League of United Latin American Citizens, the Historical Society, and a neighborhood watch association. Other team members adopted more distanced research roles in the course of following the lively and unpredictable course of political events. Whatever the depth of our involvement was, we always identified ourselves as researchers from UCLA who were studying everyday political and social life in Monterey Park.

I was primarily responsible for the last phase of research (1990–1994), which documented key political events. The results of our research were hundreds of pages of field notes, more than ninety taped interviews with local activists, reviews of Chinese and English newspapers, and quantitative data from two exit polls and the census.[4] The project depended on labor-intensive field work and the openness and patience of the people of Monterey Park. They were usually generous with their time, and most trusted us to tell more than one side of the Monterey Park story.

Capturing the many voices of Monterey Park was a challenge. We relied on the method of ethnography: observing interactions between newcomers and established residents and participating in local political networks in an effort to understand what was happening from the perspectives of the participants. The diversity of our team and the people of Monterey Park encouraged dialogue among fieldworkers and between researchers and residents, forcing us to see different perspectives and to negotiate the meaning of what we saw. During a neighborhood survey, for example, a fourth-generation Japanese American criticized an Anglo member of the team for asking an Asian American resident if he spoke English: "Would you ask any white the same question?" On another occasion, a Latino politician making the rounds at a Chinese New Year celebration sponsored by the Chamber of Commerce jokingly said to his Latino friends, "Don't bother talking to that researcher, he's only interested in Chinese." Latinos, although the largest ethnic majority in the region, often feel ignored in the discussion of Chinese immigrant and Anglo relations. Anglos also had to be understood from their own perspectives. Thus an Anglo researcher explained to a Latino colleague why a resident bristled at being called white, Anglo, or Euro-American: "He's used to being an unhyphenated 'American'—not just a piece in the ethnic mosaic, but the defining pattern."

Inevitably, our attempt to record a multitude of voices was limited by the rhythm of events, our necessarily selective observations, who we were in terms of gender, age, ethnicity, status, political beliefs, and professional roles, and how we were perceived. Some voices were inadequately represented because of the focus of our research. Addressing interactions between newcomers and established residents in politics and civic organizations, we encountered community activists, including bilingual Chinese immigrants, but not the many immigrants who lacked English or were simply too busy with survival to take on the burning concerns of more established residents. Nevertheless, recent immigrants appear in our reports on political demonstrations and neighborhood and club meetings involving their interests. Our focus on adults in local political networks tends to leave out youths, except in their interactions with adults. Key to immigrant incorporation, they are another story and another book.

Some voices may have been unheard because of our focus on ethnic empowerment and multiculturalism. A few residents active in the politics of immigration control dismissed us as deluded liberals from UCLA who could not possibly be objective. We did have opinions; it was impossible not to. For us, objectivity depended on engagement and dialogue with residents. Above all, it depended on our ability to listen and to make connections, to understand opinions and events in their own contexts.

We ended up telling what John Van Maanen has called a "critical tale," as opposed to the "realist tales" of conventional ethnography. Realist tales are about the presumably self-contained world of the research site. Critical tales address the connections between the people studied and the researchers. As outsiders, we were also insiders, part of what was studied and necessarily affecting and affected by what we found. Critical tales also address the connections between the local and the global. Monterey Park is a microcosm of larger demographic and economic changes and the intersection of race, ethnicity, and gender.[5]

Not surprisingly, our objects of investigation and perspectives changed as we studied interconnections, interactions, and the processes of change. Initially, we framed our research broadly as a study of how different ethnic groups grappled with immigration and diversity. Later, we understood that in a changing community ethnicity was something to be explained, not taken for granted, its meaning, boundaries, and political significance shifting with the economic and demographic changes that had fundamentally internationalized the local setting.

Our participation in the Ford Foundation's Changing Relations Project helped us to move away from the all-American fixation on ethnicity to look at interactions between newcomers and established residents and the larger issue of immigrant incorporation. The Ford project—a study of relations between established residents and newcomers in Philadelphia, Miami, Chicago, Houston, Garden City, Kansas, and Monterey Park, California—was launched in 1987 during the debate over reforming United States immigration policy, which raised concern about the ability of the United States to absorb immigrants.

The National Board of the Changing Relations Project argued that to understand the impact of immigration on everyday life, research and policy considerations needed to move beyond the traditional focus on the characteristics of immigrants—their values, costs, contributions, their degree of assimilation and mobility—to their interactions in society as a whole. Robert L. Bach, a member of the board, stated this theoretical perspective clearly: "The answers [about the absorptive capacity of U.S. communities] are not only about immigrants. They demand that attention be given to community conditions both newcomers and established residents face and struggle to overcome together."[6]

In Monterey Park those shared conditions included ongoing economic, political, and cultural developments in a middle-class city in a world economy undergoing rapid internationalization of capital and labor. We wanted to know how newcomers and established residents confront those conditions and to what extent newcomers were actors rather than passive reactors and adapters to established residents, their values, and their institutions.

Initially, we defined established residents as native-born Americans, and newcomers as the wave of immigrants who came to the United States and Monterey Park after the liberalization of immigration laws in 1965. Chinese immigrants were only the major part of the last wave of newcomers. Before them, there had been Latinos and Japanese Americans; before them, young whites of mixed ancestry moving into a city of Anglo old-timers.

The meaning of newcomer and established resident grew more complex as our study progressed. In Monterey Park, some prominent and politically influential established residents were relative newcomers, while some long-established residents had never achieved insider status because of their race or ethnicity. Our solution was to opt for global and local definitions. Globally, newcomers were the immigrants who arrived after 1965 in response to changes in U.S. laws and world political and economic conditions. Locally, the meaning of newcomers and established residents was settled by the people who lived in Monterey Park and had the power to say something about the matter. At this level, we came to understand that the political issue behind the labels was the incorporation of outsiders, when and under what circumstances they become citizens of a local community, and how they transform that community in the process of incorporation.

The story of Monterey Park is ultimately about social, political, and cultural participation and constructing citizenship under conditions of diversity. As with "ethnicity" and "newcomer/established resident," our understanding of that vague and overused word "diversity" would also be an outcome rather than a starting point of our study.

As an ethnically diverse research team, we came to our site certain that ethnic "diversity" was a "good thing." Many of the people we met did not feel the same way. They were not particularly responsive to abstract appeals that ignored their life situations. With few notable exceptions, they were consciously engaged not in promoting diversity and harmony, but in getting elected, getting things done, coping, confronting, and sometimes enjoying the whirl of change. They taught us that we have to ground our understanding of diversity in the concrete realities of everyday life. We had much to learn, and the people of Monterey Park had much to tell us, about the nature of conflict and cooperation between newcomers and established residents and the grassroots meanings of diversity, immigration, class, and ethnicity at this time in our history.

Chapter 1
FROM MONTEREY PARK TO LITTLE TAIPEI

Damn it, Dad, where the hell did all these Chinese come from? Shit, this isn't our town any more.

—*A Japanese American on his return to Monterey Park*

You're from Los Angeles? Isn't that near Monterey Park?

—*Heard in Taiwan*

BY UNCONGESTED freeway, Monterey Park is about ten minutes east of downtown Los Angeles. Our drive takes us past the gleaming postmodern monuments to Pacific Rim capital and beyond the black, Korea, China, Latino, and J(Japan)-towns of the central city to the west end of the commercial and residential sprawl of the San Gabriel Valley, the eastern gateway to suburbia and the desert spillovers of the megalopolis.

With only 7.7 square miles and an estimated population of about 63,000 in 1994, Monterey Park is one of 84 cities incorporated within the administratively fragmented County of Los Angeles (4,090 square miles, more than 9 million people). Not in the standard tourist guide, Monterey Park is nevertheless recognized by Chinese the world over as America's first suburban Chinatown, sometimes disdained as "Mandarin Park" by disgruntled Anglo, Latino, and Asian American old-time residents, and regularly monitored by politicians, reporters, and social scientists as a microcosm of the ethnic, economic, and political changes wrought by immigration.[1]

The ethnic transformation of Monterey Park began slowly with the migration of domestic minorities from the city to the suburbs. In 1960 Monterey Park was an Anglo town (85 percent) giving way to the suburban aspirations of primarily native-born Latinos (12 percent) and Asian Americans (3 percent). By 1970 Monterey Park had become a middle-class home for Mexican Americans from nearby working-class East Los Angeles and for Japanese Americans from enclaves in the east and west sides of L.A. and from regions of forced wartime internment and exile.

There was also a migration of Chinese from the old Chinatown located just eight miles west of Monterey Park. The migration of Asian and Latino minorities to the suburbs was the combined result of postwar economic mobility and the legal and informal erosion of discrimination in housing.

In retrospect, the process of residential integration was remarkably smooth before 1970. Ethnic newcomers had not yet tipped the ethnic balance in their favor and were not a threat to Anglo political and institutional dominance. Nevertheless, there was resistance. In the 1950s, some Asian Americans bought their homes through third parties. Others bypassed reluctant old-timers by relying on the nondiscriminatory practices of a few developers. There was one racial confrontation in 1962 when the Congress of Racial Equality picketed a developer for refusing to sell a house to an African American graduate student and his wife.[2] CORE and its local supporters won out, but few African Americans have made their homes in Monterey Park and adjacent cities in the western San Gabriel Valley. Their relative absence compared with Latinos and Asian Americans probably reflects higher levels of discrimination against African Americans and their later and different pattern of middle-class migration out of the central city.[3]

The second ethnic transformation of Monterey Park, clearly visible by the mid-1970s, was primarily the result of the immigration of Chinese and other Asians rather than the out-migration of native minorities. Their impact on the ethnic balance of Monterey Park was rapid and dramatic. In 1980 the city was almost evenly divided among Anglos (25 percent), Latinos (39 percent), and Asian Americans (35 percent). The small population of African Americans made up just over 1 percent of the community. By 1990 Asian residents had become the majority, with almost 60 percent of the population, while Anglos declined sharply to 12 percent and Latinos declined slightly to 31 percent of the total. The composition of the Asian population also shifted, the younger Chinese newcomers now decisively replacing older native-born Japanese Americans as the largest Asian group (Tables 1 and 2).[4]

Today, Monterey Park is a city completing its transition from a quiet, racially mixed bedroom suburb of aging single-family dwellings and dying commercial streets to a Pacific Rim hub with higher-density housing and a globally oriented financial and service center for a rapidly expanding regional Chinese population. The physical transition has been uneven. The city looks unfinished, caught between a Middle America of tranquil parks, tree-lined streets, and modest houses, and the encroaching restaurants, banks, supermarkets, mini-malls, condominiums, and traffic of a Chinese boom town.

The sights and sounds of the sixties and the nineties clash on the

TABLE 1 *Ethnic Change in Monterey Park, 1960–1990 (Groups as Percentage of Population)*

	1960	1970	1980	1990
Anglo	85.4	50.5	25.0	11.7
Latino	11.6	34.0	38.8	31.4
Asian/other	2.9	15.3	35.0	56.4
African American	0.1	0.2	1.2	0.5
Total	100.0	100.0	100.0	100.0

Source: Community Development Department, Monterey Park.

major commercial streets—Garvey, Garfield, and Atlantic. In 1992, on North Atlantic Boulevard, one encountered in succession: Ai Hoa supermarket (the untranslated words roughly meaning, "Loving the Chinese Homeland"; the benign Vietnamese-Chinese phrase suggests nostalgia, although some old-timers might interpret it as "Non-Chinese, keep out"); more Chinese signs with enough English to identify the Little Taipei Restaurant, Red Rose Hair Design, Flying Horse Video, Cathay Bank, Remax Realty, and Bright Optical Watch; and empty lots, formerly Fred Frey Pontiac and Pic 'N' Save, awaiting Chinese development. Further down the street, Hughes Market and Marie Callender's Restaurant remain as monuments to a "Western" past.

The large Chinese ethnic economy spreads out along the traditional commercial streets in the north of Monterey Park. North Atlantic Boulevard is the last area open to major development. In 1991 the city selected

TABLE 2 *The Changing Asian Population of Monterey Park, 1970–1990 (Groups as Percentage of Asian Population)*

	1970	1980	1990
Japanese	61.4	39.9	17.4
Chinese	29.2	40.9	63.0
Filipino	6.4	4.3	3.1
Korean	1.5	6.2	3.5
Vietnamese	—	4.6	7.8
Other	1.5	4.1	5.2
Total	100.0	100.0	100.0

Source: Monterey Park Planning Department; U.S. Bureau of the Census, 1983, 1991.
Note: In 1970, Vietnamese were not identified as such. "Other" includes Native Americans as well as unidentified Asian Pacific people.

a Taiwanese firm to do the job, but in 1994 the project was still unfinished for many reasons, including the recession and disagreement over the appropriate mix of Chinese and mainstream tenants. Recognizing the local shopping needs of established "Americans," the city hired an Anglo developer to renovate an aging shopping mall on South Atlantic Boulevard in appropriate "Mediterranean style." Located in the heavily Latino part of town next to the traditional Mexican American barrio of East Los Angeles, Atlantic Square's supermarkets, chain restaurants, and specialty shops now serve Anglos and Asian Americans as well as Latinos.

The city is segregated by "American" and "Chinese" economic zones and by income. On rare smogless days, the wealthier residents enjoy spectacular views of the San Gabriel Mountains from their hillside homes; the less affluent, living in the flats, settle for views of their neighbors' houses. Although there are traditional pockets of Latinos in the south and east of town, Anglos in the center, and Japanese Americans in the hills of the east side, the city is residentially integrated. However, the presence of Chinese and other Asian newcomers in neighborhoods has been marked by increased density—the replacement of small single-family dwellings by larger homes ("monster houses" according to some old-timers) or condominiums.

THE GLOBAL CONTEXT OF THE NEW ASIAN IMMIGRATION

Established residents, accustomed to things as they were or are imagined to have been, first experienced the new immigration as a calamity, like an earthquake, and asked, "Why did it happen, and why did it happen to us?" Missing from their focus on outsiders coming in was an understanding of how immigrants and established residents are connected in an increasingly interconnected world.

The immigration, and what *Time* magazine sensationally headlined "the Coloring of America," was not a natural disaster, or a unilateral act of outsiders.[5] It was the collective, complex, mostly unplanned result of American as well as Asian decisions regarding immigration, politics, and economic development. The case of Monterey Park needs to be understood in this global context.[6]

One decision that led to the phenomenal increase in non-European immigrants was made in the United States. The Immigration and Naturalization Act of 1965 ended discriminatory quotas favoring Europeans over Asians and people of color. The act was less the result of a coherent policy than a compromising response to different political pressures in an expanding postwar economy, including a decade of civil rights struggles against racism and the desire of business and political elites to give U.S. global power a nonracist, free-market image.[7]

Once their historic exclusion was reversed by law, Mexicans and Latin Americans became the largest group of newcomers to enter the United States legally, increasing the total Latino (immigrant and native-born) population by 53 percent from 1980 to 1990. The second-largest group were Asians. Today Asians are the fastest growing minority in America, their numbers increasing 95 percent between 1980 and 1990. In the same decade, by contrast, whites and African Americans, less affected by immigration, have increased only 6.0 and 13.2 percent respectively.[8]

The framers of the 1965 Immigration Act probably expected a continuation of the historical pattern of European immigration. At that moment, however, the labor surplus and the economic as well as political motives to emigrate were in Asia and Latin America, not in Europe. In the 1960s and 1970s, immigration from the Soviet bloc in Eastern Europe was severely restricted. The booming Western European economies were importing, not exporting, labor.

The situation was quite different for the developing countries in the Pacific Rim. They had a ready pool of emigrants formed by political instability and patterns of economic development strongly affected by U.S. influence in the region after World War II. The movement of Asian refugees across the Pacific was a direct consequence of U.S. cold war strategy and hot war involvement in civil wars in Korea, Vietnam, and Southeast Asia. It was also the indirect result of economic aid. To bolster its anticommunist allies, the United States poured millions of dollars into the friendly economies of Korea, Taiwan, Hong Kong, and the Philippines. In the process, the United States put its mark on the development of educational institutions and capitalist values, thereby ensuring the mental as well as economic preparation of elites oriented to the West.

The new immigration was also the result of decisions made entirely in Asia. The strategies of development behind the economic "miracles" in countries like South Korea and Taiwan—rapid proletarianization of rural populations, export-driven development, emphasis on higher education—created surpluses of both capital and unabsorbed labor. Liberalized immigration laws in the United States facilitated their entry.

The new laws encouraged the immigration of two different classes. Family reunification provisions continued the older and familiar movement of unskilled and semiskilled labor, thereby reinforcing the nonwhite character of the U.S. working class. However, 20 percent of the visas were allocated for professionals and other talented people whose skills were needed in the United States. Not Europeans, but Asians and other people of color, filled these quotas, thereby radically changing the racial and ethnic composition of the professional and managerial class.[9]

California has been the preferred destination of the new Asian immigrants, followed by Hawaii, Washington State, and New York State. Metropolitan Los Angeles, whose Asian population increased between 1970 and 1990 from 3 to 11 percent of the total, or from about 190,000 to 926,000 persons, has the largest concentration of Asians in the United States, larger than that of San Francisco, Honolulu, Seattle, New York, or Chicago.[10]

In Los Angeles, the arrival of an economically diverse population of Asian immigrants led to new patterns of dispersed and concentrated settlement. In the case of the Chinese, poorer and unskilled immigrants still found both employment and residence in the traditional Chinatown. However, more educated and affluent Chinese in search of better living conditions scattered throughout the county, and some settled east of Chinatown in Monterey Park and the middle class, ethnically mixed suburbs of the San Gabriel Valley.

Encompassing the small cities of Alhambra, Rosemead, Arcadia, Temple City, San Gabriel, South Pasadena, Pasadena, and Monterey Park, in 1990 the West San Gabriel Valley, with a population of nearly 350,000, was almost evenly divided among Anglo, Latino, and Asian populations. Maps 2 and 3 use census tract data to compare the geographical location in 1990 of all immigrants who arrived before 1980 with those who arrived between 1980 and 1990 in central Los Angeles County and surrounding areas.[11]

A comparison shows that Chinese immigrants arriving after 1980 were increasingly locating outside Monterey Park in the cities of Rosemead, San Gabriel, Alhambra, and Pasadena. Further east, El Monte and South El Monte reflect Latino as well as Asian immigration.

The general pattern of immigrant settlement in the central Los Angeles region is one of geographic expansion and concentration. In addition to the concentrations of Chinese immigrants in Chinatown and suburban San Gabriel Valley, Korean immigrants are found just west and south of downtown; Latinos downtown, east of downtown, and further south in regions stretching from Vernon to Lynwood; Armenians in Glendale; and Russians and Eastern Europeans in the Hollywood area.

In the 1970s Monterey Park was the major port of Chinese entry into the "Valley." At that time the city held many attractions for the newcomers: a location near the old, congested Chinatown, an established Asian population, and relatively new and affordable residential and commercial property—all vigorously marketed in Taiwan and Hong Kong by enterprising Chinese real estate and business interests who saw a future in a convenient, pleasant, and affordable suburb.

Immigrants gave us many reasons for coming to Monterey Park and the San Gabriel Valley, calling it a good place to invest capital and to raise and educate children; a familiar "Chinese" environment; and a ref-

Map 2 *Settlement Pattern of Earlier Immigrants Who Arrived Before 1980 as Percentage of Total Population by Census Tract in Central Los Angeles County, 1990*

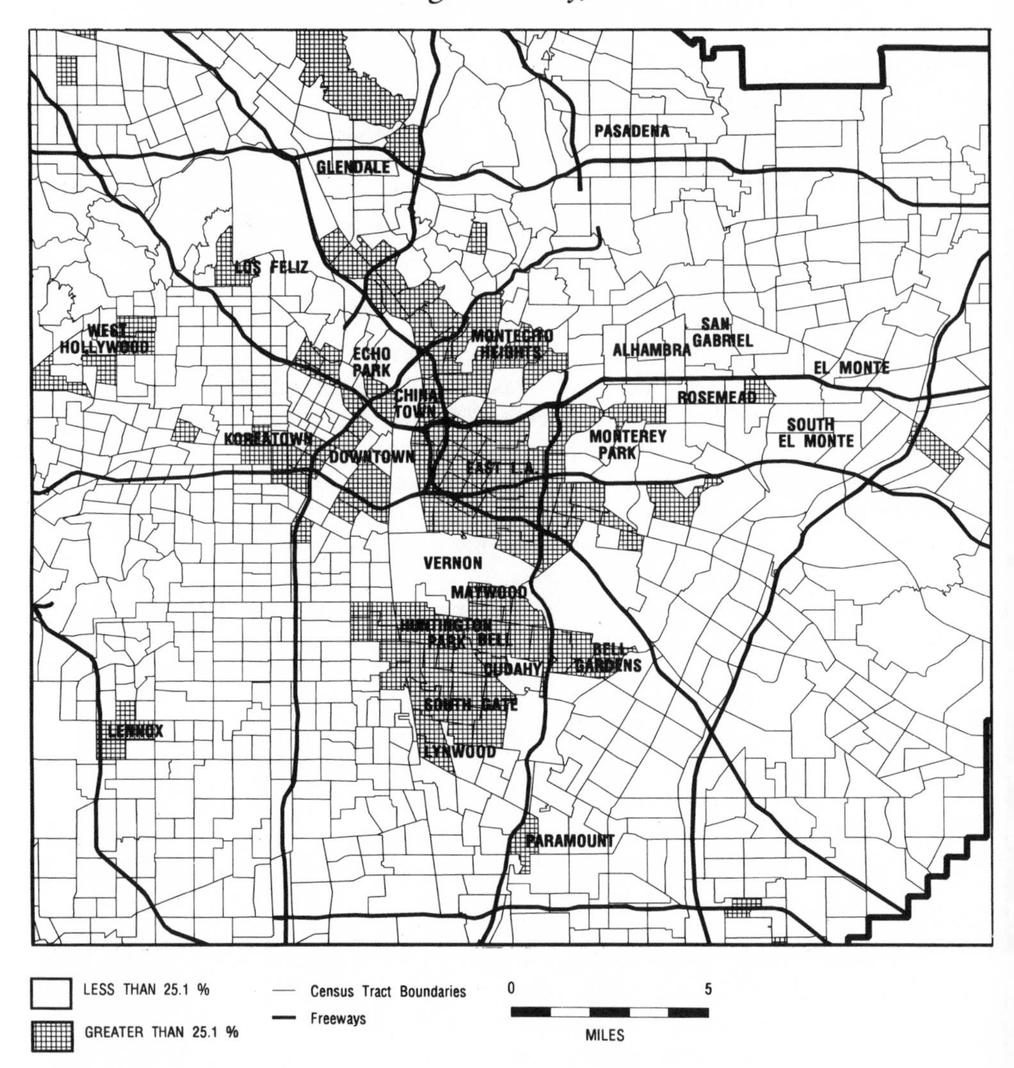

Source: Prepared by the Urban Research Section of Los Angeles County from data extracted from machine-readable Summary Tape File 3, Census of Population and Housing, U.S. Bureau of the Census, 1990.

Map 3 *Settlement Pattern of Recent Immigrants Who Arrived Between 1980 and 1990 as Percentage of Total Population by Census Tract in Central Los Angeles County, 1990*

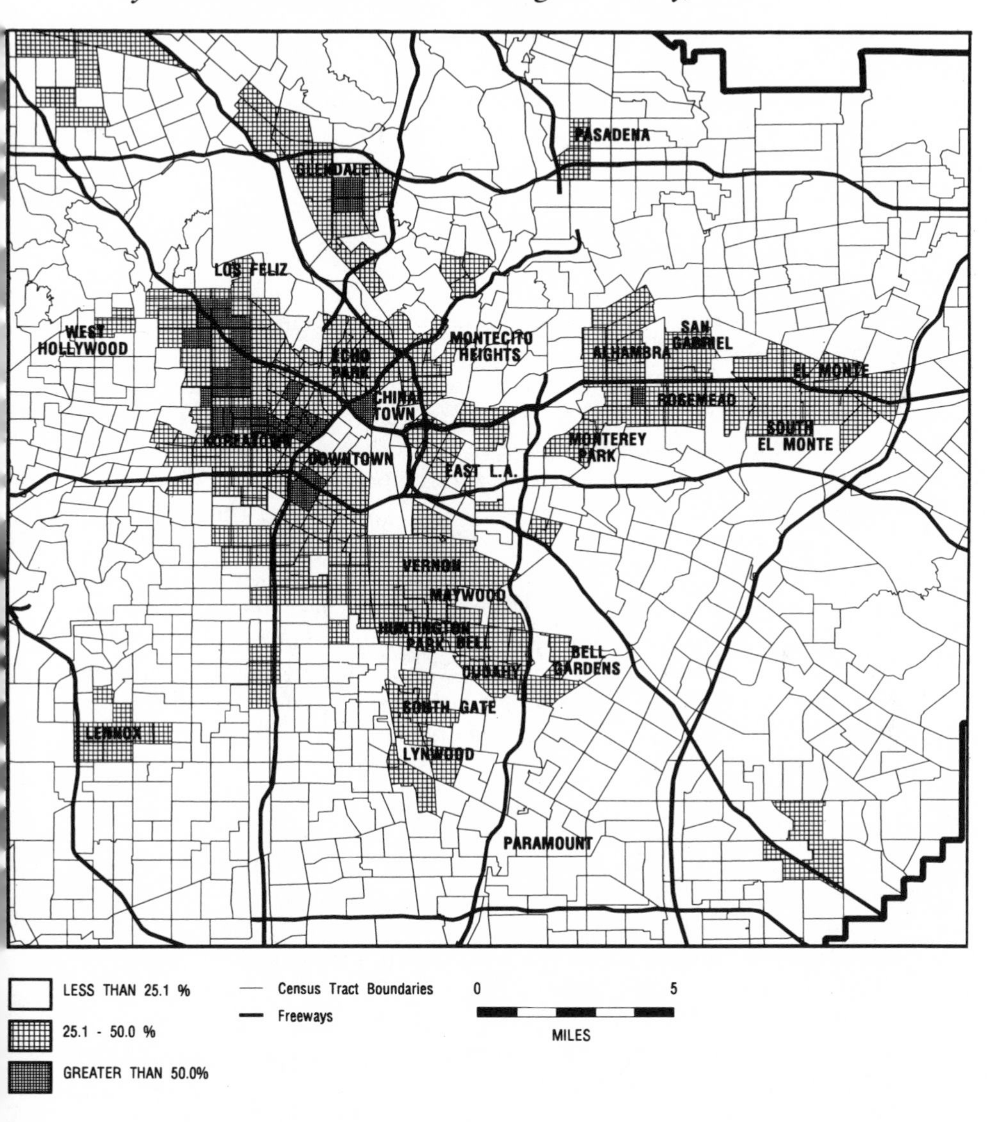

Source: Prepared by the Urban Research Section of Los Angeles County from data extracted from machine-readable Summary Tape File 3, Census of Population and Housing, U.S. Bureau of the Census, 1990.

uge from political uncertainties in Taiwan, Hong Kong, Southeast Asia, and China; they also cited family reunification as a factor. Whatever the personal reasons, they were rooted in ties already forged during World War II and immediately after, when U.S. intervention helped push anti-communist Asian nations into the modern capitalist world.

Since the arrival of these newcomers, Monterey Park exemplifies several significant characteristics of the new, post-1965 immigration: its large nonwhite and Asian component, and specifically its suburban and Chinese middle-class component, and the centrality of California and Los Angeles.

NEWCOMERS AND ESTABLISHED RESIDENTS: A SOCIAL PROFILE

The social and economic characteristics of Chinese and other Asian immigrants and established residents and the resources they collectively bring to Monterey Park and the western San Gabriel region can be gleaned from census data. We used the data set of the 1990 Census of Population and Housing: Public Use Microdata Area, representing a 5 percent sample of the housing units and the persons in them in the cities of Monterey Park (60,738), Rosemead (51,638), and the unincorporated area of South San Gabriel (7,700), a total population of 120,076. The PUMS (Public Use Microdata Sample) provides a much more detailed picture of the local population than that available for Monterey Park alone.[12] Moreover, the larger region is comparable demographically and economically to Monterey Park. Monterey Park, being a starting point and springboard for regional immigration, had a slightly larger foreign-born population than the regional sample (52 percent, as compared with 49 percent).

Estimates of Undocumented Immigrants

The census provides no data on the legal status of immigrants. Widespread publicity about profitable smuggling rings bringing in people from mainland China, combined with the scapegoating of immigrants in a time of recession, has fueled fears of a large undocumented Asian population in the San Gabriel Valley. Government estimates do not bear this out. According to the Immigration and Naturalization Service, in 1992 there were 3,379,000 unauthorized immigrants in the United States, 43 percent residing in California. By far the largest group (71 percent), come from Mexico, Central America, and Canada; Asia accounts for only 9 percent. There were an estimated 27,000 undocumented immigrants from China and Hong Kong, the most populous region of the world. About half of these resided in New York and New Jersey, and 22 percent

(6,000) in California. Thus, it is reasonable to assume that in Monterey Park and the San Gabriel Valley, we are dealing primarily with a legal and documented population of Asian and Chinese immigrants.[13]

Defining Newcomers and Established Residents

"Established resident" and "newcomer" are not fixed categories but flexible social constructions. For statistical purposes and within the limits of the available data, however, we can roughly define the ethnic portraits of newcomers and established residents in the Monterey Park region. The largest group of newcomers are Asian immigrants who came to the United States after the 1965 Immigration Act. Thus, 66 percent of the foreign-born in the Monterey Park area were Asians (the majority Chinese) and 18 percent Latinos (the majority Mexican). Only 3 percent of the foreign-born were of European descent, and about three-quarters of them immigrated before 1970. By comparison, 91 percent of Asian immigrants and 78 percent of the Latinos arrived in the United States after 1970.

The ethnic portrait of newcomers and established residents can be defined further by looking at the patterns of nativity, citizenship, fluency in English, and stability of residence within each of the major ethnic groups (Table 3). By these criteria, the majority of Anglos, Japanese Americans, and to a lesser extent Latinos qualify as established residents because they are native-born or naturalized Americans, are fluent in English, and lived in the same house between 1985 and 1989 (the year of the census). By contrast, the majority of Chinese and Vietnamese can reasonably be classified as newcomers, although their process of language

TABLE 3 *Ethnic Newcomers and Established Residents in Monterey Park, Rosemead, and South San Gabriel*

	Native-Born (%)	Citizens (%)	Same House since 1985 (%)	Speak English Well (%)	Median Age
Anglo	88	96	75	98	47
Japanese	79	84	78	78	45
Latino	65	72	55	72	26
Chinese	20	49	34	67	32
Vietnamese	17	43	20	65	26

Source: Data extracted from Census of Population and Housing, 1990: Public Use Microdata Samples, U.S. Bureau of the Census, 1992.

assimilation is well under way. Fully two-thirds of the Chinese and Vietnamese reported speaking English very well or well, and more than 40 percent were citizens.

In terms of median age, we can guess which groups will constitute the future population of the region: Chinese, Vietnamese, and Latinos. Over half of the native-born and immigrant Anglos and Japanese Americans are more than 45 years old, and these groups have been moving out of the area. The majority of Latinos, Chinese, and Vietnamese are at least ten years younger. Given the much larger number of foreign-born than native-born Chinese and Vietnamese and the youth of the former, we can reasonably assume that many of the native-born are in fact children of immigrants. Along with Latinos, they now fill the so-called majority/minority schools of the region.

The statistical picture tends to fit local perceptions. Our field observations indicate that established Anglos, Japanese Americans, and Latinos perceived Asians as the major newcomers, although there are substantial numbers of immigrants from Mexico and Central America. The focus on Asians and, particularly, Chinese may be due to their deviation from the familiar pattern of Mexican immigration and out-migration to the region. Immigrants of Mexican origin have lived in the San Gabriel Valley for generations. After Native Americans, they were the first settlers and in recent decades have shown a pattern of steady rather than sudden immigration: 30 percent immigrated before 1970, 32 percent between 1970 and 1980, and 38 percent in the next decade.[14] By comparison, foreign-born Chinese arrived in the San Gabriel region later, in larger numbers, and at an accelerating pace: 7 percent before 1970, 29 percent in the 1970s, and 64 percent in the 1980s. They were, in addition, a new kind of immigrant, racially, culturally, and economically.

A New Kind of Immigrant

Established residents, whether Anglo, Asian American, or Latino, tended to focus selectively and critically on several characteristics of the Chinese immigrants: their high status, their ability to move directly to a middle-class suburb, and their separate, thriving, and powerful ethnic economy. "Leap-frogging" from their countries of origin to middle-class suburbs and skipping expected stages of incorporation and economic and geographic mobility, the Chinese simply did not fit the traditional and acceptable portrait of the good immigrant—poor, grateful to be in the land of opportunity, and eager to fit in.

An elderly white resident expressed a frequently heard complaint: "Before, immigrants were poor. They lived in their own neighborhoods and moved into ours after they learned English, got a good job, and became accustomed to our ways. Today, the Chinese come right in with their money and their ways. We are the aliens." She went on to take particular note of a situation that seemed exceptional and inexplicable, if not objectionable, to her: Chinese newcomers driving Mercedes and conversing loudly in Mandarin or Cantonese in her American city.

Her description of a new type of immigrant was based on her knowledge and experience of earlier patterns of immigration and ethnic succession: whether white or nonwhite, newcomers arrived in the United States poor and unskilled and achieved the American dream through hard work. Although countered, for example, by the immigration to Los Angeles of educated Jews and other refugees from World War II, the stereotype had a certain reality for established white residents in Monterey Park. In the 1950s and 1960s, the nonwhite newcomers were primarily English-speaking, Americanized Mexican, Japanese, and Chinese Americans who were moving out of poorer ethnic neighborhoods into white, middle-class suburbs. The local stereotypes also captured what was exceptional about the new immigration as compared with the large working-class European immigration at the turn of century—the arrival of a nonwhite professional and managerial stratum. The census data on the Monterey Park region confirm this trend while revealing what the stereotype hides: profound ethnic and class differences among both Asian and Chinese immigrants.

Not All Asians Are "Chinos"

Locally, Latinos sometimes use the word "Chinos" for all Asians, but one word does not capture the diversity of the Chinese, let alone the Asian, immigrant population in the San Gabriel Valley. Foreign-born persons of Chinese descent constituted 69 percent of the total Asian immigrant population, but another 16 percent were Vietnamese (excluding Chinese Vietnamese), and the remaining 15 percent, in order of decreasing size, were Japanese, Filipinos, Koreans, Asian Indians, and other Asians.

The new Asian immigration has diversified and radically changed the pre-1965 profile of Asian Americans as a whole. In Monterey Park, foreign-born Chinese and Vietnamese Americans have now replaced American-born Japanese as the largest group. In the nation as a whole, Japanese Americans, with a comparatively small rate of immigration, are now the third-largest group, preceded by Chinese and Filipinos and followed closely by Asian Indian, Korean, and Vietnamese Americans.[15]

Not All Chinese Are from China

Like the Asian immigrants, Chinese newcomers are extremely diverse in their national and ethnic origins, reflecting the international scope of the Chinese diaspora: 38 percent were born in mainland China;[16] 24 percent in Vietnam; 16 percent in Taiwan; 11 percent in Hong Kong; 7 percent in other Southeast Asian nations, such as Thailand, Cambodia, Burma, and Indonesia; and 4 percent in Latin America and other parts of the world. Speaking Mandarin, Taiwanese, Cantonese, and other dialects, many find it easier to communicate across their national and cultural lines in English.

Since the census reports only place of birth rather than country of emigration, these figures underestimate the influence of the Hong Kong-based and, most particularly, the Taiwan-based immigrants in Monterey Park. Many immigrants born in mainland China were in fact refugees from the People's Republic of China and migrated to the United States from their points of exile in Asia. When the Kuomintang leaders fled mainland China and the Communist Revolution for Taiwan in 1949, they were accompanied by throngs of expatriates. After decades of residence, many of these exiles and their families, never fully integrated into Taiwanese society and fearful of both Taiwanese nationalism and mainland communism, have sought stability and prosperity in Southern California as well as in Canada and Australia. When the United States drew closer to mainland China and withdrew its official recognition of Taiwan's independence, many mainlanders in Taiwan began to see Monterey Park and the San Gabriel Valley as a good place to live, retire, invest, or perhaps send their children, with the hope that they would get an education and work there and eventually send for their parents and relatives.[17]

The U.S. Immigration and Naturalization Service provides a better picture of the Taiwan connection to Monterey Park because it reports country of emigration and point of destination by ZIP code in the United States. Although the data report intended rather than real destination, they nevertheless give some indication of the regional preferences of Chinese immigrants. Taiwanese prefer Los Angeles County and especially the neighboring San Gabriel Valley cities of Monterey Park, Rosemead, and Alhambra, over New York and San Francisco (Table 4). By contrast, the first preference of immigrants from the People's Republic of China and Hong Kong is the more traditional New York City. The preferences may reflect different social and cultural networks and the different opportunities provided by the Chinatown and new suburban economies.

The Taiwanese presence in Los Angeles and influence in the local Chinese economy and media are strong. Nevertheless, the Taiwanese label, like "Chinese," hides great diversity—for example, differences between Taiwanese natives and nationalists (who speak Taiwanese and who successfully petitioned the U.S. government to be identified as Taiwanese rather than Chinese) and mainlanders (exiles of the Chinese Rev-

TABLE 4 *Taiwanese Immigration to Selected U.S. ZIP Code Regions, Fiscal Years 1983–1990*

Location	ZIP Code	Percent
NEW YORK		(22)
New York, N.Y.	10002	6
Flushing, N.Y.	11373	16
LOS ANGELES COUNTY		(74)
Monterey Park	91754	33
Alhambra	91801	19
Rosemead	91770	7
Artesia/Cerritos	90701	15
SAN FRANCISCO COUNTY		(4)
San Francisco	94112	1
Daly City	94015	3
Total		100

Source: Immigration and Naturalization Service. Calculated from data reported in Timothy P. Fong, *The First Suburban Chinatown: The Remaking of Monterey Park, California* (Philadelphia: Temple University Press, 1994), p. 3.
Note: In Los Angeles County, Artesia/Cerritos is the largest area of Chinese suburban concentration outside the western San Gabriel Valley.

olution and friends of the Kuomintang, which ruled Taiwan as a province of China).[18]

Focusing primarily on relations between bilingual Chinese immigrants and established residents, our research does not begin to capture the ethnic and geographic complexity of the Chinese diaspora to Los Angeles. We can say with certainty only that the new Chinese immigration is diverse and that the Taiwanese wield considerable influence in the Los Angeles area.

The diversity of the new Chinese immigration stands in sharp contrast to the more homogeneous pattern of the past. The first wave of immigrants in the mid-nineteenth century brought male rural and urban workers from the vicinity of Canton. Fleeing the insecurities of a region destabilized by Western intervention, they came to seek their fortune as miners in California's frontier Gold Rush economy. As gold mining declined in the second half of the nineteenth century, Chinese came to construct railroads and irrigation systems, and work in the state's growing service and manufacturing industries. Their flow of immigration was effectively blocked by nativism and the Chinese Exclusion Act of 1882. Exclusion from the mainstream drove those who remained to create their own ethnic economies within the confines of congested Chinatowns.[19]

A second wave of Chinese immigration began slowly in the mid- and late 1940s when the pro-China climate of World War II and cold war anticommunism opened up small quotas to friends and family affected by war and revolution. Swelling after the Immigration Act of 1965, the second wave brought a population more economically and geographically diverse than that of the nineteenth century. Rather than peasants from rural China, they were urban workers, professionals, and entrepreneurs from many developing Asian nations, as well as developed ones integrated into the capitalist world economy and competitive with the United States.[20] The census figures for the Monterey Park region clearly reflect the geographic shift in Chinese patterns of immigration. Eighty percent of the Chinese who immigrated before 1965 were born in mainland China, as compared with 32 percent who arrived between 1965 and 1989.

Not All Asians Are Rich

Thus, the labels "Asian" and "Chinese" hide great ethnic, linguistic, regional, and historical differences among Chinese who have immigrated to the United States and the San Gabriel Valley. Similarly, stereotypes emphasizing the wealth of Asian newcomers erase the profound economic and class differences that exist within the Asian and Chinese populations. All Asians are not "Chinos," and not all Chinos and Asians are rich.

COMPARISON OF NATIVE-BORN AND IMMIGRANT POPULATIONS

A comparison of the region's major ethnic groups and U.S.- and foreign-born populations in terms of selected social and economic characteristics provides a complex portrait of immigrants and established residents (Tables 5 and 6).

If we compare the socioeconomic profiles of the region's major ethnic groups and make no distinctions within the very heterogeneous Asian population, then Asians as a whole have the highest status on most criteria. On par with Anglos in terms of the size of their professional/managerial stratum, Asians have a higher median household income and higher percentage of college-educated than Anglos and strikingly higher levels of education than Latinos. However, even at this level of comparison, we can detect a sign of inequality within the Asian population. The Asian poverty level is twice that of Anglos and slightly higher than that of Latinos.

Once we break down the Asian population by ethnicity and nativity,

TABLE 5 *Selected Social Characteristics of U.S.- and Foreign-Born Residents of Monterey Park, Rosemead, and South San Gabriel*

	College Graduate and Above (%)	Professional/ Managerial Occupation (%)	Median Household Income	Below Poverty Level (%)	Median Age
Anglo	15	26	$31,000	11	47
Latino	5	14	$28,900	18	26
Asian	25	26	$36,140	21	32
Chinese	25	25	$32,300	22	32
Japanese	29	33	$49,020	2	45
Vietnamese	7	10	$25,186	35	26
U.S.-born	16	25	$36,000	12	24
Foreign-born	17	18	$29,600	24	34
U.S./Anglo	17	30	$31,888	6	45
F.-B./Anglo	18	24	$32,800	6	63
U.S./Chinese	66	51	$47,407	12	7
F.-B./Chinese	23	22	$30,368	24	36
U.S./Japanese	31	38	$56,000	2	46
F.-B./Japanese	23	14	$31,000	5	47
U.S./Vietnamese	0	0	na	30	6
F.-B./Vietnamese	8	9	$25,200	35	30
U.S./Mexican	5	16	$31,650	14	20
F.-B./Mexican	4	9	$26,480	26	32

Source: Data extracted from Census of Population and Housing, 1990: Public Use Microdata Samples, U.S. Bureau of the Census, 1992.
Note: "College Graduate and Above" refers to persons 25 years old or older with a bachelor's or higher degree. "Professional/Managerial Occupations" exclude the unemployed and persons under 16. "Median Household Income" for Los Angeles County was $34,965 in 1990. "Below Poverty Level" includes persons of all ages. "Anglo" = non-Hispanic white; "Latino" = Hispanic, including Mexican; "U.S." = U.S.-born; "F.-B." = foreign-born.

a polarized pattern of economic differences emerges. Japanese Americans have higher levels of income, occupation, and education, and lower levels of poverty, than any other group, including Anglos. The Chinese, the largest Asian group, show both high education and income and a high level of poverty. The Vietnamese (excluding Vietnamese Chinese) are the poorest ethnic group in the region, with a rate of poverty about double that of Latinos and triple that of Anglos.[21]

Digging deeper into Table 5, we can see that the stereotype of high-status Asian newcomers breaks down totally when we compare the native-born and foreign-born of different ethnic groups. Vietnamese arrived with few educational and economic resources. In 1990, 35 percent

TABLE 6 *Selected Social Characteristics of Chinese Immigrants by Place of Birth and Time of Immigration in Monterey Park, Rosemead, and South San Gabriel*

	College Graduate and Above (%)	Professional/ Managerial Occupation (%)	Median Household Income	Below Poverty Level (%)	Median Age
PLACE OF BIRTH					
Hong Kong	38	31	$38,800	17	29
Taiwan	42	28	$24,388	30	31
China	21	23	$30,298	18	49
Vietnam	4	10	$24,873	38	30
Other Southeast Asia	33	31	$28,481	19	32
TIME OF IMMIGRATION					
Before 1970	31	40	$46,000	9	52
1970–1979	24	19	$40,000	14	38
1980–1990	21	21	$22,191	31	33

Source: Data extracted from Census of Population and Housing, 1990: Public Use Microdata Samples, U.S. Bureau of the Census, 1992.

were living below the poverty level, a rate about 10 percent higher than that of foreign-born Chinese and Mexicans, more than double that of U.S.-born Mexican Americans, about six times higher than that of native whites, and almost eighteen times the rate of U.S.-born Japanese Americans.

By comparison, Chinese immigrants have considerable middle-class resources, although perhaps less than one would expect given their local reputation for wealth. They have much lower levels of income, occupation, and education, and higher rates of poverty, than relatively well-off and highly educated native-born Chinese and Japanese Americans. Chinese immigrants have medium household incomes slightly lower than that of residents of European descent (native-born or foreign-born), and higher levels of poverty and college education. Except for their much higher levels of education, these Asian newcomers are also close to the middle-class economic level of American-born Mexican Americans, but better off than Mexican immigrants by all educational and economic criteria.

Our investigation of the image of "wealthy Asian newcomers" can be refined further by looking at differences among Chinese immigrants in terms of place of birth and time of immigration. Table 6 shows that the relatively young immigrants born in Taiwan, Hong Kong, and Southeast Asian countries other than Vietnam report higher levels of education than either China- or Vietnam-born Chinese. Their levels of education approach those of native-born Chinese and far exceed those of other foreign-born populations as well as non-Asians generally. In the case of Hong Kong immigrants, their median income exceeds that of both Anglo and Mexican American populations, whether foreign- or native-born. The lower status of China-born and especially Vietnam-born immigrants is not unexpected, since their populations include refugees who could not take their wealth with them when they left their countries.

Census data reporting income earned in the United States may underestimate the wealth of Chinese newcomers who have access to family wealth located in different parts of the world. In any case, their relatively high levels of education define them as middle-class and provide a key to future mobility and lower levels of poverty.[22] When Chinese immigrant cohorts who arrived before 1970, in 1970–1979, and in 1980–1989 are compared, the earlier groups are doing very well—as well as native-born Chinese Americans and Japanese Americans. We lack the information to say whether this pattern reflects mobility over time, the higher skills of earlier cohorts, or both.

In sum, do our data confirm the stereotype of wealthy and educated Asian newcomers? Statistically, Asians are polarized economically and educationally, with the Chinese from Hong Kong and Taiwan and the Japanese generally on the high-status side compared with Vietnamese and Vietnamese Chinese. However, if we focus on the Chinese, the largest Asian immigrant group in the region, they do constitute a new kind of immigrant, coming directly to suburban America with at least their middle-class educational resources intact.

In the end, the image of the wealthy newcomer is a social rather than a statistical construction related to the social position and perspective of the established residents who do the labeling. From the perspectives of moderate-income Anglos and Latinos, the Chinese who arrived with money and education may be viewed as competitors for mobility and space and potential displacers. The reaction of established Japanese and Chinese Americans toward Chinese newcomers is more ambivalent. On one hand, their numbers and potential voting power are a boon for underrepresented Asian Americans; on the other, the same factors can cause a backlash among non-Asians and threaten the positive image that established Asian Americans have generally achieved. Whatever the perception of established residents, if the local demographic trends continue, the Chinese and other Asians will have the numbers and resources to replace an aging white middle class, only to confront a large and less economically powerful Latino middle class and a more disadvantaged class being formed by Mexican, Latino, and Vietnamese newcomers.

THE NEW CHINESE ETHNIC ECONOMY

Relations between newcomers and established residents are conditioned by the number, non-European origin, and class of the new residents, structural factors that could favor either confrontation or accommodation. Relations have also been affected by the regional domination of a new Chinese economy that has refashioned the dying downtown of Monterey Park into a bustling regional and international center of an expanding suburban Chinese economy consisting of "ethnic self-employed and employers, their unpaid family workers, and their co-ethnic employees."[23] The new shops and offices spread out along the commercial streets attract Chinese customers from inside and outside Monterey Park, people of modest means and the wealthy who live in the nearby upscale cities of Arcadia and San Marino.

One of the most visible signs of a new kind of immigrant is their large and diversified ethnic economy, thriving not in Chinatown, but in a multiethnic, middle-class American suburb. Newcomers and more established Chinese Americans with close ties to the immigrant community have built an ethnic economy whose visibility dramatizes the presence of Chinese people and money. We now turn to a description of this economy and how it has both contributed to the revitalization of the region and created new problems of development affecting the lives of established residents.

The Suburban Ethnic Economy of the San Gabriel Valley

Established residents were not quite prepared for the rapidity and scale of the change. In 1977 Frederic Hsieh, a successful Chinese American realtor, was greeted with disbelief when he told a gathering of the Chamber of Commerce that "you may not know it, but this [Monterey Park] will serve as the mecca for Chinese business."[24] By the early 1980s, Chinese economic dominance was an accomplished fact. Although statistics on ethnic business ownership in Monterey Park are not available, anyone can see that signs containing Chinese characters dominate the local commercial landscape.

Some old-timers had underestimated the entrepreneurial spirit and ethnic resources of the Chinese. While they were playing poker with Hsieh, welcoming him into the Chamber of Commerce and civic organizations, and talking about the good old days, he was buying up and developing property. Born to a professional family in mainland China in 1945, raised in Hong Kong, educated at Oregon State University, he came to Los Angeles in the late 1960s to work as a city engineer. However, Hsieh soon discovered the magic of California real estate. With a little personal capital, small loans, and growing connections, he mastered the art of buying and developing property and encouraged immigrants in their entrepreneurial pursuits.

In 1972, as a young man of 27, he moved to Monterey Park. It was the right historical moment: the United States had lifted its restrictions on non-European immigrants; Chinese from Hong Kong and Taiwan, and later from Vietnam and Southeast Asia, were looking for a safe refuge for themselves and their capital. Hsieh and other entrepreneurs made Monterey Park a desirable alternative to the Los Angeles, San Francisco, and New York Chinatowns. The city had pleasant neighborhoods, proximity to downtown Los Angeles and the old Chinatown, and relatively inexpensive commercial and residential land. According to Hsieh, in the mid-1970s commercial land in Chinatown was going for fifty dollars a square foot, compared with about seven dollars in Monterey Park.

Figuring that Monterey Park would be a good place for new immigrants to develop, Hsieh established Mandarin Realty in 1973 over the old Rexell drugstore at the busy commercial intersection of Garvey and Garfield. By 1975, piecing land parcels together from empty and underused commercial lots near Atlantic Boulevard, he developed Dearfield Plaza, the city's first Chinese mall, and saved a piece of land for his own Omni Bank. Today Hsieh has many businesses in Monterey Park—real estate holdings, the Hong Kong Restaurant, a music store, a theater, and insurance and trading firms. He has even expanded his operations to Asia.

What Hsieh and other entrepreneurs collectively created in Monterey Park and in neighboring communities was an ethnic economy catering primarily to Chinese. It replaced and revitalized a sleepy downtown that had been bypassed by the growth of large regional suburban malls outside the city.

What replaced the old and vacant stores and empty lots was a mixture of familiar and unfamiliar Chinese businesses. There were, of course, restaurants. In 1994, we estimated that about two-thirds of the city's 100 restaurants were Chinese, mostly mom and pop businesses, except for a few gigantic and elegant Hong Kong–style establishments. There were mini-malls filled with small businesses selling every conceivable service and product. Banks proliferated. Our survey in 1989 indicated that 14 out of 21 were primarily owned by and run for Chinese. In 1994, the same pattern held for Monterey Park's 31 financial institutions. The size of assets has also expanded dramatically: between 1980 and 1990, bank and related deposits grew from $362,099,000 to $2,272,663,000.[25]

Chinese supermarkets have also mushroomed in Monterey Park. According to our commercial survey, six out of eight of the principal markets were Chinese-owned.[26] Built in 1981 from the ground up as part of a large chain centered in Taipei, Diho was the first American-style Chinese supermarket in the United States. Later, the Hong Kong Supermarket replaced an American-style skating rink; Hoa Binh ("Peace"), a vacant, Anglo-owned store; Quang Hoa ("Lighting Chinese"), a Japanese American–owned grocery store; Ai Hoa ("Loving the Chinese Homeland"), a big American chain, Alpha Beta Market.

While preserving their distinctive ethnic identity, the large Chinese markets have adapted to their suburban and American habitat. They do not fit the stereotype of a crowded Chinese shop with merchandise flowing onto the street. In outward appearance, except for one building with a distinctively Chinese tiled roof, supermarkets conform to familiar suburban styles in size and architecture. Inside, there are also similarities in the organization of shelves and the American-style management. Nevertheless, any "Western" shopper would find a big difference in what was sold: No rolls of film hanging from hooks (these are sold in specialty shops), but an incredible array of fresh produce not found elsewhere, live creatures from the sea, and many separately operated and franchised shops selling tea, herbs, bakery goods, books, and videos.

A few non-Chinese, having discovered the freshness and reasonable price of produce, are learning to shop in these markets that are owned by and operated for Chinese. In 1994, except for the Taiwanese-owned Diho and Hoa Binh markets, most of the owners were Chinese Vietnamese, and a majority of the managers, cashiers, and workers appeared to be from the same background. Latinos could be found in some of the lower-level jobs. In the larger stores, clerks spoke Mandarin and Cantonese to customers from the wide ethnic spectrum of Chinese who live in the region.

Less obvious to established residents who see only the visible surface of the Chinese economy is its diversity and extent. The Chinese telephone books list accountants, doctors, dentists, clinics, and every imaginable service in Monterey Park. The city is also a media center, hosting, among many smaller journals, two major Taiwanese newspapers. The *World Journal,* with a worldwide circulation, is fairly conservative, Kuomintang-oriented, and owned by the largest firm in Taiwan. The smaller *International Daily* is more liberal and was founded in the United States by a Taiwanese. The Taiwanese and Mandarin flavor of Monterey Park, sometimes called "Little Taipei," contrasts sharply with the largely Cantonese-speaking Los Angeles Chinatown. However, the entrepreneurs and customers reflect the ethnic and linguistic diversity suggested by the census of residents and households.

The Larger Context of Success

Monterey Park's Chinese economy needs to be put into a larger perspective to understand its historical significance and regional impact. The apparent success of Chinese entrepreneurs in Monterey Park and the San Gabriel Valley was not an accident or an anomaly. First, Chinese as a whole are the most successful Asian entrepreneurs in the United States. For example, Chinese American firms reported the largest gross receipts in the 1980s, followed by Korean, Japanese, Indian, Filipino, and Vietnamese American firms.[27] Chinese immigrants brought major entrepreneurial resources to the United States—high levels of education, capitalist values, banks and associations that could provide loans, and the historically learned ability of a diaspora population to survive by calling on trusted networks of family and friends.

Second, during the post-1965 wave of immigration, Los Angeles became the favorite location for Chinese businesspeople, big and small. By the mid-1980s, it was the largest Chinese business center in North America, ahead of both San Francisco and New York. The number of Chinese firms in greater Los Angeles more than doubled between 1982 and 1987, and gross receipts went up 160 percent.[28]

Third, for reasons clearly understood by pioneers like Hsieh, after 1970 Chinese business in Los Angeles broke out of its historically constricted Chinatown pattern and spread eastward into the San Gabriel Valley suburbs of Los Angeles County. An analysis of the location of businesses listed in Chinese telephone books shows that by the early 1980s, the San Gabriel Valley was replacing the City of Los Angeles and its Chinatown as the largest regional center of Chinese business. In 1983, about half of all the Chinese businesses listed in Chinese telephone books covering greater Los Angeles were located in Chinatown and about one-third in the western part of the San Gabriel Valley. In 1992, the figures were 6 percent for Chinatown and 55 percent for the Valley, with 12 percent in Monterey Park, the largest single concentration in the Valley. The regional trend was clearly in the direction of a geographically dispersed, suburban Chinese economy.[29]

The new Los Angeles pattern is both more economically diversified and more spatially dispersed than that of the regionally and industrially concentrated economies of Chinatowns. Traditionally, Chinese businesses have been associated with restaurants, groceries, and textiles relying on a proletarian work force. This is the case today in New York, which has the second-largest Chinese economy in the United States. By contrast, Chinese enterprises in Los Angeles have expanded beyond traditional niches into the areas of banking, real estate, health, education, computer technology, international trade, and other industries requiring a highly educated professional and managerial work force.[30] In her pioneering study of Taiwanese entrepreneurs in Los Angeles, Yen-Fen Tseng suggests that their heavy involvement in international trade and exchange of high-tech goods is a reflection of the growth of an interconnected Pacific Rim economy. Thus, Chinese entrepreneurs are not merely fitting into old niches; by internationalizing suburban economies, they are also actors in the restructuring and rebuilding of the recessionary economy of Los Angeles.[31]

From this larger perspective, Monterey Park is significant as an initial point in the development of a new suburban economy within a restructuring regional and global economy. Monterey Park's peak was in the mid-1980s. Today, fleeing its high land values, Chinese banks, restaurants, markets, and other services have followed the eastward movement of Chinese residents to newer and, in some cases, more affluent suburbs of the San Gabriel Valley. Initially concerned about too much Chinese business, today some city officials in Monterey Park are worrying about too little: In 1994 they commissioned a study to find out why Chinese businesses were moving out. Nevertheless, within the San Gabriel Valley, Monterey Park remains an important banking and commercial center with a wider range of services for businesses and retail customers than can be found in other suburbs. It is also a symbol of Chinese entrepreneurial success, attracting delegations from mainland China and busloads of Chinese tourists.

Conflicting Evaluations of the Ethnic Economy

For the Chinese immigrants, the geographically expanded ethnic economy is a source of wealth and employment, and an important route to mobility and incorporation into American society.[32] However, its location in ethnically mixed suburbs rather than a segregated Chinatown has created a new set of problems involving contact with local governments and established residents. Chinese entrepreneurs are learning that the free capitalist market is not so free when their investment strategies run up against limitations imposed by local governments and the growth concerns of local residents.

By the early 1980s, Chinese businesses had established their economic position in Monterey Park and revitalized the sluggish service economy of a small town that had never quite made it big. However, the rise of the Chinese ethnic economy was only a part of the wider regional problems that troubled established residents. In the 1980s rampant, speculative development was transforming suburbs that had cherished the "Leave It to Beaver" dream of safe, tranquil, and affordable communities. Like other cities in Los Angeles County, Monterey Park began experiencing gridlock, the proliferation of mini-malls and condominiums, and high-density commercial and residential overdevelopment. The demands of Asian newcomers for commercial and residential land were also fanning inflation. Affordable housing declined for renters, while owners sold out at undreamed-of prices.

What made Monterey Park unique among cities affected by the development boom of the 1980s was that development had an Asian face and the ethnic economy did not directly serve the needs of non-Chinese-speaking residents. Consequently, when the backlash against uncontrolled growth came to Monterey Park, it would be infused with nativism.

Chinese entrepreneurs would also be implicated in another problem that became painfully apparent in the 1990s as Monterey Park, like other cities, faced a financial crisis. The causes were complex: a legacy of inadequate planning and failure to raise the revenue needed for expanding city services; the California taxpayers' revolt, which placed strict limits on raising property taxes, the major source of city revenue; lowered state and federal subsidies to local governments; and, finally, a major recession.

Today, as cities compete for revenue-rich development, Monterey Park has several handicaps: a pattern of development that produces a sales tax base too low to make up for reduced property taxes; a small commercially zoned sector with narrow lots unsuitable for the large shopping malls that bring in big revenue; high land values; and rather stringent growth restrictions set by rebellious residents.

This situation was less the fault of the new Chinese economy than of the restricted possibilities for commercial growth in Monterey Park and the lack of national, state, and regional responses to the financial crisis of cities. Nevertheless, the Chinese people, as the mainspring of local growth, would also become the scapegoats for its deficiencies.

FROM A STATISTICAL TO A SOCIAL COMMUNITY

In its size, composition, and pattern of settlement, the Asian immigration into Monterey Park and the western San Gabriel Valley created a new demographic and economic order, a break in rather than a mere continuation of earlier trends. It was the local manifestation of global restructuring: the movement and increased integration of human labor and capital on a world scale.

The new order brought together in a suburban setting an ethnic mix of primarily middle-class newcomers and established residents. It created unforeseen human problems and opportunities in the areas of ethnic relations and economic development. Newcomers and established residents never intended to be neighbors. Thrown together by forces reflecting decisions made in Washington, D.C., and the capitals of Asia, they found themselves sharing the space of a potential community and confronted with new conditions and the daunting task of forging civic bonds at the points where their lives collided and intersected.[33]

The material conditions for life in Monterey Park having been laid out, the stage is now set for the actors who have played out the local drama of social change in their neighborhoods and civic organizations. Focusing on Chinese immigrants (the major contenders for future power and influence) and established Asian, Anglo, and Mexican Americans (residents rooted in local history), our story is about their struggle over economic development, language, culture, political representation, and the very meaning of ethnic and American identities in a period of extraordinary and uncertain transition. It is a tale of grassroots resistance and change.

Chapter 2

BUILDING COMMUNITY AT THE GRASSROOTS

No one promised me that Monterey Park would remain the same. When I moved here, I created change. When other people moved in, they created change. There's nothing we can do in terms of stopping the change, so you do what you can to create a sense of community. That's the most important thing. —*An elderly Anglo woman active in Monterey Park politics*

OLD-TIMERS TALK a lot about community as something they had and lost when the newcomers arrived, a geographically bounded and culturally defined network of familiar sights, sounds, and social activities.[1] Their sense of community is richly textured and entangled in their personal memories of local history—people like themselves on the block knowing each other, raising their children together, belonging to the same schools and clubs, volunteering, and getting involved in city council elections. From this perspective, the present is judged ambivalently and often negatively as a break from the good old days.

Confronted with an unexpected present, old-timers continually find ways of rediscovering, reinventing, and reaffirming the past. The Monterey Park Historical Society is flourishing. Its primarily Anglo and elderly members have expanded its museum and volunteer-run programs and collected life histories of long-established residents for the local library. To recover a buried past and keep their bearings in a sea of changing faces and structures, one elderly couple christens new buildings with the names of the familiar establishments they had erased. Thus, the donut shop replaced by a Chinese bank reentered the present as "the Chinese Donut Bank," an image reinforced by its round door. The "House of Pies" is reincarnated as "the House of Pies Chinese Restaurant."

Immigrants, the new majority, have their own versions of community, which differ sharply from those of old-timers. They too have a sense of history, but it is located in far-off places. Their Monterey Park is defined by the experience of immigration and adjustment to a new society. Monterey Park is the present, a new Chinese city of transplanted memories and authentic tastes and sounds of home, a refuge in an otherwise foreign land, and a springboard to the future. Their concept of community is bounded less by local history and city limits than by a regionally and internationally based support network of family, school, and business associations.

What is foreign to old-timers, the new and thriving commercial enclave, is for newcomers a source of pride, a symbol of success and of the contributions of immigrants to the United States. Attuned to the complaints of established residents, some Chinese would add that their achievements have come about legitimately on the free market, without welfare assistance and at no cost to taxpayers. A Chinese developer put his view this way:

> We Chinese emigrated here and became more and more dominant through the free market system. We did not "take over" this area by force, and we didn't intend to overwhelm the rest of the residents. Those who sold out their houses at a dear price were doing so willingly. They could have refused to sell their property and remain the majority in this area. I was really disgusted to read in the newspaper that some old residents claimed that they sold out because they were upset about the community quality being brought down by Chinese. . . . I think that Monterey Park is fortunate to have established a unique environment not only in Los Angeles or Southern California, but literally in this nation. The city has become identified as a land of new opportunity, a legend of a revitalized town. It has been a success story. We have made Monterey Park an important cultural and economic center.[2]

Coming together from different worlds with different languages and memories, the established residents and newcomers of Monterey Park shared a "problematic" community, a common residential and civic space, but not a sense of "we" based on identification with each other as citizens and neighbors.[3]

Community is an ambiguous and overused concept, referring broadly to social bonds forged by common experiences, interests, and struggles based on occupation, generation, ethnicity, class, living space, and other characteristics. For the purposes of our research, community came to mean the local nexus of civil society, the relationships of citizenship that extend beyond the individual and family to the residential, public, and political spheres bounded by the city and environs of Monterey Park.

Many immigrants did not seek community within the boundaries of Monterey Park because their lives, careers, families, and friends were elsewhere. Old-timers who did were often pessimistic. They believed that the changes had been too abrupt, that the population was now too diverse to maintain the earlier cohesion flowing from commonalities of language and American culture. Other residents welcomed change and were optimistic: bilingual leaders who acted as brokers between the new and the old; established residents and newcomers who saw in Monterey Park a historical opportunity to create community on a foundation of greater ethnic and cultural diversity.

What we learned about the existence and meaning of community in Monterey Park came from our ethnography of everyday life. Our observations were guided by the following kinds of questions. What was the character and extent of community building between ethnically diverse groups of newcomers and established residents in neighborhoods, public spaces (shopping centers, parks, etc.), and civic associations? To what degree and how were newcomers involved? What issues and agents brought people together? To what extent did civic associations foster immigrant incorporation and political as well as cultural empowerment?

What we found was both an absence of contact and unexpectedly high levels of cooperation that crossed ethnic and newcomer/established-resident lines. In general, contact between newcomers and established residents tended to be superficial, limited by language and structured by the urban rules of privacy and courtesy. Newcomers sometimes formed their own civic organizations, like the Chinese Parent–Teacher Association (PTA) and the Little Taipei Lions Club, which parallel those established by native-born residents. We found few settings where newcomers and established residents (outside the school population) had regular and direct contact, whether face-to-face or group-to-group.

Contact is lowest within "Little Taipei," the Chinese business and service district separated by space, language, and culture from the older, "American" Monterey Park. Contact among adults increased during public festivals and events that had been planned by diverse groups. Contact intensified in civic organizations serving seniors and youth. Community emerged most strongly when neighborhoods spontaneously mobilized to protect and defend the quality of their lives.

These sites of interaction between newcomers and established residents provided us with case studies showing the complexity and range of community building in Monterey Park in three sites: (1) city programs that involved residents through the very American value of service and volunteering; (2) senior and youth organizations that structured cooperation between newcomers and established residents; (3) neighborhood associations that united residents around their common concerns about crime and safety.

Jose Calderon lived in Monterey Park and took extensive field notes on interactions between newcomers and established residents during the course of his daily life as a husband, a father of two teenage boys, a

Latino, and a community activist. His notes included observations on organizing a neighborhood watch and supporting his sons at the Sports Club. Mary Pardo was a participant observer of women organizing to protest against the presence of a parole office in their neighborhood. I documented patterns of community building associated with the Langley Senior Center and with the city's tradition of volunteering. Occasionally, all the researchers converged on a single site and came up with very different interpretations of what was happening.

CITY PROGRAMS: MOBILIZING VOLUNTEERS

In Monterey Park, local government as the site of a struggle for power and control was often a major barrier to building a sense of community. Nevertheless, several civic projects survived the political battles of the 1980s (described below) and emerged in the 1990s as models for community building. By 1992, as a result of a voluntary move toward greater affirmative action, the city was incorporating more Asian majorities into city jobs and citizen commissions and providing more trilingual emergency and electoral services. Multiethnic contacts between residents were encouraged through family-oriented events such as park concerts, festivals (Cinco de Mayo, Chinese New Year, Fourth of July, and Play Days celebrating the city's founding) and through service to the elderly, a Child Task Force, a literacy program, Christmas in April (community mobilization to repair the homes of the needy), and Harmony Week.[4]

In all these cases, the city drew on and cultivated a major local resource and tradition: volunteering for community service. In 1992, Monterey Park had 65 groups and organizations that regularly committed volunteers and dollars to city programs. Many volunteers came as individual residents rather than members of a specific group to fill positions in one of the city's four separately managed programs: LAMP (Literacy for All in Monterey Park), the Police Reserves, the Langley Senior Citizen Center, and the Community Volunteer Office at City Hall. In addition, residents applied and were appointed by the city council to serve on Monterey Park's 12 advisory boards, commissions, and committees.

The Langley Center for seniors of diverse national and ethnic backgrounds operates with one paid director and a core of 35 full-time volunteers, aided by scores of others who perform specific services on a regular weekly or biweekly basis. The center is a bustling hub on every day of the week. In 1993 the facility drew approximately 275,000 participants, a 250 percent increase over 1985 due primarily to Chinese and Asian newcomers.[5]

When we first visited the Langley Center in 1989, most of the volunteers were established Anglo and Latino residents. At that time, the

Chinese-born director of senior housing in Monterey Park explained to us that Chinese have no tradition of volunteering.[6] We found, however, that Chinese newcomers and Japanese Americans often made generous financial contributions to community projects. Returning to the Langley Center in 1992, we noticed that several elderly Chinese Americans had joined the volunteer kitchen staff.

When we explored the population of volunteers more widely, we concluded that the pattern was increasingly multiethnic and included foreign- as well as native-born residents. In the past, the majority of volunteers had been elderly, middle-class white women who had the time to serve and were strongly identified with community organizations. In the 1990s, they are still a major component of the work force that manages the polls and makes local festivals possible. We also observed that the important service of selling food at festivals was largely performed by high school volunteers, the vast majority of whom appeared to be immigrants or the children of immigrants.

This changing pattern was also evident in Monterey Park's Community Volunteer Office, which was specifically designed to diversify and broaden the core of volunteers. While most cities incorporate volunteers into their administration, Monterey Park is one of the few cities in the San Gabriel Valley that has a structured program with a paid staff.

Founded in 1985 by the city's first majority/minority city council, the Community Volunteer Office, under the direction of Virginia Chavez, places up to three hundred volunteers yearly in city departments. Many perform clerical duties on a regular basis; others provide translating and graphic services as needed for special projects. About half come from court community-service referrals and from service-credit programs in local junior high schools. Although exact figures on the backgrounds of volunteers were not available, the director summarized what she saw as the pattern: in terms of age, most were elderly people (usually "Caucasian"), followed by youths (mostly Asian), and, lastly, the middle-aged; most were women, except for the students, who were evenly divided between males and females. Except for the relative absence of Latino volunteers, the pattern conforms increasingly to the changing demographics of the city.[7]

One of the most impressive volunteer efforts has been made for the city's literacy program (LAMP), which helps students increase their English-language skills. In 1992 there were 160 volunteers working with 300 students. The volunteers represented a cross-section of the community, from bilingual high school students to a multiethnic core of older established residents.[8] Like the Langley Center, LAMP is run with a small staff and a large corps of regular volunteers.

In a city where over half the population is foreign-born and immigrants are arriving daily, learning English is an obvious need. Although language had been for some time the most politically explosive issue in Monterey Park and residents remained sharply divided on the issues of bilingualism and language retention, they were absolutely united for different reasons on the goal of learning English. While many old-timers saw English as a symbol of national unity, newcomers knew that English was necessary for their survival and mobility. They found common ground in the concrete task of teaching English to mostly Asian immigrants.

Literacy programs turn division into unity. Starting as a one-to-one adult tutoring program, LAMP has dramatically increased its volunteers by adding high school students who were tutoring in English as a Second Language (ESL) classes. So-called developing countries have successfully mobilized their populations around literacy programs. The experience of Monterey Park shows that such programs can be combined with the American tradition of volunteering to bring together newcomers and established residents to teach English and break down the most basic barrier to interaction and participation in the community.

The city's major accomplishment in community building has been to identify several key programs and systematically involve residents in planning and carrying them out. As a result, the scope of empowerment and participation goes beyond that seen in many small cities. In Monterey Park it would be safe to say that the tradition of volunteering, often idealized by established residents as the essence of community in the old days, is being passed on to a new and more ethnically diverse present.

But does involvement in community programs and volunteering necessarily lead to the development of communality? The case of the Langley Center is instructive, illustrating one form of communality that has emerged among a very diverse group of seniors whose direct communication is limited by language and cultural differences.

THE LANGLEY CENTER: BEING TOGETHER SEPARATELY

Seniors as a group are often stereotyped as exclusionary and rigid, the least likely to overcome barriers of language and culture. Elderly Chinese, in particular, are perceived as dependent on families, isolated from the mainstream of American life, and resistant to institutional care. In Monterey Park the problem of bringing seniors together was complicated by their diversity—long-established Anglos, Japanese Americans, and Latinos, plus recently arrived Mandarin-speakers from Taiwan who were seeking the familiarity and security of a Chinese community. What the large, diverse senior population had in common was the need for housing, safety, medical care, recreation, and independent living. The Chinese were no exception, and they are adapting to institutional patterns of care uncommon in their countries of origin. The Asian custom of parental care continues in Los Angeles but functions less smoothly in the United States, where the children of the Chinese elderly, like those of other racial groups, often lack the housing and the extended helping networks that make the Asian system possible. Under these new social conditions, Chinese-speaking elderly may find more care, contacts, and independence in the senior housing and senior center of "Little Taipei" than in some isolated family unit in an American suburb surrounded by non-Chinese-speakers.[9] Indeed, Monterey Park is a major center for Chinese senior care in Los Angeles County. Their institutional housing needs are served by the Golden Age Village and Manor as well as the more racially diverse Lions Manor. Their recreational needs are served by the Langley Center.

In the Langley Center, seniors of all nationalities politely keep to their own spaces and groups: Club Amistad (Spanish-speaking), the Japanese American Club (English- and Japanese-speaking), the Chinese American Golden Age Association (mainly Mandarin), Club Bella Vista (Latinos who want to speak English), and the Monterey Park Senior Citizen Club (established residents, mainly Anglo, but with a scattering of Chinese and Latinos). Interaction is particularly difficult between Chinese-speaking newcomers and English- or Spanish-speaking established residents. Conflict is avoided and cooperation is achieved by preserving and structuring separateness even during common activities such as the daily lunch and weekly ballroom dances.

At mealtimes, about 125 members sit together at long tables but converse within their language groups. Every week, about two hundred seniors enthusiastically join in ballroom dancing. My field notes, written in 1989, described the scene of being together separately.

> The dancers seem about evenly divided between long-established Anglo, Japanese American, and Mexican American residents, and Chinese newcomers. The all-white senior citizen band, "The Memory Laners," is being led by a spirited blonde wearing cowboy clothes and sunglasses. She also plays the trumpet. There is a man at the piano and another who plays wind instruments. The mostly '40s music goes on for two hours, each dance announced on a wooden marquee in front of the stage . . . old favorites, waltzes, two-step, fox-trot. The couples (about half married, according to my tutor) took pride in their expertise. Several were exceptionally good.
>
> Standing on the sidelines, an Anglo male gave me a rundown on the different ethnic groups and how they were relating to each other: "Look on the other side of the room—the Japanese are always sit-

> ting together there." I noticed that they also danced together, even during the mixer, when people had to change partners. My informant added, "They usually don't dance with the Chinese."
>
> On the whole, couples seemed to be dancing within their own groups, with each group occupying its own space on the floor. My informant commented on the exceptions. "Whites are more likely to dance with nonwhites. We don't have a choice." (His low, conspiratorial voice indicated that I as a white person would understand that whites are a minority and lack dancing partners.)[10]

That was in 1989. Returning to the Langley ballroom in 1994, I found the scene more relaxed and less rigidly segregated. I saw more mixed couples, and a Chinese American woman, who did not lack coethnic partners, asked me to dance. As in years past, the weekly event had become a popular regional affair for both singles and couples who share a global and generational musical culture that could transcend language and racial differences.

Ethnic separateness nevertheless continues to dominate the Langley Center, since most activities are organized around ethnic clubs. To share the same building, people have to learn the rules of polite distance. When boundaries are crossed at the center through some slight breach of what another group considers proper conduct, the balance can quickly be upset.

Beth Ryan, the popular and efficient Director of the Langley Center, herself a senior and a long-established resident, explained her approach to holding her community together: "Never take anything away from anybody." Dealing with scarcity without taking anything away was a major problem. After a decade of operation, the seniors had outgrown the center. Throngs of Chinese mah jong players needed room, which could not be taken away from Anglo bridge players. The solution was to raise funds for an addition to the building, an expansion opposed by some established residents who did not want to accommodate the "invaders." With generous help from Asians, the center expanded. Today, the mah jong players have their own room, active from one to five every afternoon; so does the Chinese opera. The coexistence of presumably inflexible elders separated by race and language was accomplished with a maximum of tact, respect for differences, and skill in negotiating the rules of separateness.

This was surely one form of community building in a situation of extreme diversity. It is a pluralistic solution in which individuals and groups are presumably separate but equal. They were not in fact equal in their histories or their class, since some of the newcomers come from more educated and higher-income families than those of old-timers. Nevertheless, even these differences could be leveled on the new terrain of senior citizens.

Much of the success of the Langley Center depended on the leadership of Beth Ryan. Ryan had been a strong supporter of Barry Hatch, a local leader of Official English, a movement that many newcomers saw as anti-Chinese. In her role as Director, however, Ryan was an advocate for all seniors. Her practical task was not to exclude Chinese but to expand the center to include them. This action ultimately put her on a collision course with Hatch, who, as a city councilman, had no interest in spending money to accommodate Chinese and other Asian newcomers. Community-builders experience contradictions that reflect their varied roles and positions in society. They have to be judged by the sides they actually take in particular situations, not by labels like "white" or "conservative."

THE MONTEREY PARK SPORTS CLUB: DOING TEAMWORK

The Langley Center's model of harmony based on polite separateness would not necessarily work in other contexts, such as a sports club where young parents come together to support the training and accomplishments of their children. Here, for parents to accomplish their goals, separateness must give way to teamwork. One of the few sites in which newcomers and established residents came directly in contact with each other was the city's Sports Club for pre-teens and teenagers. Jose Calderon, as an involved parent of a teenage son, documented the interactions between newcomers and established residents from the opening ceremonies of the basketball season in December 1988 to the final tournament in May 1989.

The Sports Club was an especially interesting site because it made interactions between Latinos and Asians visible. Newspapers and studies of conflict in the San Gabriel Valley have tended to focus on clashes between politically dominant Anglos and economically dominant Asians. However, Anglos are fast becoming the minority, and the regional future will depend increasingly on relations between Latinos and Asians.

The Sports Club had traditionally been strongly Mexican American in terms of participation by youths and parents. It became a place where Anglo and Asian children and their parents learned sports and teamwork from Latinos. Like other prominent civic organizations, it was also a place for business and political contacts. Local businesses sponsored teams, and the yearbook recognized their contributions and encouraged parents to buy their products. Volunteering in the club also conferred grassroots credentials on aspiring leaders. For example, the ballot statement of David Barron, a long-time Mexican American resident, cited his service to the Sports Club as evidence of his qualification to run for City Clerk in 1988 and for councilman in 1990.[11]

The place of the Sports Club within the ethnic and political structure of Monterey Park is illustrated by a breakdown of the participants according to their ethnicity and functions during the 1988–1989 season (Table 7). The ethnicity of the young players reflected the traditional dominance of Latinos in the club, the growing presence of Asians, and the declining number of young Anglos. Latinos also dominated the ranks of coaches. However, attesting to the continued power of the Anglo minority, the Director was a prominent dentist, Stan Organ, and the majority of the politically influential commissioners were Anglos.

With his 12-year-old playing on the Lakers team, Calderon did direct participant observation, cheering in the stands and volunteering in various aspects of the program. All parents are required to volunteer their services; over time, they become integrated across ethnic and established-resident/newcomer lines as members of the larger team. Not surprisingly, the volunteers were structured according to gender. Calderon explained the pattern at the opening ceremonies:

> Some mothers of the young players had organized a bake sale at the entrance to Elder Gym. There were six women at the table—four Latinas, one Asian, and one Anglo. They said that the fundraiser was to help pay for some of the expenses of the Sports Club and that parents were required to donate at least six hours to the Club each season as referees, coaches, sponsors of pizza parties after games, and fundraisers. While the women were involved in a bake sale, the men were primarily signing up for coaching, refereeing, or playing in a fathers' basketball game.[12]

The practice of putting parents as well as children into teams also structured interaction between newcomers and established residents and

TABLE 7 *Ethnicity and Status in the Monterey Park Sports Club, 1988–1989 Basketball Season*

Ethnicity	Players	Coaches	Commissioners
Latino	45%	47%	14%
Asian American	34	19	29
Anglo	20	34	57
Other	1	—	—
Total	(232)	(38)	(7)

Source: Prepared by Jose Calderon, University of California, 1989.

eventually overcame the linguistic and ethnic separateness preserved at the senior center. At the beginning of the season, although parents of all groups sat together in support of their teams, Chinese immigrant families who did not speak English well tended to sit together, while established residents interacted more with each other and took on key roles such as scorekeeper, coach, and commissioner.

As the season went on, rooting for children on the same team created a commonality that even began to break down language barriers. The bonds were strengthened when children made friends across ethnic lines and brought their parents into the relationship.

> As I walked into Elder Gym, the parents of Larry [a Chinese boy who had become the best friend of Calderon's son, Joaquin] waved at me. I went and sat near his family. They couldn't speak English well, but we were able to communicate enough to understand that we were both hoping for a win this evening.

Other rituals of support bring parents in closer contact with their children and each other. They teach the rules of good sportsmanship, but also lay a foundation for cooperation between youths and adults of all nationalities. Calderon describes a typical scene:

> After the game, both teams get in a line and go by each other shaking hands and saying "good game." The coaches do the same. There are no real losers.
>
> Then the parents get involved. One parent brings refreshments for the players, and other parents gather around their kids and begin to talk to each other. A Chinese parent supporting the "Jazz" team placed his arm around one of the Latino parents, telling him that his son sure knew how to pass the ball "underneath." The Latino parent responded with pride, "He did have a good night, huh?"

During the championship game, the last of the season, parents were beginning to sit with each other according to team and friendship rather than nationality, and were engaging in casual conversation:

> I looked at the composition of the crowd in the stands and, as usual, saw that it was primarily Asian and Latino with a sprinkling of Anglo parents. Although there were clusters according to nationality, the pattern was primarily mixed, Asian, Latino, and Anglo parents sitting together. This was also true for the youths encircling the gymnasium and sitting in the stands. They seemed to situate themselves with friends or team supporters regardless of nationality.
>
> In the middle of the audience, I saw an elderly Anglo man (perhaps a grandparent) talking freely with another elderly Asian man. In front of me, there was a Latino family and a Chinese family sitting

> together. The women were conversing. They were talking about food. The Chinese woman was telling the Latina how she could cook a certain Chinese dish. The Latina woman responded, "But I don't cook it that way." They were very engrossed in their conversation and were not too interested in what was going on in the game. Their husbands, however, were really into the game and kept standing up and yelling at the players out on the floor. Between shouts, they would talk to each other—"That was a good play . . ." "That was a good shot." The Latino and Chinese families each had a daughter about four or five years old. They were having a great time, laughing and chattering away.

Although newcomers and established residents sometimes fought each other in City Hall, in the Sports Club they were members of a team. The link between them was their children. The motive was support and interest in their development. Teamwork and volunteering structured cooperation.

The Sports Club and the Langley Center are examples of how institutions can structure accommodation to extreme diversity in the course of serving the needs of children and the elderly. During the course of our research, we also observed more spontaneous interactions that brought newcomers and established residents of different ethnic backgrounds together to solve neighborhood problems.

THE RUSSELL AVENUE NEIGHBORHOOD WATCH ASSOCIATION

A walk down Russell Avenue in the flats of Monterey Park on a relaxed Sunday afternoon in the summer of 1989 reveals the diversity of this modest neighborhood. In the middle of the block, five young Mexican men are conversing in Spanish over beer and barbecue. Across the street, a stick of incense is burning on a doorstep strewn with bright colored circles of confetti, evidence that the Vietnamese neighbors had a celebration last night. Down the street a Chinese immigrant family, to the chagrin of their Japanese American neighbors, were removing all the trees and shrubbery from their newly acquired house. Next door, a frail and elderly white woman, a resident for 30 years, was struggling with her heavy garden hose.

The scenes reflect different communities coexisting separately. As is the case in urban areas generally, and in the urbanized residential suburbs of Los Angeles, neighborhood interaction on Russell Avenue is governed by norms of polite indifference and respect for private space. Neighbors may greet each other, talk across the fence, or watch out for trouble when household members are away. Inevitably, there are disputes about animals, noise, children—whatever does not respect boundaries and runs down the general appearance of the street.

In an ethnically mixed environment, these minor disputes can take on a racial character. An elderly white man continually complains about the "pink elephant" looming across the street, a Chinese-built and -occupied condo complex that replaced a familiar single-family dwelling: "They are running a hotel for illegal immigrants." When a Chinese neighbor complains about a cat sitting on the warm hood of her car, the owner, a young white man, warns, "There will be real trouble if anything happens to that cat." He's heard rumors that Asians eat cats.

The neighborhood is not what it used to be. Old-time residents tell us that in the 1960s, before the big wave of immigration, families on Russell Avenue raised their kids together and visited each other frequently. On the Fourth of July, there were block parties with shared food and entertainment. The stories of the good old days, whether accurate or not, function today to draw lines between us and them, the "good neighbors" and the "bad immigrants" who crowd too many people into their houses, never keep up their lawns, and will not or cannot speak English. The stories are symptoms of change, displacement, and alienation.

In the 1980s, Russell Avenue was an unlikely place for community building, yet its residents formed an active neighborhood watch association on two sides of a long block of older single-family dwellings interspersed with new condominiums. For a time at least, the barriers separating households began to break down as they organized for defense against disaster and crime.

Police-sponsored but loosely controlled neighborhood watch associations existed in Monterey Park in the early 1980s. In 1985, their numbers and activity increased in response to the notorious "Night Stalker," who had robbed and murdered women in Los Angeles and in Monterey Park. After the stalker was caught, in 1987 a 5.9 earthquake hit Monterey Park and gave neighborhood watches another reason for existing. In 1992, there were about two hundred groups led by block captains, mostly homeowners, established Anglo, Latino, and Japanese American residents, evenly divided between males and females. The Russell Avenue Watch, a particularly active association, showed that neighborhood ties could be built even on a foundation of extreme ethnic, racial, and linguistic diversity.

The Potluck

The revitalization of the Russell Avenue Neighborhood Watch was led by co-chairs Peter Chan, a naturalized citizen active in community affairs, our resident/researcher Jose Calderon, and Jim Parra, a young man raised in Monterey Park. From about 1985 to 1989, the association held meetings on an emergency basis and at least three times a year. After the earthquake of 1987, neighbors went from house to house to check on each other and offer help when needed. In 1989 the Russell Avenue association was moving toward a higher level of organization, polling neighbors through an earthquake preparedness survey and involving them in a get-acquainted block party. Several members of our research team helped residents design and conduct an earthquake survey and attended the potluck dinner in September 1989.

The results of our household survey showed the expected diversity. We contacted 42 households, reporting a total of 61 adults and 33 children. About 60 percent were homeowners. About half of the households were Latino and Anglo, and half were Asian. The majority of the latter were Chinese Americans, with a few Vietnamese and Japanese Americans. Of those who responded to a question on language, 46 percent said they preferred to speak English at home; 32 percent spoke Chinese or other Asian languages (divided between Mandarin- and Cantonese-speakers); 11 percent spoke Spanish; and 11 percent were bilingual, speaking a Chinese dialect and English.

The lower-middle- to middle-class neighborhood was clearly in transition. Twenty-seven percent were old-timers who had lived in their houses more than 11 years; 15 percent had lived there from 5 to 10 years; and 27 percent from 1 to 5 years; but 31 percent had been on the street less than a year. Less than half of the adults who responded to the questionnaire said they knew or interacted with their neighbors, and less than half of those actually knew their neighbors' names. Nevertheless, all expressed an interest in the survey and the neighborhood watch. One-quarter said they had attended a previous meeting; one-third offered their skills in case of disaster; one-half said they would attend the forthcoming potluck.[13]

The active organizing for the potluck was multiethnic, done by Calderon, Chan, a Chinese immigrant male, and two Anglo women—one an elderly long-time resident, the other a young divorcée who had recently moved to Monterey Park because it was "safe" and near her work in downtown Los Angeles. They contacted households by phone and by leaflets announcing in Chinese and English that "the best way to protect your neighborhood is to know your neighbors."

We speculated that the potluck, which required more involvement than earlier informational meetings, might be poorly attended. Behind the façade of politeness, there were Anglos and Latinos bitter about the Chinese immigration, and Chinese who felt that they had nothing in common with the "natives." About noon on the appointed Sunday, organizers set up tables and chairs on the front lawn of Calderon's modest bungalow, and wondered whether anyone would come.

As the hot September day became a cooler late afternoon, they did come, a total of 35, a few at a time. One of the first to arrive was a lone Chinese woman with her six-month-old baby. She had come from Taipei less than a year ago to join relatives. She introduced herself to another young woman from Taiwan, and they conversed over a cup of punch from McDonald's. The chairs were beginning to fill up. A refined middle-aged couple from Shanghai, an elderly and quiet couple from Mexico, two longtime residents originally from Holland, a jovial Jewish man and his wife who had lived on the street for 30 years. He jokingly tried to recruit a Chinese newcomer to his local old-timers band. Later he remarked to a friend: "I knew that Chinese would not join a band; they play violins and like orchestras."

We estimated that about half of the people who attended the potluck were Chinese or Vietnamese newcomers and the rest established Anglo and Latino residents. They spread out their international potluck on two long tables: Chinese noodles, dumplings, and moon cakes to celebrate a forthcoming festival; enchiladas and menudo; lasagna; potato salad, pies, and lemonade made by an elderly Anglo widow with fruit from her own lemon tree.

People ate, were formally introduced by the organizers, listened to a presentation on the neighborhood association, chatted informally, and in a few cases lingered long after dark. The Asian families, more limited by language, tended to remain in their own ethnic and language groups, but there were significant instances of interaction between established residents and newcomers.

During the get-acquainted ceremony, the couple from Shanghai presented a gift to their neighbor in appreciation of his quick response in calling the police when he saw a robber enter their house. The recipient was a white male in his late twenties who believed firmly in an absurd rumor that a deceased former councilman had been wiped out by the Chinese mafia. He was touched by the gesture of his Chinese neighbors. After making a few heartfelt remarks about "different kinds of people getting together to help each other," the young man walked from his position on the sidelines into the crowd and sat at a table, where he proudly displayed his gift, a tiny boat carved in teak.

There were other signs of crossings. An elderly white resident changed his anti-immigrant tune in the middle of one of his usual complaints about the irresponsible actions of the Chinese who occupied the suspicious pink condo across the street: "We're in a drought and water is restricted and they leave their sprinklers running all night." This time he caught the sympathetic ear of a Chinese newcomer. They talked easily and naturally about a neighbor's responsibility, not about the irresponsibility of Chinese strangers.

Three Perspectives

Immigrants and established residents came together and broke a few barriers in the attempt to construct a neighborhood association. The old-timers seemed quite excited about the potluck. An elderly white woman remarked that it was just like the block parties that they used to have. As an organizer, Calderon was pleased because so many different people, including many Chinese who were not fluent in English, actually attended. His field notes were enthusiastic:

> Although the character of the block has changed dramatically, these events showed the potential of the development of a new sense of community. I say "new" because it cannot be the same type or sense of community that some of the old-timers were used to. People on the block will begin to come together on the basis of working together on neighborhood problems that affect them. Perhaps, this is the way to do grassroots organizing in suburban communities and, particularly, in a multi-ethnic suburban community.

To some of the Chinese newcomers, however, the process of community building looked more complicated, since they, and not the old-timers, had to adapt to the unfamiliar forms of a potluck and neighborhood association. One of our field workers, Yen-Fen Tseng, herself a native of Taiwan, observed the difficulties of crossing barriers of custom and language from an immigrant's perspective. Even those newcomers who could speak some English gravitated toward Chinese at the potluck and seized the opportunity to speak Chinese, thereby creating that invisible wall that so annoys established residents. Tseng's field notes document another experience of the block party.

> A young Chinese woman confessed to me, "I'm afraid of talking to Americans since I can't catch their words most of the time." An elderly Chinese man who spoke quite fluent English ignored me until he found out that I was indeed Chinese. He remarked: "I didn't know you are Chinese because you were talking to Americans [a Latino and Anglo], so I did not try to approach you. Now it is just so nice to know we are all Chinese." He was talking so loudly and excitedly in Chinese that an American woman sitting near us looked at him unpleasantly.
>
> When it was time to eat, the Chinese waited until the Americans had taken food off the table. Then they moved ahead as a group, speculated about the foreign food, and generally settled on the Chinese dishes.

In other instances, however, the more assimilated Chinese helped to break down barriers by teaching the less assimilated appropriate rules of interaction. The first example, reported by Tseng, is an exchange between an English-speaking daughter and her traditional Chinese father. Breaking the old-timer rule "Speak English," he called out very loudly in Chinese to his daughter to join him and Tseng. Looking annoyed, the daughter excused herself from her friends and then complained to her father: "Couldn't you lower your voice a little bit and try not to speak Chinese in front of Americans?" Her father, perhaps feeling entitled to interrupt his children no matter what they were doing, responded: "Unfortunately, Americans don't understand the Chinese way." But the daughter insisted that it was rude to use Chinese in what she saw as an American social occasion.

The second example was audible to everyone. During the introductions, a new immigrant made the cultural mistake of mixing business and sociability. To the surprise of established residents, he announced that he owned a sports accessory business in Taiwan and began to promote his products. Although his behavior was acceptable by Taiwanese standards, Americans found it inappropriate and instrumental. Another Chinese, who apparently understood American ways, asked him ironically, "Do we get a discount for your products?" The newcomer, not sensing the negative reception, simply answered, "No." There was silence for a moment. However, his blunder was less serious than that of a young white man whose American-style joking went too far when he said: "I'm Bill and I came here to rob you." Again, a moment of silence.

These observations highlight the complexity of community building and the importance of looking at any event from several perspectives. It is necessary to go beyond counting heads to explore the kinds of interactions that are actually occurring. From the block captain's viewpoint, the fact that immigrants had come was a sign of a successful interethnic event. But from the immigrants' perspective, the gathering also reinforced the feeling of separateness, especially if they lacked language skills and knowledge of what they perceived as American ways. They did come, however, and the interaction crossed racial and cultural lines. It also brought together newcomers who were not alike—who spoke different Asian languages and had to stumble through English to communicate.

A third, official perspective about the potluck differed from that of newcomers and established residents. One of the organizers, an established Hong Kong–born Chinese immigrant, sensed that the potluck was a model for multiethnic organizing and invited the five members of the city council. The two councilmen, not particularly friendly to the diversity politics of the organizers, did not attend, but the three councilwomen did. In spite of their varied political views, ranging from extremely conservative to progressive, they had learned to cooperate and promote diversity on city commissions. For them the event was an opportunity to show their concern for interethnic harmony, drum up political support, and investigate the viability of an experiment in neighborhood organizing. They were pleased with what they saw and stayed late.

Four years later, in 1993, Russell Avenue had changed. Many old-timers, with their stories about block parties, had died or moved away, and Asian immigrants and Latinos had moved into their houses. The old neighborhood watch, however, was intact. Crime and earthquakes continued to remind residents that they had reasons to stick together.

The persistence of the neighborhood watch attests to the possibility of organizing around shared concerns about crime and safety in spite of cultural and language differences, problematic potlucks, and rapid residential turnover. Continuity in leadership, provided by Calderon and a few stalwarts, was one key to its success.

A NEIGHBORHOOD FIGHTS A PAROLE OFFICE

Established residents, not newcomers, tend to take the lead in neighborhood organizing. To be successful, however, they need to involve newcomers and teach them the political ropes. This is what occurred during a spontaneous, grassroots fight to remove a state parole office from the Highland neighborhood of Monterey Park, a hilly region of spacious single-family dwellings with a population estimated to be about 70 percent Asian and 30 percent Anglo and Latino. Here multiethnic organizers incorporated the neighborhood watch groups and block captains into a larger and autonomous structure of protest.

In July 1988 residents discovered that a parole office providing services to felons had been established in an unmarked building within half a mile of an elementary school. Their concern about crime escalated when a woman living close to the parole office was assaulted by two men who broke into her home. This set off a chain reaction of frantic phone calls and neighborhood meetings to demand that the facility be moved out of Monterey Park.

The accomplishments of the parole struggle were impressive: (1) the formation of the Concerned Citizen Organization and an official Citizen Advisory Board made up of members of neighborhood watches in the affected area; (2) mobilization of immigrants and established residents through school and neighborhood meetings, petitions, letters, and door-to-door contacts; (3) involvement of city staff and officials; and (4) in 1992 the official removal of the parole office to a less resistant community.

Mary Pardo documented the parole fight by interviewing leaders and participating in meetings.[14] Her field notes indicate three factors that worked across ethnic and immigrant/native boundaries to create a sense of community and empowerment—mobilizing concerns: crime, the safety of children, alienation from the state; mobilizers: women reaching out to immigrants and ethnic groups through their contacts in neighborhood and school organizations; and local networks, providing political experience and a site for future grassroots mobilization.

Mobilizing Fears: Crime and the State

Parents' shared concerns for the safety of their children and fear that the presence of felons would increase crime in their neighborhood overrode many differences between immigrants and established residents. Their solidarity was also reinforced by alienation from what they perceived as the arbitrary authority of the state. These sentiments were strongly expressed by a Latina activist after a year of unsuccessful protest:

> The corrections representative thinks it won't be long before the residents give up. I told him he would be hearing from us until it is moved [her voice waivers]. It is the little kids who suffer [she hesitates a moment]. I'm sorry, I get emotional about it. It would be OK if it were a high school a block away. But kids in elementary school are still too young to defend themselves.

A Chinese immigrant male who has lived in the United States for 20 years saw the parole office as an example of the state's dumping an undesirable facility on a passive minority community:

> I was so angered about the parole office, and I want to tell you that the citizens were never informed. I know why they put that office in this neighborhood. They thought the Chinese here were the silent majority, but we are a multiethnic community. They thought that we were ignorant and stupid.

Women as Grassroots Organizers

As in the neighborhood watches, established Anglo, Asian American, and Latino residents, rather than newcomers, were the leaders in mobilizing the neighborhood and organizing a community advisory board to protest against the parole office. Within this group, women—the majority of them not employed outside the home—were the major organizers. Pardo argued that their activism at the neighborhood level (and later at the city and state levels) was a direct extension of their roles and training as mothers and protectors of children and the family. A Latina activist analyzed the role of women in the parole fight:

> At the first meetings we had in Monterey Park, there were more men. But, since then, there are more women. Now most of the block

> captains are women. And I think that they were active from the PTA days. I think as time went on, the women took over. When school started, I think the PTA in the Highlands jumped in and helped, and it seemed more women were involved.

The women were also aware of how men could serve in terms of their conventional roles. For example, they agreed on the selection of a Japanese American man as Chair of the Parole Advisory Board. An elderly Latina explained their choice:

> It was kind of unanimous. We just sort of appointed him. He is a teacher at a school in L.A. and he is very bright and vocal and he kind of pulls us together. We get to talking and gossiping and we kind of get off the subject and he pulls us back on the subject. You know how women are . . . we can go all directions [laughing softly].

A younger Latina contended that women's unique approach to community involvement helps to explain their success as neighborhood organizers:

> The women have the patience. And generally, that is what it takes to sit down, take your time, and go more into detail work like calling, doing the footwork, writing down everything and following up. It's time-consuming and I think it takes patience.
>
> Men would rather just go there and make their statements. And that's why we have Ron [the chair] there. Because we need somebody to make our statements who will be heard. And of course he is vocal. So we are happy that he is our spokesman, and he's involved enough to be there. His role is figurehead, and he also steers the group when he sees us going off track. A lot of times women try to get picky, and so you have to have that combination of the two ways.

The women tended to accept these differences as natural, the way things are: Men come in and make their statements and are heard; women handle the "details" that take patience and get the work done. As the protest grew in scope and moved from the neighborhood to the city council, the women's visibility decreased. But, according to Pardo, their presence and involvement meant the difference between a broad-based neighborhood-supported movement and a protest relying on the institutional authority of priests, principals, and public officials.

Recent immigrants, whether women or men, were clearly not leaders and mobilizers at either the grassroots or the institutional level. However, they attended some meetings, particularly at schools, signed petitions, and supported the involvement of their children at school. Pardo found that the men, who were often cast in the roles of public spokespersons, minimized immigrant participation, while the women who did the actual day-to-day organizing could cite examples of immigrant participation. For example, the principal of a local elementary school, an Anglo male, perceived immigrant participation as low:

> New immigrants were not really very involved in this. This is a middle-class community. Of course, some of the residents are from Hong Kong and Taiwan, but many of the Asians who live here are second- and third-generation. For example, Cindy Yee and Ron Hirasawa were very involved in that and they are at least second- and third-generation. I am not saying that new immigrants were not interested, but maybe the language barrier precluded their involvement . . . they are in the "crank up" stage and just beginning to get involved.

A Chinese immigrant man who has lived in the United States for 20 years agreed:

> At our meetings we had two hundred people. I could count the Asian faces—about five or six families. And a lot of them were born here like Ron and Cindy. Yes, in this case [participation in city council meetings dealing with the issue], I am sorry to say, the stereotype fits. They didn't come out for it. I tell them what is happening, and you know what they say? They will move to San Marino or Arcadia where there are a lot of white people, and they will be protected. The white people will fight the bad projects.

His analysis, while no doubt true to his experience, contrasted sharply with that of women involved in the door-to-door and day-to-day organizing. They devised strategies for getting immigrants involved at the grassroots level that would not be visible to men who only attended public meetings. Two women who walked from door to door collecting signatures on petitions claimed that immigrants had turned them down only twice. With the help of a computer-minded son, they designed a flyer showing a gun with a dotted line representing a bullet moving toward a man who is being robbed.

The women explained what they did when meeting newcomers who they thought might not speak English:

> First we would go to the door, and when they didn't speak English right away, we would ask, "Does anybody speak English here?" Then we would show them the flyers and point to the little man with the gun and say, This could happen to you! We would use sign language too. They all signed the petition. But they don't come to our meetings. Seems I can only get Caucasians to come. If I had to

> do it again, I would make this more graphic. That's what we need with these people.

Two Latina organizers got their petitions translated into Chinese and passed out a thousand flyers (in Chinese and English) announcing a meeting in a predominantly Asian neighborhood. They claimed that about one-third of the parents who attended a large meeting at the Highland Elementary School were immigrants. They had a videotape of the meeting and pointed out the faces of Asians in the audience. But language was a problem, according to an organizer:

> We had Asians, Anglos and Hispanics. But it was kind of hard to get to the immigrants because of the language barrier. And they tend to be withdrawn and not ready to get involved yet. For me it was difficult. Whenever I tried to talk to some of the Chinese, I don't think I was able to communicate. Even the Asian members on the committee I don't think can communicate with the new immigrants.

The immigrants also got involved in other ways. Responding to a letter from the PTA, some allowed their children to stay after school to write a letter protesting against the parole office. A PTA co-chair reported the result, and observed that Chinese participated selectively in PTA events:

> I guess we communicated with some new immigrants because we had about ten percent of the kids who seemed to be immigrant. Usually, you can tell because the child does not speak that well. And we had to help them a lot with the letters.
>
> . . . Maybe they [Chinese parents] don't stay for the parties because they don't speak English that well. But they do give something for their kids to take to the parties. Their tendency is to stay back. And we try to talk to them and make them feel more welcome. But it is breaking down. There are some ladies that get involved, but it is really hard to understand them because they have a thick accent.

The comparison between how women and men perceived the immigrants' involvement is instructive and highlights the importance of documenting the often unnoticed role of women in creating bridges between newcomers and established residents. Only then can we begin to understand the scope of the community building that is going on.

Creating Organizers, Leaders, and an Organization for the Future

The parole fight had another consequence that ultimately enhanced interethnic contacts and increased the participation of immigrants in local political affairs. According to local tradition, an aspiring candidate for city council must show a record of community service. Grassroots participation has been the route to political office for both men and women. Immigrants were learning the lesson. In 1989 Samuel Kiang, a Highland resident and an immigrant who had lived in the United States for 10 years, announced his candidacy for city council. He cited his involvement in the parole fight as an example of his community service.

Kiang also won multiethnic support from the women who had been major activists in the struggle against the parole office. One Anglo activist commented, "Sam is bright, honest, and sincere, and it would be good to have a Chinese immigrant in city council." Kiang was elected to city council in 1990 and ever since has been a catalyst drawing more immigrants into city affairs. In 1993 he spearheaded a fight against a proposed gambling parlor in Monterey Park (see Chapter 7). Once again, he got support from his neighborhood roots. Several Asian American women and men who had been active in the parole fight mobilized their block captains and neighborhood networks to collect signatures protesting against the card club.

Thus, the parole fight offered a case study of how immigrants and established residents from different ethnic backgrounds united as neighbors for political action. Theirs was a problematic neighborhood in the process of becoming a self-conscious, organized neighborhood; the mobilizing issue was crime and alienation from the state; the grassroots mobilizers were women; the most visible leaders were men. One leader, Kiang, used his neighborhood activism as a springboard for election to the city council. The parole fight achieved its immediate goal and, in the process, created leaders and a grassroots organization for future battles.

THE PROCESS OF COMMUNITY BUILDING

Community is defined by the people who are engaged in creating and sustaining it through their everyday activities in neighborhoods, service organizations, clubs, and public events. The presence of community is the often unnoticed and precarious consequence of coping with mundane concerns in settings where the lives of newcomers and established residents intersect.

The drive for unity in Monterey Park was practical rather than idealistic. Residents discovered their similarities while cheering their kids at a basketball game or organizing to keep a parole office out of their neighborhood. The unity they achieved was less a result of an abstract belief in harmony or assimilation to a fixed set of community values than a willingness to get involved and participate. Once people were involved, cooperation was imposed by the structure of civic organizations—the team of the Sports Club that carefully breaks down ethnic boundaries, the clubs of the Langley Center that carefully preserve and protect these boundaries. Cooperation was also the more spontaneous result of joining with neighbors to prevent crime or plan for the next natural disaster. There was no one model that applied to all situations.

The examples of the Langley Center, the Sports Club, and neighborhood associations show how boundaries formed by immigrant status and ethnicity can be crossed and diverse populations mobilized around shared concerns for safety and serving the needs of youth, the elderly, and immigrants. Success depended on the efforts of a few tireless organizers and a host of people willing to volunteer at the grassroots level of city life. The organizers were established Anglo, Latino, and Asian American residents, frequently women who have extended their concern for the welfare of their family to the neighborhood and city. Newcomers acted as supporters, their activity sometimes mediated by bilingual middlemen and -women.

Although the results are ephemeral, local, and situational, grassroots community building can have longer-term consequences. Their numbers diminishing, established activists in Monterey Park need newcomers and try to involve them in their causes. Those who become involved learn how Americans mobilize to get things done. In this way the work of neighborhood and civic organizations can function to incorporate newcomers and channel them toward greater civic and political participation.

The participation of newcomers has been associated with both continuity and discontinuity in the character of civic organizations. Continuity is expressed in the value of service and participation as the basis of community, the role of women as grassroots facilitators of cooperation, and the persistence of forms of civic and neighborhood organizations developed in the city's past.

Discontinuity is expressed in the diverse ethnic backgrounds of the participants and their challenge to traditional Anglo dominance. The discontinuity associated with the new immigration has been most stark in the local political realm, where established residents and newcomers compete for representation and control over the city's destiny. We turn now to the impact of immigration on city politics—the challenge to the old-boy white network of control, the rise of new political actors, and the movement from a politics of resistance to incorporation of newcomers into a more ethnically diverse and representative local political system.

Chapter 3
POLITICAL BREAKS AND TRANSITIONS

The old power structure is gone. What we are seeing today is a disorganized situation that's trying to organize. We are looking for an organization that will do what the old one did . . . provide candidates and structure. I think the battle royale *is on in terms of who's controlling the city.*
—*A white woman who is a longtime Monterey Park resident*

OUR INITIATION into the rough and tumble of Monterey Park politics began in 1988 in the city council chamber. On that stage—and a dramaturgical metaphor is appropriate—we began to identify major political issues and actors. Their trails led us offstage to the individuals, social networks, organizations, and events that made up the political arena of the city and the changing sites of our ethnography. What we saw on and off stage were signs of a political break—the decline of the aging white power structure; the political rise of women, minorities, and grassroots leaders; and a "battle *royale*" for control of the city council and the destiny of the city.

Sitting through long hours of debate in the council chamber and moving out into the political community, we tried in vain to pinpoint a key organization, an old-boy network, a group of leaders who could determine the candidates and policies of the Monterey Park city council. Instead of a coherent political structure, we found a shifting set of networks touching many sites: the city council, neighborhood organizations, civic and political clubs, and public events and festivals. The political center had fallen out. We had arrived at a moment of transition. Its course was unclear: A rebellion of disgruntled old-timers against newcomers and developers? The replacement of Anglo by Chinese power? A new ethnic diversity of uncertain political direction?

"HARD-BALL" CITY POLITICS

The city council was the visible arena of offstage pressure and negotiation. The battle lines continually reformed: today, council members against council members and the City Manager; tomorrow, factions of residents against each other, the city, and their elected representatives. Every other Monday night at seven o'clock, the five council members, the City Attorney, and assorted staff covered a never-ending agenda, which began patriotically with the pledge of allegiance before erupting into often acrimonious conflict. The council had voted mercifully to end meetings at eleven, but the time often extended into the early hours of the morning. A white "headlight" flashed ineffectually whenever speakers from the floor exceeded their three minutes. There seemed to be no limit to the lengthy speeches of the male council members.

During heated debates, residents filled the auditorium's 200 padded red seats, stood at the rear, protested at the podium, and intently watched for council votes to appear on the electronic scoreboard. It was a theater of polarization. The smallest technical details became points of contention; "oral communications," an occasion for speeches greeted with wisecracks, claps, or hisses from a chorus of council watchers. Field notes taken in the winter of 1989 captured the raucous atmosphere:

> A white woman about sixty, a council regular, a tireless advocate of environmental issues and fighter to clean up the city dumps, steps to the podium to support recycling. (A voice from the chorus of regulars: "Here comes the dumps again.")
>
> A gray haired Latino in his fifties reads a letter in support of the police chief, who is under political attack. Identifying residents by their ethnicity, he commends the chief for working well with the multicultural population of Monterey Park—Asians, Europeans, and Latinos. (A disapproving voice from the council chorus: "Aren't they all Americans?" For some old-timers "ethnicity" and "multiculturalism" are fighting words because they mean division.)[1]

Our observations repeatedly captured the freely expressed concern of the "regulars," mainly Anglo residents, that the council and City Manager were not accountable to the voters and not dealing adequately with the effects of economic growth and immigration on the quality of city life. What we were witnessing was a challenge to the local system of governance and its complicity with the rampant, market-driven development of a once-sleepy bedroom community.

Paradoxically, the very forms of governance that the Progressive Movement promoted in the first decades of the century against the collusion of business and party bosses had created new forms of collusion and unaccountability, shrouded in a value-neutral professionalism that had effectively disenfranchised local citizens. In his analysis of the California homeowners' tax revolt in the 1970s, Clarence Lo accurately described the situation in suburban cities:

> The suburban landscape was dominated not by the partisan machine but rather by a bureaucratic structure of government, founded with the best intentions of honest and efficient administration. But unbeknownst to progressive reformers, plans for rational administration had turned into a behemoth of unresponsiveness.[2]

Incorporated as a city in 1916, Monterey Park, like many cities in California, has been governed since the late 1940s by the council–manager system, one of the fruits of the Progressive Movement.[3] The Office of the City Manager describes the formal legislative structure as follows:

> The City Council is responsible to the electorate to be the policy-making body of the City and enacts laws, votes appropriations and provides direction to the City Manager, the various citizen commissions and the City Attorney. The City's five Council members are elected at large for four-year, overlapping terms of office. The Council reorganizes every nine and one-half months and elects one of its members to serve as Mayor. The Mayor presides over all the Council meetings and is the ceremonial head of the City for official functions. . . . The City Council also serves as governing board of Monterey Park's Community Redevelopment Agency. . . . To assist in their policy-making role, the City Council has appointed non-paid citizens' commissions, boards and committees to serve in an advisory capacity and to review and make recommendations on alternative priorities, policies and legislation affecting specific areas of community life.[4]

In theory, the council–manager system was a reform designed to separate politics from professional governance. The City Manager is supposed to run the show. The low-paid, part-time council members, while offering advice, would lack the time, knowledge, resources, or interest to control or interfere in important day-to-day decisions. In practice, at least in California, this system tended to hide and perpetuate power and squash local opposition. Today, strong mayors, interfering councils, and angry citizens have laid siege to the system.[5]

Monterey Park offers one example of the regional decline of the city manager system and the repoliticization and democratization of local politics. Residents, in rebellion over demographic and economic changes, struggle to control city council. The council battles among its members to control the City Manager. Although a nonelected position rotating on a nine-month basis among the five council members, the position of Mayor has assumed increased political significance in the community and media. The new Mayor sends out thousands of invitations to well-attended inaugural shows featuring the symbols of power and connections.

The City Manager is beholden to the changing and quirky politics of the council and fears for his job (all so far have been male). Both he and the council are torn between residents' demands for controlled growth, better services, and low taxes and the city's need for increased sales revenues (derived from development) to raise funds depleted by taxpayer revolts, recession, and uncertain federal and state support. Monterey Park shares a California dilemma: The same homeowners who voted for Proposition 13 and limits on property taxes, the major source of city funds, are also deeply suspicious of commercial development, a source of sales taxes needed to replace shrinking revenues.

In the politically tense climate of the late 1980s, the city staff were reluctant to talk to researchers, fearful that they would be drawn more deeply into the maelstrom. We never got an interview with Mark Lewis, then City Manager. Hired in 1988, he was fired by the city council in 1991 after a series of coups by established residents. Thereupon, he furthered the process of politicization by attempting, unsuccessfully, to sue the council for misconduct. One member of his staff who did offer an observation summed up the atmosphere in City Hall as "hard-ball politics." From his perspective, by "meddling" in the "profession" of governance, politically involved council members and residents were undermining stability and job security for city managers and staff.

THE DEMISE OF THE "OLD-BOY" NETWORK

In Monterey Park the stability of the city manager system had rested on the existence of a fairly stable local power structure, an old-boy network of established and predominantly white business and professional people. From the 1940s to the mid-1970s, the power structure was coherent enough to select candidates, run their campaigns, and keep city government on an even keel. The roster of council members shows a continuity rooted in friendship networks and membership in the same clubs.

Fiscally conservative Republicans and protectors of local business tended to dominate city politics until the late 1960s, and remained a powerful force until the mid-1970s. Some served long council terms—James Bradshaw from 1940 to 1960, Rod Irvine from 1955 to 1968.

These men organized their power socially through their connections to such civic associations as the Monterey Park Lions Club, Kiwanis Club, Rotary Club, and Chamber of Commerce. The Lions Club had been especially influential in determining and supporting candidates for city council. A critical but respectful member explained the club's influential, if parochial, role in city politics:

> The power structure at Garvey and Garfield [the commercial corner of the local business establishment] were essentially the people who

were the Lions Club. It was a mechanism, a social mechanism through which the city functioned. The club was very large in its heyday, and also very particular as to who became a member and who didn't. They were the ones who determined who the hell was going to run for city council and who wasn't. With that kind of authority they could determine whether or not Bullock's [a large department store] could get a piece of ground to build a shopping center on, and the decision was "no," because it was going to hurt the local merchants. Those were the decisions that were made that prevented the city from growing.[6]

In the early 1970s, in spite of its proximity to downtown Los Angeles, Monterey Park was still a pleasant economic backwater, its commercial property underdeveloped and undervalued. A longtime resident, who was definitely outside the old-boy business network, described her impression of the business area in that period:

You know, you sometimes wonder when people talk about the "good old days." Well, I'm going to tell you the business district looked terrible. It looked like a disaster area. Eighty percent of the stores were vacant. The owners would be glad to let us use vacant stores for meetings just to avoid vandalizing.

By the mid-1970s the commercial landscape of Monterey Park had changed. Chinese real estate interests had bought vacant commercial land on Atlantic Boulevard from large property owners; on Garvey and Garfield, businessmen were selling their small stores to Asian newcomers at a handsome profit. Aging and outnumbered, the former business leaders had lost the economic base of their power and, with it, their interest in and ability to influence local elections.

Established residents whose lives spanned the transformation recognized a clear political break associated with immigration and economic development. A middle-aged white male businessman, who deplored what he saw as the short-sighted, anti-Asian attitudes of some of the old-timers, offered a credible theory of their political decline:

It was the time when Fred Hsieh was buying up a lot of property. He wasn't the only one. There were others who were here before him, but I look at Fred Hsieh's involvement as a kind of watershed. Three things occurred simultaneously.

The first thing that happened was the beginning of this gargantuan rate of inflation, where all of a sudden property values of the previous decade or two bore no relationship to current values. So all of a sudden you had folks who had purchased property for a song whose property was worth a hundred thousand dollars, and they

> were going crazy. And the second thing that occurred at the same time was the wave of migration from the Far East. Third, the power structure had matured. But their control had been so absolute and narrow that they failed to look forward to the future, and they had not created a cadre of younger folks to take over. So as they got older and decided to retire and pull out and got less interested . . . they left behind them a vacuum . . . but as nature abhors a vacuum, that vacuum was filled in terms of new leadership.[7]

Today the old white male power structure lives in memory. The Monterey Park Lions Club still symbolizes community service and past political glory. Members talk nostalgically about the saner times of responsible city politics. They speak with pride about how their chapter originated "White Cane Days" (now an international fundraising event for the blind), and built Lions Manor for the elderly and extensive facilities at Barnes Park.

Every June the Lions Club holds its annual pancake breakfast fundraiser in Barnes Park. Every morning the political past is ritually celebrated when old-timers from the Monterey Park Lions and Rotary clubs come together with a scattering of younger civic leaders for breakfast and political talk at the "Kaffee Klatch." When we began our study in 1988, the Kaffee Klatch met regularly from nine to ten at the Paris Restaurant in Monterey Park. It was an old-timers' institution, an authentic, hometown, ham and eggs 1950s-style eatery with maple tables, red plastic booths, and pictures of American country scenes.

A year later, the Kaffee Klatch was meeting at the Olympic Restaurant in the neighboring city of Alhambra. The Vietnamese-run "Hawaiian Restaurant" had supplanted the Anglo-style but recently Chinese-owned Paris Restaurant, noodles had replaced scrambled eggs, and the Kaffee Klatch crowd had left town for a real American breakfast. While finishing off his Olympian plate of eggs, a veteran member of the Lions Club and Kaffee Klatch explained the move:

> I used to eat Chinese food once in a while, but I haven't done it for years because I'm just so fed up with the Chinese I don't want any of them. It's a kind of protest. If I was in another town I might go to a Chinese restaurant, but in this town I haven't been in one for a good many years.
>
> The Paris Restaurant was the only English, or only Caucasian, restaurant in town. And now there isn't any. That's the reason we came over here.[8]

The function of the club declined along with the number of Caucasian restaurants. Hal Fiebelkorn, who started attending breakfast meetings in 1943, and for years has written a local column entitled "The Kaffee Klatch," contrasted the club and government of today and yesterday:

> Every self-respecting city must have a Kaffee Klatch. Call it a "Breakfast Club," a "Discussion Group" or a "Spit and Argue Club," a town cannot succeed without the guidance that comes from these groups. . . . The Kaffee Klatch has changed. Where once fiery attorneys, concerned doctors, energetic real estate brokers and hardened businessmen gathered to castigate the city council and the planning commission, they have now turned their attention to the number of miles per gallon they get from their recreation vehicles and the latest reports of their doctors.
>
> But even though they have attained some measure of tolerance, every once in a while the juices begin to flow and tempers are raised as they bemoan the good old days when government existed for the people.[9]

To survive today, the old clubs needed to recruit business and professional newcomers. With the attrition of old-timer business and professional members, some civic organizations, like the local Kiwanis Club, have become predominantly Chinese. Others, like the Chamber of Commerce, have a poor record in recruiting Chinese businessmen and -women and have tended to maintain established resident, non-Asian control at their highest leadership levels. The once politically influential Monterey Park Lions Club has remained a bastion of old-timers who can no longer call city elections. Meanwhile Taiwanese newcomers have formed their own Little Taipei Lions Club and are becoming a presence in civic affairs.

The old white business elite has disappeared, along with its ability to wield power through civic organizations, but the political function of civic organizations remains. Candidates for city council—whether immigrant or American-born, Chinese, Anglo, or Latino—know that membership in the Chamber of Commerce or the Boys and Girls Club and volunteer work for service organizations establish their qualifications for public office. Locally, established residents call this service "paying your dues," a necessary part of forming a changing network of the people who count socially and politically.

Asian immigrants have helped to sustain and revitalize the class base of civic organizations. The presence of Chinese American businessmen and -women has strengthened and internationalized the conservative class interests once represented by the more parochial, white old-timers. This has not escaped the notice of local Republicans, who would like to capture a larger conservative vote in a traditionally Democratic region. They know from their own research what social scientists have reported:

that the majority of Chinese newcomers who become citizens, unlike established Japanese American, Latino, and Anglo residents, tend to have no party affiliation or to register as Republicans.[10]

THE LEGACY OF THE DEMOCRATS

The conservative old-timers were not all-powerful. Before the big immigration of the 1970s and 1980s, they had been challenged by progressive and ethnic contenders for power. The challengers were part of an earlier wave of newcomers—young business and professional people attracted by affordable housing during the suburban building boom of the 1950s and 1960s.

The newcomers were very different from the old-boy business elite whose base was in local property. They had less interest in buying and selling property than in using it to enhance the quality of their suburban life. One of the postwar newcomers who was active in Monterey Park politics from the mid-1950s to 1970 contrasted the philosophies of the two groups that played a political role in Monterey Park before the Chinese immigration:

> What we [the newcomers] were trying to do was to create a community environment that was an extension of our homes, something positive. Practical businessmen [the local business-based old-timers], their attitude toward development was "Let them put it up, it's their money and it means sales tax for us."[11]

Having different relations to property, the old-timers and the politically active newcomers held different conceptions of community development, and they organized their power differently. The newcomers built their power less through the old service organizations than through political clubs and campaigns for better parks, libraries, and "quality" (high standards) development. Their most progressive wing could be found among the members of the Monterey Park Democratic Club, which included a strong Jewish contingent along with other Anglos and a smaller number of Latinos and Japanese Americans.

Together they built the largest and most liberal Democratic club in the San Gabriel Valley. Chartered in 1949, at its peak (the mid-1950s to the mid-1970s) the club had up to two hundred members who were active in state politics and ran their own candidates against the more conservative Republican members of city council.[12] An elderly Anglo woman described the political climate of the club and the activist atmosphere of Monterey Park in the 1960s:

> I remember when we first moved here, I thought I'd moved to heaven. I was getting very interested in politics by that time. I grew

up in Orange County in a staunch Republican family. But I began to see that I didn't agree with that point of view. I thought there were a lot of things that needed changing, and I wanted to get active in doing something about it. When I came here I found an active Democratic club and the Women's International League for Peace and Freedom. People put yard signs out before elections and walked precincts. People really talked about politics here, and they didn't down there [in Orange County], and I thought that was so wonderful.

I remember one of the first [Democratic club] meetings I came to in Monterey Park. There was a Mexican American, a Japanese American, a black man, Jewish people, people from different backgrounds. I was so happy with it because I was brought up in the Methodist Church, and we were taught that was the right way to be, you know, that all men are brothers, but it wasn't practiced. You just paid lip service to it. Up here it was practiced. I'd like to keep it that way.[13]

The Democrats made inroads in city council in the 1950s and began to wield significant local power by the late 1960s. In the 1960s, they fought successfully for a Community Relations Commission in Monterey Park and, to the chagrin of some old-timers, welcomed Latino and Asian American newcomers and campaigned vigorously for fair housing in their community and in the state. The Monterey Park Democratic Club also organized the campaigns for most of the liberals and ethnic minorities who were elected to the city council before a new brand of leaders emerged in the late 1970s: the liberal Democrat George Brown, Jr. (1954–1958); the first Asian on city council, a Korean American, Alfred H. Song (1960–1962); a Jewish leader of the Monterey Park Democratic Club, Gershon Lewis (1962–1974); the first Japanese American on the council, George Ige (1970–1978). (Matthew Martinez, the first Mexican American councilman [1974–1982], was an exception. He started out as a Republican and received strong local support from the conservative Lions Club before joining the regional Democratic establishment.)

Living in mainly Democratic state and federal districts, these aspiring politicians used the Monterey Park city council as a stepping stone to higher office. Song moved on to the California Senate and Assembly. In 1995, Brown and Martinez were serving in the United States House of Representatives.

Thus, between the late 1950s and the mid-1970s, there were two major power groups in Monterey Park politics. The dominant one was conservative and rooted in the local business interests of old-timers whose vision of the city predated the postwar suburban explosion. The second, more cosmopolitan and liberal, expressed the interests of postwar newcomers—young Anglo, Latino, and Asian American families who cared above all about the quality of their suburban life.

The political influence of the second group survived the new Asian immigration, both reacting against and adapting to the changes. Their political evolution paralleled that of Democrats in other American communities confronted with ethnic change in their own backyards. Some moved to the right and resisted change; others actively supported and organized for the new minorities who had become majorities.[14]

One important sign of this political change was the expansion of Democratic clubs from one to three. For most of the period before the new immigration, there was only the Monterey Park Democratic Club (MPDC). In the mid-1980s, two new clubs formed: the West San Gabriel Valley Asian Pacific Democratic Club and the United Democratic Club (UDC). The organizations represented divergent political responses to demographic and economic restructuring. The development of the Asian club, as we shall see later, was primarily a historical response to the opportunity for ethnic power opened up by an unprecedented suburban concentration of Asians. The divisions between the two primarily white clubs reflected leadership conflicts and different attitudes about economic development and ethnic power.

The MPDC followed up its early support of minority rights by coming down strongly on the side of ethnic diversity, actively supporting Asian empowerment and interethnic coalitions. For example, Ruth Willner, a longtime leader of the club, helped run the successful campaigns for city council of Lily Chen (1982), Judy Chu (1988), and Sam Kiang (1990). The MPDC maintained close ties with the new Asian club, and members were active in organizing against local attempts to pass an "Official English" ordinance in the city and to impose language and sign restrictions on Chinese newcomers.

The UDC, while strongly supporting Latino candidates in Latino-dominated state and national races, has made environmental and development issues rather than ethnic representation its priority. The club is a mixture of moderates and liberals; some members have worked with Republicans on local growth-control issues, going so far as to support a right-wing advocate of Official English for city office and oppose an Asian Democrat, Lily Chen, in her 1986 bid for council reelection on the grounds that she was "pro-development."

A member of the UDC condemned members of the old club as "misguided old-leftists who were so old when the left-wing thing collapsed that they couldn't give up on it and listen to reason. So they support any non-Anglo candidate without evaluating what kind of candidate it is."[15]

For their part, some members of the old club contended that the UDC lost its liberal and Democratic credentials by giving support to conservative and nativist Republicans because they were politically correct on the issue of slow growth. In 1987 the UDC's alleged bipartisan politics led the Los Angeles County Democratic Central Committee, with the help of several malcontents within the UDC ranks, to temporarily deny renewal of the club's charter. The charges included having at least one Republican sign the charter application and jointly sponsoring an ad with the Monterey Park Republican Club. The latter incident involved the 1987 move to recall two council members because of their support for the "racially motivated" Official English ordinance. The ad criticized the recall as an attempt "to punish a difference of opinion."[16]

Given the ambiguity of the issues and motives behind the charges against the UDC, the charter was renewed. The local party squabbles were symptomatic of a larger problem—the Democrats' lack of a consensus on how to deal with new economic and racial tensions.[17] The politics of integration that many had espoused in the 1960s did not fit the conditions of the 1980s and 1990s. The ethnic problem was no longer one of "integrating" disadvantaged minorities into dominant white institutions, but of adapting these institutions to minorities and immigrants. Some Democrats strongly supported this agenda. Others opposed it, agreeing with conservatives that ethnic empowerment and affirmative action were anti-American and divisive slogans used to promote "special interests." The responses of local Democrats to the new diversity were as diverse as those of the other political players who arose out of the ashes of the old political order. The traditional political practices and labels were no longer working.

THE NEW POLITICAL PLAYERS

With the old white conservative business elite in retreat and their Democratic challengers in disarray, the doors to city governance were temporarily left open to established residents and newcomers who had not been part of the old political order. The new activists fell into five general groups: (1) advocates of slow growth and nativists who wanted to limit economic and demographic changes according to their vision of a less urban and more homogeneous past; (2) younger multiethnic businessmen bent on establishing and politically legitimating their control over economic development; (3) progressives or radical Democrats who saw the changes in Monterey Park as an opportunity to build economic and multiethnic empowerment for the future; (4) minorities and immigrants who wanted civil rights and political representation; and (5) women of many different political persuasions who were asserting their political voices and leadership. These players represented overlapping responses to the demographic and economic restructuring of the city.

Nativists and Slow-Growth Advocates

The slow-growth movement emerged locally to protest against the collusion between local government and developers and the unwanted results of uncontrolled economic development and immigration. Their leaders and activists were overwhelmingly Anglo and elderly, although their programs drew strong support from established Latino and Asian American residents.

While slow-growth advocates targeted developers and defended what they interpreted as the interests of homeowners, a second group wanted to defend America and target immigrants and foreign capital as the primary cause of the decline in national power and quality of local life. Their political objective was to restrict immigration, bilingualism, and the use of foreign languages, particularly Chinese, on business signs and on official occasions.

Differing in their immediate objectives, the nativists and the slow-growth advocates had several things in common. They espoused populism through their grassroots appeal to the little guys against big government, big developers, and big, uncontrolled structural changes. They agreed on the importance of controlled economic growth and were united in their desire to restrict development and preserve their conception of a more livable past. Both groups were on a collision course with the champions of growth. In a city where developers were frequently Asian, however, nativism and slow growth, ethnic and economic issues, were often conflated and could lead to racial polarization.

One of our most important research tasks was to trace the relationship between nativism and slow growth. Were they respectively the reactionary and the progressive side of populism, or were they variant defenses of white and middle-class privilege against the influx of nonwhite immigrants? What effects did these movements have on the course of political conflict and consensus, particularly on power relations between newcomers and established residents, ethnic groups, and classes?

Growth Advocates

Pro-growth interests ranged from high-powered developers and land speculators, who often lived outside the city and favored unfettered market-driven growth, to local businessmen and -women who recognized the need for planned development. The pro-growth group was multiethnic and included both native- and foreign-born. Collectively, they could promote either harmony or conflict between Monterey Park's diverse residents. Already "integrated" as a business class, they could unite to oppose xenophobia or, in their desire to fight growth controls, play the "racial card" by arguing that slow growth equaled nativism. By this reduction, slow growth was translated to mean "no growth," anti-immigrant, and "NIMBY"—that is, no developers and no Chinese in my backyard.

Progressive Multiculturalists

Slow-growth and pro-growth advocates had to contend with Monterey Park's left Democrats, or progressives. They included elderly, established progressives, some from the old MPDC, and younger Latino, Anglo, and Asian American newcomers with a history of community organizing. The latter group consisted of first-, second-, and third-generation Americans who had recently moved to Monterey Park to become active players in the building of a more democratic and multicultural America.

Placing a positive value on multiculturalism, ethnic empowerment, and multiethnic alliances around issues of representation and community control over development, they combined the developers' antiracist message with the slow-growth demand for economic empowerment of local residents. We shall see that these priorities created the possibility of political alliances with either multicultural business interests or the more xenophobic but populist advocates of controlled growth. The progressives' role in the evolution of a politics of diversity in Monterey Park is an important part of our story.

Minorities and Immigrants

When we began our study in 1988, the media tended to focus on Monterey Park as a hotbed of nativist reaction to immigration. Less noticeable at the time was another tendency that cut across this dichotomy—the emergence of minority politics and interethnic alliances. The sudden transformation of the people and economy of the region created fears of displacement among some established Anglo residents, but also hopes for empowerment on the part of Asian newcomers and established but unrepresented Latinos and Asian Americans. Their demand for ethnic and immigrant representation set another political tendency in motion in Monterey Park.

In implementing their demands for greater representation, minorities and immigrants also founded their own organizations to legitimate the role of ethnic politics. Their strategies for empowerment took two sometimes conflicting directions. The first was nationalistic, organizing strictly within particular ethnic and immigrant groups; the second strategy favored the formation of multiethnic alliances, a response to the improbability that any single group could command a political majority in the ethnically fragmented terrain of the San Gabriel Valley.

A major focus of our research was the impact of emerging ethnic politics on relations between newcomers and established residents and the general course of political conflict and accommodation. The development of ethnic politics was part of the political restructuring of Monterey Park, a tendency that could work for either ethnic conflict or harmony as the political process unfolded.

Women

One new group of activists cut across all the others and formed the leadership base of growing grassroots politics. Always loyal workers behind the men who had led city council, in the current period of economic and demographic change women were becoming elected leaders in their own right.

The "old-boy" network had indeed consisted of boys. Of the 59 council members who held office in Monterey Park between 1916 and 1975, only 2 were women, and one was filling out the term of her late husband. During a period of political change between 1976 and 1994, 7 of the 17 council members were women. Between 1988 and 1994, women held three seats in the five-member council.

A mixture of established residents and newcomers, American-born, foreign-born, Latino, Anglo, and Asian, the women were, with some notable exceptions, united less by ideology than by a pragmatic political style. In a community torn by ethnic conflict, the strength of their most effective leaders was their ability to rise above factionalism and egotism to negotiate policies and institutions for an ethnically diverse city.

This rise of women was another political break with the past. One armchair historian correctly dated this break to the defeat of the last candidate of the Lions Club in 1976:

> When the last member of the Lions Club, Hal Fiebelkorn, ran for office and was defeated by Louise Davis in 1976, that was one of the indications of breaking the grip of the old establishment in the city of Monterey Park. If you go back and look at the members of the city council, leading back in the late thirties, you'll see that in this town the majority were members of the Lions Club. But Louise Davis was a community member who decided to become active. She was not connected to the power structure. She managed to get elected because the power structure had lost its political clout in terms of being able to get out the vote.[18]

Louise Davis agreed that her election was a break from tradition:

> This was the first time I ever ran for anything. There hadn't been a woman on this council for twenty-five years. There was another woman who ran against me, a really outstanding woman—she was president of the Chamber of Commerce at the time. She was supported by the Lions Club people, and she also lost. So that was really the turning point there.[19]

Davis contrasted her own grassroots qualifications with those of the more moneyed and well-connected:

> I was visible in the community because of my involvement with the PTA and other groups. And I had also been appointed by the mayor to head our Bicentennial Committee. And also, in 1975, I was designated as the outstanding citizen of the year by the American Legion. So I had really a lot going. But politics never really crossed my mind until—I believe it was the end of seventy-five, or maybe seventy-six, that the city council decided to eliminate our free ambulance service. I joined a community committee to oppose this because I just felt that it would be too expensive for ordinary people to pay for ambulance service.

Two incumbent seats opened up, and people started to ask Louise, "Why don't you run?" She lacked the conventional resources, but power was building up at the grassroots. Davis explains:

> It was kind of a joke at first—it was always a joke to a lot of people, you know, that I was running for office. Because, number one, I did not have a lot of money. I spent only twenty-five hundred dollars on the campaign. Number two, I was older. I had seven children. I hadn't been in politics. But I guess the timing was right, and I was in the grassroots. I had always been visible in the community—City Beautiful, pictures out there with the broom in my hand, you know. All those things were going on, which, really, I never knew would accumulate to be background for me. Besides that, I walked every block of the city [during election campaigns], which I always do, because I have to compensate for lack of funds.[20]

Starting from the grassroots and never severing her connections with them, Davis proved to be a strong and tenacious leader. She remained in city council for two terms (1976–1984) and was elected City Treasurer twice in 1988 and 1992. Her case shows how women used the political opening created by the breakdown of the old order to make a transition from family and community support to political office. A volunteer, then a leader in such organizations as the Langley Center, the Historical Society, the Soroptimist Club, and the UDC, Davis has been a conservative yet moderating voice of established residents. Unconnected to the business establishment, she was closely attuned to the concerns of residents who had become increasingly critical of big government, big developers, and the new immigration.

Davis' route to power via the roles of homemaker and volunteer was followed by councilwomen like Betty Couch (1988–1992), Marie Purvis (1990), and Rita Valenzuela (1992), whose political aspirations were circumscribed by the neighborhood and the city. But there was another route to women's power. Lily Chen (1982–1986) and Judy Chu (1988) came to the city council through their professional careers and multiethnic and inter-community networks. Chu is an American-born professor of psychology at East Los Angeles Community College. A relative newcomer to Monterey Park, she has a record as a community activist and Democrat whose progressive politics were honed in the civil rights and antiwar movements. Chen was born in China into a prominent Beijing family. She is a county administrator and a moderate Democrat with strong connections in the Chinese immigrant community. Both of these professional women had a political reach that extended far beyond Monterey Park to the wider Asian and Chinese communities, and they aspired to higher office.

FOUR LEVELS OF POLITICAL STRUGGLE

Women and other political actors who filled the vacuum left by the old power structure represented four separate but interrelated struggles whose outcome would decide the direction of political change and the meaning of ethnic and American identities in Monterey Park.

Gender Power

The struggle of women for leadership and representation came first. This was not the consequence of a formal feminist movement, or a deliberate war against male supremacy, but rather an extension of their traditional concern for family and neighborhood.[21] Taking advantage of the opening brought about by demographic and economic changes and the weakening of the white old-boy network, women were extending and deepening their political involvement. We saw women of different ethnic backgrounds and political persuasions pushing themselves up from the grassroots toward more formal leadership. A key issue for us was whether their leadership styles were different from those of men and, if so, what effect these different styles might have on the course of conflict and consensus in a multiethnic city. The mediating role of women in city council and in neighborhood politics and civic organizations is described in Chapters 2, 6, and 7.

Class Power

The second major level of conflict was the class struggle between homeowners and developers (and their supporters in city government) for control over land use and economic growth. On one side were the local forces for slow or controlled growth; on the other, the more regionally and globally based forces for unrestricted, market-driven development.

Our use of the terms "class" and "class struggle" needs to be understood in its residential and suburban context.[22] In general, classes define the pattern of control over the forces that create wealth: labor, land, resources, and instruments of production. In Monterey Park, a middle-income bedroom community, the most visible class struggle during our study was between homeowners and property users (residents whose primary concern was land use and the quality of suburban life) on one hand and big property owners, developers, and speculators (people who buy and invest in property for profit) on the other. Here the issues were overdevelopment, congestion, traffic, and increased density. Class struggle over land use and abuse was also manifested in local protests against the state and industry as the perceived agents of environmental problems such as toxic dumping, toxic spraying to eradicate the Mediterranean fruit fly (the "medfly" being the latest pest of big growers), and a proposed card casino. The organized slow-growth movement is analyzed in Chapter 4, but class struggle over development is a strand that runs through our story.

Ethnic and Immigrant Power and Identity

The third important struggle in Monterey Park was the one for ethnic power and identity within a changing ethnic/racial hierarchy. Here, in contrast to the class hierarchy, social and political positions are defined not by ownership/nonownership of wealth-producing property, but by race and ethnicity, differently imagined and evaluated biological (racial) and cultural/historical (ethnic) differences. In recent decades the more positive term "ethnicity" has been publicly favored over "race," a concept implying invidious and innate phenotypical and genetic distinctions. Since the major dividing line between residents remains white versus nonwhite, however, race and ethnicity merge in practice, and our text will use "race" or "ethnicity" as the social context requires.[23]

Unlike class, which is more or less fixed by determinant patterns of ownership, race and ethnicity are more flexible and changeable social and political constructions. For example, one effect of the new immigration and diversity was to increase ethnic political consciousness, a tendency shared by Anglos facing their own minoritization. The new immigration and increased diversity also brought about a shift in the racial/ethnic fault line from majority/minority (white/nonwhite relations) to interethnic relations between Asian newcomers, Asian Americans, Latinos, and Anglos and between diverse national groups within the heterogeneous Asian population (e.g., mainland Chinese, Taiwanese, Chinese Vietnamese, Vietnamese, Korean). Another change was the reconstruction of Pan-Chinese and Pan-Asian identities as different Asian populations searched for ways of increasing their political representation.[24] The rise of ethnic and interethnic politics is discussed in Chapters 5 through 8.

Incorporation of Newcomers: Citizenship

The power struggle between established residents and immigrants was the latest and most dramatic historical episode in an ongoing process of conflict and accommodation between newcomers and old-timers. After World War II, during a time of population explosion and geographic mobility, younger, mostly white newcomers confronted older, more established white residents. Their differences reflected a clash of lifestyles as a small, almost rural town became part of an expanding suburban Los Angeles. By the 1960s, the newcomers increasingly included American-born Japanese and Mexican Americans, whose differences with established white residents were affected by race and ethnicity. After the mid-1970s, newcomers were above all Chinese and other Asian immigrants, while the established residents were Latinos and Asian Americans as well as Anglos. This time, the clash between established residents and newcomers was tainted with nativism as well as racism.

Relations between newcomers and established residents are inevitably affected by all the things that divide Americans—lifestyle, race, ethnicity, class, and immigration. Yet newcomer/established-resident relations have their own dynamic not directly reducible to these divisions.[25] Fundamentally, the tension between established residents and newcomers turns on citizenship in a broad, rather than narrowly legal, sense—the criteria for being included in a local community.

From the viewpoint of established residents, these criteria for citizenship include length of time in the community, participation in civic and political groups, and ability to speak English. Local values dictate that promotion to the category of established resident depends on how long one has been in the community and what one does for it, rather than who one is. In practice, who one is always counts, and the weight given to ascribed criteria varies according to the status of the persons who judge and are judged. At one extreme, conservative whites may exclude all nonwhites from insider status regardless of their American birth, length of residence, and level of participation. At another extreme, some newcomers may imagine that having the money to buy in is all that counts. Currently, the formula for local citizenship is highly contestable and negotiable in Monterey Park, where no single group has the power to define and impose its standards unilaterally on newcomers.

Finally, in a situation involving differences in language, political relations between established residents and newcomers are rarely direct. Though unable to vote or directly intervene in politics, newcomers nevertheless strongly affect local politics by their large, growing, and highly visible presence. Their power is mediated and brokered by established immigrants: bilingual middlemen and -women with the resources to inform immigrants through the foreign-language press and media, churches, and other organizations and, at crucial points, organize and mobilize them for protest.

Our research, responding to growing concerns about immigrant incorporation, initially focused on political relations between newcomers and established residents. We wanted to know whether this division was the primary basis of conflict in a city radically changed by immigration. At the beginning of our research (the mid-1980s to 1990, described in Chapters 4 to 6), this seemed to be the case; the tone of political discourse was set by anti-immigrant, nativist forces. By the end of our research (1990–1994, described in Chapter 7), newcomers had moved from a position of defense to offense and were setting agendas and affecting a variety of political and economic decisions. This tendency reinforced newcomer/established-resident conflict from a different side. The larger political picture, however, was characterized by an incredibly complex set of shifting class and ethnic alliances that tended to supersede the clash between newcomers and established residents.

To our list of local struggles—women versus men, homeowners and property users versus property owners, white versus nonwhite, ethnic versus ethnic, and newcomers versus established residents—others could be added. Some members of the aging population of established residents, for example, were concerned that younger newcomers cost the government more than they contributed in taxes and revenues. We also noticed generational political divisions between first- and second-generation Asian Americans and Asian immigrants. These divisions are reported in Chapters 5 and 7.

THE MEANING OF THE POLITICAL BREAK

In the 1980s, the emergence of women and other political actors and the leaning of population and the economy toward people of Chinese and Asian descent provided the material foundation for a major political break in Monterey Park. The old white power structure was in full decline, weakened by age, size, and the loss of its economic base to new Asian entrepreneurs. Replacing the old-timers were grassroots rebels, some resisting and others pushing for change: established residents who wanted to turn back the clock; women who thought they could do a better job than men; ethnic minorities bent on empowerment; and a multiethnic business elite eager to translate its resources into governmental power.

Together these forces carved out the political options for a multiethnic community transformed by the new Asian immigration. The tradition of white, male, business domination of local politics was at stake. Would it be maintained? Would it be ethnically modified, its class and gender base preserved under the rule of Chinese American males? Or would newcomers and established residents bring about a fundamental political transformation in the direction of greater ethnic and gender representation and more control over local economic development?

Also at stake was the relative interethnic harmony that had been achieved under the aegis of Anglos before the new Asian immigration restructured the old ethnic and economic hierarchies. Would the old forms of white-sponsored accommodation collapse into political conflict based on ethnicity and divisions between newcomers and established residents? Would those forms be reimposed in a surge of nativism and Americanism? Or would new forms of coalition and cooperation grow from the soil of diversity in a city where Latino and Asian minorities had become the numerical majorities?

The answers lie in the evolving political process and its effects on the structure of power and political relations between immigrant newcomers and the multiethnic population of established residents. During the course of our study from the mid-1980s to the early 1990s, the political process evolved from an initial stage of cooperation between immigrant newcomers and established residents at elite levels, to conflict rising from the grassroots, and, finally, greater levels of accommodation as well as new points of conflict. Each of these stages was associated with a different alignment of class and ethnic forces and different levels of political conflict and accommodation between newcomers and established residents.

Chapter 4

THE BACKLASH: SLOW GROWTH AND ENGLISH ONLY

Will the last American to leave Monterey Park please bring the flag?
—Large sign prominently displayed at a Monterey Park service station in the early 1980s

I came here to buy a home, not a ticket to development. The underlying philosophical question is, who owns the city? The town belongs to the people who live here. *—Joseph Rubin, a leader of the growth-control movement*

Until attitudes change, we will have racial tension. Monterey Park will be a Chinese community. You can't buck this trend over time. Don't be Indian fighters. You will win some battles, but lose the war.
—Frederic Hsieh, real estate investor and developer

THE QUOTATIONS that begin this chapter express three different reactions to community change, three levels of discourse that framed the terms of conflict between newcomers and old-timers and between ethnic groups in Monterey Park in the mid-1980s.[1] The anonymous slogan, with its image of foreign invasion, conveys an unambiguous anti-immigrant nativism. Rubin speaks the populist language of growth control. For him, uncontrolled economic development rather than immigration as such is the problem in Monterey Park. Control over land use should be wrested from the developers and compliant city officials and put in the hands of the people who live in the city. Hsieh, an immigrant who was one of the first promoters of Chinese ownership of property in Monterey Park, perceives resistance to Chinese newcomers, expressed in both racism and restrictions on the free market, as the major problem and barrier to peace in Monterey Park.

The intersection of these tendencies defines the politics of resistance and defense that evolved in Monterey Park after a brief honeymoon between local leaders and entrepreneurial newcomers.

THE RISE AND RAPID FALL OF THE "ALL-AMERICA CITY"

In 1985 the National Municipal League and the newspaper *USA Today* awarded Monterey Park the title of "All-America City" for its innovative programs involving immigrants and established residents of all ethnic groups in the solution of civic problems. The city council had solicited the award and proudly basked in the resulting publicity. Councilman David Almada explained how the city had met the challenge of immigration:

> During the 1970's, almost overnight, Monterey Park experienced an explosion in residents from the Far East. Up to 90 percent of the enrollment in our elementary schools became Asian students whose primary language spoken at home was something other than English. Better than 50 percent of the businesses in commercial areas were being purchased by various Asian interests and some 60 to 80 percent of new home purchases were being made by Asian residents. . . . Suddenly, we were not just a community of interesting ethnic backgrounds—but a city with real language and cultural differences. The language problem became more than the occasional Spanish and Japanese difficulties of a few senior citizens and mushroomed into a daily coping with Mandarin, Cantonese, Vietnamese, Korean as well as a multitude of other Asian dialects.
>
> In the late 1970's, Monterey Park residents—newcomers and old timers—rolled up their sleeves and reached out to one another . . . opening up communications and insuring that residents and business people continue to work and participate as a united community.[2]

The evidence presented of a people united was impressive. Harmony was visible in city services that addressed the diverse needs of very diverse residents. Following Monterey Park's tradition of volunteerism, a multiethnic corps of established residents and newcomers were giving their time to city boards and commissions, tutoring Chinese-speakers in a literacy program, and acting as translators for the police. There were active Taiwanese and Japanese Sister City programs, yearly ethnic festivals, and the highly successful and volunteer-run Langley Senior Center serving Latinos, Chinese Americans, Japanese Americans, and Anglos.

Never had city government been so diverse. The City Manager, Lloyd de Llamas, was Mexican American; the Treasurer, George Ige, was Japanese American. Of the five council members, Louise Davis was an Anglo; David Almada and Rudy Peralta were Mexican Americans; G. Monty Manibog was a Filipino American; and Lily Lee Chen was a Chinese American.

Chen's inauguration as Mayor on November 28, 1983, was acclaimed by the Chinese and national press as a sign of the political ascendancy of Asian Americans: "Lily Lee Chen, her speech still accented with her native Chinese, her career written up in China's People's Daily, was sworn in tonight as the first female Chinese-American mayor in the United States, a symbol of the growing numbers and political sophistication of Asian-Americans."[3] From China to the United States, little Monterey Park, with its multiethnic population and its international ties, was being recognized as a positive model for a new Pacific Rim society.[4]

The official image of harmony was soon tarnished by political events. In 1986, a year after the "All-America" award, Almada, Chen, and Peralta were swept out of office and replaced by three long-established Anglo residents: Barry Hatch, Chris Houseman, and Patricia Reichenberger. The electoral result was to return the city council to white control. The new contenders for power had damned the old council for its pro-developer stance. Houseman, a young law student and a progressive Democrat, clearly stated the case in his official campaign statement: "For four years the Council has allowed reckless development—high rise hotels in neighborhoods, parking structures and office buildings overlooking backyards, unneeded condominiums."

Reichenberger, a middle-aged businesswoman who supported legislation to make English the official language of the city, state, and nation, argued that the community had changed for the worse: "Monterey Park has changed since I was a young girl, manifesting itself in traffic congestion, a glut of poorly planned 'mini-malls,' crowded parking lots and cluttered business areas."

Hatch, a social science teacher in his early fifties and a forceful advocate of Official English, added a touch of Americanism to his message of slow growth: "The Spirit of America lives in the hearts of many of our residents. It was the spirit that motivated Americans to create the family unit, the customs, and the laws that forged our great country. . . . I will renew this spirit. . . . I will provide incentives and opportunities for our newcomers to see what makes America great."

The fourth candidate, who ultimately lost the election, was Frank Arcuri, the nativist voice of the *Citizen's Voice,* a small local newspaper of "investigative journalism." Arcuri explicitly linked the issues of growth, immigration, and Americanism in his ballot statement:

> We must do something about Monterey Park's haphazard, uncontrolled growth. We need a moratorium on residential condominium and commercial construction. . . . We need to make English our official language and we must require the use of English on all business and advertising signs. I will work towards solving our problems

> without thinking of how my decisions will get me the Hispanic, Asian, Black or White vote. . . . I believe that our American heritage comes before any ethnic loyalty. We must join together to plan our city's future, not as members of different 'multi ethnic communities,' but as Americans.[5]

The ballot statements point to the two sentiments that fueled the backlash against the city council. The overt sentiment was *populist,* defending the interests of ordinary citizens against big developers and big government. The covert sentiment was *nativist,* blaming growth problems on the Chinese newcomers and extending the fight for control over economic development to control over the language of business signs, official discourse, and, ultimately, the definition of what is American.

The records of the defeated incumbents, Almada, Chen, and Peralta, had actually been mixed on the issues of language and development. They had opposed two slow-growth propositions that were subsequently passed by referendum, and they allowed many variances from building codes. Under mounting pressure, however, they increasingly voiced the need for controlled, quality development. Moreover, they were being blamed unjustly for a pattern of unrestricted, market-driven development that had formed before their terms of office. As for language, the council had already sponsored a mild ordinance requiring some English on Chinese commercial signs—an ordinance proposed by the Chinese-born Councilwoman Lily Chen.

It did not much matter whether the minority incumbents were fully guilty as charged. The slow-growth rebels had taken power, and council heads were on the block. The minority incumbents were defeated not because they were fanatically pro-developer or insensitive to language issues in the city, but because, in the eyes of their opponents, they were going along with, rather than aggressively opposing, the dominant demographic and economic trends.

Growth control was the overt economic and class issue behind the defeat of the minority council, but in 1986 the issue quickly took on nativist overtones as the new, Anglo-dominated council relentlessly pursued a combination of nativist and slow-growth policies. One of the first acts of the council majority was to declare a temporary moratorium on the construction of commercial buildings, apartments, and condominiums. Another was to oppose a housing project for the elderly sponsored by Taiwanese developers. Since the restrictions directly affected the housing and investments of Asian newcomers, it was not surprising that some newcomers divined racial motives. One Chinese American whose plan to build ten condominiums was blocked by the moratorium publicly suggested that the issue was really "race conflict—a lot of people don't want to see too many Orientals move in."[6]

A week after the building moratorium, the nativist side of the established-resident reaction resurfaced. At 1:30 a.m. on June 2, 1986, after the watchful public had retired, three out of the four Anglos on the five-member city council voted for Resolution 9004:[7]

> NOW, THEREFORE, THE CITY COUNCIL OF THE CITY OF MONTEREY PARK, CALIFORNIA, DOES RESOLVE AS FOLLOWS:
> 1. That it opposes the so-called Sanctuary Movement as a violation of United States immigration law, and denounces, as creating poor role models for this nation's political leadership, those city councils that have declared their cities as "sanctuaries" for illegal aliens;
> 2. That the City of Monterey Park will never become nor support any city that does become a "sanctuary" city;
> 3. That the Monterey Park Police Department will cooperate with the INS in regard to illegal aliens;
> 4. That the City of Monterey Park urgently requests that the United States Congress pass legislation to control United States borders and to remove aliens who are residing in the United States illegally;
> 5. That the City of Monterey Park supports legislation to make English the Official Language of the United States.[8]

With the passing of a resolution linking opposition to sanctuary and illegal immigration with support for Official English (a broader attack on all immigrants), and with the implementation of a moratorium on building, the city entered into a stage of official backlash against more than a decade of demographic and economic change. Praised as a model of multiculturalism and economic revitalization in 1985, Monterey Park a year later became a widely publicized site for rebellion against diversity and development. What follows is an analysis of the forces behind the defeat of minority candidates in 1986 and the rapid demise of the "All-America City."

RESENTMENT AND RESISTANCE

What the official story of harmony did not mention was the resentment felt by many established residents against the changes that had transformed Monterey Park from a tranquil suburb to a bustling hub of Pacific Rim commerce and immigration. For them, the "All-America City" award was a fantasy of self-promotion on the part of ambitious council members and a bid for publicity that hid the darker side of community change: the invasion of their small-town America by mini-malls, condos, congestion, jumbo signs in Chinese, fancy cars erratically driven by arrogant newcomers, and foreign stores that did not need or want the business of established Americans. Recalling the "harmony" period, one of the Anglos on the new council remarked that "there was so much hostility" in the city that the award was taken as "a big joke."[9] In their enthusiasm for services for the newcomers, the promoters and recipients of the award had been out of touch with the fears and needs of some of the old-timers. In an interview, Lloyd de Llamas, the City Manager at the time, stated that the minorities ousted from the city council

> did make a tremendous contribution in encouraging and making opportunities for new residents to become involved in the community and making sure that our services met the needs of immigrant residents. . . . Unfortunately, we were concentrating so much on the newcomers' needs that we hadn't really thought about the old-timers and the growing resentment.[10]

The council should have heeded the results of the opinion survey sponsored by the Monterey Park Community Relations Commission in December 1985. The evidence of established-resident hostility and resentment belied the official story of harmony.[11] Under the direction of a professor from nearby California State University, members of the commission, citizen volunteers, and representatives of the Chinatown Service Center went to large markets and stores to canvass the racial attitudes and the quality of life of 263 people, a cross-section of local residents.

On the positive side, the study found that Asian Americans, Latinos, and Anglos agreed that "Monterey Park is a good community in which to make a home, raise children and invest in the future," and they had favorable views of their immediate neighborhoods. On the negative side, all groups recognized rising racial discrimination.

Anglos in particular perceived prejudice directed against them by Asians in schools and businesses. They were also more likely than either Asian Americans or Latinos to complain about changes brought by the immigrants: the direction of economic development, businesses catering to Asians, foreign-language signs, and bilingualism in the schools. By contrast, although Asians were clearly dissatisfied with the racial situation in Monterey Park, they were less sensitive than Anglos about being victims of racial prejudice and were generally satisfied with their perceived acceptance into the community.

The differences are not too difficult to understand. Newcomers could feel at home in a city where they spoke Chinese while eating, shopping, and seeking services in establishments catering to Chinese—the very advantages that aroused feelings of alienation and displacement in old-timers who longed for the "good old days." Our interviews with established residents—Japanese American and Latino as well as Anglo—gave ample anecdotal evidence of alienation and resentment toward newcomers. These sentiments were most pronounced in the telling and retelling of in-group stories about the out-group immigrants. By drawing lines between established residents, the "good immigrants" of yesteryear, and the "bad immigrants" of today, these we/they stories functioned to legitimate the virtues and status of the "real" Americans over the newcomers.

With varying degrees of "fear and loathing," the stories drew on a list of undesirable Chinese traits: "they can't drive; they bring in crime and drugs, evade the law, and get special privileges; they're rude, they push and talk loudly; they stick together in their own organizations, won't learn English, won't adapt to our ways; they care only about money and trying to buy us out." Good Americans, by contrast, are friendly, neighborly, and courteous; they volunteer and feel a sense of community responsibility. The list sounds familiar. It had been applied variously to Mexicans, Jews, and other newcomers in the past.

Alienation was also a theme in local jokes, as in the following variation on the theme of being lost in one's own country: "At an Alcoholics Anonymous meeting a recovering alcoholic begins telling how he went on a binge, blacked out, and woke up in a strange city where all signs were written in Chinese and no English language. Was he in China? No, it was Monterey Park, U.S.A."[12]

We found few old-timers who did not comment on the foreignness of Monterey Park. An elderly Anglo woman wearing a conspicuous pin in the shape of the American flag complained about the lack of shopping areas:

> We can't walk downtown to get anything. Not to a grocery store. On Garvey and Garfield, it's all Oriental grocery stores . . . stacks of rice in the window. The store I worked in during the [Second World] War, Oriental; they're all Oriental, every one of them. We're not against them, but they want to buy our city, take our city. Everything that's loose, they buy. They buy a taco stand, they can't make tacos. But they come in with money, and they have cash money.[13]

Perceived Chinese separateness irked an elderly second-generation Japanese American (or Nisei) who has learned to survive in Anglo-dominated Monterey Park by keeping a low ethnic profile:

> The Chinese immigrants do not want to be a part of American society. They want to create a Hong Kong of the West. They are creating their own community. It is OK if the Chinese want to retain their culture, but they should learn our ways and learn to get along when they are in contact with non-Chinese.[14]

A longtime Latino resident, in his thirties and marginally employed, echoed the theme of displacement when asked by a campaign worker whether he would support a Latino candidate in the next city council race:

> It's too late. There aren't many of us left. This was a nice Latino neighborhood once. Now the Chinese-run parts store on the next corner doesn't want my business. Look at the two new houses across the street, single-family dwellings, but six Chinese families live in one and four in the other. My kids can't get into the preschool because the immigrants have taken all the places. Besides, how can you learn anything with all those languages? This is not Monterey Park; it's Mandarin Park.[15]

Confronted with a "Mandarin Park" in their home town, some established residents claimed that they were victims of reverse discrimination—that the Chinese, not the Anglos, were racist. A white middle-aged female, a Democrat active in local politics, told us her own experience:

> What do you tell a person when they say that they walk into a beauty shop on North Garfield and they say, "No, no, only do Asians." What do you say when a couple goes into a triple A restaurant and asks for Chinese food, and they tell them, "No, no serve whites." What do you say when the people at the little herb shop on Alhambra and Garvey say, "What do you want in here? Get out." Now you tell me where the racism is. You tell me when I stand in the lines at Hughes [one of the remaining major "American" supermarkets], and they take the basket and run it into the back of my legs. Who is the racist? People don't see that until you really live in this city. . . . You see some Chinese telling me to fuck off when they run the red light and I am going through the green—hey![16]

The perceptions expressed in these interviews were not universally held, but they fueled the backlash. Residents with a positive view of change were predisposed to cross boundaries and tell different stories about newcomers. Jose Calderon told about his experience in a local Chinese–Vietnamese mini-market:

> After we had finished getting the products we needed, we moved to a checkout line where about a half-dozen people were waiting. As we stood at the end of the line, one of the employees (who was helping another checker) noticed us. I looked at her and she looked at me smiling. At that moment, something happened which had never happened before. As though we were someone special, she motioned for us to come to an open counter. I hesitated. I didn't want to cut in before all the people in front of us. But they were smiling and mo-

> tioned us to go to the open counter. Their gestures let me know that we had a much smaller order than they did. The cashier quickly rang up and bagged our groceries and said, "Thank you." As we left the store, I turned and noticed that the counter was closed again and that the woman who had helped us had gone back to helping the other cashier. When we got into the car, I said to my wife, Rose, "Did you see that? They treated us like we were their family."[17]

Calderon's experience would surprise, but not likely convince, an old-timer who hates the sight of "Oriental" markets in his neighborhood and does not initiate or want contact with the foreigners. What were we to make of these contradictory stories about newcomers? We did not run around the city trying to check out their accuracy on the false assumption that the real truth about newcomers could be determined without reference to the people who constructed the stories and the contexts in which they were told. Our task was to understand how the stories were situated and shaped in everyday interactions.

Trusted in-group interaction in a multiethnic city marked by language and spatial segregation invariably produced we/they stories. Calderon's broadened sense of "we" was the result of his determined and sustained intergroup interactions. A more surprising finding, which will become clear as the larger story unfolds, was that because resentment is situational, such attitudes are subject to change. Thus, we observed that the same Anglos who complained to other Anglos about the behavior of Chinese shopkeepers could be exceptionally friendly to Chinese newcomers in their neighborhoods and clubs. They were not being confused and inconsistent. Life in a multiethnic community is complex. Different situations produce different responses.

Often based on misinformation and colored by prejudice, negative stories about newcomers were nevertheless grounded in an experienced reality that cannot be dismissed as prejudice or cured by invoking the wonders of multiculturalism. The alienation of some old-timers was an understandable if regrettable result of a clash between their proprietary attitudes about their city and the scale of change—the size of the immigration, the visibility of wealthy, well-educated, Chinese-speaking immigrants with the ability to fashion a new kind of city. These changes, as well as the attitudes and actions of old-timers, need to be addressed to uncover the roots of conflict between newcomers and established residents. Both groups were victims as well as actors in a wider play of social change.

The tales of established-resident alienation tapped a reservoir of hostility behind the official façade of harmony. The hostility found expression in various strategies of resistance to newcomers and to the changes associated with their arrival.

Some of the strategies, which will be discussed in detail later, were relatively benign attempts to control and manage local symbols of the city's history and American identity from an old-timer viewpoint. Other strategies for resisting and managing change were more aggressive, reaching beyond demonstrations of American culture and history to outright control over newcomers. In the late 1970s and 1980s, slow-growth and nativist movements emerged and converged into a powerful backlash against change.

THE GROWTH-CONTROL MOVEMENT: DEVELOPMENT WITH AN ASIAN FACE

In Monterey Park, as in other cities across the United States, local politics are fundamentally about the class struggle for control over land use, economic growth, and revenues. On one side stand the business elites and their friends in government, organized to maximize profit from land investments; on the other side stand residents who want some control over land use in order to protect their homes and the quality of their residential space (land use, services, crime, the environment).[18]

The city is a "growth machine" for developers in search of profits and for city officials in search of revenues. Generally, the growth machine has been victorious. Such has certainly been the case in Southern California, for over a hundred years the celebrated and uncontested terrain of development.

During the post–World War II building boom, the interests of middle-class residents and developers meshed. The land capitalists encouraged and realized homeowner dreams of suburban tranquility in the sprawling housing tracts that ravaged the pastoral and desert outposts of Los Angeles. By the late seventies, however, during the orgy of financial and real estate speculation, those dreams were turning into nightmares. Homeowners, having bought into the dream, were not about to sacrifice it to the next phase of "progress."

The homeowners' first action was to challenge the high taxes on their superinflated property. Organizing from the grassroots, small homeowners initiated a tax revolt that led to the passage of a statewide referendum in 1978, the notorious Proposition 13, the model for property tax limitation for the nation as a whole. Steeled in the antitax campaign, local rebels next took on the developers and accommodating politicians, blaming them for the problems of unplanned and unregulated development. From the comfort of their living rooms in big and small cities in Southern California, respectable homeowners challenged California's powerful land development industry. They flooded municipal elections with propositions limiting development. In 1985 the citizens of Los Angeles passed Proposition U, which promised to cut future commercial density in half. According to Mike Davis, a local historian of "homegrown revolution," of the 76 growth-control measures put on the California ballots between 1986 and 1988, nearly half originated in Southern California; and of the half from Southern California, 70 percent were successful.[19]

Monterey Park residents were among the vanguard of the larger revolts against high taxes and out-of-control growth. The Monterey Park Taxpayers Association was a local force in the fight for property tax limitation in the late 1970s. In 1981, angry neighbors formed the Sequoia Park Homeowners Association to oppose the city council's decision to rezone a single-family site for the development of condominiums. Successfully gathering the necessary signatures, they forced a special municipal election to approve the development (Proposition A). For the residents of Sequoia Park, the rezoning meant overcrowding, traffic, higher taxes, and a boondoggle for a developer. Apparently, the voters agreed, and rejected Proposition A.

Later in 1981 the one-issue Sequoia Park Homeowners' Association became RAMP, the Residents Association of Monterey Park, which was devoted to a relentless campaign against what members saw as the city-wide pattern of rampant and uncontrolled development. RAMP's core of leadership was white, middle-class, middle-aged, Republican and Democratic. With strong support across ethnic groups, they successfully fought to place stringent controls on the city's commercial and residential development. Their strategy was to get their people elected to city council and to go directly to the voters to pass slow-growth propositions.

In 1982, over the opposition of the growth-oriented city council, city voters passed two slow-growth propositions. Proposition K limited residential units to no more than a hundred per year; Proposition L was even more radical in its long-term implications. It required a special election for any zone change involving more than an acre of land. RAMP also pushed to place slow-growth advocates on the city's influential Planning Commission and endorsed candidates for city council, achieving a slow-growth majority in 1986. This majority held sway in city council until 1990, when more business-friendly candidates began to get elected.

A crowning achievement of the movement to control and plan city growth came in 1987 when the city endorsed the comprehensive redevelopment plan formulated by a citizens' Community Design Advisory Committee. The same year, in a special election, voters by 4 to 1 margins passed four propositions (based on the committee plan) regulating building height, clarifying development standards, and specifying areas for redevelopment. In 1990, the voters extended an earlier ordinance to control the number of new residential units, even as they elected a more strongly pro-growth council.

Overall the slow-growth movement in Monterey Park had wide support among homeowners and produced results.[20] Its success in the long run, however, was limited by three economic factors. First, the movement achieved its political force after much of the rapid and chaotic market-driven development had already taken place. Second, by the late 1980s slow growth was losing its popular appeal as recession and fiscal crisis rekindled the emphasis on finding revenue-rich development. Third, developers ultimately had more staying power than locally based slow-growth movements. Nevertheless, homeowners and residents had established their right and ability to intervene in land-use decisions.

The controlled-growth movement had contradictory effects on interethnic harmony in Monterey Park, uniting residents in an economic struggle while tending to divide them into Chinese newcomer and established-resident camps. The contradiction was built into the ethnic character of regional economic development and into the populist and nativist character of the controlled-growth movement.

Irv Gilman, a former councilman and full-time political gadfly, captured the populist side of the taxpayers' and slow-growth revolts in one of his many letters to the editor of the *Monterey Park Progress:*

> I believe that Monterey Park is divided into two parts. The largest part is the voter who keeps sending loud, clear, unmistakable messages to city hall about development in our community. The second part is the misguided city council, an insensitive chamber of commerce, greedy developers and a bunch of good old boys. Actually, the second group can be bunched together as the establishment—an elite group that is either deaf or has decided the voters are just too dumb to vote right.[21]

The philosophy sounds populist in its grassroots appeal to the "people" in general in their fight against big developers and big government. The politics are antiestablishment, yet pragmatic and nonpartisan, crossing conventional lines dividing Democrats from Republicans.

Some observers have argued that the populism of slow-growth, environmental, and tax- and term-limitation movements are fundamentally progressive in that they threaten the power of capitalism, the state, and, in the case of growth control, unregulated market forces and the one form of private property that cities can regulate, the use of commercial and residential land.[22]

However, slow growth is not inherently progressive. In the words of the historian Mike Davis:

> Slow growth, in other words, is about homeowner control of land use and much more. Seen in the context of the suburban sociology of Southern California, it is merely the latest incarnation of middle-class political subjectivity that fitfully constitutes and reconstitutes itself every few years around the defense of household equity and residential privilege.[23]

Davis cites the role of white homeowners' associations in enforcing restrictive covenants until they were ruled unconstitutional by the U.S. Supreme Court in 1948, and their cooperating with developers to build racially and class-segregated communities thereafter. Today, in a period of massive immigration, "slow growth" may be the code phrase for the current phase of middle-class exclusionism, keeping out immigrants and minorities as well as the poor by restricting the development of condominiums, apartments, and high-density development. From this perspective, slow growth is the union of the NIMBY spirit ("not in my backyard") and the Know-Nothing nativists of the nineteenth century.

Gilman's letter to the editor and RAMP's political statements focused entirely on land use rather than immigration and ethnicity. Nevertheless, there was something special about growth politics in Monterey Park that shaded into middle-class exclusionism. Growth had an Asian face. Tipping the population and property ownership in their favor, immigrants from Taiwan, China, Hong Kong, and Southeast Asia were the major forces behind the rapid development and redevelopment of residential and commercial land. Consequently, appeals for slow growth would inevitably target Chinese newcomers.

The connection did not escape Chinese businessmen. Frederic Hsieh, frequently credited with pioneering Chinese investment in Monterey Park, argued that the slow-growth movement there was a racially motivated attack on Chinese and free-enterprise capitalism:

> This is a free society. I should be able to do what I want with my property. My situation is like that of being the last person on a plane. You are already on and want to keep me out so that you have more room, but I have bought my ticket and have my rights like everybody else. . . . People in the slow-growth movement say they are not racist and that their restrictions apply to everyone, but the everyone just happens to be Chinese.[24]

Joseph Rubin, a leader of RAMP, had a ready answer for the developers and land speculators:

> The charge of racism is a handy one in Monterey Park. Given the situation, the way to attack someone is to charge him with being a racist. And here the developers use it, and that's no surprise, right? So the fact that we were involved in organizing the Residents' Association, we were labeled as being racists.[25]

Hsieh dismisses the movement's antidevelopment intent and labels it racist and anticapitalist; Rubin dismisses the charges of racism as the developers' ploy to discredit their enemies. But in a racially divided society, there is no such thing as a completely race-free economic issue. The debate over growth took on a more overt nativist tone when the issue was not simply whether there should be development, but who should develop and for what groups.

Established residents—Anglos, Latinos, and Asian Americans—frequently complained about the decline of "American" shopping in Monterey Park. In the late 1980s, the complaint centered on the redevelopment of the old Atlantic Square Mall. A vocal group wanted to make sure that the job would be done by an Anglo developer in a non-Chinese style. Prominent members of RAMP supported the plan, which was passed by the majority-white city council.

Field notes taken by Leland Saito in 1989 during public hearings on Atlantic Square revealed the anti-Chinese tone underlying what some established residents meant by a "good" development.

> A young Anglo man active in the struggle to provide a strong local definition to Atlantic Square asked: "What's the theme? Things have changed so fast that our roots are blurred. We have to go back to the history of the town."
>
> What he meant by "roots" was "European," not Asian. The topic turned to the kind of restaurants wanted for the redeveloped mall. Bob Champion, the developer, remarked that the city had around 120 restaurants. A resident called out: "We could use a few GOOD restaurants." Another resident softly echoed his words: "Yes, a few good ones."
>
> People come from all over Los Angeles to eat at Monterey Park's many Chinese restaurants. But these residents had enough of that. For them "good" meant chain restaurants like the Velvet Turtle and the Red Onion, something American, not Chinese and Chinese American.

An Anglo developed Atlantic Square in conventional "Western" style, but not without a considerable subsidy borne by the city and taxpayers. Many established residents were satisfied with the result. Others felt that the project was a costly folly and that the city could have cut a much better deal with Chinese capital.[26]

The issue of economic development could not be color-blind in a city where some ethnic groups were declining and trying to hold on to their familiar turf, while the new majority were fashioning the city to suit their own tastes. The style and purpose as well as the amount of development had become an issue of ethnic and American identity.

In sum, the politics of the slow-growth movement were complex and contradictory, combining a reaction against uncontrolled development in general with opposition to Chinese-directed development in particular. The balance of these economic and ethnic concerns was greatly affected by RAMP's association with the members of another movement that had a directly negative effect on intergroup relations in Monterey Park—Official English.

THE POLITICS OF LANGUAGE CONTROL

If growth control was relatively progressive in its defense of people over profit, the Official English movement in the nation and in Monterey Park was relatively reactionary in its get-tough defense of English and Anglo/European culture over the language and culture of immigrants and minorities.

According to its leaders, the movement's purpose was to heal and unify a divided country by giving a special legal status to the language they saw as the historical basis of national unity. Fearing the loss of a common language in the swirl of immigration, they argued for the exclusive use of English in public and governmental discourse. Labeling the movement "English Only," progressives argued that it would deprive immigrants of the bilingual tools needed for their empowerment and assimilation. Chinese immigrants tended to see language control as another manifestation of nativism:

> In a way, the native residents do not respect the new immigrants. Not only did the established residents try to stop the immigrants from moving in; they also tried to gang up against the Chinese, for example, by proposing "English Only" and limiting the use of Chinese on signs, acts which disregarded the freedom of speech protected by the Constitution.[27]

In retrospect, Monterey Park offers a case study of what happens to relations between immigrants and established residents when Official English comes to town.

Aims and Accomplishments of Official English

Language politics first came to Monterey Park in the early 1980s as a local response to the proliferation of Chinese commercial signs without

English words to identify the name or nature of the business. For the Chinese merchants, such signs were a legitimate way of attracting their largely Chinese-speaking customers, and a form of advertising protected by the First Amendment. By contrast, some old-timers interpreted Chinese signs as a bold symbol of the takeover of American business and the decline of the English language.

Frank Arcuri, a tenacious and pugnacious local leader of Official English, was explicit about the connection between signs and the immigrant invasion. In a letter to the *Monterey Progress* in 1985, he complained that "Asian businesses are crowding out American businesses in Monterey Park and Alhambra. . . . Stores that post signs that are 80 percent Chinese make us feel like strangers in our own land."[28]

The sign issue erupted again and again in city council meetings between 1982 and 1985 as Arcuri and other residents demanded a strong English-sign ordinance. The city council, which then had a Chinese/Latino majority, was not sympathetic to the anti-Chinese tones of the demands. Nevertheless, Councilwoman Chen tried to defuse conflict, first by asking Chinese businessmen voluntarily to add English to their signs, and then by proposing an ordinance requiring an English address on all signs. By 1986 Monterey Park had adopted an informal rule of at least 50 percent English on all signs.

The most volatile language controversy emerged in 1985 when Monterey Park almost became the first city in the United States to put an Official English measure on the municipal ballot. The referendum was intended as a kind of pretest for the tactics of U.S. English, a national organization that was working to pass a ballot initiative in California. Founded in 1983 by an obscure Michigan ophthalmologist, John Tanton, and California's Republican Senator, S. I. Hayakawa, U.S. English sought to control what it saw as the destructive tide of bilingualism and multiculturalism. Its tactic was to establish English as the official language of the United States through amendments to the U.S. and state constitutions, the repeal of laws mandating multilingual ballots, restricting funds for bilingual education, and immigration control.

In consultation with U.S. English, Frank Arcuri and Barry Hatch led a petition drive in 1985 to put an Official English referendum before the voters of Monterey Park. They collected 3,200 signatures, about 40 percent of them, according to Hatch, from Latinos and Asian Americans. Much to their chagrin, the City Attorney ruled that the petition was invalid because it did not contain the exact text of the proposed ballot measure.

The battle was not over. In 1986, three white Official English advocates on the city council passed Resolution 9004, which combined opposition to immigration with support for Official English. Vociferous and organized local opposition led one member of the council to change his vote, and the resolution was rescinded. Later in 1986, however, California voters had their say when they overwhelmingly passed Proposition 63, which declared English the official language of the state. The measure included an ambiguous provision that allowed anyone living or doing business in the state to sue the state or local governments for actions that diminish or ignore "the role of English as the common language of the State of California."

Anti-immigrant politics in Monterey Park flared up again in 1989, when Hatch took advantage of his position on the city council to pursue his anti-immigrant campaign. Hatch saw himself as the embattled defender of the unifying principles of "Americanism"—English, the family, God, the nation, the neighborhood. For him, the unity and strength of America were being undermined by special interests, power blocs of minorities, immigrants, and their liberal defenders in government, education, and the media.

He countered these threats with a two-pronged strategy: on one hand calling for a national moratorium on immigration as well as restrictions on the public expression of Chinese language and culture; on the other hand imposing his patriotic vision of America on public places and events: City Hall, the city's parks, and civic events and festivals. He was particularly proud of having revived the moribund Fourth of July celebration to reinforce core American values in the face of immigration and change.

The Leaders of Official English

What precisely were the politics of Official English? Like those of growth control, they were complex, contradictory, not neatly fitting into the conventional liberal/conservative spectrum. A patriotic side appealed to the desire for a national unity that transcended race and ethnicity. A populist side addressed the feelings of alienation and powerlessness of ordinary people faced with global economic and demographic disruptions of their everyday lives. An explicitly xenophobic side played on the racial fears of established residents and targeted immigrants as the source of the nation's problems. Whites, in particular, would be attentive to the message that Anglo/European culture was being sold out by self-interested bureaucrats and money-makers and wiped out by Latino and Asian newcomers.

In unraveling the politics of Official English, we need to separate national and local leaders from supporters. The leaders were clearly xenophobic. Their message was about unity, but the subtext implied race—the need to control the immigrant masses of Latino and Asian newcomers who wanted to keep their own culture and would not learn English.[29]

At the national level, leaders of U.S. English avoided making connections that would brand them as nativists. John Tanton even had some liberal credentials through his activism in the ecology and population control movements. On the other hand, he also headed the conservative Federation for American Immigration Reform (FAIR) and had ties to other anti-immigrant groups, such as Americans for Border Control and Californians for Population Stability. The national success of U.S. English was in part the result of Tanton's tactical decision to keep quiet about his anti-immigrant views and concentrate on the positive message of language unity.[30]

Arcuri and Hatch, the much publicized local leaders of Official English in Monterey Park, were less subtle about their conservative politics. For them American unity clearly meant adherence to the language and traditions of white European domination. Patriotism meant not being afraid to stand up for America against the real racists, as they saw it, whose ideology of diversity, bilingualism, and multiculturalism was turning the melting pot into an unmeltable mix. Speaking in city council just before California passed its official English initiative, Arcuri left no doubt about his view of the internal enemies:

> If passed, the initiative could have an immediate impact on thousands of city, county, and state jobs. Great! Isn't that wonderful. There'll be a hell of a lot of bureaucrats unemployed, and basically they are the people that are against this official English. Those professional minorities who have profited from this bilingual program that has devastated our state economy, that has drained us dry. Who are the professional minorities? They got their names listed here. We got [California] Assembly Speaker Willie Brown, he endorsed this [a statement opposing Proposition 63]. He's with the Black Democratic Caucus. Who's the racist here? The Japanese American Citizen League. The Asian Pacific American Coalition. Mayor Tom Bradley. Who else? Oh, yes, that group that really does represent the professional minorities of America, that's the American Civil Liberties Union.
>
> What we have to do is unify ourselves as a nation. We have to declare that we want one official language, not a bilingual culture or bilingual society, and this is what will keep us together as Americans.[31]

Arcuri's style was physical and belligerent. A stocky, middle-aged, Italian American originally from the east coast, in Monterey Park he was a photographer who fashioned himself into an investigative journalist.

Apparently of modest means, he published a local newspaper, the *Citizen's Voice,* as his personal platform for launching attacks against his enemies, who included the "Dragon ladies" (Lily Chen and Judy Chu of the city council) and Asian immigrants unwilling to assimilate into American society. At public meetings Arcuri engaged in shouting and shoving matches that resulted in arrests, law suits, and extended publicity.

Hatch had more political and social capital. He eventually separated himself from Arcuri's political antics and, unlike Arcuri, got elected to city council. A tall, gray-haired man with a deep ministerial voice, he was born in Monterey Park into a Mormon family. In his youth, Hatch had served as a missionary in Hong Kong, where he learned Cantonese. Now in his fifties, he taught social science at a predominantly Latino school in nearby Bell Gardens. Personable in conversation, he was rigid and unyielding on the topic of immigration.

> We have no handle on the destiny of America. It's been altered by the fact that everybody, including Congress, has blinders on, and people are coming in at will. I mean, there's no stopping the Asians for one. There's no stopping the Latinos for another. Now who's next? And there'll never be a time in our future that we're going to say "close the gates." We cannot close the gates, because once we've allowed half of Taiwan to empty onto our shores and a good third of Mexico and Central America, are we going to say no to the continent of Africa or to the Russians? The Russians will unload hundreds of thousands and possibly millions before they're through.[32]

For Hatch, the newcomers brought problems: disease, crime, radically different languages and customs, higher public expenses and taxes, and competition for jobs and services.

This message had appeal first of all because it addressed genuine problems avoided in the official celebration of diversity—massive demographic changes, economic dislocations, the declining quality of life, and the powerlessness of ordinary people to influence change. Second, the local leaders, at least until they became media stars, were themselves ordinary people, homegrown activists and long-established residents without ties to local wealth and power.

The Diverse Supporters of Official English

The mixed messages of language politics encouraged a broad and diverse base of support. Initially, the advisory board of U.S. English included respectable civil libertarians like Norman Cousins, Walter Cronkite, and Gore Vidal, although they withdrew in embarrassment when they understood the coded racial politics of the organization. The movement has been very successful throughout the country. As of 1990, Official English measures had passed by large majorities in 17 states and were being considered in others.[33]

What American, regardless of race or ethnicity, does not appreciate the value of speaking English? Nevertheless, not everyone in racially divided America was susceptible to a color-blind appeal to unity. Many appear to have suspected that "in an English Only America, only English speakers would enjoy equal rights, including the right to speech itself."[34] In California and Texas, Latinos and liberals were much more likely to reject Official English measures than either Anglos or conservatives.[35]

Examining the vote for California's Official English measure by precinct in Monterey Park, we found a similar but more complex ethnic pattern. While support was strongest in precincts that were heavily Anglo and weakest in heavily Latino precincts, the heavily Asian precincts fell in between the two. The behavior of Asian voters may have reflected the strong Americanism of second- and third-generation Japanese Americans and the conservatism of foreign-born Chinese Americans.[36]

From our interviews with Anglo activists and observations in Monterey Park, we found strong opposition to Official English and language restrictions from left liberals and libertarian Republicans; strong support from Reagan and Bush conservatives; and ambivalent support from moderate Democrats. In the context of Monterey Park, "moderate" meant liberal to fiscally conservative on economic issues, but conservative when it came to diversity and ethnic politics. The "moderate Democrats" were of particular interest because they also tend to support the slow-growth movement and probably came closest to representing the white Democratic vote in the city and region as a whole.

Many Democrats had clearly grown conservative on racial matters. They would say that they had moved to racially mixed Monterey Park because they did not want to live in a white ghetto. They had supported the civil rights movement in the 1960s. Today they believed that Monterey Park had lost its racial balance and become too Asian. Meanwhile, the national political system had moved far away from their ideals of integration and equality of opportunity toward the divisive policies of racial preferences and bilingualism.

Some Anglos bristled whenever they heard Chinese Americans talk about "their candidate, Judy Chu," or "Sam Kiang"—"Aren't they supposed to represent us too?" They could not understand why Asian Democrats preferred to form their own club rather than integrate into their club as Democrats. For them, race was not a legitimate reason for political distinctions or differential treatment. There should be citizens who vote on issues, not ethnic blocs that form their own organizations and political constituencies. They did not recognize a need for nonwhites to organize on a racial and ethnic basis to oppose the history of white dominance, discrimination, and their own second-class citizenship.

Although our local Democrats would probably reject the parallel, their discourse resembled that of "neoconservatives" like Nathan Glazer, Norman Podhoretz, Irving Kristol, and Arthur Schlesinger, all liberals who moved right in the late 1970s and 1980s.[37] Neoconservatism, not racism, pervaded the reasoning of Democratic leaders of the slow-growth movement. Bothered by the racial tensions Hatch had stirred up, they nevertheless believed that racial divisions had no legitimate place in American political life. Their attitudes toward Official English were ambivalent. One leader expressed his views as follows:

> I tell you, I drift back and forth. Now I think I am in favor of Official English. As was Norman Cousins and lots of, you know, learned, liberal people in America who felt that it was important that we keep the tradition of the English language in the United States. But it's tagged as English Only. Now, if there is such a thing as English Only, yes, that's a racist thing, and I would be very much opposed to that. But I am not necessarily opposed to English as the official language. And it was passed overwhelmingly in this state, it was passed overwhelmingly in Monterey Park. And I have not yet seen the evils that were predicted. The horrendous things like people calling for help from the Fire Department and not getting help because they can't speak English. Nothing happened. Now, that's what Barry Hatch espoused. OK? And that is not necessarily racism.[38]

His remarks were correct in one sense. The approval of Official English in California did not, as some opponents had predicted, lead to "blood in the streets." In Monterey Park, however, the struggle over Official English did not foster the unity predicted by its supporters. On the contrary, it widened the gulf between newcomers and established residents and between ethnic groups.

THE CONTRADICTORY CHARACTER OF RESISTANCE

Objecting to rapid demographic and economic changes, many established residents felt alienated from what their city had become, and they resented newcomers as the agents of its transformation. At the political level, these attitudes coalesced into two overlapping strategies of resistance: the demand for control over economic development and the demand for Official English as the symbol of unity challenged by immigration.

Both movements of resistance were politically complex and contradictory, combining the popular demand for citizen control over development and the meaning of America with the xenophobic fear of Asian newcomers. Thus, the fight against developers was also a fight against the Chinese, who had become the major economic force in the region; the call for Official English was also a threat to the growing Chinese community, whose languages and cultures were becoming part of America. The conflation of nativist and populist tendencies (and, by extension, racial and class issues) within the slow-growth and Official English movements was exacerbated by alliances between their leaders.

Established residents' complex and contradictory responses to change were not the result of confusion or the latest incarnation of middle-class exclusionism. Race, ethnicity, and class were interconnected in the minds of residents because they were interconnected in the transformation of Monterey Park: The many dimensions of change did have an Asian face. The balance of the political tendencies within established-resident movements and their effects on group relations—whether they veered toward anti-immigrant nativism or antiestablishment populism, whether they divided or united newcomers and established residents into one community—would depend on the course of political struggle.[39]

The defeat of Chen, Almada, and Peralta in the city council races of 1986 marked a stage of reaction and conflict that lasted until 1990. This stage was characterized by racial politics: the reduction of economic struggles over growth and cultural struggles over language to a basic conflict between Chinese newcomers and established residents. The overtly anti-immigrant element in local politics became dominant when the new and predominantly white city council passed Resolution 9004 in 1986, and Hatch began to use his office to promote the causes of language and immigration control.

Hatch and the Official English movement were not unopposed. Across the spectrum of class, ethnicity, and nativity, a group of residents emerged to fight against "English Only" and for the language rights of minorities and immigrants. They ushered in another stage in the evolution of a politics of diversity.

Chapter **5**

THE STRUGGLE FOR MINORITY AND IMMIGRANT RIGHTS

I think the problem begins with your initial attitude toward change. If you look at it as an opportunity to broaden your horizons and to share experiences and ideas, it's an opportunity. But too many of the old-timers have taken the attitude that there is an infringement on their rights. And when you start with that attitude, you run into trouble everywhere you turn.
—*A long-established Latina resident*

The problem is the power struggle of the minority, not *wanting to let the majority of the population assume democratic rights.*
—*A recent Latina resident and community activist*

MONTEREY PARK spawned nativists and slow-growth rebels, but also multiculturalists who took a stand against the xenophobic politics of the mid-1980s. Their diverse class backgrounds, changing organization, and tactics had contradictory effects on the course of group conflict. In 1986, the promoters of cultural diversity came together defensively in Citizens for Harmony in Monterey Park (CHAMP), a coalition of conservative businesspeople and radical professionals, to oppose the city council's Official English resolution. Later the same year, CHAMP split along class lines. The business-dominated faction with broader support formed a new group, A Better Cityhood (ABC), to recall two council members on the grounds of racism. Meanwhile, progressives within CHAMP, moving away from the diverse tactics of recall, united to support a Chinese American, Judy Chu, for city council. Her election in 1988 signaled the rise of ethnic politics and interethnic alliances on issues of controlled growth and ethnic representation, two tendencies countering the political division between established residents and newcomers.

CAPITALISTS AND PROGRESSIVES UNITE AGAINST NATIVISM

The anti-immigrant and pro–Official English resolution passed in June 1986 divided the "All-America City" into warring factions. CHAMP quickly mobilized to overturn the resolution as an expression of racism and a violation of First Amendment rights. The alliance of middle-class white leaders in the growth-control and Official English movements had engendered its opposite—an interethnic and interclass coalition of businesspeople and progressive professionals.

The leading force in CHAMP were progressives ranging in age from the thirties to the sixties. One of the four co-chairs was Ruth Willner, a 30-year resident, veteran activist, and leader of the Monterey Park Democratic Club. She supported increased minority representation in city government and had campaigned in 1982 for Lily Chen. The second co-chair was Jose Calderon, a sociology graduate student in his mid-thirties who had recently moved to the city with his family. Calderon, a Mexican immigrant who came to the United States as a child, had been an activist in the Chicano and civil rights movements. He was also a founder of the recently formed West San Gabriel Valley League of United Latin American Citizens (LULAC), an organization that encouraged multiethnic alliances on progressive issues. The third co-chair was Mike Eng, American-born and of Chinese descent. Similar to Calderon in age and politics, and a recent arrival in Monterey Park, Eng was a lawyer active in civil rights and immigration law. He was also one of the founders of a new force in local politics, the West San Gabriel Valley Asian Pacific Democratic Club.

These three co-chairs were left of center on issues of economic justice and minority rights. Willner represented the radical legacy of older Democrats who had long been influential in local politics. Calderon and Eng, professionals and community activists, were part of a younger generation who had cut their teeth in the civil rights and antiwar movements and were now fighting for the empowerment of the new majority and the building of progressive interethnic alliances.

The fourth co-chair, Kevin Smith, was the son of a local developer and the husband of a Mexican American. Representing a more economically conservative tendency, Smith's participation, with that of Asian and Latino businesspeople, made CHAMP a multiclass and multiethnic organization expressing the new economic and ethnic complexity of the region's population. Absent from the organization were the Anglo leaders of the growth-control movement.

Developers and progressives each had their own reasons for opposing the nativist tendencies of the Official English and slow-growth movements. The progressives opposed them in the name of social justice and the empowerment of minorities. The developers were particularly concerned about ethnic and language restrictions on free enterprise.

The influence of progressives in CHAMP kept out some potential supporters. A local Republican businessman explained why he did not join the coalition:

> I wanted to use CHAMP to reach out to the Chinese business community. By dint of money, political clout, and influence, they could provide a great deal of leadership, a voice in saying, "Enough of this bullshit." But CHAMP was more liberally oriented, they did not want to do that. They wanted to go back to the street tactics of the sixties, and I couldn't endure that.[1]

The progressives, for their part, were uncomfortable with the motives of their capitalist allies. They would have made strange bedfellows in the civil rights era of the 1960s, when rich meant white and minority meant poor. But things were different in the 1980s. The arrival of rich as well as middle-class and poor immigrants had changed the ethnic composition of the classes and the political character of the struggle for minority rights.

The alliance held benefits for both sides. Faced with the double threat of xenophobia and slow growth, an ethnically mixed group of developers and businessmen needed allies who could teach them how to defend their economic interests with the language and tactics of civil rights. In exchange for a weakened class perspective, the progressives got powerful allies, financial support, and practical training in building an antiracist alliance during a period of political conservatism. Thus, a professional/business coalition against racism emerged in a "middle-class" town, where the new immigration had blurred the historical connection between racial and economic inequality.

CHAMP did its political work. Targeting the two major "American" and the more numerous Chinese supermarkets, members collected about five thousand signatures on a petition demanding that the city council rescind the infamous anti-immigrant resolution. Sixty-seven percent of the signers were residents, and, of these, 81 percent were Chinese, 13 percent Latinos, and 6 percent Anglos.[2] A sign painted on a petitioner's table gave a clear message: "M.P., The All-America City or M.P., The All-Racist City. Petition to Rescind 9004."

The political pressure worked. One white council member who had supported Official English changed his vote. Pro-growth and not anti-Chinese, Cam Briglio was more conflicted than his colleagues Barry Hatch and Patricia Reichenberger. Resolution 9004 was rescinded in October 1986. The following month, when 73 percent of California voters supported Official English, the vote in Monterey Park was close—53 percent for and 47 percent against. The political education provided by CHAMP may have dampened voters' enthusiasm for Official English.

The statewide victory for Proposition 63 nevertheless encouraged local leaders to rally to the cause of Americanism against the foreign takeover. In one instance, council members objected to the raising of the Taiwanese flag at City Hall during the Yung Ho Sister City's celebration of "Ten Ten Day," a national holiday celebrating the overthrow of the Manchu dynasty by the Nationalist Chinese. With the Taiwanese flag in mind, the Anglo-dominated city council passed an ordinance banning all foreign flags from the two flagpoles in front of City Hall.

THE CAMPAIGN TO RECALL OFFICIAL ENGLISH LEADERS

The next big fight involving racial conflict was waged in 1987 by ABC, a new group led by Kevin Smith, a developer who had been a member of CHAMP, and Steven Tan, a Chinese American who owned an insurance business. ABC's members and employees collected the number of signatures needed to hold an unprecedented special election to recall Patricia Reichenberger and Barry Hatch, the two council members who had steadfastly supported the city's Official English resolution. The charge was racism, but Hatch and Reichenberger's association with slow growth offered the developers an opportunity to strike both movements with one antiracist blow. Thus, the idea of a recall, originally discussed at the grassroots, was taken up by pro-growth factors and used for their purposes.

Led and financed by business interests, ABC nevertheless picked up support from some progressive Anglo, Latino, and Asian Americans who sincerely believed that racism as manifested in slow growth and Official English was the primary problem in Monterey Park. One prominent endorser of ABC and the recall movement was David Almada, a former councilman, a high school principal, and, in the eyes of some old-timers, an unreconstructed Chicano revolutionary.

His radical past notwithstanding, as an incumbent in the 1986 city council race Almada had been labeled pro-developer by the slow-growth opposition. His defeat by Anglo opponents reaffirmed his feeling of racial injustice and cemented his desire to recall the culprits. He also turned toward ethnic political organizing as the head of the Hispanic Round Table, a group formed in the mid-1980s specifically to promote Latino candidates and Latino political interests in Monterey Park.

ABC's attack on Hatch and Reichenberger solidified the alliance between the slow-growth and Official English camps. The leaders of RAMP concentrated all their energies on saving the council members from recall. Their tactic was to expose the greedy developers who, they claimed, were using racial politics as a smokescreen for their business interests. But if developers ignored the economic self-interest behind their campaign against racism, RAMP, like Hatch, ignored the racism within its own ranks.

The statements on the recall ballot reflected these tactical decisions. The ABC side charged their opponents with racism, while the latter defended themselves by exposing the class motives of their accusers:

> STATEMENT OF REASONS FOR THE PROPOSED RECALL OF BARRY L. HATCH
> His racially motivated vote in support of Resolution "9004" may subject every Hispanic and Asian to immigration checks by the police department while in Monterey Park. This racist resolution also openly challenges our constitutional right of "Freedom of Speech." It has severely divided a community proud of its multi-ethnic and multi-cultured residency. This blatant racial resolution has promoted hatred among the Asian, Anglo, and Hispanic residents of Monterey Park.
>
> ANSWER TO STATEMENT OF REASONS FOR PROPOSED RECALL OF BARRY L. HATCH
> The proposed recall is directed by developers who are extremely angry for my part in the moratorium on building construction to allow a master plan for properly developing our city. . . . What greatly concerns me is that the developers will promote racism and hatred to hide their greed for building profitable condos until the last available square inch in Monterey Park is gone. . . . Resolution 9004 requests the United States Government to strengthen and support immigration laws and to support English as the common language of America.

Although, as noted above, developers were dominant financial backers of ABC, only one identifiable developer signed the recall statement.[3] The other four signers were middle-class professionals and Democrats who believed that racism was not simply a figment of developer propaganda.

In the largest turnout in the city's history, the voters—Anglo, Asian American, and Latino, American- and foreign-born—defeated the recall move by 62 percent. Contrary to ABC's expectations, established residents united against them rather than the two Anglos charged with racism. Lacking data on individual voters, we must turn to our interviews and observations to explain this result. First, RAMP and other supporters of Hatch and Reichenberger had done an effective job of reducing ABC to developers and questioning the economic motives behind the recall. The word "developer" raised a red flag for the many voters who mistrusted big business and favored greater control over growth.

Second, voters saw no crime in their council members' decision to stand up for Official English, a popular idea in no way limited to white racists. Besides, Hatch and Reichenberger were not fixed ideologically on one issue, but had strong records on the populist issue of controlled growth. Third, ABC's heavy-handed use of racism won it enemies even among minorities otherwise sensitive to discrimination. Opponents of the recall made well-publicized claims that paid volunteers were telling assimilated, middle-class, and English-speaking Latino residents that the city council was out to deport them to Mexico.[4] In the end, the recall campaign was simply a bad idea in an ethnically fragmented city tired of the divisive course of racial politics.

ETHNICITY AS A FORCE IN LOCAL POLITICS

The defeat of the recall movement in 1987 appeared to be a defeat for the developers and a mandate for the slow-growth movement, which had now "officially" cleared itself of the charge of racism. The way seemed clear for a slow-growth victory in April 1988, when two pro-growth candidates would be up for reelection. Now that racism had been exposed as a ploy of developers, RAMP leaders reasoned that they had only to field their candidates to get interethnic support for an absolute slow-growth majority of five council members.

But racial tension had not disappeared. Hatch was free to propagate his anti-immigrant views in city council. RAMP had not disengaged itself from his racially divisive politics or adequately dealt with the xenophobic tendencies within its own movement. Besides, immigrants and minorities wanted more representation on the city council. Expecting victory for slow growth, RAMP overestimated its interethnic support and underestimated the strength of the desire for ethnic representation among Asian Americans and Latinos.

Monterey Park had been a multiethnic community since the gradual arrival of upwardly mobile Latinos and Japanese Americans in the 1960s. This tradition of multiethnicity was revered by many residents in Monterey Park as a positive foundation for interethnic harmony. However, the ethnic balance of forces had changed dramatically since the good old days and opened up new political opportunities for ethnic organization and representation. The situation in the 1980s was qualitatively different from that of the late 1950s, 1960s, and early 1970s—the difference between partial integration and diversity, between tokenism under Anglo tutelage and the struggle for ethnically organized and supported power. The rise of Asians to numerical dominance strengthened Asian American power in particular, but Latinos also gained politically from their numbers in the wider San Gabriel and East Los Angeles region.

Asian American Politics

The break with the past was most marked in the Asian American population, whose political opportunities had grown with their new majority status. Our interviews with residents indicated that, until the late 1970s, Japanese and Chinese Americans maintained a low political profile and generally integrated themselves into a political structure and civic organizations dominated by Anglos. While some important regional service organizations, like the (Japanese American) Eastside Optimist Club, maintained a strong sense of Japanese American identity, there were no specifically Japanese or Chinese American political organizations in Monterey Park.

Before the new immigration, some highly respected Asian Americans were represented in the influential structure of service and political clubs. Alfred Song and George Ige had been elected to city council (in 1960 and 1970, respectively). However, their presence depended on the financial and political largesse of the politically more powerful Anglo population. They were not candidates of an organized movement for Asian power.

Song, the first Asian city councilman in Monterey Park and a California State Senator in the 1970s, bluntly summed up the non-Asian character of his own political support:

> In all of the years that I have campaigned for elective office, I have never had the help, financial or otherwise, of any organized Oriental group; whatever their origin may be—Korean, Japanese, Chinese, Filipino or any others. Even individual assistance has been very rare: in twenty years, I think I could count the individual Asians who have come to my assistance on one hand and still have a couple of fingers left over.[5]

The pattern of Asian dependence on local Anglo backing was broken in 1976 with the election to city council of G. Monty Manibog, a Filipino American lawyer. The break was even more marked with the election of Lily Chen, a Chinese-born county administrator, in 1982. This was a turning point in the development of explicitly Asian American politics in the region. Initially depending on their local connections and Anglo sponsorship, Asian Americans buttressed this support with generous financial contributions from business and professional people who lived outside the city. Their Asian constituency extended beyond Monterey Park to a regionally based Chinese population who saw the local election as a test-case for the development of Chinese and Asian American power in Los Angeles, California, and the United States.

The arrival of Asian ethnic politics can also be documented in the formation in the mid-1980s of the West San Gabriel Valley Asian Pacific Democratic Club and immigrant political organizations, as well as the drive to register Asian American citizens and organize noncitizens for mass mobilizations and other forms of political pressure.

Latino Politics

The new trend toward increased ethnic and interethnic social and political organizing could also be found among Latinos, the majority being native-born Americans of Mexican descent. Because of the heavy concentration of Latinos in the San Gabriel Valley, in the last two decades the region has been viewed by organizers as one of the nation's most important arenas for Latino representation. The Southwest Voter Registration Education Project has been particularly active in the drive for political involvement among Latinos and their election to state and national office. In 1994 the Latinos of Monterey Park and the San Gabriel Valley were represented at county, state, and national levels by Los Angeles County Supervisor Gloria Molina (representing a district newly redrawn in 1991 by court order to allow for Latino representation), State Senator Charles Calderon, State Assemblywoman Diane Martinez, and Representative Matthew Martinez.

The political representation of Latinos within Monterey Park has been much less impressive. Although they are the majority in the San Gabriel Valley region, Latinos are the second-largest group in Monterey Park and in political competition with the larger Asian American population.[6]

The historical pattern of Mexican American political participation has been both similar to and different from that of Asian Americans. Before 1980, both groups lacked representation in Monterey Park. No Mexican American was elected to city council until the election of Matthew Martinez in 1974, although Latinos then constituted about one-third of the city's population. Like Asian candidates of that period, he depended heavily on sponsorship from the Anglo political structure. A Republican, Martinez entered politics with the support of the conservative Monterey Park Lions Club. Changing his registration to Democrat, he was elected to Congress in 1982 as the selected candidate of Representatives Henry Waxman and Howard Berman, Westside Los Angeles politicians who are the nucleus of one of the country's most powerful regional Democratic groupings.[7]

Until the 1980s Latinos in Monterey Park lacked any formally organized local political presence. Drawing on his interviews with grassroots

Mexican American activists in Monterey Park, Jose Calderon argues that Latino power was based informally in certain club structures rather than formally vested in city council politics:

> It is in the neighborhood civic and sports groups where Mexican Americans have politically organized themselves. However, all of the activists are quick to point out that their organizing has not been along ethnic lines. Instead, they indicate that living in a middle-class community that is multiethnic results in their joining long-established groups which are also multiethnic.[8]

Although this pattern of informal power continues, Latinos have been getting more involved in Monterey Park politics. By the mid-1980s, Latinos had formed the Hispanic Round Table and the more regionally based West San Gabriel Valley Chapter of LULAC. In 1994, the chapter continued to be involved in ethnic and interethnic politics. Although the Hispanic Round Table is no longer, its electoral goals are being fulfilled. In 1994, out of five city council members, two were Mexican Americans and one an American of Spanish descent.

MUNICIPAL ELECTIONS OF 1988

Ethnic power was on the rise in Monterey Park, and had become at least as significant as the nativist current. The 1988 municipal election gave us the opportunity to see whether ethnicity was a factor in how people voted. Indeed, the city council race was both a testing ground for the issues of growth and ethnic representation and a rich opportunity for ethnographic research. We observed and sometimes participated in many facets of the election, from strategy meetings and fundraisers to community-sponsored forums and the elections themselves. We walked precincts with candidates Betty Couch and Judy Chu to get a sense of their messages and reception. On election day, we helped conduct an exit poll and analyzed the results. Combining ethnographic observations of the political process with the exit poll, we were able to get a close look at how candidates and voters were lining up in the political process.

Candidates and Issues

On the slow-growth side, the Anglo-led RAMP forces, confident of a sweeping victory, sponsored two Anglo candidates: Betty Couch and George Ristic. They ran on a clear-cut platform of controlled growth and citizens' participation. Ristic, a 56-year-old retired school administrator and businessman, had lived in Monterey Park for 30 years and had served on the city's Planning Commission. A newcomer to city politics, he ran a lackluster campaign. As a founding member of RAMP, a leader in the controlled-growth fight, the chair of the Parks and Recreation Commission, and a resident for 17 of her 43 years, Couch was a more visible and popular figure. She was a civic-minded woman whose rise to the city council followed her grassroots involvement in community service as a mother, neighbor, and hard-working volunteer. Moreover, she ran a vigorous door-to-door campaign. Both Couch and Ristic were fiscal conservatives and had been supporters of Official English.

The development forces backing the ABC coalition got behind the incumbent, Cam Briglio, who was 55 years old. Briglio had some virtues in the eyes of the pro-developer forces. He was a pro-growth businessman and, under pressure from CHAMP, had changed his vote from "yea" to "nay" on the city's controversial anti-immigrant resolution. Perhaps fearing that no Asian could win in the current anti-immigrant climate, the developers did not run an Asian candidate for city council. The incumbent G. Monty Manibog, who was Filipino and generally pro-development, ran instead for City Treasurer.

True to their multiethnic image and in a play for the Latino vote, however, the development forces added to their ticket a local Latino businessman, 36-year-old Fred Balderrama. A longtime resident, Balderrama had been active in the Chamber of Commerce and civic organizations, but lacked an organized base of support.

Representing a multiethnic, pro-business ticket, Balderrama and Briglio proclaimed the need for city revenues and quality development. Relying on a flood of signs and flyers, rather than door-to-door precinct walking, they did not run grassroots campaigns. This was a mistake in a changing community where old-boy networks and endorsements could no longer determine victory. Candidates had to go directly to neighbors and civic organizations to pitch their lines.

The new force in the election was Judy Chu, 34 years old, a native-born Chinese American, a progressive, and a professor of psychology at Monterey Park's East Los Angeles College. Although a relative newcomer to Monterey Park, Chu had strong credentials because of her education, membership in the Eastside Optimists and Soroptimists of Monterey Park, and years of work in organizations that served the city, such as the Garvey School Board, Red Cross, United Way, and Family Counseling Service.

Rejecting developer support and stressing ethnic harmony, she introduced a new political direction: the possibility of interethnic cooperation on the side of growth control. A vocal critic of Hatch, she was a potential ally of RAMP. Such a coalition could threaten the association of growth control with Anglo nativism and forcefully undercut the developers' claim that the slow-growth movement was basically racist and anti-Chinese.

For any of this to happen, Chu would have to be embraced by the less xenophobic forces within the slow-growth movement. She was, however, a political unknown, and RAMP neither opposed nor endorsed her. Moderates suspected that she was first and foremost a Chinese candidate. Indeed, Chu received strong financial backing from Chinese eager for representation, although members of the Chinese business community had reservations about her positions on development. Her cadre of campaign organizers and workers came from the multicultural and progressive forces that had led the old CHAMP coalition. Practicing what she preached, Chu conducted a vigorous, well-organized grassroots campaign involving Asian, Latino, and Anglo volunteers.

Three candidates for city council lacked a strong campaign organization and base of support: Frank Arcuri, the belligerent fighter for Official English on the right wing of the slow-growth movement; Marie Purvis, 47, a local businesswoman active in the Chamber of Commerce; and Victoria Wu, 48, an eccentric Hong Kong–born acupuncturist without wide support. These candidates did not have the organization or the funds to mount an effective and expensive grassroots or mailer campaign.

Wishing to avoid controversy and to maximize support, none of the council candidates directly raised the issue of racism beyond bland references to promoting unity and "healing wounds." Their overt concerns were to keep taxes down, fight overdevelopment and congestion, and promote "quality development" rich in needed sales revenues. But given the recent history of racial conflict and the continued rule of Anglos in a city that was almost 90 percent minority, the covert issues for many voters were ethnic domination and immigrants.

The election of April 12, 1988, was an opportunity to tap the strength of ethnic and development concerns. The candidates offered the voters distinct choices: slow economic growth with nativist undertones (Couch and Ristic); slow growth and overt nativism (Arcuri); market-driven growth with ethnic diversity (Balderrama and Briglio); controlled growth and ethnic harmony (Chu). Our exit poll allowed us to match ethnicity and other social factors like income, education, age, political preference, and nativity with candidate choice, producing a clear picture of voting patterns. If the trends held as RAMP expected, the two white slow-growth candidates would win with the interethnic support of established residents. This did not happen as RAMP had planned.

Ethnic Tensions at the Polls

We became aware of ethnic tensions during the election from interactions with poll organizers, voters, and precinct workers. Everyone involved in the conduct of the poll and the election seemed to be expecting conflict. The poll was organized by the Asian Pacific American Voter

Registration Project, a group of young and progressive Asian professionals from Monterey Park and the wider Los Angeles region. Deliberately oversampling the Asian voters, their aim was to find out more about this population as part of a broader strategy of building Asian American power. Given the racial climate in the city, the organizers did not want to draw attention to themselves as Asians organizing Asians, and in constructing the exit poll questionnaire they carefully avoided asking voters any questions about the volatile issues of development and language.[9] Nevertheless, they had their eyes on Monterey Park as a crucible for emerging Asian American politics. In designing and conducting the poll, they received friendly technical assistance and direction from the Southwest Voter Research Institute, which already had years of experience in the fight to register and empower Latinos. Asians were learning from the political experience of Latinos, who no doubt had learned from African Americans before them.

Ethnic fears and tensions rose when it was time to take the poll and confront voters and precinct workers. The latter were mainly elderly, long-established Anglo women who had served year after year because they believed in the American system and volunteering to help it work. In 1988, they seemed nervous as they encountered first-time immigrant voters and pollsters who descended on all twenty of the city's precincts during the peak morning and evening hours.

We, the pollsters, were predominantly Asian, a fact which did not go unnoticed. Moreover, the precinct workers were understandably suspicious of us as interfering outsiders. Like many other residents in Monterey Park, they had had their fill of microscopic scrutiny and negative publicity. Later we learned that city officials had given them a minimal briefing about the poll without instructing them to cooperate. This information gap was also the fault of the exit poll organizers, who in their efforts to avoid controversy had evaded rather than promoted communication. Such were the times. Aspiring politicians were not yet accustomed to open, interethnic communication.

There was reason for concern. A year before, during the controversial recall election, the City Clerk's office was besieged with complaints arising from disputes between precinct workers and poll watchers representing the pro-recall forces. Chinese voters complained about feeling unwelcome and being asked for special identification. Precinct workers felt intimidated by Chinese-speaking poll watchers, and established residents repeated bizarre stories about newcomers registering their dogs on absentee ballots.[10] The city intervened at four polling places to resolve disputes, and police stood guard at the Lions Manor retirement apartments.

Nothing like this happened during the council elections of 1988.

Sensitivity to race and ethnicity ran high, but tense incidents were minor. The pollsters experienced some hostility and resistance to our presence. At every precinct at least one elderly Anglo would tell us that how he (or she) voted was none of our business and that the questionnaire was an infringement of his privacy and his rights as an American. One elderly white man, after spending an hour watching our every move for poll violations, called City Hall to protest against our presence. Several Latino residents objected to being ethnically categorized: "Aren't we all Americans?" A Latina activist objected to the Southwest Voter Research Institute's decision to help with an Asian-organized poll: "Why should we cooperate with people who are taking over?" Asian American voters either avoided us or answered our questions without objection. As pollsters, we summed up our reception and the relations between Asian newcomers and established residents as ranging from "suspicious to reluctantly cordial."

Election Results

The biggest surprise was the victory of Judy Chu. The pre-campaign gossip among both Asians and Anglo leaders was that "the city was not yet ready for a Chinese candidate." Chu came in first, with 24.5 percent of the vote. The second winner was the strongest RAMP candidate, Betty Couch, with 19.8 percent of the vote.

The losers were George Ristic, the second slow-growth candidate (17 percent); the developers' Latino candidate, Fred Balderrama (14.5 percent); and the developers' incumbent candidate, Cam Briglio (10 percent). Other candidates received less than 10 percent of the vote.

Although RAMP got only one of its slow-growth candidates elected, the election of Chu and Couch was a decisive defeat for the developers, made more bitter because the growth-control leadership was now multiethnic. The election was also a defeat for Frank Arcuri—but not for nativism, since Hatch would not face reelection until 1990.

The 1988 election significantly altered the city council, which now contained one minority and three women. All espoused a policy of controlled growth, but they differed strongly on minority and immigrant issues.

How do we explain the victory of a Chinese American candidate and the defeat of RAMP's second candidate during a period of apparent racial backlash? Who were the voters in terms of ethnicity, nativity, economic status, and political affiliation, and how did they line up on the candidates and the issues they represented? Would we find a political division between native-born and immigrant residents, the former favoring candidates reacting against change, the latter favoring the two Chinese candidates and the promise of ethnic representation? Or was candidate choice related to ethnicity across the board, Latinos voting for Latinos, Anglos for Anglos, and Asians for Asians? Or would class interests prevail, with higher-income citizens, regardless of their ethnicity or nativity, siding with unfettered growth, and lower- and middle-income residents opting for candidates who promised greater citizen control over development?

Voter Registration and Turnout Patterns

Before explaining the patterns of candidate choice, the registered voters need to be identified in relation to the population as a whole. Using data provided by the Asian Pacific American Voter Registration Project and the Southwest Voter Research Institute to identify ethnicity, we estimated that 30 percent of the registered voters were Latino, 30 percent Anglo, and 39 percent Asian. Fifty-nine percent of the Asians were Chinese, and 37 percent were Japanese, mainly American-born and long-time residents.[11]

As is generally the case in multiethnic Los Angeles, voters were not representative of the population as a whole. Anglos, constituting only 16 percent of the population, were overrepresented as registered voters, while Asians, with about 51 percent of the population, were underrepresented. Nevertheless, the Asian American rate of registration had increased 10 percent between 1984 and 1988.[12] One obvious factor favoring the low registration of Chinese was their high proportion of immigrants and noncitizens.

Profile of Voters in the Exit Poll

Deliberately designed to oversample Asians in order to have a clearer picture of differences within this ethnically heterogeneous population, the exit poll was not representative of the voters as a whole: 57 percent Asian (35 percent Chinese and 22 percent Japanese American), 24 percent Anglo, and 19 percent Latino.

As could be predicted, Chinese Americans were primarily immigrants. Seventy-three percent were foreign-born, a sharp contrast to Japanese Americans (6 percent), Anglos (9 percent), and Latinos (15 percent). The Chinese differed significantly from mainly second- and third-generation residents in several other respects: They were younger, had higher levels of income (with the exception of Japanese Americans) and education, and were more likely to vote Republican or have no party affiliation in a region that was strongly Democratic. The differences between Latinos and Chinese were particularly striking. Seventy-one percent of the Chinese had a college degree, compared with 28 percent of Latinos; 51 percent had family incomes over $50,000, compared with 31 percent of Latinos; 24 percent were Democrats, compared with 80 percent of Latinos. Thus, Chinese voters, primarily immigrants, had a distinctive social and political profile that differed sharply from that of other ethnic groups, particularly Latinos. The Chinese voters definitely did not fit the stereotype of the poor, working-class immigrant (Table 8).

Ethnic and Cross-Ethnic Voting Patterns

Nevertheless, in the 1988 elections these sharp status differences between immigrants and native-born residents were less associated with candidate choice than were ethnic voting patterns that intersected divisions between newcomers and established residents. Asians voted for Asians: 9 out of 10 Chinese and 7 out of 10 Japanese Americans voted for Chu; 63 percent of the Latinos supported the Latino candidate, Balderrama.

TABLE 8 *Candidate Preference and Voter Profile by Ethnicity, Monterey Park Municipal Elections, April 12, 1988*

Candidates	Chinese American (%)	Japanese American (%)	Latino (%)	Anglo (%)
Chinese				
Chu	89	75	35	30
Wu	22	2	1	1
Slow-Growth				
Couch	12	28	19	45
Ristic	8	22	15	45
Pro-Growth				
Balderrama	17	21	63	17
Briglio	15	19	19	14
VOTER CHARACTERISTICS				
Age 45 +	42	71	61	77
Foreign-born	73	6	15	9
College +	71	42	28	41
Income $50,000 +	51	46	31	33
PARTY AFFILIATION				
Democrat	24	60	80	59
Republican	45	30	16	35
Independent/none	30	10	4	6
RESPONDENTS (*N*)	397	247	216	266

Source: Data extracted from the exit poll of the 1988 municipal elections, conducted by the Southwest Voter Research Institute and the Asian Pacific American Voter Registration Project.

Note: Numbers do not add up to 100 percent because of "no answers" and because voters had two candidate choices.

Anglos spread their votes around more, although the largest bloc of 45 percent went to the two major Anglo candidates, Couch and Ristic.

According to our analysis, knowing a voter's ethnic status was a significant (at the .01 level) predictor of candidate choice in the cases of Chu, Couch, and Balderrama. Age, sex, education, income, and immigrant status were not significantly related to candidate choice.

An equally important finding was the extent of cross-ethnic voting. In a community marked by tension between longtime residents and Chinese immigrants, and one where Chinese are less than one-quarter of the electorate, the voters gave their strongest support to Chu. Seventy-five percent of the Japanese Americans, primarily English-speaking and second- and third-generation Americans, voted for her. She drew between 30 and 35 percent of the votes in our Latino and Anglo samples. Couch did particularly well (28 percent) among Japanese Americans, who were also strong supporters of controlled growth. Chu and Couch needed these cross-over votes to win an election in a city where no one ethnic group had a majority of voters. Because Chu's campaign opened up the possibility of an interethnic alliance on the issue of growth control, we wanted to know whether voters with two candidate choices tended to select both Chu and Couch, who professed growth control positions. This pattern existed only to a limited extent, as we shall see below.

The complexity of ethnic and interethnic voting patterns emerges only when we examine the weight and probable meaning of particular political tendencies within each major ethnic group, with its own diversity and experience of incorporation in the United States and Monterey Park. Based on our ethnographic and electoral data, that analysis follows.

The Chinese: The Primacy of Ethnic Representation

Chu did not specifically target or cater to the Chinese vote. Her emphasis was on interethnic harmony. She rejected all financial support from developers, including Chinese developers. Nevertheless, she clearly got the Chinese vote. Why? Chinese voters were single-minded about having some representation in a community where Asians are a numerical majority and a political minority. More than any other group, the Chinese maximized their choice by "bullet voting." Twenty-four percent of her Chinese supporters voted for Chu only. Thirty-five percent cast both votes for Chu and Wu.

The desire for ethnic representation overrode all other major social and political differences among Chinese. Established residents tend to exaggerate the homogeneity of the Chinese and to build stereotypes of monolithic power because of the high visibility of some high-status immigrants. However, the Chinese of Monterey Park are extremely diverse in social status as well as national origin, language, and length of residence in the United States. For example, the Chinese in our sample were almost equally divided between Mandarin- and Cantonese-speakers. The former were more likely to be new residents; the latter, more established in the community.

Nevertheless, for the sake of the election, Chinese unity persisted in spite of great diversity. Evidence of this came from the strong interest in Chu shown by the wider Chinese community outside Monterey Park. Chu was invited to their functions; they attended her fundraisers and contributed even though she was not running in their districts. Two major regional Chinese-language newspapers—the conservative, pro-Taiwanese *Chinese Daily News/World Journal* and the more liberal (at least in terms of foreign policy) *Central Daily News*—gave her favorable coverage. Divided on international issues, they united on the need for local representation. While both papers reported the developers' fear that Chu was not loyal to their cause, their editorial consensus was positive. She had a good professional image, which could serve the Chinese community as a whole. The Chinese voters apparently agreed.

However, the exit poll also reveals potentially important cross-currents within the Chinese community. The one factor that was significantly related to differences in candidate choice was length of residence in the United States. The more recent immigrants tended to vote only for ethnic representation, while the more established Chinese took into account other political considerations. For example, the more recent immigrants voted both for Wu, an immigrant, and Chu, a Chinese American. The more established residents tended to vote for Chu alone or in combination with a non-Chinese candidate. Thirty-nine percent of the Chu supporters also voted for a Chinese-friendly but anti-Chu developer candidate, Balderrama or Briglio; 21 percent cast their second vote for a slow-growth candidate, Couch or Ristic. As for the 11 percent of the Chinese in our sample who voted against Chu, 49 percent voted pro-development; the next-largest group, 34 percent, voted slow-growth.

From these results, we can draw two conclusions. First, the Chinese were voting primarily for ethnic representation. Second, there are profound differences within the Chinese community, particularly between newcomers or immigrants and established residents. Later we will see that these differences assumed greater importance over time as more Chinese Americans gained office. The current trend of ethnic voting tells us nothing about how the Chinese will vote in the future when they have a choice among Asian candidates who reflect the heterogeneity of Chinese and Asian citizens.

Japanese Americans: A Vote for Asian American Representation and Slow Growth

The Japanese Americans show a complex pattern of ethnic and cross-ethnic voting. Why did they support a Chinese candidate? In Monterey

Park, the Japanese seem to have more in common with old-resident Anglos and Latinos than with Chinese immigrants. Ninety-four percent of our Japanese respondents were American-born, compared with 27 percent of the Chinese (see Table 8). Japanese Americans are in fact certified old residents who may well dislike the changes associated with the new Chinese immigration—overdevelopment and an anti-Asian backlash on the part of established residents who do not distinguish between Chinese newcomers and Japanese American old-timers.

The apparent anomaly of old residents' supporting a Chinese candidate indicates the existence of two major and, at this time, contradictory political currents within the Japanese American community. The majority current supported a vote for Asian American representation. However, there was also a strong slow-growth, old-resident, and, probably, anti-Chinese current. Fifty percent of our respondents gave their support to Couch and Ristic, second only to the Anglo support for Couch. Put more strongly, 60 percent of those Japanese Americans who did not support Chu cast their vote for Couch. By contrast, only 23 percent of the Chu supporters cast their second vote for Couch. After the election, leaders of RAMP, surprised by Chu's vote, admitted that they had overestimated Japanese American support for slow-growth candidates and underestimated their desire for Asian American representation.

Our analysis of the exit poll data suggests that these cross-currents reflect different populations with different concerns. For example, those Japanese American voters who did not support Chu tended to fit the social profile of an old resident. They were significantly (at the .05 level) more likely to be older and less educated than the Chu supporters. Based on our observations and interviews in Monterey Park, we would hypothesize that lower education and older age may be related to a conservative, old-resident view of the community, to an attachment to the way things were before the Chinese immigrants arrived.

These cross-currents are also built into the contradictory status of Japanese Americans in Monterey Park as old residents and Asians. They speak English, have assimilated, and are welcomed by Anglos as "good, quiet, neighbors." But assimilation and residential proximity have not erased their separateness. The two groups stay pretty much to themselves socially. In local political life, the Japanese maintain a low profile and are underrepresented, while the Anglos have put their distinctive stamp on local issues.

Thus, the Japanese Americans are both established and politically underrepresented residents. In the absence of a Japanese American candidate, Judy Chu was a good Asian American choice. As one resident commented, "She is not Japanese, but at least she is not a FOB [fresh off the boat] Chinese immigrant." Influential Japanese American leaders gave their support to Chu, and the majority of voters followed suit. The result was probably a vote for an Asian American rather than for a Chinese candidate. As Chinese power grows in the city, time will tell whether Japanese Americans will support a candidate whom they identify as representing Chinese immigrants rather than Asian Americans as a whole.

Latinos: A Strong Ethnic and Chu Vote

How do we explain the vote of second- and third-generation Latino voters who, like the Japanese Americans, probably moved out of the central city for a quiet and comfortable existence in a racially mixed, middle-class suburb? The second-largest ethnic group in Monterey Park, they seem to get lost in the Anglo–Asian dialogue.

Although the majority of Latino voters supported the Latino candidate, their ethnic vote was weaker and more ambivalent than that of the Chinese and Japanese. Chu was a strong second political choice: 35 percent, followed by 19 percent for Couch, and 19 percent for Balderrama's running mate, Briglio. Moreover, support for Chu was strong among both Balderrama and non-Balderrama voters. Forty-six percent of the Balderrama voters gave Chu their second vote, as compared with 21 percent for Briglio, and 12 percent for Couch. Non-Balderrama and, presumably, slow-growth supporters voted 35 percent for Chu, followed closely by 26 percent for Couch, and 12 percent for Briglio.

The ethnic vote, the relatively strong support for Chu, and the weaker support for Couch and slow-growth politics can be understood in terms of the social characteristics and historical experience of Latinos in Monterey Park. A vote for Balderrama made sense simply because Latinos, like the Chinese and Japanese, lacked political representation. But a less than enthusiastic endorsement of Balderrama was also understandable. His pro-development politics had little to offer to old-resident, strongly Democratic Latinos without significant business interests in the community.

But why the particular pattern of cross-ethnic voting? Why did the Latino voters support Chu more strongly than Couch? One might have expected them to support a slow-growth Anglo candidate over a Chinese American who symbolizes the changes in the city. Typically assimilated, English-speaking, and middle-class, Latinos, like Japanese Americans, tend to be old residents. As such, they often complain about the effects of growth and immigration on the quality of community life. Moreover, as the "first" residents of California, Americans of Mexican descent may have a special prejudice against the Chinese, whose apparent success as a "model minority" and greater collective prosperity threaten them with yet another historical demotion on their own territory.

After years of Anglo discrimination, however, Latinos also have reason to band together with Asians to claim their majority status. Like the Japanese and Chinese Americans, some Latinos in Monterey Park associate the slow-growth movement with Anglo domination and anti-immigrant bias. In 1986 two prominent Latino councilmen as well as a Chinese American had been voted out of office with the help of RAMP and the slow-growth movement. Moreover, many Latinos had united with Chinese newcomers to oppose Official English as a threat to their language and culture.

In the historical context of Latino–Anglo conflict, we can understand both the pattern of ethnic voting and the preference for a candidate who stressed ethnic harmony. Besides, Chu's campaign had dedicated Latino organizers and volunteers who went door to door in Latino districts. Her victory no doubt depended on the success of this Latino–Chinese alliance.

Anglos: The Slow-Growth Stronghold

The slow-growth Anglo candidates got major support from Anglo voters. Can this be interpreted as an Anglo ethnic vote? To what degree was there also significant cross-ethnic voting among Anglos? In Monterey Park, a case could be made for slow growth as basically an Anglo nativist movement. While established residents, regardless of their ethnicity, have given support to slow-growth candidates and measures, it was the Anglo old guard who led and emotionally took up the fight. Accustomed to being the politically dominant group and the unhyphenated Americans in a city experiencing ethnic transformation, Anglos may be doing their own ethnic voting by championing the ostensibly ethnically neutral but exclusionary politics of slow growth and Official English.

Nevertheless, Anglos, like Asian Americans and Latinos, cannot be stereotyped. They also engaged in complicated patterns of voting across ethnic lines. Fifty-five percent did not vote for Couch, the major slow-growth candidate. Her opponents gave their votes to Chu (44 percent) or to the developer candidates Balderrama (21 percent) and Briglio (12 percent). Altogether, 30 percent of Anglo voters supported Chu. This pattern shows considerable support for a Chinese American candidate.

Who were the Chu supporters among Anglos? We know that they tended not to be Couch and slow-growth supporters. Our exit poll data indicate that Anglos who voted for Chu were significantly more likely than non–Chu supporters to be Democrats, have higher education, and speak a foreign language at home. In other words, they tended to have a progressive and cosmopolitan rather than an old-resident profile. Like other "ethnics," they cross-voted enough to affect the overall election results.

Thus, the comparisons between different ethnic categories tell a complex story of how the economic issues of growth are transformed into the politics of ethnicity by each group's historical experience of domination, oppression, and competition. For the Anglo minority, the growth control movement shaded into nativism; for Asians, into a manifestation of racism. Latinos, caught between a history of Anglo class and ethnic oppression and the fear of future Asian power, understood both the Asian and Anglo viewpoints. The story becomes even more complex when we examine differences within these three groups.

THE EMERGENCE OF ETHNIC AND INTERETHNIC POLITICS

By the mid-1980s the nativist and racist tendencies within the primarily white and native-born leadership of the growth-control and Official English movements had created their antithesis: pro-immigrant and anti-racist multiethnic coalitions of immigrant and native-born business and professional leaders. This particular line-up of forces exacerbated the racial and immigrant components of conflict.

The high point of tensions occurred in 1986, when the city council passed its Official English resolution, and in 1987, when the developer-financed ABC tried to recall two "racist" council members. The Monterey Park voters showed their sophistication by rejecting the recall and the temptation to reduce the complexities of local politics to race.

The progressive elements of CHAMP, having broken from their business allies who formed ABC, were developing an alternative to the politics of racial polarization by supporting Chu in the 1988 city council race. Her election set the conditions for a move away from confrontations between newcomers and established residents toward ethnic and immigrant empowerment and interethnic alliances on ethnic and economic issues. It also revealed two political tendencies that cut across the division between newcomers and established residents. The first was the struggle of ethnic minorities for representation. A major finding of our exit poll was that ethnicity, not nativity or other social factors, was the statistically significant predictor of candidate choice. This tendency would prove to be a mixed blessing: Necessary for achieving representation of the unrepresented, ethnic organizing and voting as an end in itself can foster competition and conflict.

A second political tendency in the 1988 election was cross-over or interethnic voting on issues of representation and economic development. Asians, whether native-born or immigrant, united to support a Chinese American candidate, while Latinos and Anglos rallied to her message of controlled growth and harmony. Similarly, the Anglo slow-growth leader Couch won with major support outside her solidly Anglo base.

The 1988 election also saw the emergence of a new type of leadership. In previous elections, Latinos, Asian Americans, and Anglos had united to support slow-growth measures, but no leader had brought together the goals of diversity and controlled growth into one program. The achievement of Judy Chu and her progressive supporters from CHAMP was to offer a multiethnic and progressive foundation for the controlled-growth movement, the possibility of a multiethnic class alliance against developers to counter the existing multiethnic alliance of developers. For such a movement to develop, two political realignments would have to take place. First, the progressive multiculturalists had to separate themselves from developers. This began to happen when a faction of CHAMP failed to support their business-oriented allies in the recall effort, and when Chu refused developer support.

Second, the alliance of slow-growth and Official English leaders had to break up. This had not happened. Reacting to ABC's charges of racism, RAMP leaders rallied against the recall. A political struggle on many fronts would be required before established residents and progressive leaders in the controlled-growth movement would distance themselves from Hatch's nativist politics and look for ethnic and immigrant allies. This struggle began to take place between the council elections of 1988 and 1990. The result was the breakup of the alliance between RAMP and Hatch, the weakening of nativist tendencies, and the increased representation of women, ethnic groups, and immigrants in local politics—moving the city away from ethnic conflict and Anglo domination and toward an uncharted and undefined course of multiethnic democracy.

FROM NATIVISM TO ETHNIC AND INTERETHNIC POLITICS

The times are changing and you cannot go against the wind.
—A naturalized Chinese American woman active in promoting interethnic cooperation

SPRING, 1988: The scene is the Monterey Park city council chamber. Seated behind microphones on a long dais are the five council members: two Anglo men and two Anglo women, all variously identified with the politics of slow growth and Official English and a lone Chinese American woman, an advocate of harmony and "managed" growth. Although Asian Americans and Latinos constitute more than 80 percent of Monterey Park's population, the city staff and elected officials are predominantly white.

Facing the council members in choice front-center seats, a "jury" of mostly white and elderly council watchers scrutinizes the proceedings. This is their turf. One of the "regulars," leaning on her cane as she moves slowly toward the podium to register her opinion, comments to the assemblage, "I feel at home here." Recent immigrants do not feel at home in the city council. They attend irregularly, in the defense of specific causes, often taking advantage of the safety of large numbers.

SPRING, 1990: Three of the Anglo council members, including a militant advocate of restrictions on immigrants, have been retired by a recent election. The new council now consists of two women elected in 1988, an Anglo and a Chinese American, both advocates of controlled growth, and three newly elected, business-friendly members—an Anglo woman, a Latino, and a foreign-born Chinese American male. They have come together to celebrate the mayoral inauguration of the Chinese American councilwoman, Judy Chu.[1]

At least for tonight, Chinese newcomers do not have that sense of being unwanted in City Hall. The elderly council watcher who two years ago had announced that she felt at home in the chambers is now struggling to find a seat. Arriving early and in great numbers, newcomers have occupied her customary perch and scattered the regulars to the periphery of action. Not deterred, she asserts her seniority by sitting up front in a section normally reserved for city staff.

Everywhere mingling with established residents are well-dressed immigrants, many recording the event on film. Large baskets of flowers with red-ribboned Chinese messages of good luck line the dais, in grave danger of being toppled by the entertainers: a gyrating Chinese dragon, a fan-waving Japanese American woman dressed in a traditional kimono, an energetic troupe of Mexican American folk dancers. Public officials are present to sanction the event—a local rabbi, state Attorney General John Van de Kamp, Secretary of State March Fong Eu, and Dr. Omero Suarez, President of Monterey Park's East Los Angeles College, Latino territory with a fast-growing Asian student population.

With these gestures, diversity and multiculturalism were being institutionalized in the Monterey Park council, which only two years before was the bastion of established-resident reaction to the new Asian immigration. The multicultural celebration of a Chinese American Mayor, the defeat of a leader of anti-immigrant policies, the election of a Chinese immigrant and a Latino—these events dramatized major political changes: the containment, at least temporarily, of an anti-immigrant backlash, the decline of Anglo dominance, and the empowerment of minorities and immigrants. This chapter is about the people and the political process that brought about these changes from 1988 to 1990.

HATCH'S LAST STAND

The election of Judy Chu to the Monterey Park city council in 1988 introduced a new political tendency that combined the implicit promise of Asian representation with explicit support for managed growth within a framework of diversity. Challenging the developers' association of slow growth with racism, Chu was in effect proposing that a bridge could be built between Asian, Anglo, and Latino residents on issues of economic development.

But interethnic bridges are difficult to build and notoriously unstable. In 1989, xenophobia continued to set the tone of city politics as Councilman Barry Hatch took advantage of his tenure as Mayor to promote his anti-immigrant policies. On the stage of city council, Hatch played the role of the embattled defender of American unity based on reverence for family, God, the community, and the English language. He believed that American unity and strength were being threatened by special interests, power blocs of minorities, illegal immigrants, criminals, and their defenders in the liberal establishment of government, education, and the media. As councilman in a city of immigrants, he used official Monterey Park stationery to send an anti-immigrant message to each presidential candidate:

> As a candidate for office in the government of this great nation, you are ignoring the most serious threat the United States has ever faced. The runaway invasion of this sovereign nation by illegal aliens, drug runners, terrorists and criminals is rapidly placing in jeopardy the safety and quality of life of our citizens. . . . We want, and the nation demands, leaders with principles, patriotism and realism. Control our borders—preserve our nation. If you cannot support America, we cannot support you.[2]

While the overt message was about illegal aliens and criminals, the subtext was about the growing number of nonwhite Americans. From his election in 1986, Hatch consistently introduced a xenophobic agenda into local politics. By 1989, however, this strategy was severely compromised. Hatch's demand that the city require two-thirds English on all business signs eventually produced an ordinance requiring only a slightly higher proportion of English on the local signage. His move to fire the city's independent and progressive library board was overturned by a federal court order. In spite of his complaints about the increasing number of Chinese books in the local library, the staff accepted a gift of 10,000 Chinese books from Taiwan. He did not even succeed in erecting a statue of George Washington as a lesson in Americanism for newcomers. Finally in 1990 Hatch was defeated in an election where the biggest vote-getter was Samuel Kiang, a first-generation Chinese American who was clearly pro-immigrant.

Hatch's removal from city office symbolized the decline of overt nativism and a move toward greater ethnic democracy. How did this come about? Drawing on the results of an exit poll from the 1990 city council elections and ethnographic observations of everyday events, we can begin to construct the political process behind the defeat of Hatch himself and the political tendency he represented. It is a complex story of increased empowerment of Latinos and Asian Americans and shifting interethnic alliances on the issues of growth, diversity, and representation.

ETHNOGRAPHIC EVIDENCE OF OPPOSITION

Our field observations indicated that Hatch was in trouble before his bid for reelection in 1990. While he was pursuing his anti-immigrant policies in city council, his supporters were backing away and his opposition was moving from a position of defense to one of offense. Chinese newcomers, or, more accurately, their leaders in the immigrant and native-born communities, were organizing for resistance and empowerment. They were joined by a small but visible group of grassroots activists—established Anglo, Latino, and Asian American residents who were fed up with racial tension. Another continuing force of opposition were the developers, still playing up the link between Hatch's slow-growth and nativist policies, and working behind the scenes to replace him with ethnically diverse candidates sensitive to the needs of big business.

Meanwhile, Hatch was losing his slow-growth allies. He was becoming a political liability. The mostly Anglo leaders of growth control were eager for ethnic support, a course opened up by Chu and others. Even Hatch's conservative Republican friends were concluding that immigrant-bashing interfered with their recruitment of potentially Republican Latinos and Asians. Thus, the initial nativist reaction of established residents was being undermined by political realism and the increased empowerment of minorities and newcomers.

Grassroots Resistance

The dynamics of grassroots opposition to Hatch emerge in the field notes of Mary Pardo, who regularly attended council meetings to follow the political involvement of women. Her field notes from the summer of 1989 highlight the role of women—Latina, Anglo, and Chinese—in resisting the patriarch of Americanism.

The setting is the final city council meeting to decide on Hatch's proposal to erect a George Washington monument. Three women speak against the project. The first is a middle-aged Chinese immigrant and longtime resident. A Republican, she has become a strong supporter of Chu and multiculturalist politics. Lately, she has been attending meetings of the Asian Pacific American Democratic Club and has been active in building interethnic bridges. She wants to assert her patriotism and oppose the monument: "I have lived in Monterey Park for twenty years. I am also a member of the Parks and Recreation Commission. As an immigrant, I truly respect the land of freedom. I am all for erecting the George Washington monument. But the monument should be erected through private donations."

Next to speak is an elderly Anglo woman, a member of the politically progressive Monterey Park Democratic Club. Her tactic is to evade the controversial issue of Americanism and oppose the monument strictly on the basis of costs and priorities, a pragmatic approach popular across the political spectrum: "I have circulated a petition many times. But this time, I got signatures very easily from a cross-section of the community. This leads me to believe that ninety percent of the city is opposed to using city monies for the monument. I also asked people how they

Immigrant workers passing Chinese and English signs on North Atlantic Boulevard, Fourth of July, 1994.

EVERYDAY LIFE IN MONTEREY PARK

Photos by Martin A. Sugarman

An old-timer in front of bungalow, Summer 1994.

New luxury development, Summer 1994.

East meets West in an Asian American home, Summer 1994.

Chinese supermarket and Asian businesses, North Atlantic Boulevard, Summer 1994.

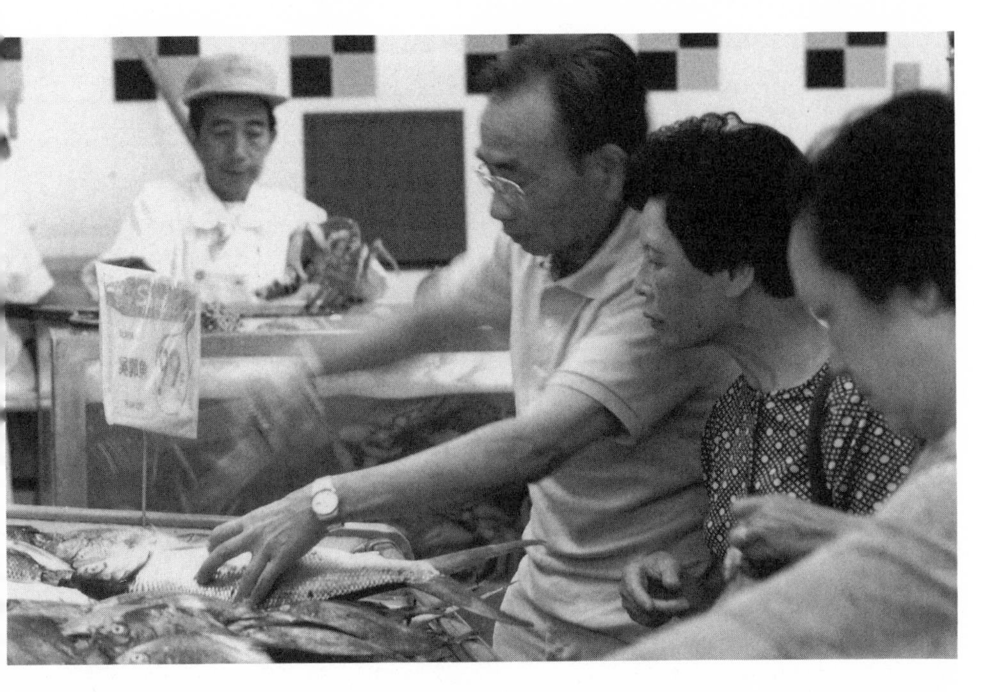

Shopping at a Chinese supermarket, Summer 1994.

Shopping in Atlantic Square, Summer 1994.

Children of immigrants studying calculus in the Bruggemeyer Memorial Library, Summer 1994.

An English class offered by Literacy for All of Monterey Park (LAMP), a city program run with the help of volunteers, Summer 1994.

Dancing to the mellow sounds of the "Memory Laners" at the Langley Senior Citizen Center, Summer 1994.

Doing a line dance at the Langley Senior Citizen Center, Summer 1994.

Meeting of the Spanish-speaking Club Amistad at the Langley Senior Citizen Center, Summer 1994.

The Monterey Park Concert Band, performing at the Fourth of July celebration in Barnes Park, 1992.

Mixed audience and mixed reactions to the entertainment, Barnes Park, Fourth of July, 1992.

Princess Staci Jung, Queen Jennifer Zepeda, Princess Gina Dietrich (from left to right): members of the court in the Miss Monterey Park Pageant, sponsored by the Monterey Park Chamber of Commerce, Fourth of July, 1992.

Hot dogs for sale, Barnes Park, Fourth of July, 1992.

Tending the barbecue, Barnes Park, Fourth of July, 1992.

Friends joining a mother's celebration for one recently married son and another about to enter military service, Garvey Ranch Park, Summer 1994.

would prefer the money be spent. Here are some of the responses: help the handicapped, for child care, for the police, for the library, the parks, the hungry. There are many needs in our community."

Next, a middle aged Latina resident speaks. She has fought for Latino representation on the city council. Now she dares to confront Hatch's concept of patriotism: "I oppose the statue and mean no disrespect for George Washington. Being an American is not having a statue in front of City Hall or wrapping yourself in a flag, but having two brothers and uncles [war victims] buried in a cemetery. And it is also standing up to city council and speaking out."

Hatch's reaction is a classical display of how to lose battles by condescension. Drawing a line between his true Americanism and the self-interest of everyone else, he speaks aggressively, not shouting, but agitated and scolding:

> You know that there is a twenty-foot statue of Confucius at Cal State Los Angeles [the nearby state university]? Where are our American philosophers?
>
> What are people's agendas? I served in the military too, you know. What is the motive of coming up here and talking about what love of country means? I think these are very disturbing attitudes.
>
> What do you mean patriotism isn't wrapping yourself in a flag? Hispanics from all over can say, "Viva la Raza," but they're not going back home. I want to bring a formal recognition, a statue here, and I am embarrassed by the attitudes [adamant tone]. I am appalled by these views. Why didn't some of you come up and oppose the thousands of dollars being spent on a video technician? We have volunteers, but no, they had to spend twenty thousand dollars on a full-time technician. How much are we spending on new immigrants? How about spending a few dollars on men who made this great country possible? All of you are so self-centered. (An Asian video camera operator in the back of the auditorium gives an audible "humph" and laughs.)

Hatch's remarks were directed primarily to the comments of the Latina and Chinese American speakers. Returning to her seat and fuming, the Latina confided to Pardo: "See, this is what he does. I'm going to walk out of here. I'm not going to sit here and listen to this."[3]

Interviewed later, the Chinese American speaker reflected:

> A lot of Chinese people do not like to get involved, especially in our City Hall, because someone can embarrass you. That makes you feel uncomfortable. Like me, I don't feel it. I just go there and fight

> back. If you insult me, I let you know it, and I won't let you push me around. It really takes some courage. At least if you don't have a language handicap, you can speak back.

She had learned from her own experience as an immigrant who once had to "go with the wind"—adapt to the pattern of Anglo dominance.

> I went to city council not because I am against the monument but because Hatch raised it to a racial issue. After I spoke against it, he gave a lecture. He said that at Cal State L.A. there is a statue of Confucius. He said that he asked some young students how it felt to have Confucius looking down on them. He is the one that looks down on people. He brings out this Confucius statue right after I spoke. That made me have a bad feeling.[4]

In the end, the city council voted against Hatch and the Washington statue but, as a compromise, decided to hold a celebration for new citizens. The event, like the George Washington monument, was a flop. Only one Chinese immigrant was there to receive a flag from the welcoming natives.

At a community meeting, two residents exchanged perceptions of this nonevent. An Anglo woman, very active in community affairs, saw the failure as another example of "our reaching out" and getting no response:

> I was very disappointed when they had the program at Barnes Park. I wasn't on the committee, but I'm sure they worked very hard. They sent out invitations. The park looked beautiful with the flags. And there were about twenty people there. I don't know what happened, but something fell through. That's a celebration where nobody took part. Three women council people attended. They had all these flags ready to give out, and presentations, and certificates, and there was just this one little Chinese lady, and that's all. And the American Legion baked cakes and made punch. I'll tell you, we all had plenty of cake that day.

A Chinese immigrant in his late thirties, a citizen and a Monterey Park resident for about a decade, politely offered an explanation of Chinese American resistance:

> I saw announcements in the local Chinese newspaper. They do cover well the city activities. I can offer just right off my hat the reason why there was a small turnout, only one person. The people's perception of the city is wrong. . . . What happened in the city council is that there are a lot of negatives against the Chinese people. So people just feel that whatever the city does is against us. Actually

there are a lot of good programs that the city has put out. But people just, you know, have the perception that they're against us.[5]

Councilwomen Unite Against Hatch

Resistance to Hatch was not limited to Chinese newcomers and grassroots activists; it was also being forged within the council by three very different women: Betty Couch, an Anglo and conservative Republican leader of RAMP; Patricia Reichenberger, an Anglo and a conservative Democrat who had once been close to Hatch and had been a strong supporter of Official English; and the progressive, Chinese American Judy Chu. Three factors strengthened their political unity during the council debates of 1988–1990: Hatch's rigid ideology and demeaning political style, Chu's strategy of nonpartisan consensus building, and the willingness of the councilwomen to cooperate and compromise on an issue-by-issue basis.

Unbending in his opinions and unresponsive to compromise, Hatch harangued the women whenever they failed to support his no-growth and no-immigration positions. His reaction was predictable in the case of the liberal Chu, but he also belittled and insulted his more conservative potential allies.

While Hatch competed in speechmaking with Councilman Chris Houseman, the councilwomen quietly researched city issues and banded together for protection against harassment. At one point when Hatch was serving as Mayor, the verbal harassment grew so intense that the three women sent him separate letters threatening to walk out of the council chamber if he did not stop his personal attacks. When he used city stationery to express his views on restricting immigration, the women passed a rule restricting city stationery to official business.

The women also united as peacemakers and doers. Chu generally supported Couch and Reichenberger's growth-control stands. In turn, the more conservative councilwomen supported policies that fostered interethnic harmony: working out a compromise on Chinese-language signs, bringing more Asians and Latinos into the moribund but potentially influential Human Relations Commission, selecting a liberal Japanese American for a post on the important Planning Commission, and supporting an Asian Youth Project to address the problems of immigrant children living in the United States without their parents.[6]

The councilwomen achieved consensus by finding common ground. Chu was a master of the process. She gained support for her liberal agenda by appealing to the conservative principles of her sisters. For example, rather than fight over racial quotas in a community already sharply divided on ethnic lines, the women increased minority representation on city commissions by stressing qualifications; and there were well-qualified Asian and Latino applicants. Chu won support for the Asian Youth Project by going to the United Way and businesses for financial help and not depending on scarce city funds. Couch balked at supporting Chu's proposal for a municipal child care center but, after intense lobbying by child care supporters, cast a "yes" vote because federal money had been earmarked for the center. Finally, only Hatch opposed the child care center on ideological grounds: Families and not "Big Brother" should take care of children. Today the child care center is thriving and financially independent.

Thus, in the mundane deliberations of city council, two conservative Anglo women and a progressive Chinese American woman united to improve the quality of life in a multiethnic community. Chu opened up new political space for an interethnic alliance around shared concerns. Her efforts were also intended to normalize and legitimate the Chinese in the eyes of Anglo and Latino residents: "Through me, they can see the Chinese not as evil people who want to take over, but as people who can provide leadership in a responsible way."[7]

Chu was apparently successful in sending this message to her sisters on city council. Together they exposed the divisiveness of Hatch's approach to women, minorities, and newcomers. Moreover, the internal battles within the council, whose five members supported controlled growth, revealed a serious split within that movement. The leaders and followers of slow growth who had united behind Hatch during the recall effort were now beginning to question his leadership and, more generally, the negative impact of his anti-immigrant policies on a city of immigrants.

Undermining the Hatch/Slow-Growth Alliance

In 1986, the leaders of RAMP had endorsed Hatch's election to city council because he spoke out forcefully for growth control. Facing reelection four years later, he had become a liability for the movement, and particularly for the liberal elements, who found themselves in the embarrassing position of harboring a right-wing anti-immigrant Republican. A Democratic leader of RAMP stated the problem in an interview:

> Supporting him may have been a tactical mistake in the sense that we don't need that sort of person there representing us now. . . . he caused enough trouble during his period in office so that we were busy working on things other than development. The recall in particular was a tremendous amount of effort that we spent to save his butt.[8]

Disenchanted with Hatch, the Anglo leaders of the growth-control movement needed Asian and Latino allies whose presence could counter the developers' charge that regulated growth was in essence xenophobic. Overestimating their own strength and underestimating the demand for ethnic leadership, RAMP did not support Chu in the 1988 election and expected her to lose. A year later, a leader of RAMP applauded her victory:

> As it turned out in retrospect, I think the results [of the election] were excellent because the problem in supporting Judy Chu was she didn't have a track record, but she has been true to her originally stated positions. So from RAMP's standpoint she's been a very good councilperson, someone who at this point we could easily support. She had already requested support [at the time of the election], so she had overcome the idea that she couldn't get along with us, right? We had to get over the idea that we couldn't get along with her. But now that has been resolved, there's no reason why we should not represent a unified force.[9]

The RAMP/Chu alliance was uneasy; getting along and breaking down ethnic and racial barriers would come slowly and unevenly. In 1989, the painful process of constructing diversity could be observed on several occasions when slow-growth advocates in the mostly Anglo United Democratic Club (UDC) attended meetings of the West San Gabriel Valley Asian Pacific Democratic Club.

For most Anglos, ethnic harmony required integration into their existing organizations. Now, faced with the existence of the Asian Democratic club, they could either accept it and strengthen their own power base through alliances and coalitions or become isolated and obsolete in a situation where they were no longer the majority, or even a model for the new ethnic majorities. In 1989, Anglo Democrats called for joint meetings with the expectation that Asians would be eager to meet with them and iron out misunderstandings. Initially, the results were disappointing. Members of the UDC complained that they were rebuffed in their attempts to arrange meetings with the Asian club. Members of the Asian club complained that they had no interest in returning to the days when they had to follow a white agenda or give Anglos lessons about racism. One member thought that the interest of Anglos in attending their meetings was "patronizing, an attitude of, 'Why don't you educate us about Asians?'" Another said jokingly, "I know why they're interested in meeting with us. . . . we're [Asians] coming out from everywhere!"

Nevertheless, there were some joint meetings. The West San Gabriel Valley Asian Pacific Democratic Club invited the UDC, the Monterey Park Democratic Club (MPDC), and the League of United Latin American Citizens (LULAC) to attend a banquet to install new officers, a forum on immigration, and a presentation of some results of our research. We had become participants as well as observers.

Interactions among the different clubs were particularly lively during the immigration forum. To the surprise of some members of the Asian club, the UDC showed up at the forum on time, before the Asians arrived, "late as usual." That meeting turned into an exchange of information about immigration laws and trends, a topic unfamiliar to many of the Anglos. An Anglo woman, expressing a familiar concern about the large size of the new immigration, said: "Let me play the devil's advocate. My father came from France. He had nine brothers and sisters. What would have happened if they all got married and emigrated? It would have emptied the country." A Chinese American woman countered by pointing out that for many years the United States had expressly excluded Chinese in favor of Europeans. The sides were far apart, but the Anglo guests clearly enjoyed the face-to-face exchange and continued the discussion after the meeting.

A more stressful interethnic encounter took place a month later when members of the two Monterey Park Democratic clubs and LULAC attended a banquet to install the new officers of the Asian American club. Members of the feuding UDC and MPDC sat at separate tables. The ethnically conscious MPDC had been involved with the Asian club since its founding, and members were comfortable in that setting. The members of the UDC, as outsiders, were pleased at being inside and laughing at the "in jokes" of Mike Eng, the former president of the Asian club and Judy Chu's husband. Nevertheless, one researcher observed that they were visibly uncomfortable when listening to the guest speaker, Warren Furutani, a member of the Los Angeles School Board. His topic was strategies for enhancing Asian power:

> They didn't seem to be too happy about Warren Furutani's talk. At times, Warren speaks in the agitational way of the '60's, and I could tell that some of the United Democratic Club members were a bit disturbed when his tone of voice went up a few notches. A few individuals, at the table, looked at each other and rolled up their eyes when Warren began to talk about the experiment of power-sharing between teachers and administrators in the Los Angeles Unified School District. When people clapped in the middle of Warren's speech, not one of the members at the United Democratic Club table joined in. Only a few clapped when he finished. Overall, their support seemed somewhat cool. This wasn't true for the Monterey Park Democratic Club table, or for any other table which I observed. They all seemed very excited about what Warren had to say.[10]

After the meeting a UDC member expressed his ambivalence about the event:

> We have been trying to break down the doors for a long time. This was important as a social event; first you have to get to know people. But I would like a real political discussion. For example, I would like to ask, Why do you want to form your own club? Why is your membership for Asians only? [The membership brochure stated that anyone could belong, but only Asians would have full voting rights.]
>
> . . . He [Furutani] said he wasn't going to make a hard-hitting, pragmatic speech, but that is just what it was . . . all about how to increase Asian representation. I think that political differences are more important than ethnic ones. We are in an interesting period when Monterey Park will see the emergence of new alliances.[11]

The installation banquet was a testing of the waters. By inviting Anglo and Latino Democrats to their meeting, defined by their agenda, the Asian club leaders reinforced their legitimacy as a separate organization. For the members of the UDC, the encounter was an uncomfortable education in the reality of minority politics.

It was also another step away from the politics of xenophobia toward greater contact and cooperation with the minority and immigrant communities. Tactics, if not principle, demanded it.

Hatch as a Republican Liability

As some Anglo Democrats within the controlled-growth movement began to distance themselves from Hatch and accept Chu as an ally, many conservative Anglos remained suspicious of her agenda. As one local leader in the Republican Party put it: "Chu is doing OK, but I don't think she has shown her true colors yet. Also, I suspect that her motive is to use us as a stepping stone to higher political offices."[12]

Conservative Republicans did not, however, have to embrace Chu and liberalism in order to distance themselves from Hatch. It was not in their interest to stir up ethnic divisions in an ethnically plural community with a large foreign-born and minority population. One Republican who had been involved in the Southern California campaign for Official English strongly advised the national office of U.S. English not to intervene in Monterey Park politics or side with Hatch, who had complained about too many Chinese books in the library and had led the effort to reduce the authority of the progressive library board. The liberal national organization People for the American Way had already intervened to help the board in its suit against the city.

> They [U.S. English] were interested in the conflict with our library and, you know, the Friends of the American Way and all that. And they wanted to come in and to do something. I wrote to them and I talked to them on the phone too, and I said, Just stay out of Monterey Park. Leave Monterey Park alone. We are at the point now where all these things have subsided. The people I've talked to, and I talked with a lot of Chinese, and they said that they really want to put this behind them. They're trying to integrate into the community. You know, we are such a diverse community. We're doing many things that people who don't live here don't understand, and you can't come from Washington in here and think that you're going do something for the City of Monterey Park. Stay away. We are working things out. And they had a board meeting and they agreed to stay away.

There was another reason for backing away from Hatch and his confrontational nativism. Republicans could not afford to alienate middle-class Asians and Latinos, the new majority of the population and a potential base for Republican power in a historically Democratic district. To quote our astute local Republican again:

> When we stop to think about it, the Mexicans identify with the Republican Party because of everything the party stands for. We have found that in this district, especially, the people that have voted—the Mexicans who have voted, the Mexican Americans—have voted for the English Only initiative. They have voted for the death penalty. And they have voted for Governor Deukmejian, and they've voted for Ronald Reagan. Those things, you know, are in our studies. And then, with the Asians that come here, the Chinese, they identify with the Republican Party a great deal too.[13]

Old-Timers Reject Divisive Politics

By late 1989, the political climate was changing. In 1987, residents had turned out in record numbers to save Hatch from recall. Two years later, the same Hatch sympathizers were describing him as too "divisive," "against everything," and without "positive solutions to anything." They had had enough warfare and wanted to get on with solving the community's many problems.

We found this mood of ambivalence toward immigration and anti-immigrant politics in an unlikely place, the "Homecoming Day celebration." Once a year established residents of Monterey Park come together with old-timers who have fled (called laughingly, by one participant, "the betrayers") to renew once-strong community ties. Several hundred people, overwhelmingly Anglos, wined, dined, reminisced about the golden past, and joked about a bewildering present and future. These were the people who might have been sympathetic to Hatch.

Strategically sitting at different round tables in the dining room of Luminarias Restaurant, we observed reactions to a "roast" delivered by an elderly Anglo businessman who had been a member of the city's pre-immigration power structure. His jokes expressed ambivalence toward both newcomers and xenophobes:

> Monterey Park is speeding up the assimilation process. You might say that this is a "melting wok." (Fair amount of audience laughter.) I enjoy the city, my neighbors. There are many new residents and a dwindling supply of old residents. Smiles are an integral part of the Oriental faces. I enjoy seeing them, except at stop signs. (Lots of laughter. A middle-aged Latina whispers to one of our researchers, "Because they go right through stop signs.") Barry Hatch has gotten us lots of attention. He says that he's interested in promoting the use of the English language. Well, I've seen him at city council meetings, and presumably he's speaking in English, but I don't know what the hell he's talking about; and I'm probably better off than those who do. (A fair amount of laughter, although a very senior Anglo woman at our table remarks disapprovingly, "That's naughty.")[14]

Thus, from the voices in the field we began to understand the reasons for Hatch's growing isolation and the rejection of his militant nativist politics. His rigid refusal to negotiate drew a line between "real Americans" and "the others"—the immigrants and ethnic minorities. This polarizing strategy paralyzed civic life in a community where no single ethnic group had the numerical or political strength to define who and what Americans are. Hatch alienated many Chinese immigrants, established minorities, and politically progressive forces, who saw him as racist. Even established residents who might dearly love to turn back the clock began to understand that he was a political liability in a multiethnic community where direct confrontation on issues of race and immigration meant war. Such were the tendencies we observed before the 1990 election. They translated into an electoral defeat for Hatch and the installation of a more multiethnic city council.

THE MUNICIPAL ELECTIONS OF 1990

The Candidates

A major issue in the 1990 municipal election was whether Barry Hatch would be reelected to city council along with the conservative Patricia Reichenberger. After beating the 1987 recall, Hatch stepped up his anti-immigrant activities in the city council, while Reichenberger softened her stance, stating that it had been a mistake to support Official English because the issue proved too divisive. Now, faced with reelection in a political atmosphere unfriendly to any incumbents, they both avoided the topics of language and immigration and emphasized their controlled-growth records.

Four candidates opposed Hatch and Reichenberger. Two were leaders of the local Chamber of Commerce who had lost the 1988 elections, Fred Balderrama and Marie Purvis. This time around they had well-organized campaigns and the advantage of attacking the incumbents for the city's increased indebtedness and antibusiness attitudes. Purvis had strong support among established Anglo residents. Balderrama cultivated his connections to Latino residents and Chinese businessmen.

The third candidate for city council was David Barron, a Latino, who had been elected City Clerk in 1988. Not specifically targeting the Latino vote, he ran a low-key controlled-growth campaign designed to appeal to all groups.

The surprise candidate was Samuel Kiang, a 40-year-old engineer and lawyer and an immigrant from Hong Kong. He was politically unknown and inexperienced except for his involvement in the neighborhood struggle to remove a parole office described in Chapter 2. Taking a leave from work, he campaigned vigorously, reaching out for support among community leaders in all ethnic groups and regularly walking door-to-door in the city's precincts. Privately, Kiang admitted that his main goal was to defeat Hatch, whose anti-Chinese attitudes were giving Monterey Park a bad reputation nationally and internationally, and who overlooked the fact that the Chinese were doing everything in their power to assimilate.[15] Publicly, Kiang avoided any reference to ethnic politics, although he was clearly a Chinese American candidate out to get the Asian and anti-Hatch votes. Following the popular controlled-growth line, he spoke for quality, revenue-rich, and managed development. Not impressed by Kiang's credentials, RAMP circulated a campaign flyer that called him a developer's candidate: "Business donors are *99.6%* of the total, and sources from *outside of Monterey Park* are over *60%,* both in numbers and $. Kiang said that the 'business community' will 'feel better' with him on the Council to speak to."[16]

By the end of his campaign, Kiang had collected more money than any other candidate: $42,487, the highest amount ever reported for a Monterey Park election.[17] However, the amount and source of money were not conclusive proof that he was a developer's candidate. In a situation where Chinese Americans lacked representation, Chinese businesspeople had recently supported a wide range of candidates, including Judy Chu, who favored controlled growth. Kiang would certainly listen sympathetically to the complaints of the Chinese business community, but it remained to be seen whether he was in fact a developer's candidate.

Thus, the political and ethnic profiles of the candidates running for three open positions on city council in 1990 were as follows: two Anglos associated with both slow-growth and nativist tendencies (Hatch and Reichenberger); one slow-growth Latino (Barron) running a multiethnic campaign; two business-friendly candidates, an Anglo (Purvis) and a Latino (Balderrama); one Chinese American candidate who was a political wild card (Kiang).

The campaign literature for the 1990 election showed one dramatic change compared with 1988. Every candidate except Hatch cultivated important multiethnic endorsements in a play for cross-over votes. Balderrama was the biggest player of the "endorsement game." One of his many flyers had the headline "Everyone's Choice, Balderrama," and listed 24 endorsements from national and state officials and ethnic leaders ranging from the Vice-Chairperson of the National Democratic Party and the Lieutenant Governor of California, to a former Monterey Park Chief of Police and the President of the Chinese Consolidated Benevolent Association. The local endorsements, which included 11 Asians, 10 Latinos, and 2 Anglos, gave the distinct impression that Balderrama was a Latino who was friendly to the Chinese community.

Endorsements: A Realignment of Political Forces

Our ethnographic observations before the election campaign had indicated that Hatch was losing supporters from the slow-growth movement. This trend was apparent during the campaign. As expected, RAMP rejected Kiang, Purvis, and Balderrama as pro-business, and endorsed Barron and Reichenberger as authentic "controlled-growth" candidates. To the surprise of some voters, RAMP did not endorse Hatch. Deeply divided in their own evaluation of his anti-immigrant and language politics, RAMP faulted him only for his extremist antigrowth policies: "At times, however, he has behaved like a 'No Growth' advocate. He has been stubborn and uncompromising—unwilling to work with other Councilmembers to come up with reasonable solutions in controlled growth matters."[18]

RAMP's choice of words is instructive. "No growth," with its connotation of xenophobia and resistance to change, was widely used by developers against the slow-growth movement. Now slow-growth leaders were using the same language to purge a xenophobe from their own ranks. The RAMP wording also implies a changed position on development. No longer outsiders, but represented on the city council and commissions and confronted with the need for growth that would increase revenues, RAMP was rejecting the "slow-growth" label for the more negotiable concept of "controlled" or "managed" growth.

RAMP's language and pattern of endorsements reflected important political realignments within the slow-growth movement: the rejection and isolation of a former nativist ally, the endorsement of a Latino, and an adoption of a less rigid position on economic development. The shift away from nativist NIMBYism was less a change in ideology than a pragmatic adjustment to demographic and economic realities. There were still xenophobes within the slow-growth movement, but they needed minorities and newcomers to continue the struggle against uncontrolled development.

Meanwhile, outside the "controlled-growth" movement, the Democratic clubs and ethnic organizations were also splitting their endorsements along the intersecting fault lines of growth and racial politics. One line seemed to favor ethnic politics over growth concerns; a second line tried to combine the goals of ethnic representation and controlled growth; a third reflected division and indecision.

The primarily Anglo UDC, favoring growth controls but divided on the ethnic issues, endorsed no candidates. By contrast, the primarily Anglo MPDC, consistent with its previous support of Asian candidates, championed Kiang. In fact, his campaign organizer was Ruth Willner, a MPDC member who had previously helped Lily Chen and Judy Chu win council seats.

The liberal West San Gabriel Valley Asian Pacific Democratic Club, pursuing the complex and sometimes contradictory policies of Asian empowerment and controlled development, endorsed both the controlled-growth Barron and Kiang, whose position on the development issue was ambiguous. Mexican American Democratic leaders were divided in their support for the Latino and Chinese candidates. Pursuing a policy of progressive interethnic alliances, Jose Calderon, a founder of the local chapter of LULAC, supported Kiang and Barron, but did not endorse Balderrama because of his developer connections. David Almada, whose defeat in the 1986 election was largely orchestrated by RAMP, rejected RAMP's candidate Barron for the pro-business Balderrama. The Republican Club of Monterey Park was the only prominent group to endorse Hatch, the lone Republican among the candidates, although some Republican leaders had clearly backed away from his anti-immigrant politics.

Election Day: Signs of Greater Ethnic Harmony

Our observations of political alignments before and during the election campaign of 1990 indicated a decisive move away from racial polarization toward complex and shifting patterns of interethnic alliances. Our observations made while conducting an exit poll on election day revealed a higher level of ethnic harmony than appeared in the elections of 1987 and 1988.

The mostly white precinct workers seemed calm and cooperative toward the ethnically mixed voters and multicolored team of pollsters.

When Leland Saito, a member of our research team, briefed the poll workers about our questionnaire before the election, they expressed friendly interest. On election day, some of the same precinct workers who had been suspicious in 1988 were cooperative, some even sharing coffee and cookies with tired pollsters. Moreover, our questionnaire items about language policies elicited few objections. In 1988, the researchers had rejected any such questions lest they arouse controversy.

The reactions of the precinct workers meant that diversity had become a familiar, if sometimes annoying, facet of everyday life. Our research team, similarly, by 1990 had become a familiar, if sometimes annoying, fixture on the political scene. There were, of course, old-timers who thought that any poll was somehow "un-American," since "how I vote is nobody's business." There were also some language difficulties and signs of mutual uneasiness when first-time Chinese voters confronted the mostly Anglo guardians of the American electoral system. We observed one incident of freely expressed prejudice when a white woman in charge of a polling place responded to a white researcher's "How are things going?" with: "They're voting for the Chink!" One does not have to dig deep to find prejudiced opinions, especially in co-ethnic encounters, but the rule of the day was caution in public language and interethnic practice, and accommodation to the reality of a growing Asian presence.

Election Results

Our goal was to explain three major results of the 1990 municipal elections: the defeat of Barry Hatch, a symbol of the nativist side of Official English and slow-growth politics; the election of Samuel Kiang, who drew the largest vote, followed by Fred Balderrama and Marie Purvis; and the apparent contradiction represented by solid support for Proposition S, which extended controls over residential development, combined with rejection of growth-control candidates Hatch, Reichenberger, and Barron.

The 1990 election dramatically altered the political and ethnic composition of the city council. Hatch was removed from the stage. A probusiness majority replaced a slow-growth majority. An ethnic majority replaced a white majority. The female/male ratio of three to two achieved in 1988 remained constant, attesting to the key role of women in local politics.

Was the movement away from Anglo, male domination and anti-immigrant politicians toward greater diversity primarily an expression of the changing demographics of the voting population? Did Hatch lose because there were no longer enough Anglo and established-resident voters to support him, while Kiang gained because Asian voters and newcomers now dominated the polls? Or was the outcome a result of a convergence of tendencies within a multiethnic electorate?

Our answers are based primarily on an analysis of the results of an exit poll. Knowing who the individual voters were and how they voted allowed us to measure the statistical association between their social and attitudinal characteristics (our independent variables) and their candidate choice and vote on Proposition S (our dependent variables).[19] Above all, we were interested in the social and attitudinal factors associated with Hatch's defeat, Kiang's victory, and support for Proposition S.

Multiethnic Voters: An Uneven Pattern of Empowerment

A glimpse at the ethnic characteristics of voters in general and those voters who responded to our poll quickly dispels the hypothesis that Hatch lost and Kiang won because the Chinese newcomers had finally prevailed against the forces of white and established-resident resistance to change. Chinese American voters remained politically underrepresented in Little Taipei, while Anglos were overrepresented in terms of their proportion of the general population. The voting population was multiethnic. The electoral result depended on both ethnic and interethnic voting patterns.

According to one analysis that identified ethnicity by family name, the breakdown of citizens who voted in the 1990 municipal election was as follows: Latino, 25 percent; Chinese American, 24 percent; Japanese American, 12 percent; other Asian (primarily Korean and Vietnamese), 9 percent; other (primarily Anglo) 30 percent.[20] The poll results based on the voters' self-identification came very close to this result (Table 9).

The pattern of ethnic empowerment in Monterey Park is uneven, but

TABLE 9 *Patterns of Ethnic Empowerment, Montery Park Municipal Elections, April 10, 1990*

	% of Population	% Who Voted	% in Exit Poll
Anglo	12	30	36
Latino	31	25	26
Chinese American	36	24	25
Japanese American	10	12	13

Source: U.S. Bureau of the Census, 1990; Political Data, Burbank, Calif., May 13, 1993; exit poll of the 1990 Monterey Park municipal elections, conducted by John Horton, Department of Sociology, University of California at Los Angeles.

much less so than in the neighboring multiethnic megapolis, Los Angeles. There, the much touted coloring of the population has not extended to the electoral arena, where the Anglo minority remains solidly in control. The mayoral election of 1993 exemplified the relative absence of nonwhite voters. The *Los Angeles Times* laid out the statistics:

> Non-Latino whites, who make up 42% of the city's voting-age population and 65% of its registered voters, cast fully 72% of the ballots. . . . Blacks, 13% of the voting-age population and 21% of the registered voters, cast 12% of the ballots. . . . Latinos, 34% of the voting-age group but only 11% of the total registration, were 10% of the turnout. Asians, 11% of the voting-age population and only 3% of the total registration, cast 4% of the ballots.[21]

Under these circumstances, the ethnic majorities remain political minorities. The non-Latino white minority determined the election by casting 67 percent of their vote for Richard Riordan, a white Republican. By contrast, 86 percent of black, 69 percent of Asian, and 57 percent of Latino voters supported Michael Woo (a Chinese American and a liberal who preached the gospel of interethnic cooperation), but lacked the voting power to elect him.[22]

As in Los Angeles, the Anglo minority in Monterey Park have a lot of electoral power. The difference is that the Anglos of Monterey Park have to share power. In this sense, the small city offers an example of what could happen politically in the large city if Anglo power declines and minority power increases.

Profile of Ethnic Voters

To understand the voting behavior of the various ethnic groups in Monterey Park, or indeed whether ethnicity was a significant factor in candidate choice, we first examined the social characteristics of the various ethnic groups. We then tried to determine whether ethnicity and other characteristics such as income and education were statistically related to voting behavior.

Not surprisingly, our findings about the social characteristics of the various ethnic groups in the 1990 poll were almost identical to those of 1988. Seventy-four percent of the Chinese voters were foreign-born, compared with 20 percent of the Latinos, 6 percent of the Anglos, and 1 percent of the Japanese Americans. The Chinese American voters were an immigrant population and relative newcomers to the city.

Chinese voters also tended to have a distinct social and political profile. As a whole, they were younger, more educated, more affluent, and more Republican than established Latino and Anglo residents. Furthermore, they were less supportive of the slow-growth cause and more supportive of bilingual education. In terms of education and income, the biggest status gap was between Latinos and Chinese Americans (Table 10).

Ethnicity and Candidate Choice

Replicating a major finding of the 1988 poll, we found that ethnicity was the single most important determinant of candidate choice in Monterey Park. Knowing a voter's ethnicity was a significant predictor (at the .001 level) of candidate choice. The result was obtained by controlling for seven independent variables at the same time: ethnicity, education, income, gender, length of residence in the United States, opinion on bilingual education, and position on ballot Proposition S.[23]

Each candidate was most favored by members of his or her ethnic group. However, the relationship between ethnicity (defined by voters' ethnic self-identification) and candidate choice was stronger for some candidates than for others. The order from strongest to weakest association was: Kiang, Reichenberger, Hatch, Purvis, Barron, and Balderrama; that is, knowing a voter's ethnicity was a much better predictor of candidate selection in Kiang's case than in Balderrama's. This is not difficult to explain. Kiang drew his largest base of support from Asian Americans, while Balderrama was a second choice of all the major ethnic groups.

Ethnic voting was also stronger within some populations than others. It was strongest for the Chinese, clearly the result of the political situation and not some innate ethnic trait. Chinese were acutely aware that they lacked representation and rallied around the one Chinese candidate: 90 percent cast their votes for Kiang, and 44 percent voted for Kiang only, a practice that maximized their ethnic vote.

Since old-timers sometimes criticize bullet voting as an unfair strategy, we tried to determine what factors were actually involved. For all residents, length of residence in Monterey Park (possibly an indication of familiarity with local politics) was a factor: The longer voters lived in the city, the less likely they were to vote for one candidate only. In the case of Chinese Americans, we found that only 25 percent of those who had lived in the city more than 30 years did bullet voting. However, Chinese Americans are relative newcomers; only 18 percent had lived in Monterey Park for over 30 years. Another related factor was nativity. Only 18 percent of native-born Chinese Americans voted for Kiang only, compared with 51 percent of Chinese immigrants. More was involved here than length of residence. As an immigrant with close ties to the Chinese-speaking community, Kiang could provide needed representation for Chinese immigrants.

The pattern of ethnic voting was also very strong for Japanese Americans, primarily long-term residents with a low rate of bullet voting.

TABLE 10 *Candidate Preference and Voter Profile by Ethnicity, Monterey Park Municipal Elections, April 10, 1990*

	Chinese American (%)	Japanese American (%)	Latino (%)	Anglo (%)
ALL VOTERS	25	13	26	36
CANDIDATES				
Kiang	90	69	30	40
Purvis	26	34	48	53
Reichenberger	15	36	21	44
Hatch	10	25	19	37
Balderrama	36	44	67	45
Barron	19	37	47	42
VOTER CHARACTERISTICS				
Age 45+	33	57	48	69
Foreign-born	74	1	20	6
College+	66	43	23	36
Income $50,000+	54	50	31	35
LENGTH OF RESIDENCE IN M.P. (30 YEARS+)	18	37	42	56
PARTY AFFILIATION				
Democrat	22	59	80	59
Republican	47	37	15	35
Independent/none	22	1	3	3
SUPPORT FOR PROPOSITION S				
Yes	51	70	65	67
No	22	15	19	19
Didn't vote	13	8	9	7
No response	14	7	7	7
SUPPORT FOR BILINGUAL EDUCATION				
Yes	68	40	57	41
No	20	45	29	46
Undecided	7	11	11	12
NUMBER OF VOTES				
1	44	18	23	13
2	10	14	14	10
3	41	62	53	70
RESPONDENTS (*N*) (ABSOLUTE NUMBERS: TOTAL 974)	239	131	255	349

Source: Data extracted from exit poll of the 1990 Monterey Park municipal elections by John Horton and Yen-Fen Tseng, Department of Sociology, University of California at Los Angeles.
Note: Numbers do not add up to 100 percent because of "no answers" and because voters had three candidate choices.

Lacking an ethnic candidate but wanting greater Asian American representation, 69 percent of the Japanese Americans voted for Kiang, 6 percent less than voted for Chu in 1988. Chu, a third-generation Chinese American, may have been more acceptable to native-born Japanese Americans than a Chinese immigrant. A campaign worker for Kiang reported to one of our researchers that he encountered less support from Japanese Americans than he had expected: "When you are an immigrant, no matter how long you have been here, they [Japanese Americans] always view you as Chinese, not an Asian American, because the Asian identity only works for more established Asian Americans."[24]

Ethnic voting was also fairly strong for Latinos, who had no representation in the political arena. Sixty-seven percent in our poll voted for Balderrama, a slight increase over the 63 percent he received in 1988. The second Latino, Barron, was the third choice, after longtime resident Marie Purvis. Balderrama, unlike Barron, had run a high-powered campaign targeting his constituency, and he was associated with Purvis in the local Chamber of Commerce.

Anglos, although generally preferring Anglo candidates, were most likely to spread their votes around ethnically and to vote for more than one candidate. Many Anglos would proudly explain this as the result of their belief in voting for issues rather than ethnicity. Their objection to ethnic voting, however, also stems from their history of assured political and ethnic domination. This was changing in Monterey Park, but Anglos were still a formidable political force, and in 1990 three out of six candidates were Anglos.

The Balance of Ethnic and Interethnic Currents

Although a voter's ethnicity was the best single predictor of candidate choice, it cannot fully explain the election results in a city where no single bloc of ethnic voters dominated and many issues cut across ethnic lines. The results reflect complex ethnic and interethnic currents. The balance of these forces favored a shift away from racially divisive politics toward greater ethnic representation, interethnic voting on specific candidates and issues, and an increased ability to separate class issues of growth from nativist issues of immigrant and ethnic exclusion.

Hatch lost because he was the last choice of all ethnic groups. In an election in which voters had three choices among six candidates, Kiang won because he got significant support in all ethnic groups: the first choice of Chinese and Japanese Americans, the fourth of Latinos, and the fifth (but not the sixth) of Anglos.

The vote for Kiang tended to be a vote against Hatch, and vice versa. Only 10 percent of the Japanese Americans who supported Kiang also voted for Hatch. They apparently shared Kiang's opposition to

Hatch and his anti-immigrant stance. We find the same pattern among Latinos (only 7 percent of those who voted for Kiang supported Hatch) and among Anglos. Thus, a strong antinativist and pro-diversity current ran across ethnic lines to elect Kiang and defeat Hatch, who stood at opposite poles of the debate over immigration and diversity.

One question in our poll helped us to tap attitudes toward diversity: "Do you support public spending for bilingual education for non-English-speaking students?" We had hypothesized that support of public spending for bilingual education would separate the nativists from the multiculturalists and be associated with candidate choice. This proved to be the case. Knowing a voter's position on bilingual education was a statistically significant predictor of candidate choice in the specific cases of Reichenberger, Hatch, and Kiang, candidates who had expressed strong opinions about such issues. Those who supported bilingual education were more likely to vote for Kiang, but least likely to vote for Reichenberger and Hatch. This outcome makes sense because language issues had been the greatest source of conflict in Monterey Park and marked an important ideological divide between these candidates.

Ethnic groups varied greatly in their acceptance of bilingualism as defined by our question, Chinese and Latinos being most favorable, and Anglos and Japanese Americans being most opposed.[25] Length of residence in Monterey Park was also involved: Old-timers were more likely to be opposed than relative newcomers. The correlation between attitude toward bilingualism and candidate preference was most striking when we compared the profiles of Anglo voters who voted for Hatch (37 percent) and Kiang (40 percent). Among Anglos, 60 percent of the Hatch supporters were opposed to bilingualism, compared with 30 percent of those who supported Kiang. Hatch voters also generally preferred Anglo candidates, another indication of their xenophobia. Only 15 percent of the Anglos for Hatch made Kiang their second or third choice; only 14 percent of those Anglos who supported Kiang cast a vote for Hatch. Like the Chinese, Anglos who voted for Kiang tended to support the winning ticket, which included Balderrama and Purvis (Table 11).

Less striking than the pattern of candidate choice and attitude toward bilingualism were social differences between Anglo Hatch and Kiang supporters. The latter were wealthier; 49 percent of Kiang voters reported incomes over $50,000, as compared with 33 percent for Hatch voters. Kiang's Anglo supporters were also better-educated and younger. These differences, although not great, may roughly correspond to the social characteristics of locally grounded as opposed to more cosmopolitan residents.

Finally, the majority of both Kiang and Hatch supporters among Anglos favored Proposition S, the controlled-growth measure, although

TABLE 11 *Comparison of Anglo Supporters of Hatch and Kiang in Monterey Park Municipal Elections, April 10, 1990*

	Hatch Voters (%)	Kiang Voters (%)
CANDIDATE CHOICES		
Purvis	35	56
Barron	35	35
Balderrama	27	56
Kiang	15	—
Reichenberger	59	24
Hatch	—	14
VOTER CHARACTERISTICS		
College +	35	47
Income $50,000+	33	49
Age 45+	75	61
SUPPORT FOR BILINGUAL EDUCATION		
Yes	29	54
No	60	30
Undecided	11	14
SUPPORT FOR PROPOSITION S		
Yes	74	66
No	17	23
RESPONDENTS (*N*)	121	133

Source: Data extracted from exit poll of the 1990 Monterey Park municipal elections by John Horton and Yen-Fen Tseng, Department of Sociology, University of California at Los Angeles.

Hatch supporters were most strongly in favor. This result can be generalized. Proposition S won because it was supported by the majority of all ethnic groups, including the Chinese who were the direct target of nativist elements within the controlled-growth movement. Residents voted for Proposition S not because of their ethnicity, but because they cared about development. Moreover, the longer they had lived in Monterey Park, the more they cared. This applied also to the Chinese. Sixty-one percent of the old-timers (resident in Monterey Park for 20 years or more) supported Proposition S; 22 percent opposed it; and 17 percent did not respond. By comparison, the results for newcomers (resident less than 20 years) were: 44 percent "yes," 22 percent "no," and 34 percent "don't know."

The support for Proposition S revealed an apparent contradiction in the election results. On the one hand, the majority of the voters supported a slow-growth measure on the ballot; on the other hand, they rejected three candidates (Hatch, Reichenberger, and Barron) who had espoused slow-growth policies, while supporting three candidates (Kiang, Balderrama, and Purvis) with no record of support for slow-growth issues. This was not in fact contradictory. Ethnic considerations were probably paramount in the judgments of the candidates, particularly in the polarized cases of Hatch and Kiang, whereas economic considerations determined voter support for controlled growth. The voters were demonstrating a sophisticated ability to separate economic and ethnic issues, whose conflation in the practice of local nativists had resulted in the scapegoating of Chinese newcomers in general for economic problems caused by developers and speculators. Contrary to the propaganda of some developers, the movement for greater control over the community was not inherently racist or xenophobic.

TOWARD THE POLITICS OF DIVERSITY

The electoral data for 1988–1990 revealed important political outcomes. The ethnographic evidence described how they came about through a complex process of shifting positions and alliances on the issues of immigration, economic development, and ethnic power. Together the electoral and ethnographic evidence points to a transition from a period of tension between newcomers and established residents and between white minorities and nonwhite majorities toward greater accommodation and harmony.

One factor behind this transition was the continuing development of minority politics, the tendency to organize and vote for ethnic representation and against nativist policies and candidates. A second factor was the increased ability of residents to separate slow-growth from nativist struggles, class from ethnic issues. The incentive for the break was practical and points to a third factor in the evolution of local politics: the need for interethnic alliances on candidates and issues in a multiethnic city where no single group could determine elections.

Our story of the political transition from nativism to greater ethnic empowerment does not end with the waning of xenophobic reactions to economic and demographic change. Ethnic conflict had subsided by 1990, but the problems of ethnic, racial, and class control had not gone away; they were merely rearticulated into a different pattern with a different potential for conflict.

With the defeat of Barry Hatch and overt nativism, it was easier to contemplate and mobilize interethnic support on the side of community control over big business and big government. If Anglo domination and nativism had subsided, however, a new multiethnic political order had yet to be constructed. Would political diversity collapse into ethnic competition and political Balkanization, the very lack of community that the doomsayers had always predicted? Or would Monterey Park move toward ethnic empowerment, with interethnic consensus on political goals and the democratic means of achieving them?

We have no answers and can only identify the evolution of tendencies within the ongoing political process. The next phase of our research, from 1990 through 1993, revealed another stage in the difficult transition from Anglo political domination to the construction of a politics of diversity. Having in a profound sense gone beyond xenophobia and nativism, citizens were beginning to recognize, define, and confront the dilemmas of building community amidst diversity.

Chapter 7
THE DILEMMAS OF DIVERSITY

Rather than celebrate diversity, how we are different from each other, we should celebrate how we are alike. Diversity is divisive.
—An elderly Anglo woman active in Monterey Park politics

In Los Angeles, we need to develop a politics that recognizes the importance of ethnicity without elevating it into the only standard of governance. . . . We need a social contract that assures diversity and something else. We need a political structure that can fit the pieces together in such a way that alliances can be made and changed.
—Xandra Kayden, Center for Politics and Policy, the Claremont Colleges (1993)

WITH THE defeat of Barry Hatch and the installation of a majority/minority council in the spring of 1990–two Chinese Americans, one Latino, and two Anglos—local activists were saying, "Now we have a good development plan for the city, and we have gone beyond ethnic conflict." Indeed, there were many signs that Monterey Park had regained its title as the "All-America" city, a model of multiculturalism and controlled development.

The business-oriented members of the council had pledged allegiance to managed growth. Interethnic cooperation rather than confrontation seemed to be the council norm. The multiethnic Community Relations Commission was preparing for its second annual Harmony Week, featuring, among other programs, awards for students who wrote the best essays on "the person who taught me the most about multiculturalism."

Used to political fireworks, city council watchers were nodding off in boredom. But, ever suspicious of local government, they began to complain that council members were inaccessible and working behind closed doors to undermine the city's hard-won growth regulations by approving too many building variances. Councilwoman Couch, the most consistent defender of controlled growth, even expressed nostalgia for the old, divisive council: "My stomach is turning. Even though there was rudeness and arguing with the other council, there were high [development] standards."[1]

As it happened, the council watchers' slumber was disturbed first not by the revival of the growth machine, but rather by the issue of affirmative action and ethnic empowerment. Having moved beyond established-resident resistance to the very existence of newcomers and their language, residents now had to work out the practical meaning of their presence and incorporation into the political process.

The challenge for activists was to build interethnic alliances around issues of representation and development in a situation where unrepresented minorities and newcomers were jostling for position within the shifting ethnic hierarchy. The political dilemma was how to balance diversity—the respect for ethnic differences and the recognition of the legitimacy of organizing on an ethnic basis—with a sense of common goals and struggles that crossed ethnic boundaries.

A major barrier to a sense of community and interethnic cooperation had been the exclusionary Americanism of old-timers, particularly Anglos. Their containment strategies had set the racially divisive tone of politics and put newcomers and minorities on the defensive. Now, with the decline of Anglo power and nativism, immigrants and underrepresented minorities had entered the local political arena.

They were becoming proactive in demanding their right to representation and refining the art of demonstrations to make up for their lack of citizenship and voting power. Would their empowerment strategies strengthen interethnic connections by making a wide bid for support or inflame ethnic divisions by substituting ethnic politics for nativism? Would the result of ethnic diversity be more ethnic war and the Balkanization of political life predicted by conservatives or the realization of the liberal's dream of harmony amid ethnic diversity?

The political history of Monterey Park between 1991 and 1993 did not conform to either the liberal or the conservative script. People were discovering for themselves the dilemmas of diversity and working out their own practical solutions. The uneven, ongoing process can be seen in three key moments of political struggle and mobilization: in 1991, a confrontation between Councilwoman Chu and Councilman Kiang and between an ethnically diverse group of established residents and Chinese immigrants on issues of affirmative action; in 1992, Chu's reelection and the defeat of Chinese immigrant contenders; in 1993, the mobilization of Latinos and Chinese to block a card club, proposed by a Taiwanese developer and supported by a group of Anglos associated with RAMP.

Together these cases illustrate the gains and problems of the evolving politics of diversity. The major gains were the increased political involvement of ethnic groups and immigrants and the growing sophistication of residents in developing alliances across ethnic boundaries. The problems were the divisiveness of narrowly ethnic politics, whether in the form of nativism or ethnic nationalism; divisions between native-born and immigrants in the diverse Chinese community; the clash between citizens and the noncitizen majority, between extraelectoral and electoral politics; and ethnic and racial divisions within the movement to control development.

ESTABLISHED RESIDENTS CONFRONT IMMIGRANT POWER (1991)

Although the balance of forces in the city council elected in 1990 had shifted from nativism toward diversity, the potential for conflict remained. On one side were the two conservative Anglo councilwomen, Marie Purvis and Betty Couch, defenders of the rights of established residents; on the other side, an ethnic bloc consisting of Judy Chu, Fred Balderrama, and Sam Kiang, defenders of the rights of immigrants and minorities.

The established-resident side was bent on firing the City Manager, Mark Lewis, who had already survived several coup attempts. This time, in addition to charges of overspending and poor staff relations, there was concern that his enthusiasm for economic development and affirmative action conflicted with the city's controlled-growth mandate and legal hiring policies. However, the council majority of Kiang, Chu, and Balderrama continued to support the beleaguered Lewis, whose survival depended on keeping their votes on his side and courting Chinese support through his contacts and affirmative action policies.

A second issue also threatened to divide established residents from newcomers. In May 1991, the council's majority had approved pay incentives for hiring bilingual (English and Spanish or Chinese) police dispatchers on the "911" emergency line. The City Manager championed the plan and took the unusual step of defending it before the Personnel Board. In July 1991, the primarily Anglo board rejected it as violating its system of employee classification and discriminating against employees who do not speak Chinese or Spanish. The Monterey Park General Employees' Association also opposed the bilingual proposal. Frustrated in his efforts on behalf of affirmative action, Kiang, taking a proactive stand for the needs of elderly and non-English-speaking immigrants, urged the council to override the authority of the Personnel Board and immediately implement the plan to hire bilingual dispatchers.

The stage was set for a confrontation that would reactivate divisions between established residents and newcomers and expose divisions within the growing Chinese community. The ensuing fight over the fairness and legality of policies and procedures quickly escalated into a racial issue. The peace was broken, and Monterey Park returned to front-page news as a city torn by ethnic conflict.

Ironically, Judy Chu, the staunch defender of Chinese rights and interethnic harmony, set off the spark on July 22, 1991, when she unexpectedly cast the deciding vote to fire Lewis. This was a painful decision. Lewis had been supportive of Chu and the Chinese community, and she had defended him in the past. But, sensitive to the concerns of established residents who formed a vital part of her interethnic network of support, Chu conducted an independent investigation of the City Manager and concluded that the charges against him were valid. According to Chu, Lewis had shown blatant favoritism by giving special perks to his allies and passing over non-Asians in hiring an Asian American. Over 40 percent of Lewis' senior staff had resigned, and a few were coming forward to denounce him.

At about the same time, although supportive of hiring bilingual dispatchers, Chu objected to Kiang's plan to take authority away from the Personnel Board, and offered her own proposal. She could not have predicted the quick and strong reaction. In responding to the concerns of many established residents about legality and the protection of employee and citizen rights, she found herself denounced as the instant enemy of the Chinese people.

Chinese Protest Chu

For three days, hundreds of immigrants, mostly elderly Chinese, many bused in from outside the city, picketed City Hall and protested against Lewis' firing and Chu's alleged opposition to bilingual dispatchers. Some of their placards called for Chu's recall in Chinese and English. The demonstrations were organized by Abel Pa, the President of the privately owned Southern California Chinese Radio Broadcasting company. His station was thriving as the new communication and command center in the latest battle against anti-Chinese activity in Monterey Park.

Another center of communication and interpretation of events was the Chinese press. Usually more preoccupied with homeland than local events, the two major papers ran daily stories on the rapidly unfolding drama. More attentive to the Chinese-speaking Kiang than the American-born and non-Chinese-speaking Chu, and ever alert to signs of discrimination, the papers initially tended to side with Lewis and Kiang against Chu. For example, the *Chinese Daily News* framed the conflict as one between established residents and the immigrant community:

> The two councilpersons of the Monterey Park City Council who support the rights of native residents gained the support of the Chinese councilwoman Judy Chu on July 22. They plan to take a series of steps to "force down" the City Manager Mark Lewis. . . . Has Judy Chu changed direction? Is she planning to climb up the [politi-

> cal] ladder? Mr. Lin, a Monterey Park resident who is concerned with city governance, points out that Chu intends to run for some electoral position on a state level after her current term is over. He says that this might be the main reason why Chu is changing her attitude. Lin figures that Chu would need the votes from the Anglo community and that is why she is supporting the policies and actions of the Anglos. Chu strongly denies this. She emphasizes that her action is based on matters of fact, and she has nothing personally against Lewis. On the other hand, Kiang feels that Lewis has been done an injustice. He thinks that the city manager faced strong pressure from the Anglo community for supporting the bilingual 911 proposal. Kiang urged Chinese residents to go to the city council to show support for Lewis.[2]

Chu's critics in the Chinese community saw her two decisions as linked, and as evidence that she was siding with the two Anglo councilwomen and the old-timers against the rights of the Chinese.

The English and Asian American press gave fuller and more favorable coverage to the Chu side.[3] Her defenders argued that it was preposterous to call her "anti-Chinese," given her long record of service to the Chinese and immigrant community. Chu had consistently supported the hiring of bilingual dispatchers and was critical only of an implementation plan that would violate city procedures. As for Lewis, his firing was strictly a matter of professional misconduct. Her defenders said that it was not Chu who was responsible for racial conflict; rather, her jealous competitors for influence within the Chinese community (in particular Kiang and former councilwoman Lily Chen) were playing "racial politics"—that is, infusing race into nonracial issues.

Polarization of Immigrants and Established Residents

The split between Chu and Kiang translated into polarization between newcomers and established residents during the city council's open forums on the City Manager and bilingual controversies. Most of the Chinese immigrants supported the immediate implementation of bilingual dispatchers and denounced Lewis' firing. Established residents denounced Lewis and Kiang for violating the rights of employees and residents. The sides spoke past each other; there was no middle ground. Field notes taken during the open forum on Kiang's proposal to override the Personnel Board capture the tone of the confrontation:

> The language issue has surfaced again, only this time established residents and not Chinese immigrants are on the defensive. The immigrants fill the whole central section of the council chamber. This is

their issue. They want Chinese dispatchers for the 911 emergency telephone line now. The ordinance is opposed by the city's Personnel Board, union, Judy Chu, and the two Anglo councilwomen. Immigrants who do not speak English do not fear to express their support and ask that the proceedings be translated into Mandarin so that they can participate more freely.

Mrs. Yang speaks her mind: "We don't understand the proceedings. We want a translation in Mandarin."

Mayor Betty Couch responds: "Our problem is we need to understand English. Any Hispanic could demand the same thing. We can't translate for everyone." But when a citizen offers English translations, the mayor reluctantly accepts in spite of her Official English principles.

The debate heats up. An established Chinese immigrant sees racism in the opposition to bilingual dispatchers: "What's being expressed is along racial lines. The city spends millions and can't spend a few bucks for the 60 percent who live here. Chinese don't have problems when they go to Hughes Market, color doesn't matter there, but it does in City Hall."

A longtime Anglo resident talks of reverse racism: "Is the only way to be American to hire by numbers and quotas? This is disturbing; it's the politics of color."[4]

During the next open forum, on Lewis' firing, there were many fewer Chinese in the audience: Defending the City Manager, even one friendly to affirmative action, was of less immediate interest than demanding bilingual dispatchers. Moreover, the Chinese-speakers were less united than before. Of the 11 who spoke, 6 immigrants opposed the firing, and 2 wanted further investigation. One immigrant, a longtime resident, and 2 American-born Chinese supported the firing, denouncing the use of "racial politics" by Chu's Chinese competitors.

The 11 Anglo and 4 Latino speakers all supported the firing. The consensus of these established residents was remarkable, given their history of ideological differences on the questions of diversity and affirmative action. They were about equally divided between those known to be liberal to left on political and racial issues; moderates who were liberal or conservative in national politics, but rather xenophobic; and committed nativists. They had different reasons for opposing Lewis and Kiang.

Stepping up to the podium, Barry Hatch opposed affirmative action and bilingualism on principle: "I talked about a language [English] in which everybody could communicate. Now you have to be bilingual. Be honest, send him [Lewis] on his way." By contrast, Jose Calderon criticized the City Manager's practice of affirmative action: "I support affirmative action, but it must be done for the community as a whole. Poor management under the guise of affirmative action polarizes the community. Because one group is a majority, we don't throw away the rights of others."

Many speakers were surprised at finding themselves on the same side. Old enemies were talking to each other, and Hatch publicly thanked Chu for finally voting to fire Lewis. Progressives, moderates, and nativists, Anglos, Latinos, and Asian Americans, all united as established residents to support the firing of the City Manager and oppose an "unfair" hiring policy. Their other target was Kiang, who "put the rights of Chinese newcomers first," above those of employees and residents as a whole.

Thus, Monterey Park once again was polarized between natives and newcomers. After moderates and progressives had struggled to build a middle ground of negotiation and accommodation, had the center fallen out and given way to ethnic conflict?

A New Stage in Political Development

There were similarities between the Official English battles of the mid-1980s and the conflict over affirmative action and bilingualism in 1991. Both involved issues of language and ethnic domination, raised charges of racial politics, and created deep fissures between newcomers and established residents. However, there were also fundamental differences that pointed to a new developmental stage in a politics of diversity.

This time round, the newcomers had grown more powerful and had moved from a position of defense to offense. During the battle over Official English and Chinese signs in the mid- to late 1980s, they were primarily reactive, defending themselves against perceived anti-immigrant policies. In 1991, they were demanding bilingual emergency dispatchers and had formed more proactive immigrant groups, like the Chinese Political Action Committee, bent on extending their power rather than merely reacting to policies of containment. These groups were less dependent on the good will and support of established residents, including Asian Americans.

To the shock of old-timers, the Chinese were also adopting the tactics of the old civil rights movements, bringing immigrants who were not yet citizens into American politics. They were mobilized by the new political groups and by influential individuals who had access to Chinese media. Their numbers translated directly into pressure and influence through contributions, demonstrations, and presence at public hearings. Their actions in 1991 shattered any remaining stereotypes about Asians as compliant or tending to avoid local politics or conform to its patterns of control.

Established residents were now on the defensive. By 1991, the defeated Hatch had moved out of Monterey Park and taken his anti-immigrant fight to a more receptive audience. The politics of nativism and backlash no longer dominated or limited the range of established residents' concerns about ethnic power. The choice was no longer between hating and celebrating Chinese newcomers; they could now be recognized as residents wanting empowerment. While some residents continued to reject any expression of ethnic power as reverse discrimination, others supported it, but not as a zero-sum game that would diminish the rights of other residents. This position was expressed in the public forum on hiring practices and seemed to have support among Latinos, Anglos, Japanese Americans, and Chinese Americans who wanted their rights protected in a city that was becoming Chinese.

The events of 1991 eventually led to a compromise that advanced affirmative action while taking into account some of the concerns of established residents. A supporter of immigrant rights analyzed the situation cynically in a conversation at City Hall: "It's a trade-off. Judy [Chu] goes for the [Kiang's] ordinance tonight; they'll [the council] sacrifice Lewis tomorrow."

That was precisely what happened. Established residents got part of what they wanted: Lewis' firing and closer attention to the way affirmative action was being implemented. Immigrants achieved their most immediate affirmative action demand, bilingual dispatchers, when Chu sided with Councilmen Kiang and Balderrama to override the opposition of the Personnel Board and develop an affirmative action policy.

In October 1991, the council majority adopted a program to hire bilingual firefighters and 911 emergency dispatchers. Later, city officials met with Los Angeles County officials to develop a policy to recruit more minority employees. The result has been a more aggressive approach to hiring minority and bilingual Spanish-, Cantonese-, and Mandarin-speaking employees. Between 1990 and 1992, the city had added Chinese to the police department and hired three Chinese to top managerial positions—Assistant City Manager, head of the library, and head of Executive Managerial Services. Nevertheless, as elsewhere in the United States, the city staff, council, and residents have yet to thrash out an affirmative action policy that is acceptable to all groups.

The Casualties and Causes of Conflict

Because the negotiations came late, all sides were injured by the conflict. The biggest loser was interethnic unity. Kiang's aggressive stance may have lost him the support of established residents who concluded that he was "nationalistic," working only for "his people." Chu, by voting to fire Lewis, pleased established residents, but may have lost support from immigrants who were looking for someone they could count on unconditionally. Chinese political unity was also a major casualty. In the future, no Chinese American candidates could take for granted the Asian unity that had swept both Chu and Kiang into office. The conflict between second-generation Chu and first-generation Kiang had revealed deep cleavages within the Chinese community. The more recent immigrants tended to stand alone in support of Kiang and Lewis, while more established Chinese Americans, attuned to the subtleties of local politics, joined an ethnically diverse group of established residents in support of Chu.

Local theories blamed the conflict and division on ambitious politicians who had deliberately or inadvertently played "racial politics," stirring up support for themselves by imputing racial motives in situations that had nothing to do with race. For example, Kiang's opponents said he was playing racial politics in the hot summer of 1991 when he told the city council audience, just before the vote on the bilingual dispatchers: "I ask people to put aside their prejudice and support the proposal."

Politicians can and do manipulate racial tensions, but they cannot create tensions that are not already there. The dubious assumption behind charges of racial politics is that racism is being inserted instrumentally into issues that have nothing to do with race. In Monterey Park, almost all issues have something to do with race. Thus, Kiang's charge of "prejudice" was inflammatory, but prejudice was in fact one element in the opposition to his proposal.

No issue is colorless in a multiethnic society. Race, class, and other components of political issues can be separated only by confronting them and struggling to sort them out through negotiation and compromise. This did not happen in 1991 until the conflict was well under way. There was a failure of leadership, and, consequently, complex issues were reduced to their racial and ethnic elements.

In her final statement before the council voted on Kiang's proposal, Chu identified this failure of leadership: "What I've learned is that we need a dialogue before reaching this point of polarization." Acting alone, and by her own admission failing to talk out the issue with the individuals and communities affected by her decisions, Chu inadvertently dropped a bomb in the political arena when she voted to fire the City Manager. She had, in effect, not followed her own agenda of interethnic communication and consultation.

Under these circumstances, Chu's political competitors, who had the attention of the Chinese media, had only to utter the buzz word "anti-Chinese" to arouse the fear and protest of immigrants. In turn, the insensitivity of some immigrants to the fears of established residents about their own minoritization courted a backlash. Thus a complex of issues not exclusively racial in nature quickly got distilled into a battle between established, English-speaking residents and Chinese-speaking immigrants.

The Dialectic of Ethnic and Interethnic Politics

In the 1991 confrontation over affirmative action, the actions of Chu and Kiang exemplified the growing practices of ethnic and interethnic organizing. While Kiang championed the ethnic interests of immigrants, Chu emphasized her interethnic ties with established residents.

Residents are tempted to attribute these strategies to self-interest or ethnic traits. In this view Chu works with many groups out of political opportunism, while Kiang's nationalism is an expression of Chinese separatism and feelings of superiority. However, the preference for one strategy or another has more to do with social and historical circumstances. The history of discrimination in the United States has been the cause of ethnic organizing. In multiethnic Monterey Park, getting represented and getting things done require both ethnic and interethnic organizing.[5] The selection of strategies also reflects different life experiences, political goals, and constituencies.

As a professor in a local university and a board member of several community organizations, Chu was accustomed to working in multiethnic settings. She was a member of the West San Gabriel Valley Asian Pacific Democratic Club, which was engaged in forging an Asian American political identity from diverse Asian groups and fostering interethnic alliances with Latinos on progressive issues and candidates. The thrust of her ethnic and interethnic organizing would be to bring immigrants into the mainstream of Asian American and American politics.

Working as a lawyer for an immigrant clientele, Kiang had closer economic, linguistic, and cultural bonds to first-generation Chinese Americans. Although he got his grassroots political training as a member of an interethnic group that successfully fought to drive a state parole office from Monterey Park, once in the city council he was the loudest voice for Chinese immigrants.

Chu stressed interaction and harmony between ethnic groups and wanted Monterey Park to be a model of diversity. She believed that her survival as councilwoman and her chance of gaining higher office required interethnic support, which she cultivated during her campaigns along with support from American-born Chinese and immigrants. There was no doubt that she pleased established residents in 1991 when she cast the deciding vote to fire the City Manager. She practiced the art of interethnic cooperation among the women on city council, founded the city's Harmony Week, and was active in building regional coalitions between Latinos and Asians. Kiang had other priorities. In an interview he said that as a councilman he "really wanted to turn Monterey Park into something that, first of all, the Chinese can be proud of, then the community can be proud of. The whole nation can look at it and see that this is an immigrant community, and it's really a model community."[6]

Other differences reflected potential splits within the Chinese community: generation (Kiang was born in China; Chu in the United States), language skills (Kiang spoke several dialects of Chinese as well as English; Chu was primarily English-speaking), political orientation (Chu was progressive and for managed growth; Kiang was a more conservative Democrat and viewed Chinese commercial development more favorably).

The differences between Chu and Kiang's positions on interethnic alliances perhaps depended less on principle than on where each stood within the rapidly developing Asian and Chinese American communities in the United States. When asked about the value of interethnic as opposed to ethnic organizing, Kiang replied:

> It depends on what stage you are talking about. Of course, for the Chinese community, we are still new to this political game, and we have to organize ourselves first. Every meeting we talk about working with other ethnic groups, but it's not that easy. We can't even organize ourselves, how could we work with the others? Different groups have different agendas. I am sure that one of these days we will get there, but for the time being, it is more important to be able to organize ourselves.[7]

In Monterey Park, there was a reasonable basis for both ethnic and interethnic strategies. On one hand, there was a large, heterogeneous community of Chinese newcomers whose potential for local power depended on organizing and building unity around their common Chinese identity and immigrant status. On the other hand, the ethnic mix of voters in Monterey Park and the surrounding San Gabriel Valley means that Chinese cannot be assured of office unless they win support across ethnic and newcomer/established-resident boundaries.

The problem for established residents suspicious of the very mention of ethnicity is to understand the social causes of ethnic and interethnic organization. The problem for politicians in a multiethnic society, like Kiang and Chu, is to balance ethnic and interethnic concerns. Kiang's avowedly pro-Chinese stance frightened Anglo, Latino, and some established Asian American residents. They united against him as being "too Chinese," a "Chinese Barry Hatch." Because of her multiculturalism and the danger of spreading herself too thin, Chu had the greater problem of image control. When she supported Asian causes, the more xenophobic established residents would find her too pro-Chinese. When she sided with established residents, Chinese newcomers could see her as too "mainstream," "American," not Chinese enough, or even "anti-Chinese."

As researchers, our purpose was not to pronounce judgments on "nationalist" and interethnic organizing, but to situate them in local politics and assess their effects on relations between groups. The clash between established residents and immigrants and between Chu's mainstream strategy and Kiang's nationalism exposed divisions within the Chinese community and political tendencies that could affect the struggle for empowerment in the immediate future.

Was newcomer power united and powerful enough to translate into electoral victory without support from established American-born Asian, Latino, and Anglo residents? Or did Asian empowerment require what Chu practiced, mainstreaming through interethnic alliances, or perhaps other forms of political struggle? The 1992 municipal elections would be the first test of the competing strategies of empowerment.

THE MUNICIPAL ELECTIONS OF 1992

With five Chinese Americans, four Latinos, and three Anglos on the city's first trilingual ballot, the Monterey Park elections of April 1992 were the most diverse in the city's history, decisive evidence of the decline of Anglo political dominance. Chinese newspapers speculated hopefully that the city might become the first on the U.S. mainland to have a Chinese American majority on its city council. The *Citizen's Voice,* a small, strident, and widely distributed publication, cried out against the "Chinese takeover": "Asian Apartheid Goal of Chinese Media. They Want an Asian Majority on Next City Council."[8] Some established residents were frightened at the prospect.

Monterey Park was but one example, albeit an advanced one, of a transition occurring throughout Los Angeles County, where disenfranchised minorities were challenging traditional Anglo domination in city councils by turning their stunning population gains into electoral power. Dramatizing the trend toward ethnic power in the 61 municipal elections of Los Angeles County in April 1992, a headline in the *Los Angeles Times* proclaimed: "Minorities Poised for Gains at Ballot Box."[9]

In the ethnically mixed suburban cities of the San Gabriel Valley—El Monte, Rosemead, Azuza, West Covina, Baldwin Park, and Monterey Park—Latinos, the largest single group in the Valley, were fighting to increase their representation. First-ever Chinese candidates, representing the smaller but faster-growing Asian population, were running for city councils in South Pasadena, West Covina, and San Marino.

South of Monterey Park and the San Gabriel Valley, in the once-prosperous industrial white working-class heartland of Los Angeles, poor working-class Latinos, their numbers swelled by immigration to over 80 percent of the population, were challenging their Anglo-dominated city councils. In March, just a month before the 1992 elections, there had been a revolution in Bell Gardens. Twenty years after becoming the majority of the city's population, Latinos attained political representation. They had boldly recalled and replaced four Anglo council members.[10] Their victory inspired the struggles for Latino power in the neighboring cities of Bell, Cudahy, Huntington Park, Maywood, and South Gate. Arturo Vargas, head of community education and public policy for the Mexican American Legal Defense Educational Fund (MALDEF), captured the spirit and hope for change: "My gut reaction is: 'Finally!' It is extremely exciting to our community that people are taking an activist approach to government."[11]

An expression of a new political diversity, these municipal elections in Los Angeles County were also tests of strategies for ethnic empowerment. Could candidates win by targeting their own or by appealing to several different communities and soliciting cross-over votes? Could they assume that their own constituted a unified ethnic bloc? In southeast Los Angeles, where Latinos were the clear numerical majority, candidates could make a direct appeal to their ethnic constituency. In the more ethnically mixed suburbs of San Gabriel Valley, most candidates, at least publicly, avoided ethnic appeals.[12]

In private strategy sessions, however, candidates calculated the ethnic votes. They knew from experience what our exit polls of the 1988 and 1990 Monterey Park elections had revealed—that ethnicity was an important factor in candidate choice. But was it sufficient for getting candidates elected in a multiethnic community? Councilman Kiang thought that the ethnic numbers were favorable to a Chinese victory in Monterey Park. Having personally counted names on registration lists during his own campaign in 1990, he estimated that Chinese Americans constituted at least 25 percent of the registered voters. Given a high turnout and consensus on "voting ethnic" for the two council seats, they could vote in a Chinese majority. Councilwoman Chu was less sure. For the first time, several Chinese candidates were competing with each other for two council seats. Aware of political and ethnic divisions within the Chinese and established-resident communities, Chu knew that the only winning strategy was an interethnic appeal. Our analysis of the line-up of candidates, endorsements, and election results suggests that she was correct, at least for the political conditions of 1992.

The Candidates: The Growing Presence of Chinese Immigrants

The candidates for Monterey Park's municipal election of 1992 represented a rainbow of colors. The declining and aging population of Anglos did not produce a viable candidate for the city council. The incumbent Betty Couch declined to run. The other two Anglo candidates for city council were unlikely to draw wide support: the belligerent nativist Frank Arcuri was making his third bid for power; John Casperson was an only-in-Los Angeles phenomenon new to local politics. An out-of-town developer, his head shaved in honor of his conversion to Buddhism, Casperson moved to Monterey Park just in time to file for his candidacy. He talked a lot about crime and patriotism, while reaching out for the Chinese immigrant vote through his Chinese wife's connections and her program *China TV* on local Channel 18.

The strongest Anglo candidate, Louise Davis, was running for her second term as City Treasurer. It would be interesting to see how this former councilwoman and popular grassroots leader would fare against a Chinese contender.

Of the three first-time grassroots Hispanic candidates, none had political experience, but all were long-established residents. There were five Chinese American candidates, including Chu. This represented a dramatic change: When Chu announced her intention to run for city council in 1988 during a period of backlash, some of her advisors wondered if it was too soon for an Asian candidate to win. Only one Chinese, Kiang, ran for office in 1990. Now, in 1992, Chinese candidates were running against each other and members of other groups in a competition for two council seats.

The Chinese candidates were different from the Anglos and Latinos. Lawyers, professors, accountants, and other professionals, they generally had higher levels of education. They also had the best-financed campaigns. Unlike old-timer Anglos, who depended on local support, the Chinese American candidates tapped the regional wealth of an underrepresented Asian population eager for a political voice.

In 1992, Chinese candidates also benefited from changes encouraging the political involvement of Asian newcomers. Kiang spearheaded a successful campaign to print electoral material in Chinese, Spanish, and English; thus, Monterey Park became the second city in California, after San Francisco, to provide election material in Chinese.

Another benefit for Chinese candidates and a sign of immigrant activism was the involvement of Chinese political groups in organizing traditional candidate forums, something that would have been unthinkable only a few years before. In the past, forums were put on only by Anglo and multiethnic service and political clubs like the Soroptimist International of Monterey Park, the League of Women Voters, and the two Anglo Democratic clubs, the MPDC and the UDC. In 1992 the Chinese American Professional Society, the Taiwanese American Citizens League, the Chinese American Political Alliance (in conjunction with Asian Americans for a Better Community, the Chinese Political Action Committee, the Chinese American Association of Southern California, and the Organization of Chinese Americans, Los Angeles Chapter), and KSCI (TV Channel 18) sponsored four separate forums. Some organizations (like the Taiwanese American Citizens League) were well established; others (like the Chinese American Political Alliance, Asian Americans for a Better Community, and the Chinese Political Action Committee) were new manifestations of immigrant involvement in local affairs. The television event attested to the political influence of the Chinese media and was the first bilingual candidate forum in Monterey Park. The forums and election were well reported by the two largest Chinese papers in the region, the *Chinese Daily News/World Journal* and the *International Daily News*. As if to celebrate the legitimate arrival of Chinese in suburbia, 1992 also witnessed a Chinese New Year's parade, co-sponsored by Monterey Park and neighboring Alhambra, a city that was becoming Chinese.

The Chinese Candidates: Immigrant and Ethnic Versus Mainstream and Interethnic Politics

Unified in their desire for Asian and Chinese representation, the Chinese American candidates were divided by national background and political strategy. Nativity was taking on particular political significance as their local Chinese political involvement spread increasingly from its initial base in native-born Asian Americans to first-generation Chinese Americans. Of the five candidates, only Chu was American-born.

In the summer of 1991, generation had been a factor in the split between the American-born and English-speaking Chu and the Chinese-born and bilingual Kiang. It was the social foundation for the political line between Asian American and immigrant politics, interethnic and ethnic politics. In the elections of April 1992, these generational differences translated into two different campaign strategies. The first-generation Chinese, relying on their ethnic base, tended to target Chinese voters. Chu, courting the votes of Asian American and other established residents as well as Chinese newcomers, followed the path of "mainstream and interethnic" politics.

The strongest of the three immigrant candidates was Bonnie Wai, an articulate lawyer, community volunteer, and commissioner on the city's Residential Design Review Board. Raised in the United States (a member of the so-called 1.5 generation), she had the potential to reach beyond a Chinese constituency. Like all the candidates, she emphasized issues of concern to the whole community, but, following Kiang's path, her major electoral strategy was to target and get out the Chinese and Asian votes. Early in the campaign, her supporters had conducted an aggressive campaign to register Asian Americans. Wai hoped to win as a result of a heavy Asian American turnout.[13]

The Chu Campaign: Juggling Chinese, Asian American, and Established-Resident Interests

In contrast to the immigrant candidates, Chu was both an incumbent with a long history of community involvement and a rising star in Asian American politics. Resisting the temptation to run for an open State Assembly seat, in 1992 she declared her candidacy for city council even though no incumbent had met with the approval of angry voters since 1984. Her campaign strategy of reaching across ethnic divisions was based on an ideological commitment to interethnic harmony and a practical plan for winning the votes of a multiethnic electorate.

To succeed, Chu had to juggle at least two agendas. One was for everyone, particularly those who could be united across ethnic lines around quality-of-life issues and managed development. Another agenda was for Chinese and Asian Americans who had long been excluded from the "everyone" list.

With two agendas, she ran the risk that both immigrants and established residents would accuse her of duplicity and political ambition. Some Chinese expected her to be their candidate and be especially attentive to their neglected needs; everybody else expected her to represent them as abstract citizens regardless of color, gender, or other factors. The apparent contradiction was built into the situation of an Asian American running for office in a multiethnic community with a rising Chinese immigrant population.

Chu's solution to this structural contradiction was to organize interethnically, through her contacts with Anglos and Latinos within the established-resident population, and to organize ethnically on two generational fronts: through Chinese immigrant organizations and her network of progressive Asian American Democrats. This dual strategy of mainstream and ethnic organizing was reflected in her campaign. The task was to make the strategies work together.

Above all, Chu had to avoid any direct ethnic appeals. In a press interview, she frankly explained why: "The strength of a leader is in their ability to represent everybody. This is an extremely important issue to people who are not Chinese, especially because of the ethnic feelings here."[14] This message was reflected in her official ballot statement, which was attentive to the fears and needs of old-timers:

> Fighting for your concerns is my number one priority. I want to provide a diversity of needed stores to increase sales and tax revenue, introduce social services to homebound elderly, keep the Garvey Reservoir empty [after an earthquake, it had developed a leak], and reduce the robbery rate. Most importantly, my commitment to you

is to be fair in fighting for the concerns of all the people of Monterey Park as we work to improve the quality of life in our community.[15]

Here the appeal to everyone contains a special recognition of established residents and their alienation from a Chinese economy that did not in fact provide sufficient revenue for city services. The word "diversity" must be decoded. One meaning is diversity in types of businesses and the need for large department and discount stores that could bring in the sales taxes not being provided by the banks and mini-malls of the ethnic economy. A second meaning is diversity in type of shopping. The Chinese ethnic economy grew at the expense of the "American"-style shopping familiar to established residents. In the past, Chu had shown her commitment to established residents by supporting what could be an unprofitable revitalization of an aging American-style shopping center.

Her campaign showed an attempt to balance established-resident and newcomer concerns and resources. Following the pattern established by Chinese candidates in Monterey Park and other cities in the San Gabriel Valley, Chu's campaign relied heavily on absentee ballots and money from the larger regional Chinese population. However, she used these ethnic resources to maximize her interethnic appeal.

In her 1982 and 1986 campaigns, Lily Chen, the first successful Chinese candidate for city council, discovered the value of mail ballots in getting out the votes of Chinese who might (because of language difficulties, for example) be reluctant to engage in an unfamiliar electoral process managed by established residents. Kiang had spectacular results with mail ballots in 1990: a return rate of 65 percent, 30 percent of his total vote.[16]

Initially, established residents complained that the Chinese use of mail ballots was both undemocratic and too successful by far. Over time, however, local campaigners discovered that what worked for the Chinese might work for them. In 1992, the candidates who could afford to do so sent out absentee ballots, and more were sent out than at any previous time in the city's history. Chu, confident of her interethnic support, targeted all frequent voters, not just Chinese and Asian Americans, with mail ballots. She wanted and needed their support.

The use of ethnic tactics to further interethnic support was apparent also in Chu's fundraising. Established residents were understandably wary about the superior ability of Chinese to raise funds for local elections. Dollars do buy elections, and Chu was a stellar fundraiser. In 1988, having raised $35,032, she outspent all the other candidates. Two years later, in 1990, Kiang raised $42,844. In 1992, with $46,000, Chu had become the top fundraiser among the candidates running for election in the San Gabriel region. In Monterey Park, following the Chinese pattern, Chu's Chinese competitors raised between $29,000 and $42,000 (Wai was a close second to Chu), compared with zero to $10,000 for the Latino and Anglo candidates.[17]

With her fundraising feats, Chu ran the risk of displeasing established residents. She cut these risks by investing her Asian capital wisely to build interethnic support. She spread her literature widely and interethnically. She headed a strong, well-financed and well-organized grassroots campaign with enthusiastic Asian, Latino, and Anglo organizers and volunteers. Women were especially well represented. Day after day, Chu walked in all the precincts and knocked on doors of frequent voters, whatever their ethnicity. Thus, she combined money and grassroots power, Asian resources and mainstream politics.

The Issues: Development and Diversity

Behind the bland promises of all candidates to serve everyone and improve their quality of life, two fundamental and divisive issues were at stake in the election: the future course of commercial development and ethnic representation.

Since the mid-1980s, a strong slow-growth movement had imposed stringent controls on residential and commercial development, a homeowners' revolution against the tide of uncontrolled growth. Now, in 1992, hard times were on the side of the growth machine, with its seductive offer to fill the city's empty coffers with the revenues from developer-controlled growth. An important issue behind the campaign rhetoric was whether slow growth would continue to have a voice on the city council. Since the last election in 1990, reliable support for controlled growth had dwindled to Couch and Chu, and both were up for reelection.

On the ballot, moreover, was a proposition to loosen the city's tight restrictions on building height in the case of a proposed Taiwanese-financed mall. One of the victories of the slow-growth movement was the requirement that citizens vote on such changes. Now they were being asked to vote on a proposition that represented a compromise between slow-growth and growth forces, an example of the evolution from a no-growth rebellion to a policy of negotiated, managed growth.

A second major issue was the course of ethnic succession, and what it would mean for future community development. Would Chinese and other Asian Americans unite as they had in the past, this time to elect two Chinese to the vacant council seats and thereby create a Chinese American majority on city council? Would the Latinos and Anglos increase their council representation? Coming only months after a conflict that revived tensions between established residents and newcomers, the election was also a test of the strength of interethnic voting. Would voters cross immigrant and ethnic lines to vote for Chu, the master of interethnic politics?

The Pattern of Candidate Endorsements

Local endorsements for candidates in the 1992 election generally reflected the split between newcomers and established residents. Among the Chinese immigrant candidates, Wai made the greatest effort to reach out to the multiethnic established-resident community. Her highly professional campaign literature addressed established residents' concerns and listed four ethnically diverse local endorsers and two moderate Democratic representatives from her district: U.S. Representative Matthew Martinez and State Senator Charles Calderon.

However, the most telling indication of her base was the strong endorsement of Sam Kiang. Although a Democrat, she received no support from the Asian and primarily Anglo Democratic clubs, and RAMP dismissed her (on slight evidence) as a developer's candidate. This pattern of support would probably make her more attractive to Chinese immigrants than to established residents.

As for Chu, her mainstream strategy may have offended nationalists in the Chinese community, but it clearly expanded her support among established residents. As in her 1988 campaign, she could count on strong support among progressive Asians, Latinos, and Anglos. She did not get an endorsement from Kiang. What Chu did get in 1992 that she lacked in 1988 was the endorsement of prominent Anglo leaders.

Appearing on one of Chu's campaign flyers distributed citywide was the picture of Louise Davis, the longtime grassroots activist and favorite of established Anglo residents. Chu also had the support of retiring Councilwoman Couch. A fiscally conservative Republican and unswerving leader of slow growth, Couch had learned to work with and respect Chu when they served together on city council.

The biggest boost to Chu and to a Latina candidate, Rita Valenzuela,[18] and a blow to other candidates, arrived on doorsteps just before the election: the endorsement of RAMP. Although RAMP was waning along with the slow-growth movement in general, its election newsletter, *The Record,* commanded interest for its research and analysis of candidates' stances on the popular issue of controlled development.

About Chu, the first Chinese American candidate RAMP had ever endorsed, *The Record* said:

> Four years of experience has taught Judy Chu a lot about the City Council—and has taught us a lot about her . . .

> - She kept her promise to work to improve development standards.
> - She kept her promise to work to bring the community together.
> - She kept all of her promises. Imagine that!
>
> But there's something else that makes her an unusual politician—Judy is smart. Sure, she has the university degrees, but that's not what makes the difference—she uses her common sense, and she has the good instincts—to do the right thing. We need to keep her on the City Council.[19]

Candidates endorsed by *The Record* had been moderately successful in the past. The first newsletter appeared in 1986 to endorse three Anglo slow-growth candidates and condemn the alleged "pro-developer" record of the three minority incumbents. The Anglos (including Barry Hatch) won.

In 1992, RAMP's endorsement of two minority candidates freed it from the taint of nativism and racism. The decision was a decisive sign of a trend that we had observed before the election: the movement away from nativism toward interethnic alliances on the issue of controlled growth. RAMP's action was a practical accommodation to demographic changes and the absence of viable and available Anglo candidates. More importantly, as we have argued, the political change was the result of increased contact with potential allies among minorities and political struggle against nativist tendencies within the slow-growth movement.

RAMP thus endorsed Chu and Valenzuela as a multiethnic growth-control ticket. For City Treasurer, it endorsed the growth-control sympathizer Louise Davis over the politically unknown first-generation Chinese candidate. Expressing a more flexible attitude toward development, RAMP also endorsed the ballot proposition to increase building height limits.

A Victory for Negotiated Development and Interethnic Politics

The 1992 election appeared to be a victory for negotiated growth and diversity. The leaders of the slow-growth movement seemed to have widened their ethnic and ideological alliances. Fifty-five percent of the voters supported the RAMP-endorsed measure to waive height regulations on a specific development.

Demonstrating again how far the city had moved since 1986, the victors in the council race were two minorities: Chu (26.7 percent) and Valenzuela (21.1 percent). Wai was a distant third (13.7 percent). But hard-core resistance to "the Asian takeover" had not altogether disappeared: Acuri came in fourth (10.7 percent). The other five candidates got less than 10 percent, and the two remaining Chinese candidates came in last. The old-timer Louise Davis received the biggest vote (71 percent) in her race against Chester Chau (29 percent) for City Treasurer.

With the election of Chu and Valenzuela, the controlled-growth minority might be able to hold its own against the mounting pressure to loosen the strict controls imposed by the slow-growth movement. But if the course of development was in doubt, the trend toward greater ethnic diversity was not. The new council reflected the demographics of the city: two Latinos, two Chinese Americans, and one Anglo.

The Regional Trend

The subsidence of slow-growth fever and the coloring of city council were replicated throughout Los Angeles County. Only three commercial development measures were submitted to voters in the county's 61 municipal elections, and they were defeated.

The regional transition from Anglo power to diversity in cities affected by Latino and Asian immigration was the most striking pattern of the Los Angeles County municipal elections in 1992. Generally applauding this trend, the *Los Angeles Times* declared, "Ethnic Diversity Is an Election Winner."[20] First-time Chinese American candidates were elected to city councils in West Covina and South Pasadena, thus extending their representation beyond its initial base in Monterey Park and Alhambra to other cities in the San Gabriel Valley. However, a Chinese American candidate was defeated in the posh suburb of San Marino.

First-time Latino candidates won city council seats in four other valley cities. In Baldwin Park, Latinos gained a first-ever council majority in a city whose population was 72 percent Latino. Challenging Anglo rule in the heavily Latino cities south of the San Gabriel Valley, Latinos also won a first-ever majority in South Gate, a city that according to the 1990 census was 83 percent Latino. In Bell Gardens, Latinos held on to their majority representation. They picked up one seat each in Cudahy (89 percent Latino) and Maywood (93 percent Latino), cities where Anglos had dominated city councils 5 to 1.[21]

A Setback for the Chinese or a Victory for Interethnic Politics?

The political history of Monterey Park reflects the regional tendency for new Asian and Latino majorities to challenge and replace Anglo leaders. It also reveals the complexity of a transition affected by resistance, differences within ethnic communities, and the importance of issues that intersect them.

These factors need to be taken into account in understanding the election results. Was the electorate's failure to vote in two Chinese American candidates a sign of backlash against Chinese newcomers? Or was the election of Chu and Valenzuela, an incumbent and a long-established resident, a victory for diversity and interethnic politics?

For the Chinese who had hoped that Monterey Park would become the first city in the United States to have a Chinese majority on its city council, the election results were a setback. All of the Chinese immigrant candidates were defeated by two U.S.-born candidates. Wai suggested that backlash was one factor in her own defeat: "I think people in Monterey Park are not ready to have an Asian American majority on the city council. . . . I sensed a lot of hostility and resentment."[22]

Her theory contains an element of truth. The conflicts of 1991 revived divisions between established residents and newcomers and probably heightened established-resident hostility. Kiang offered another explanation—the Chinese tendency to avoid politics. Constituting about 25 percent of the registered voters, they could have united to win two council seats, but "Chinese don't vote. They just don't vote."[23]

There are problems with Kiang's interpretation of voting behavior. According to calculations of ethnicity based on the voters' names, Chinese Americans represented 23 percent of the registered voters and 27 percent of those who voted. Asians (a category comprising Chinese, Japanese, Korean, and Vietnamese Americans) were 46 percent of the registered voters and 51 percent of those who voted in 1992 (Table 12). At least in Monterey Park, Chinese and Asian Americans vote about as much as Anglos, although they are probably less likely to register to vote.

Kiang's assumptions about ethnic voting patterns were challenged by a Chinese American resident of Monterey Park who wrote in a letter to the editor of the *Los Angeles Times:*

> I take strong exception to that characterization [that Chinese don't vote], not only because it is completely false, but because Mayor

TABLE 12 *Ethnic Composition of Registered Voters in 1993 and Turnout in the Monterey Park Municipal Elections, April 14, 1992*

	Registered Voters (%)	Voted in 1992 (%)
Chinese American	23	27
Japanese American	12	13
Korean American	7	8
Vietnamese American	4	3
Latino	30	21
Anglo/Other	24	28

Source: Political Data, Burbank, Calif., May 18, 1993.

> Kiang operates under the misconception that Chinese Americans vote along ethnic lines. The voters of Monterey Park (including Chinese voters) are a little more intelligent than Mayor Kiang gives them credit. The voters made their decision and elected Judy Chu and Rita Valenzuela, two eminently qualified and experienced leaders who demonstrated their talents to the electorate in Monterey Park. I, for one, voted in that election and am quite happy and satisfied with the results.[24]

According to our exit polls, Chinese voted for Chinese in 1988 and 1990 in situations where they lacked representation and had few qualified Chinese candidates. In 1992, with two Chinese Americans on the city council and five Chinese candidates, Chinese voters did not vote strictly on an ethnic basis.

Unfortunately, we did not conduct an exit poll in 1992, which would have allowed us to match candidate choice and voter characteristics. However, indirect evidence from the 1990 exit polls points to differences among Chinese voters that may have had a political effect in 1992.

The differences between Kiang, Chu, and the other Chinese American candidates reflected a basic division between Chinese oriented primarily to the established multiethnic community and Chinese oriented primarily to the Chinese community. The generational split apparent in the conflicts over bilingual dispatchers in 1991 and in the elections of 1992 prompted us to take another look at our data on Chinese American voters from the 1990 exit poll. We found marked political differences between American-born Chinese, immigrants who had resided in Monterey Park for more than 10 years, and immigrants with less than 10 years of residence.

The more "American" they were by birth and residence, the more Chinese voters resembled other established Latino, Japanese American, and Anglo voters in their tendency to spread their votes around rather than vote only for their ethnic candidate, to favor growth control (Proposition S), to be critical of bilingual education, and to be identified with a political party. Thus, the election of 1992 highlighted generational and political differences between Chinese Americans, and such differences probably divided the Chinese vote—the more established Chinese Americans opting for Chu and an established Latino resident over a Chinese immigrant without significant local experience; the less established Chinese Americans voting for two Chinese candidates (Table 13).

The Victory for Interethnic Politics

If we are correct, the election results in multiethnic Monterey Park represented a victory for candidates who were able to capture both ethnic and

TABLE 13 *Political Profile of Chinese American Voters by Nativity and Length of Residence, the Monterey Park Municipal Elections, April 10, 1990*

	Newcomers (%)	Old-Timers (%)	American-Born (%)
CANDIDATE CHOICES			
Kiang	95	89	85
Balderrama	25	42	41
Hatch	7	13	46
NUMBER OF VOTES			
1	59	42	23
2	3	10	21
3	28	44	56
SUPPORT FOR PROPOSITION S			
Yes	38	53	69
No	22	22	23
Didn't vote/No response	40	25	8
SUPPORT FOR BILINGUAL EDUCATION			
Yes	80	62	59
No	9	24	33
Undecided/No answer	11	14	8
FAMILY INCOME			
$40,000 or more	53	72	NA
$20,000 or less	17	5	NA
RESPONDENTS	41.4 (99)	33.1 (79)	25.5 (61)

Source: Data extracted from exit poll of the 1990 Monterey Park municipal elections by John Horton and Yen-Fen Tseng, Department of Sociology, University of California at Los Angeles.
Note: "Newcomers" were defined as immigrants with less than 10 years of residence in Monterey Park, and "Old-Timers" as immigrants residing in the city more than 10 years. Years of residence in the city were not taken into account in the case of the "American-Born."

interethnic support. Thus Valenzuela and Chu won because they had such support; the other Chinese candidates lost because they lacked interethnic and unified ethnic support.

This interpretation is borne out indirectly when we examine how candidates fared at the precinct level. Chu came in first in 11 out of 19 precincts and second in all others, except for one heavily Latino precinct, where she came in third. She was the first choice in 7 out of 9 precincts where Asians constituted over 50 percent of the voters, and first choice in 4 out of the 10 mixed precincts where no single ethnic group had the majority of votes. Also, Chu made inroads into heavily Anglo precincts, capturing one more than in her 1988 election.[25]

Valenzuela won in 7 precincts: 3 predominantly Latino, 1 predominantly Asian, and 3 that were mixed. She came in second in 10 precincts and third in 2 others. Her first base of support was Latino, while Chu's was Asian, but both clearly won with the addition of cross-ethnic voting. Billed as a ticket by RAMP, Chu and Valenzuela seemed to benefit from association with each other, and each shared the other's ethnic base. Wherever Valenzuela came in first, Chu tended to come in second, and vice versa.

The precinct pattern of the Chinese immigrant candidates, in stark contrast, showed weak across-the-board support. Wai, the candidate with the third-largest vote, came in second in only 1 and third in 3, of the 9 majority-Asian precincts. She was the fourth, fifth, and sixth choice in all but 1 mixed precinct; and the fifth, sixth, and seventh choice in the 3 strongly Latino precincts.

Generally, the native-born candidates got a cross-ethnic vote. The support for the immigrant Chinese candidates was limited to Asian areas, and in none of these did they beat Chu.

Implications of the 1992 Municipal Elections

The elections of 1992 were a test of strategies for empowerment in a diverse and multiethnic city. Was reliance on ethnic power or interethnic alliances the route to victory? To some extent, all the candidates wisely pursued both strategies, but the two candidates who won, Chu and Valenzuela, were most successful in garnering both ethnic and interethnic support for their platforms of community involvement and controlled growth.

The Chinese immigrant candidates gave priority to the Chinese vote, and they lost. The Chinese were not numerous enough or united enough to elect two candidates to office. Moreover, many established residents were not inclined to vote for the Chinese immigrant candidates, who had not paid their dues in community service and political life, and may have been victims of a backlash against the previous year's demonstrations of immigrant power.

In Monterey Park, however, the boundaries between immigrants and established residents and between ethnic groups were notoriously unstable, breaking down and reforming with changing political circumstances and opportunities. The ethnic and cultural divisions between Japanese Americans and Chinese Americans broke down in 1988 when they united as Asian Americans to elect Chu; in 1990 voters crossed the divide between newcomers and old-timers and between ethnic groups to elect Kiang and remove Hatch from office. The political divisions between established residents and Chinese newcomers were reactivated during the battle over bilingual dispatchers in 1991 and expressed in 1992 with the defeat of Chinese immigrant candidates—only to be weakened in 1993 when Chinese Americans, Latinos, and Anglos united to save their neighborhoods from the threat of a gambling casino.

THE CARD CLUB BATTLE (1993)

The setting is the packed and raucous city council meeting of February 22, 1993. Tonight the council members will listen to public opinion and vote on the resolution introduced by Councilman Kiang "to take all steps necessary to keep gambling establishments illegal" in Monterey Park. The resolution reaffirms and strengthens an existing municipal code against gambling. By mobilizing community support and pressuring for compliance on city council, Kiang and his allies hope to stop the BCTC Development Corporation from going ahead with its plans to build a $30-million card club in Monterey Park.[26]

Approximately seven hundred people from Monterey Park and areas potentially affected by a card parlor fill the council chamber and flow into adjoining spaces.[27] Some press into an antechamber to watch the fireworks through a long, open sliding glass door. Others turn the spacious halls into a people's forum—a bustling space to watch the televised meeting, pass out no-gambling petitions, and form lively discussion groups with friends and strangers.

Greatly outnumbered and feeling like a besieged minority, the supporters of the card club gather in angry clutches at the peripheries. Standing in the back of the antechamber at the Coke machine with several other elderly Anglo friends, Irv Gilman, former councilman and leader of RAMP, is conspicuously ignoring the meeting and offering words of warning: "The crime isn't gambling, but the budget. These people are a moral majority who are against Monterey Park. You want my predictions? [Unless we solve the budget crisis] . . . the council will cut fire and police and we'll be a million in the hole. You asked, 'Does RAMP have a position on the casino?' [He looked puzzled.] This is not a growth issue!"

Working the crowd and collecting copy for the *Citizen's Voice,* Frank Arcuri dismisses the protestors as "a bunch of outsiders and communists."

Irritated by the noise, a group of Latinos and Chinese against gambling start shaking their protest signs and strain to hear what is going on in the council chamber. Their orange placards with black letters in English, Spanish, and Chinese send an interethnic message of community empowerment: "Save Our Neighborhood." Other symbols inject a note of moral condemnation: a "no" sign superimposed over a devil with a pitchfork lurking behind an Ace of Spades, Queen of Hearts, King of Clubs, and 10 of Diamonds—a losing poker hand. To the consternation of the City Attorney and Mayor Balderrama, larger versions of the signs have been pasted on the council dais, and the vociferous majority and Councilman Kiang make it clear that they will stay there.

After a half-hour of delays and haggling over the agenda, the "oral communications" begin, extending the meeting from seven o'clock to almost midnight. Of the 66 residents who stand at the microphone for their three minutes of free speech, 54 oppose gambling in Monterey Park, 6 support the card parlor, and 6 claim neutrality. Given the intimidating opposition, the neutrals look suspiciously like supporters of the card club.

Budget Crises and the Lure of Card Clubs in Los Angeles County

The council meeting of 1993 was a more dramatic and better-attended replay of a 1981 attempt to consider legalizing gambling in Monterey Park. At that time Councilmen Irv Gilman and Harry Couch (husband of Betty Couch), activists in the tax-limitation and slow-growth movements, unsuccessfully floated the idea of capturing needed revenue through legalized gambling.[28]

By the 1990s, Southern California cities, their budgets drained by recession, overspending, tax revolts, and the withdrawal of state and federal bailouts, were once again weighing the benefits and social costs of card clubs.[29] This time, in an atmosphere of recession rather than growth, no-tax rebels hungry for city revenues and developers hungry for quick profit united in an effort to sell gambling to residents fearful of crime and big developers.

The officials of BCTC, a Taiwanese-owned company, reasoned that the city was a promising site. Asians were good customers of existing clubs, but they had no facilities conveniently located in Monterey Park, where BCTC had an inside track to development. Monterey Park had already selected BCTC to plan an $80-million retail and mixed-use "quality" development that was potentially revenue-rich but cost the city virtually nothing. This would go in Monterey Park's last large undeveloped commercial zone. BCTC was also doing a good job on local public relations. While the young Chinese owner remained out of sight, his affable Anglo Vice-President, J. Richard Myers, was busily charming old-timers. By the time of the gambling controversy, he had become a key member of the Chamber of Commerce and the President of the Monterey Park Boys and Girls Club.

Even the best-laid plans can be thwarted by hard-ball politics. Some residents, sensitive to manipulation by developers, became uncharmed when BCTC's quality project did not materialize and the company turned to a card club for profit. In addition, they were put off by the latest scientific methods of persuasion. Preparing the way for a club, the company had hired a public relations firm to survey local opinion and to create opinion by inviting selected residents to attend focus groups on solutions to the city's problems. Their attendance at these promotional meetings was rewarded with a payment of 45 dollars. Myers summarized their findings as follows: "Although we are still assessing the situation, it has become evident that many community leaders and a large percentage of the citizens of our City believe that a card club entertainment center, if strictly regulated by the City, could provide a means of preserving and improving the quality of life in Monterey Park, which may otherwise be jeopardized by the looming budget crisis."[30]

Kiang and others disagreed. In the words of one rebel, "This is one battle that you [BCTC and developers generally] are going to lose."[31] The message was resoundingly delivered at the city council meeting to debate Kiang's resolution against gambling.

"*Save Our Neighborhood*—Digamos No! A El Casino"

The pro- and antigambling forces had very different messages and backgrounds. All twelve of the pro-gambling and neutral speakers at the council meeting were from Monterey Park, and the majority were middle-class Anglos. They spoke for themselves, although several were local leaders with their own constituencies.

Defending the card club were former Councilwoman Couch and her mother-in-law, Evelyn Diederich, both fiscally conservative founders of RAMP, which was too divided to take an official stand. Some members opposed gambling as a quality-of-life issue; others supported it as a revenue issue. The popular City Treasurer, Louise Davis, claiming neutrality, argued for a fairer public hearing. As a councilwoman, she had opposed the card club when it was proposed in 1981. Now, during a time of budget crisis, she was clearly more open to reconsidering the idea.

The speakers opposed to gambling were more numerous and multiethnic, organized from the grassroots, regionally based, and equally divided between primarily working-class Latinos and middle-class Asian Americans (chiefly Chinese Americans) and Anglos. Seventy-two percent were residents of Monterey Park, while the rest came from neighboring East Los Angeles, Alhambra, and Rosemead. The Latinos, in particular, represented organized groups—churches, neighborhood associations, small businesses, and the elderly. The Chinese and Anglos tended to speak out against gambling as individual citizens, although some represented churches and the elderly.

Much in evidence were Latinos from the church-sponsored, Saul Alinsky–inspired United Neighborhood Organizations (UNO). Their militant presence conveyed the threat of a widened protest against any card parlor bordering the barrio of East Los Angeles. Their opposition was strengthened by the voices of three former Monterey Park councilmen (David Almada, Chris Houseman, and Rudy Peralta) and well-known grassroots activists (including Jose Calderon, Lucia Su, and Ruth Willner), and by letters of support from Los Angeles County Supervisor Gloria Molina, California Assemblywoman Diane Martinez, and other officials in neighboring cities.

They testified to the social costs of gambling: crime, the arrival of big money with power to corrupt public officials, the "tarnishing" of the image of a middle-class bedroom suburb, and the threat to the working-class corner of Monterey Park where the club would be located. Some of the opposition spoke out of religious conviction. James H. K. Lau, M.D., Chair of the Community Concern Committee and member of the Board of the Chinese Evangelical Free Church, said in a written statement to the council:

> To allow for the setting up of a casino means that the City Council encourages greediness and unethical pastime at the expense of financial necessity. The narrow focus on increase in revenue reflects that the city government is short sighted, pragmatic and has no concern for the long-term development of our community.

Former Councilman Houseman eloquently tied opposition to the history of a city that was founded in 1916 to prevent "victimization by outside interests" who wanted to dump garbage on their turf: "It's part of our history, our founding principles, our heritage as people of Monterey Park to be vigilant about the interests and schemes of others who usually don't take into account the interests of average residents."

By contrast, the speakers for the card club rejected moral and political appeals and made their case on pragmatic and financial grounds: Like it or not, gambling was here to stay. The best citizens made regular treks to casinos in Nevada, card clubs in Los Angeles, and bingo games in local churches and senior centers. The less respectable had no difficulty finding high-stakes gambling in Monterey Park. Given the situation, why not recognize gambling, rely on the reputable BCTC to build a facility, and watch the revenue come in to solve the city's budget crisis and build a stronger police department? This argument was forcefully made by Diederich, a veteran of RAMP:

> People who spoke don't realize the financial crisis. The city will never cut enough to matter. We'll have to pay more taxes. . . . The paper said that a million dollars is spent for illegal gambling in the San Gabriel Valley. Why won't we let people who want to gamble pay our taxes? If this is a moral issue, why don't they fight to close down bars? People drink all evening and go out and drive, and that's dangerous. The gamblers just go out broke after paying a big lump of taxes. . . . The casino would be located away from homes in the Southwest part of the city, next to East L.A. in a rough area where no restaurant will go because of bad elements. Let the gambler pay the taxes.

Racial and Class Motives for Opposition and Support

The words of supporters and opponents reflected different perspectives on development based on ethnic divisions between old-timers, minorities, and immigrants, as well as class divisions between a sheltered middle-class zone and the working-class zone where the card club would be located. The opposition tended to see racial and class interests behind the "objective" and "pragmatic" arguments for the gambling facility.

Privately, some residents suspected an anti-immigrant and anti-Chinese element behind the enthusiasm for a card club. A young Chinese American male, raised in the United States and a resident of Monterey Park for 25 years, asked: "Who's for gambling? Old residents of European descent. Their children have grown up, they think that they are already paying too many taxes and see the casino as a way of preventing more." A middle-aged American-born Chinese woman, a long-time resident, agreed: "The old whites are for the project. They only see the Chinese as people who love money, as gamblers, and people who cause crime, people who should pay to solve the city's budget crisis."[32]

While middle-class Chinese opponents of gambling were quick to find racial and nativist motives, Latinos, identifying with the plight of poorer populations who would have to live near the proposed card club, invoked the language of class discrimination: "I'm speaking not just for my parish, but for the little people, the poor. UNO is organized to bring power to the little people, and they will gather together and oppose" the facility, said the Reverend Arnold Gonzalez from Our Lady of Soledad parish in Los Angeles, a member of UNO. Jose Calderon said, "Investors rob the poor; it's the immigrants and the poor who get hurt." And a preschool teacher from East Los Angeles, Dora Luna, described the proposed gambling parlor as "a false model for our children in an area already crime-ridden."

For their part, Anglo supporters of the card club also read between the lines and saw themselves as victims of discrimination. They resented and feared the "undemocratic," "dictatorial" tactics of outside groups, minorities, and radicals. One longtime resident, Norman F. Schoff, insisted in a written statement to the city council that

> city projects and goals *cannot* be the right and privilege of an appointed few. . . . We cannot put the burden of choice on the shoulders of the City Council or the backs of a few irrational citizens. . . . I suggest that a public forum be called, after thorough research has been done and the results of the information acquired be supplied to the general public. That is the way our "government of the people, by the people and for the people" is supposed to operate.

Other supporters of the card parlor held Kiang responsible for deliberately fomenting racial division. During the council meeting, they were passing among each other copies of a newspaper editorial with a yellow-highlighted passage that read:

> The issue of 911 [hiring bilingual dispatchers], and especially the Mark Lewis issue shouldn't have become one involving race, thus some have questioned the motives of Kiang and the city manager, as well as the part they may have played in stirring up of emotions in the Chinese and non-Chinese communities.

Written on the editorial was a comment: "Kiang is doing it again! But now, it's the card parlor that will divide the city."[33]

By contrast, the opponents of gambling claimed that their show of organized, grassroots protest was, to use Judy Chu's words, "democracy in action." In this case, democracy meant the direct and self-directed action of historically underrepresented minorities, even those who lacked citizenship or local residency. Given that any decision regarding a card parlor could affect their lives, shouldn't they organize to make their voices heard in a forum ordinarily controlled by a relatively unrepresentative corps of regular voters? Was this "mob rule" or "democracy in action"?

The answer depended on the situation and one's position in a community undergoing ethnic and political change. Old-timers who saw outsiders threatening their status and power wanted the issue of gambling settled through an election. But the majority of people of color were outside the electoral system and would exercise democracy in direct political action.

A Temporary Victory for the Antigambling Forces

In the end, the "democracy in action" of the more numerous opponents of legalized gambling won out over the "electoral democracy" advocated by the supporters. At least for the moment, the plan for a card club was stopped before it could be voted on in a special election. Kiang's antigambling resolution before the city council was strongly endorsed by Chu. Under fire, the three reluctant members, Valenzuela, Balderrama, and Purvis, bowed to the army of protest and approved an amended resolution pledging to "take all steps legally permissible to keep gambling establishments illegal" in Monterey Park.[34]

BCTC also gave in to "democracy in action." Several weeks after the protest at city council, the company decided not to push for a local referendum that could override the city's antigambling ordinance. According to Myers, "It was too close a business decision to invest half a million dollars on a campaign."[35] Judging from the electoral response elsewhere, this was a wise decision. By August 1993, voters in five cities in Orange and Los Angeles counties had voted against proposed card clubs.[36]

The Political Significance of the Gambling Controversy

The casino tempest was significant in several respects. First, it engendered unusually strong grassroots participation that culminated in what local observers claimed was the largest protest in the city's history. It was certainly the largest that we had seen. Second, the protest involved an unprecedented level of interethnic, interclass, and immigrant/established-resident unity. Power flowed from the convergence of grassroots organizing and leadership by and among Latinos, Chinese, and Anglos. Particularly noteworthy was the strong presence and cooperation of two previously separated and sometimes antagonistic groups: working-class Latinos from East Los Angeles and the poorer sections of Monterey Park, and middle-class Chinese and Japanese Americans from Monterey Park. Asians were particularly sensitive to the danger that gambling would tarnish the image of America's first majority-Asian city; Latinos, to the location of the facility in their community.

The alliance merged different class styles of grassroots politics. Latinos from East Los Angeles brought a tradition of militant working-class and church-supported collective organizing and a philosophy of empowerment. Middle-class residents from Monterey Park brought the power of their networks, the skills of individuals involved in issue-specific, neighborhood organizing, and the knack for working within the system.[37] Mitchell and Gloria Ing, young professionals and long-term residents, printed their own flyers, walked door-to-door in their ethnically mixed neighborhood near the proposed club, and visited churches and

PTA meetings. They joined forces with other young professionals like Cindy Yee and Betty Gin Tom. Activists from another neighborhood, they distributed petitions through block committees that had been formed during the fight against the state parole office. Their team collected more than a thousand names in a week's time, another example of the significance of women in organizing at the grassroots level.

Elsewhere in Monterey Park, Phyllis Rabins, a well-known environmental activist, contacted her networks, which extended to County Supervisor Molina. Longtime Latina activists Tina Martin and Mary Soto contacted their networks in Monterey Park and East Los Angeles. Councilman Kiang mobilized residents through his press conference, council resolution, and visits to many local churches. Irv and Ruth Willner, leaders of the MPDC, worked with Kiang to coordinate disparate groups and individuals into a new organization, Residents Against Gambling in Monterey Park, capable of mobilizing protest against any future plans to legalize gambling.

In spite of the differences in class, ethnic background, and political style, the protestors shared the determination to protect their neighborhoods against the unwanted project of a big developer. Improving the depressed quality of local life had been a constant struggle in working-class neighborhoods, which were often the dumping grounds for facilities unacceptable to more affluent and powerful residents in the suburbs. By the 1980s, increasingly urbanized suburbs like Monterey Park were no longer safe havens from unwanted development, but fought to maintain an already high quality of life. The protest against gambling was significant in uniting neighborhoods ordinarily separated by class and parochialism. The protestors recognized that their problems were regional and that, in this instance, they were on the same side in the class struggle over land use.

Finally, the mass involvement of Latinos and Asian Americans in the casino battle signaled both the democratization of the movement for control over development and the continuing salience of ethnic divisions within it. Throughout most of the 1980s, the leaders of the controlled-growth movement were Anglo. In 1993, the leaders of the protest against gambling were multiethnic, a point dramatically brought home when a long-established Chinese American resident said publicly in accented English: "Asians like gambling, particularly Chinese, but not in their backyards."[38] Her statement belied stereotypes of Chinese narrowly focused on making money and unconcerned about community welfare. One does not have to be white to be a NIMBY.

The demand for control over one's own backyard came with the territory and the structure of economic and governmental power. At one level, it is a simple class issue dividing homeowners and property users from property profiteers. In Monterey Park, however, the territory had become more ethnically diverse and the movement for control over development both more representative and more divided. Several prominent leaders of RAMP, as they had in the past, supported the card club. To be located outside their neighborhoods and promising increased revenues without higher taxes for homeowners, it was for them a good development.

The clash over the gambling facility reminded us that ethnicity as well as class counts in determining what is and is not a development issue. Ironically, given the history of development issues in Monterey Park, Chinese and Latinos were united against a Chinese developer and his supporters, who included a contingent of Anglo leaders of the controlled-growth movement. Was the mantle of leadership in the populist struggle over land use passing from a small group of whites to a multiethnic coalition?

FROM ETHNIC TO INTERETHNIC POLITICS

The internationalization of Monterey Park led to the decline of Anglo control and the rise of ethnic and immigrant organizing for representation and power. By 1993, it was becoming clear that ethnic politics were a regular feature of political life. Growing ethnic diversity, continuing ethnic discrimination, lack of representation, the state's tendency to allocate rewards and punishments on an ethnic basis—all these factors favored ethnic political organizing. Class inequalities between the major nonwhite majorities, particularly between poorer Latinos and more affluent Chinese American populations, also tended to express themselves in ethnic terms.

However, the arrival of diversity and the politics of ethnicity did not inevitably result in permanent competition and conflict among Latinos, Anglos, and Asian Americans or between newcomers and established residents. What we saw—and this may be our most important finding—was the fluidity of ethnic political divisions and an unstable pattern of interethnic alliances that continually shifted around changing issues of representation and community development.

Ethnic politics have received a great deal of positive and negative attention. Brokers of ethnic power, as well as corporate purveyors of diversity, tend to applaud each increase in ethnic representation as a sign of greater democracy but fail to identify the integument holding the pieces together. Democracy requires a common bond of citizenship. This bond is a central concern of conservatives, who deplore ethnic counting as a sign of Balkanization and the decline of national unity. Their solution, conformity to the tradition of white, Euro-American dominance, will not be acceptable in an ethnically diverse society, but their critique of ethnic politics identifies a genuine dilemma often ignored by liberals. Something else besides self-interest based on ethnic identification is needed to secure the mosaic of diversity.

In Monterey Park, that "something else" included the practice of working together in civic organizations and forming interethnic alliances in the political arena. This practice did not come easily, nor was its stability assured. Established residents, particularly Anglos bent on remaining the dominant force, had to move beyond resistance to newcomers to accommodation and negotiation. This required a political fight that in 1990 resulted in the electoral defeat of the city's most influential nativist leader and opened the way to greater ethnic and immigrant representation.

Ethnic contenders also had to move beyond ethnicity toward interethnic cooperation. It did not happen in 1991, when conflicts between established residents and newcomers flared over the firing of "the Chinese-friendly" City Manager and the hiring of bilingual dispatchers. This time, ethnic division was initiated less by nativism than by ethnic nationalism. The aggressive efforts of Councilman Kiang and other Chinese leaders on behalf of newcomers created a backlash that probably contributed to the defeat of Chinese immigrant candidates in 1992.

In 1993, the sides changed again as Latinos, Anglos, and Chinese (both immigrants and established residents) allied under Kiang's leadership in a successful effort to block legalized gambling. The victory signaled greater participation of ethnic groups in the struggle to control community development, but also some ethnically based differences over the meaning of development and appropriate methods of political participation.

During this period, the gain for the politics of diversity was the willingness and ability of residents to come together across ethnic and even class lines to work on issues of representation and development. Interethnic organizing was very effective in the battle against gambling and in the election of Judy Chu. The concept was catching on. In 1991, in their section of a book prepared for the city's seventy-fifth anniversary, Chinese residents called for "a Residents' Association and Commerce Union composed of each ethnic group. The purpose is to help advise on problems, to channel communication with the city government, to draft workable proposals to help establish a harmonious community."[39]

Such a group has yet to appear, but interethnic alliances now form regularly around issues of growth and development. They also formed in the regional electoral arena—for example, on the issue of redistricting to enhance ethnic representation. Given Chinese Americans' residential dispersal within the ethnically fragmented landscape of the San Gabriel Valley, their ethnic representation is difficult to achieve without coalitions with other Asians and the numerically and politically stronger Latinos who currently dominate county, state, and federal elected offices in the region that contains Monterey Park.[40]

If the experience of Monterey Park is any indication, such coalitions and alliances will be short-lived. In city politics, alliances have been notoriously situational, issue-specific, and unstable. A political friend today is often an enemy tomorrow, when a new issue arises. The art of making alliances depends less on the belief in harmony and unity than on the changing need for interethnic allies.

Interethnic alliances also come about because ethnic identity, as an expression of a person's position and political alignments, does not consist of set attributes but malleable social and political constructions. Another way of understanding the emergence of political diversity and the formation of ethnic divisions and alliances is to describe the formation of the culture of diversity, the changing and ambivalent formation of ethnic and American identities, another important chapter in the Monterey Park story.

Chapter 8

THE CRISIS OF AMERICAN, ETHNIC, AND IMMIGRANT IDENTITIES

A lot of white people in this society . . . say, "We're all Americans. Why can't we call everyone American?" I'd like to see that happen. It is my dream that my son and my daughter, that's what they're going to call themselves. . . . But in the meantime, we need to deal with some basic things, if we are honest with ourselves. For a long, long time, Americans have been defined as white European Americans. I am a Chinese American, not antiwhite. . . . "American" does not include me, only a part of me.

—Chinese American male at a public forum during Harmony Week, 1991

MANY OF the whites in the audience were not happy to hear someone raise "the racial thing" after a pleasant morning of "harmony." The speaker was reacting to a white resident's wish that Monterey Park would not become entirely Chinese but would remain diverse. As we left the meeting, the disturbance still on our minds, a Chinese American companion remarked ironically, "What's wrong with Monterey Park being Chinese? Aren't we all Americans?"

One way of keeping peace in Monterey Park is to avoid talking publicly about ethnic and racial tension, except perhaps to say that "the conflict is behind us now." Angered by a white man's suggestion that Monterey Park was becoming too Chinese, a Chinese American resident broke the rule of public silence. For a moment, the contradictions of being an American and nonwhite were revealed at a personal level—longing to be American without qualification, wanting his Chinese heritage to be recognized as part of his American identity, and feeling exclusion from full citizenship because of that heritage.

In Monterey Park, the conflicts and contradictions of being ethnic and American are never far from the surface, for white Americans as well as minorities and newcomers. They fear to talk openly across ethnic and racial lines because words not carefully chosen may get them in trouble. Worse, the old discourse and terminology for interethnic relations can no longer be taken for granted. The younger generation of Asian Americans do not like being called "Orientals." Conservative whites wince at being called "Anglos," or "Euro-Americans," and insist that they are "Americans." And what is a third-generation American of Mexican descent—an "American," a "Mexican American," "Hispanic," "Latino," or "Chicano"?

The situation gets even more complicated in the heterogeneous Chinese community. Asserting their independence from mainland China, natives of Taiwan may prefer to call themselves Taiwanese rather than Chinese. And are Chinese from Vietnam "Vietnamese" or "ethnic Chinese"? When and under what circumstances do they become "Chinese," "Chinese Americans," or simply "Americans"?

What do "minority" and "majority" mean when "ethnic" minorities are majorities and "whites" have become minorities without ethnicity? Most Los Angeles public schools are now classified as "majority minority." The Alhambra School District, which draws students from Monterey Park because the city does not have its own high schools, classifies its minority of white students as "others," a residual, colorless category alongside the majority/minorities of Asians and Hispanics.

The terminological confusion indicates social change. The arrival of large numbers of relatively high-status Asian immigrants changed the ethnic balance in Monterey Park and challenged the way residents define themselves and others. The ethnic pecking order was upset, throwing the whole system of stratification—the ethnic composition of classes and ethnic ranking—into disarray.

Under these conditions, residents were forced to reexamine their social identities. The very meaning of fundamental concepts like American, ethnic, minority, and majority became a contested and negotiable issue. The rapid demographic change was thus accompanied by a transition in the ways residents defined themselves and others as ethnic groups and Americans. The transition was social and political, evolving through interaction between diverse groups in the struggle to find a position in the local, national, and global hierarchies of worth and power.

In Monterey Park, the formation of American and ethnic identities is another chapter in the story of resistance, empowerment, and incorporation, told here from the experience and perspectives of residents who bear the often socially imposed labels of Anglo, Latino, Asian American, and immigrant.[1]

UNHYPHENATED AMERICANS: BECOMING ETHNIC

"In Boston, I always thought of myself as Latin, so I was surprised to find that in Los Angeles I was an Anglo," a second-generation Italian

American woman told us. "I'm proud of my ethnicity, but we are all Americans," said a second-generation Irish American male. And a child of a Chinese–Anglo marriage described his ethnic background as follows: "My father is Chinese, my mother is nothing."

In the ethnic mosaic of Monterey Park and the western San Gabriel Valley, many Anglo old-timers are experiencing nothing less than a crisis of identity—the fear of being engulfed and extinguished as *the Americans*.[2] Accustomed to thinking of themselves as majority Americans distinct from, if not superior to, minority ethnic and racial groups, they now find themselves a minority without ethnicity in a society seemingly bent on organizing around ethnic power. The old, taken-for-granted ways of defining themselves and others as Americans no longer function. Listening to the sounds of Chinese and seeing residents organize for Asian and Latino power, they ask themselves: "Where have all the Americans gone? We feel like strangers in our own town."

The established resident of Italian descent who became an Anglo by moving from the east coast to California, the American of Irish descent who bemoaned the disintegration of America into ethnic groups, and the child of a mixed Chinese and Anglo marriage who sees his Anglo mother as having no identity were responding to conflicting historical movements that have contributed to the local crisis of American identity. The children of the great European immigration tended to lose their specific ethnic identities in exchange for an unhyphenated American identity, a sign of absorption into the Anglo-American melting pot. Since the wave of Asian immigration and the increase in the non-European and nonwhite population, these Americans now reluctantly face the loss of their unhyphenated American identity in exchange for no identity (the "other") or some unacceptable, reconstructed racial ("white") or ethnic identity ("Anglo" or "European American"), a sign that they are an odd piece in the ethnic mosaic that has replaced the melting pot.

Many white Americans believe in the melting pot and are loath to give it up, although it did not work for nonwhites, who were never allowed to escape their status as minorities and second-class Americans. Responding to continued segregation, discrimination, civil rights movements, and riots, social scientists, as well as activists and the liberal establishment, now recognize the persistence of ethnicity in American life and question the traditional model of assimilation and the melting pot.[3] One issue in their debate is the salience of ethnic identities and the conditions for their maintenance, disappearance, or transformation.[4] Some authors argue strongly for the revival of ethnicity;[5] others dismiss this argument as greatly exaggerated.[6] Whatever the disagreements, academics increasingly emphasize the changing social construction of ethnicity and race for all groups, including whites.

From this perspective, ethnicity both retreats and persists. It depends on the population (the experience of whites is different from that of nonwhites), the time (1950 is not 1990), and place (Boston is not Los Angeles). The stigma of ethnicity did tend to disappear and the melting pot did work for white European Americans. At least, this was the case in Monterey Park and Southern California. For white Americans of Italian, Greek, or Jewish descent, a ticket from the ethnically stratified older cities on the east coast to Los Angeles could mean mobility, becoming a core American.

Entry into the dominant group had little to do with cultural traits and a lot to do with the character of the regional ethnic and racial hierarchy. Micaela Di Leonardo points out that Italians had higher status in California than in Boston because of the earlier presence of distinct racial groups on the west coast: "These groups filled the most proletarian jobs and suffered the most from white ideological constructions of them as dirty, incompetent, lazy, and ambitionless. Italians, Irish, and French Canadians filled these slots in Boston."[7] Her point is well taken. The melting pot worked rather well for whites in California because the dividing line was racial, between whites and nonwhites, rather than between Anglo-Saxons and other whites.

Thus, in California and in Monterey Park, the white Americans could drop their hyphens because hyphens were reserved for nonwhites. While this meant a certain loss of identity, the sense of being Italian or Jewish, and was a blow to the status of Anglos, who now had to share their label with lesser Europeans, it represented a collective gain in status for all European Americans: the privilege of identifying with the dominant racial group and becoming an unqualified American. Of course, invidious differences among whites did not disappear (certainly not for non-European whites), but over time they became more symbolic, a personal adornment, rather than a social obstacle to working and living wherever one wanted.[8]

Their social identities reconstituted by the white melting pot, California "Anglos" had become accustomed to thinking of themselves as Americans without qualification. Now the historical process was undermining their American identity and throwing them unwillingly into the maelstrom of ethnic politics. With the new, post-1965 immigration and a change in the ethnic composition of the local class system, they are confronted with the "browning" of America and their own minoritization. To make matters worse, in Monterey Park they encountered high-status nonwhites apparently quite capable of living successful, separate lives without Anglo help and guidance.

Life and politics in the land of golden opportunity in the 1980s and 1990s left many Anglos with a dilemma: how to deal with being a minority with a majority mentality in an ethnically diverse and internationalizing society. As *the Americans,* they found themselves on the decline and on the defensive without an ethnic culture of resistance and empowerment to express their fears and aspirations.

The most extreme response to the Anglo crisis of identity takes the form of racial war, attacks on immigrants, and calls for white power. Monterey Park contained no visible skinheads or KKK. The closest thing to white-power advocates were the conservative leaders of Official English. However much they thought white, they talked American and wielded their American identity like a club to keep the newcomers in line and contain change.

To legitimate their claim to a privileged position in an uncertain present, they invoked their real or imagined past, their dubious status as the first Americans, their patriotism, their language and culture, as models that newcomers must emulate. While addressing a widespread desire for peace and unity, their response, as we have seen, was divisive. The motive was fear of Asian or Latino "takeover." Their call to unity masked and perpetuated the reality of class and racial domination that had created the ethnic organizing that they so much deplored.

The response of some white liberals to the new diversity was not very different. While generally rejecting the forced assimilationist model of the right, they also deplored any sign of ethnic segregation and continued to preach the sixties message of integration. They could not understand why minorities and newcomers would want to form separate organizations rather than integrate into their clubs and groups. On this issue, it was hard to separate white conservatives from white liberals; both were unprepared to address their whiteness and accept an American identity that was not white and European at its roots.

In an interview, an Anglo woman active in local Democratic politics had three specific complaints about Asian power:

> It's a political game for Asians to take political posts across the U.S. They identify how many positions are won. It is scary. And it is no longer, "You are an American in America." It is that "You are an Asian and you are from Asia." . . . Non-Asians cannot be voting members of the Western San Gabriel Asian Pacific Democratic Club, but anyone can join the Monterey Park Democratic Club and the United Democratic Club. . . . The Chinese play up to Judy Chu as the Chinese candidate and refer to her as "*Our* councilwoman." You never hear an Anglo say "*Our* Anglo candidate."

What she and others do not understand is that ethnic Americans organize their own groups when they believe that established all-American organizations are Anglo-dominated and unresponsive to the realities of ethnic inequality. The fundamental objection to ethnic politics extends to Latinos as well as Asians. An example can be taken from a local forum held in February 1991 for candidates running for office in the redrawn Los Angeles County First District, which includes Monterey Park. The district was created by court order following charges that the all-Anglo Los Angeles County Board of Supervisors, in violation of the federal Voting Rights Act, had gerrymandered the district to disenfranchise the county's three million Latinos. The major candidates for the new First District were Latinos, and a Latino was expected to win.

At the forum, to the horror of several "regular Americans," State Senator Art Torres violated their rule of meritocracy and displayed racism when he admitted that he had told an all-white city council in an all-Latino city in Los Angeles County that he'd "like to see more faces like his own up there." After the forum, a local leader of Official English complained to Torres about making his ethnicity a basis for political representation: "I said to him, 'You don't look Mexican, you're American.' He just flipped his tie in my face and answered, 'If I didn't have this tie on, I'd be nobody.'"

For many white Americans, while the public demonstration of cultural differences among Americans may be acceptable or even desirable, an emphasis on ethnic politics is un-American. It violates the universal American norm of fair play and status earned by merit rather than race. However, the criticism of ethnic politics without a rectification of ethnic inequalities only reinforces a pattern of Anglo domination under the guise of fair play, nondiscrimination, and national unity.

This is difficult for the dominant ethnic group to understand. But those who have not left the city and fled to a whiter enclave are beginning to understand. Perhaps our most important finding about local white identity was the existence of discourse probably uncommon in regions of the country where whites are the numerical and political majority. We heard the frequent, if reluctant, willingness of unhyphenated Americans to call themselves "whites," "Anglos," or even "European Americans," thereby acknowledging pluralism and diversity while accepting a new ethnic tag for themselves. Certainly in the eyes of many non-white, hyphenated Americans, the whites were not *Americans,* but *European Americans,* and that may well become their new ethnic identity in multiethnic America.[9]

HYPHENATED AMERICANS: THE FIRST WAVE OF NEWCOMERS

"My Dad didn't come to Monterey Park to be a Chicano, he just wanted to get out of East Los Angeles [the barrio], buy a house, and find good schools for his kids. When I was going to school here, I had friends from all races. I never thought about being a minority. Now that I'm into politics, I'm a Latino. I understand it, but I'm ambivalent about it."

The speaker is a male born in Monterey Park of an Anglo mother and a Mexican American father. Like Anglos, established Asian and Mexican Americans in Monterey Park were experiencing a crisis of American and ethnic identity, but of a different kind with quite different reactions and results.

From the post–World War II period until the mid-1970s, upward mobility into a suburban community and accommodation to Anglo political and cultural domination had tended to minimize their ethnicity and maximize their sense of being Americans like everyone else. By the 1980s, however, the new immigration was simultaneously reinforcing their sense of being established Americans, different from the newcomers, and making them more conscious of being hyphenated Americans.

Being established residents, they might resent the new immigration and draw a line between themselves as Americans and the newcomers from another land. But the Anglo-led nativist attacks on the cultural and economic rights of immigrants reflected on all minorities and exposed their already ambiguous status. Moreover, the immigration had challenged white domination, increased the numbers and resources of minorities, and thereby, with the help of the state's emphasis on ethnic representation, opened up new opportunities for their empowerment as ethnic Americans.

The situation challenged old ways of thinking about American and ethnic identities and suggested new possibilities. Would the hyphenated Americans side with nationalism and Americanism against the newcomers? Would they reassert their ethnic identities as Asians and Hispanics and organize politically on that basis? Or would they negotiate a more diverse definition of Americans with newcomers and established residents? As we have seen, Asian Americans and Mexican Americans pursued all of these options in Monterey Park, but in different ways and for different reasons.

Mexican Americans

"On legal papers where it says 'Hispanic' and 'Oriental,' and 'check one,' I always check 'other' and write in 'American, Mexican descent,' because I was born here, but my roots are in Mexico. My culture is Mexican,"[10] a second-generation Mexican American woman in her forties, resident in Monterey Park for 22 years, told us.

A Mexican American male in his forties, a 30-year resident, said: "I just call myself an American. I don't really think about my race. Once in a while, I think I am Latino when someone brings it up. I've had customers who have talked to me on the phone, but have never met me, and then one comes down to meet me, and I come up and when I say, 'I'm Joe,' and he goes, 'No, I'm looking for the owner,' and I say, 'Well, I'm the owner,' and he's kind of shocked that I'm not white."[11]

Native-born, longtime Mexican American residents of Monterey Park emphasized that they were Americans and, like Americans, made their political decisions on the basis of issues and qualifications, not ethnic identity. Their experience in the city had supported this view, but not without contradictions that could arouse a sense of being Mexican American, Latino, or Hispanic. During the late 1970s and 1980s, these contradictions and ethnic consciousness were on the rise, challenging the more accommodationist views formed in an earlier period of Anglo domination.

Summing up his interviews with middle-aged, established Mexican American political leaders in Monterey Park, Jose Calderon concluded that they are very much like what Chicano scholars have called the "Mexican-American generation"—middle class, middle-of-the-road, assimilationist, not deeply identified with their Mexican roots.[12] Many had lost fluency in Spanish and a strong sense of their Latino heritage and saw little political relevance in having a Latino, Mexican American, or Hispanic identity. For example, a fifth-generation Latino who referred to himself as a "Californian," descended from the original and occasionally prosperous Mexican settlers, said this about his Hispanic identity:

> Hispanic? It's just a nice category. It doesn't mean anything to me. It is a way to classify yourself. . . . I eat Mexican food, but I don't speak the language. But, retain my culture—retained what culture? My parents consider themselves Californians. You know I belong to—am active in the California Historical Society, in the Southwest group and those kinds of things. Well, you know, I'm not too sure what else it would mean.

This pattern of accommodation was a reasonable response to the experience of upward mobility into an ethnically mixed suburban community politically dominated by Anglos. For many Mexican Americans who lived in the nearby barrio of East Los Angeles, a move to Monterey Park symbolized and still symbolizes separation from the ethnic and political core and the attainment of middle-class status. A professional man in his thirties, a third-generation American, generalized about his own move:

> Once you become educated, you leave your community and move to the next step up, and that to me was Monterey Park because it was

> still close to East Los Angeles, where all the politics were going on. I wanted a better place. . . . I don't think Hispanics like to move far away from the family. So Monterey Park is like the next economic step up the ladder. I know it used to be called East L.A. Beverly Hills.

Mobility had consequences, not unlike those experienced by white ethnics. Looking back on their history in Monterey Park, longtime Mexican American residents often speculate about the loss of ethnic identity and concerns. A middle-aged developer put it this way:

> Monterey Park is not only a middle-class city, it's a middle-class status for Mexican Americans, and it's a status we've not enjoyed for too many years. And I think a lot of people have the feeling that I am here, I've got it made, and I've arrived. I've achieved. I am into the melting pot, and I'm just as good as anybody else or as much an American as anybody else.
>
> He went on to suggest that this American-first identity was a barrier to social and political unity among local Mexican Americans:

> I don't see that much getting together among Latinos. Everyone seems to want to go his own way. When we do get together, it is not in a political sense—more like at Las Vegas night. After that, we don't see each other, sometimes for a year. I don't see that many networks either, except for, maybe, the Latin Club at Langley Center.
>
> There are a lot of Hispanics in Monterey Park who are "white Latinos." If they had a choice to vote for an Hispanic or a Jones, they would vote for Jones. These white Latinos consider themselves middle-class or upper-class. They average thirty thousand dollars a year. But all of them don't turn away. Some monied Latinos will give money to elections. Some will even help Latinos who are running. But the ones I am talking about are the ones who don't want to be called "Chicano." The ones who say, "I'm an American citizen." The barrier to the unity of Latinos is the white Latino.

A middle-aged but less affluent Latina active in local politics explained that for her the melting pot meant pressure to be Anglo:

> I noticed that the Mexican people that lived here were prone to be Anglicized. For example, the food. The sandwiches, the roasts, the enchiladas were forgotten. . . . Sometimes I feel you have to talk Anglo, act Anglo, you almost have to be Anglo. I think being married to one helped me a lot in Monterey Park.[13]

By the 1970s, there was ample evidence that the melting pot was working for Mexican Americans at the social and cultural levels. Social clubs and civic organizations were integrated. Young Mexican American families who began to move in after World War II and the Korean War were raising their children alongside Anglos and Japanese Americans in the same schools and neighborhoods.

As we have seen, however, social assimilation did not mean political empowerment. There were no local Latino political organizations and few social ones outside the two clubs in the Langley Center for senior citizens and the Sports Club, where there was strong Mexican American participation. Although approximately one-third of the city's population by 1980, Mexican Americans constituted an ethnically unorganized, politically invisible, and underrepresented force in local politics.

The new immigration challenged the American and ethnic identities of local Mexican Americans that had emerged under earlier demographic and political conditions. The massive numerical increase in the regional Latino population, the decline in local Anglo domination, the expansion of Asian numerical and economic power, and the potential expansion of Asian political power led to a contradictory mix of nativist, nationalist, and multicultural responses.

As we have noted, some America-first Latinos who strongly identified with Monterey Park before the immigration supported local controlled-growth movements, which newcomers often construed as anti-immigrant. Interviews and open-ended responses to the 1990 exit poll indicated that many Latinos also felt displaced by the presence of large numbers of high-status Asian immigrants. In a multiethnic community, their attitudes seemed to translate into supporting Latino candidates and making distinctions among Chinese American candidates rather than voting against all Chinese. For example, Latinos gave numerically important support to Chu in her 1988 and 1992 city council races, but in 1990 were least likely among established residents to support Kiang, and probably contributed to his defeat in 1994.

Negative attitudes toward immigrants cemented bonds between Anglos and Latinos as regular Americans trying to hold their ground against the new immigrants. However, contradictions within the nativist movement strengthened the Latinos' ethnic identity and drove them toward selective support of Asians on the issues of immigrant and minority rights. There was suspicion that the Americanism of Anglo leaders in the Official English movement hid a dislike for all people of color, not just Chinese and recent immigrants.

A Latina active in interethnic politics explained why some local Mexican Americans were, but should not be, anti-Chinese: "Hispanics will vote anti-Chinese because they are looking at the Asian immigrants taking over. But if those [anti-immigrant] people discriminate against Chinese, what makes them think they will treat us any different?"[14] Following the same line of reasoning, a Latino businessman saw the anti-Chinese attitude as a rerun of earlier discrimination against other minorities in Monterey Park. Notice that he sometimes makes distinctions among Asians and sometimes lumps them together:

> They used to blame the Latinos for all the problems in Monterey Park. Latinos caused all the accidents. Latinos are terrible drivers. No insurance, causing all the congestions in the streets. Then the Japanese moved in. They started blaming the Japanese . . . and now they have the Chinese, and they're blaming them for the traffic. Lousy drivers. Just basically everything is blamed on them. They're shakers, unlike the Mexicans and Japanese. They wanted to own the property and do business in Monterey Park. A lot of people are offended by that. They have visions that all the Asians come here with big suitcases full of money. I look at all the people I know and I ask them how do they make it. They came out here poor, you know, nothing. Busted their butts and made a living. A lot of people here are offended that the Asians drive their Mercedes, and they own big homes, nice suits, and all that. I guess if the Asians weren't successful then maybe they wouldn't be blaming them so much for all the problems in the city.[15]

Racism turned one Latina away from the local slow-growth movement:

> They would call me up and tell me you better come to the council meeting tonight because "they" are going to come [threateningly]—"The Chinks will be there." I began to feel that if they say that about them, what do they feel about me?
>
> In the beginning when they had these meetings on development, I attended one near where I live and walked in, and they were discussing what should be done. They were coming up with a petition, and I went to see if I could be included. And I pleaded and I begged, and this guy's mother looked at him and said, "I think you should consider her because she is white."[16]

Another Latina activist who lived in the modest "flats" of Monterey Park criticized the slow-growth movement on class as well as racial grounds:

> Let me tell you a little story about RAMP. They're up on the hill. Do you see any condos on the hill? All the no-growth and slow-growth has to do with the hills. It didn't stop any of the construction going on down here.

> . . . I think it's too late for them, because these people [the Chinese immigrants] have already come in and dug in their heels. . . . Now it's a question of the last RAMP to leave Monterey Park is going to be the one to go out with the [American] flag. That's their attitude. Because the flag belongs to them; anybody else is just intruding.[17]

Such alienation from local Anglo-led movements set some Latinos on the course of ethnic and interethnic organizing. Indeed, our exit polls of 1988 and 1990 showed that ethnicity was the single most important force predicting their vote.

Two indigenous groups, the Hispanic Round Table and the West San Gabriel Valley LULAC, emerged in the 1980s with leadership and membership from Monterey Park. These organizations expressed newer, less assimilationist tendencies rooted in the radicalism of the 1960s, but tempered by the diversity of the 1990s. If the old dialogue in the Chicano movement was between nationalist and class politics, the new dialogue was between the politics of nationalism and the politics of multiethnic alliances.

In 1986, the defeat of city council incumbents Almada and Peralta, led by slow-growth leaders, sparked ethnic organizing and the formation of the Hispanic Round Table. As one member explained: "We realized that we did not have a voice. We had no one to represent us, so we formed a group and decided to stick together." The purpose of the group was to discuss Mexican American issues and work for local representation. Another member saw ethnic organizing as a counter to the Anglo backlash and the old accommodationist attitude of Mexican Americans:

> I think when a minority is starting to become the majority people are more threatened and you have to realize that and fight it and not give in to it. I think my father's generation gave in to it. They said, I want to live here. I want a better life for my kids. So OK don't speak Spanish. Don't make any waves; don't identify.

While the members of the Hispanic Round Table were exploring ethnic organizing, a new chapter of LULAC explored an interethnic "working-class/professional alliance." Jose Calderon, its founder, explained the purpose of the organization:

> LULAC organized ethnically but advanced the idea that its individual members support candidates, whether Latino or not, on the basis of their political agenda. With this organization framework, LULAC actively worked to build multi-ethnic unity, particularly with Asian leaders and new Chinese immigrants. . . . It sought to go beyond unity based simply on cultural understanding to one that also in-

cluded building ties with other ethnic groups around the political issues which were facing the larger community.[18]

The existence of the two organizations showed that the new immigration had spurred increased political consciousness and organizing in a region where accommodation and fitting in had been the middle-class political mode. Latinos' rising power was also expressed in local elections. In 1994, Mexican Americans were the majority on the Monterey Park city council.

Japanese Americans and Asian Americans

"Well, if I had a choice I would say I am an American. You know, I wouldn't hyphenate myself," an elderly Nisei told us. "It depends on how you are looking at things. To another Japanese, it's obvious that I am Japanese, so I'd be Japanese American. I get annoyed by people who are non-Japanese asking me whether I am American or Japanese. I always tell them, well, you know, you're European American, and I am Japanese American."[19]

Like the Mexican Americans of Monterey Park, established second- and third-generation Japanese Americans would probably prefer to be called unhyphenated Americans. Their experience of moving up and fitting into an Anglo-dominated middle-class suburb weakened their ethnic identities and strengthened their sense of being Americans. However, the Asian immigration changed the ethnic balance and accommodations that residents had worked out. For established, American-born Asian Americans, the newcomers were both a resource for increased Asian empowerment and a source of increased anti-Asian hostility that could spill over onto them. In either case, the situation meant another historical turning point, another crisis in the struggle for a self-determined American identity.

We begin with the accommodations Japanese Americans had already made to living in Monterey Park and explain how they were challenged by the presence of Chinese immigrants.

To prove oneself a loyal American was an especially urgent task for Japanese Americans who made their lives and careers in the wake of World War II. Against the legacy of racism, they struggled to enter the American mainstream by being patriotic and hard-working. A World War II veteran told us what being American meant to his generation:

> The whole thing for the Japanese Americans in World War II, I'm not saying a hundred percent, but the vast majority, was to go out and prove that we were good Americans. And we never looked at America as a matter of race. I think we all looked at it as something in the mind and heart—in other words, that we would be treated

equal and that we have certain rights. You know, those things we fought for, or else why the hell would people come to this country from all over the world? It's the only country in the world where you have such a mixed bag of people. It's the freedom that we have.

In the 1950s and 1960s, Japanese American veterans took advantage of housing benefits to move out of their older and more congested Crenshaw, West Los Angeles, and East Los Angeles neighborhoods and buy new homes in suburban Monterey Park. Slowly, without pressure or fanfare, primarily American-born Japanese Americans moved in and blended into mixed white and Latino neighborhoods, giving Monterey Park the second-largest concentration of Japanese Americans in Los Angeles County.

Being able to live peacefully and prosperously in suburban Monterey Park was a symbol of what they had achieved as loyal Americans. A retired Nisei who had lived in the city for more than 30 years expressed his pride in the community's accomplishments:

I think the Japanese as a whole in Monterey Park have done well culturally, not only economically. In all ways they have contributed. They were the first group of Asians to move in here, and being that it was right after the war, they wanted an area where they could come and buy a home and send their kids to school, be proud of what they're going to do. I felt that way too; that's why I'm glad my kids went to high school and graduated and didn't goof off. The Japanese have done a lot for the city, in the sense that they've never done anything to stick out, nothing bad, just constructive things.

They made a name for themselves, and nobody gave us anything; the government didn't give us money to start businesses, like they did for the Koreans. They've made a name for themselves and got the respect of the American people. For their behavior, they won the respect of other Americans.

The Japanese Americans accommodated to life in an ethnically mixed but Anglo-dominated town by fitting in and proving they were good Americans without demanding special privileges and making waves. Often stereotyped as a Japanese cultural trait, this tendency is best understood as a historical adaptation to the racist conditions of the times.[20] During World War II, U.S.-born as well as first-generation Japanese Americans on the west coast were treated like enemy aliens, uprooted from their homes and businesses, and sent to relocation camps. Although many of their sons fought loyally for America, they did not have full naturalization rights until 1952.

In the eyes of Anglos, the Japanese Americans who moved into

Monterey Park in the 1950s and 1960s were a "model minority"—self-supporting and hard-working, patriotic, and good neighbors who kept a low profile and neat yards. But, as with Mexican Americans, respect and toleration did not translate into local political power. Beyond voting, Japanese Americans and the smaller number of other Asian Americans tended to stay out of politics and never constituted themselves as an organized political force. Only one Japanese American was ever elected to the Monterey Park city council.

The Nisei whom we interviewed generally believed that their behavior paid off in peaceful, nondiscriminatory relations with their ethnically mixed neighbors until the late 1970s. A Nisei woman who moved to Monterey Park in the early 1960s marked the turning point and its particular effect on Japanese Americans: "It was much more friendly atmosphere back then [1960s and 1970s]. We didn't feel any prejudice when we first came here. All the prejudice things sort of cropped up after the Taiwanese came."

In response to a question on our 1990 exit poll, "What is the greatest problem facing people in Monterey Park," an elderly Nisei woman who had lived in Monterey Park for 33 years explained that the Chinese spoiled what the Japanese Americans had achieved in terms of acceptance by whites:

> The biggest problem today is rude people from the old country behaving and driving cars the way they used to in the Orient. We Americans of Oriental ancestry worked hard to be accepted by the Caucasian majority. This is being ruined by many, not all, of the immigrants' antisocial behavior.

A new, unacceptable stereotype of the rude Asian was replacing the acceptable stereotype of the quiet, unassuming Asian. Since Anglos and Latinos generally could not distinguish one Asian from another, resentment against Chinese immigrants also affected established Japanese and Chinese Americans. They called it getting the "Asian flack." The flack ranged from racial slurs to hate crimes, which the Los Angeles County Human Relations Commission reported to be on the rise.

The slurs were common enough to be part of everyday life and discourse, dividing Asians from non-Asians and from each other. The stereotypes even crept into jokes, as internalized racism. A Japanese American reported that his wife jokingly calls him a "dumb Chinaman" whenever he makes a foolish move in traffic. Japanese and Chinese Americans have been direct victims of scapegoating by non-Asian residents. Every Asian American we interviewed had stories to tell. A Nisei woman reported that, minding her own business in a fabric store, she was suddenly assaulted by "a blond, blue-eyed Caucasian lady" who twisted her arm and fled while shouting, "Go back to China where you came from." The victim wore a cast on her wrist for a month. She did not pursue her attacker because "it might make things worse."[21]

Some established Chinese Americans also experienced the anti-immigrant backlash, as a 30-thirty-year old resident explained:

> We get this Asian flack from the upper-class Asians here. They flaunt their money and drive around in their Mercedes. Now, all Asians look alike and so they [non-Asians] think every Asian they see is rich. I am second-generation, but they don't see the difference.
>
> Here's a good example. My girlfriend, who is also Chinese American, and I were in Hughes Market. And there were these two Anglos in their fifties next to us. You know that one looked at us, then turned to the other and said, "They are even taking over this area." They didn't even lower their voices or try to hide what they were saying. Now, how did they know if we spoke English or not?

Leland Saito, a member of our research team and a Yonsei, or fourth-generation Japanese American, encountered an even more hostile reaction from an Anglo male sitting at the bar in the local American Legion Hall:

> I stopped, turned around, and told him my name, mentioned that I lived in Montebello and was a student at UCLA. He said that it was a good school "before all you people started going there. It's just like Monterey Park." I asked him what did he mean by that? He said that UCLA must be 90 percent Chinese. Then, when I told him that I was Japanese, he replied, "I killed my first one in 1942." But later, when he was talking to the bartender about the Nisei veterans who used the hall, he said that Nisei were OK because they were born here.

Racial slights coexisting with stereotyped images of "model minorities" have long been part of growing up Asian American in the United States, but the new immigration and the "yellow backlash" have caused a particular crisis for established and American-born Japanese and Asian Americans. The balance of ethnic forces and attitudes that had created and sustained patterns of survival were no longer present. In response to these changes, Japanese and Chinese Americans were forced to reaffirm or renegotiate their ethnic and American identities. As with Mexican Americans, they could become more American and nativist (siding with established residents as Americans against newcomers), more ethnic (Japanese American, Chinese American, or Asian American), or more ambivalent, developing flexible identities suitable to their different relations in a complex community.

American-born, English-speaking, and elderly Japanese Americans shared many of the concerns of Anglos when it came to defending American identity against ethnic divisions. Many in both groups complained about Chinese signs and language. According to our exit poll of 1990, the majority of Anglos and Japanese Americans were against government support for bilingual education.

Some Japanese chose to distinguish themselves from the newcomers. A Nisei man explained his position in an interview:

> Some stranger who lives on the other side of Monterey Park sees me and figures that I'm Chinese, and that is kind of a bad thing for us because I don't want them to think that I'm Chinese. First of all, I think that we can speak English a lot better than the Chinese. Overall, scholastically, we're as good as they are. And I think we probably behave better in public. We're not boisterous and pushy in public. I mean you don't see a Japanese person crowding in line or talking at the top of his voice. [Laughing] I think I'm going to go into business and make a big button, like the ones they had during World War II, which said, "I'm Chinese, not a Jap." My button will say, "I'm Japanese, not Chinese."

A few Nisei sided with the nativism espoused by Barry Hatch and Frank Acuri, convinced that they were Americans first and ethnic second, and that status should be determined by merit rather than ethnicity. They found it difficult to explain away the anti-Asian outbursts of their white political allies. One evasion was to appeal to the social position, personality, or even the ethnicity of the nativist leaders: "I know Barry Hatch. He's a schoolteacher and can't be prejudiced." "Frank Arcuri? He was misinterpreted. He's just a loud-mouthed Italian who doesn't express himself the way he wanted. What he meant is that the Chinese should speak English, if possible, in public places." Another strategy was to argue that racism was a false charge trumped up by developers against the patriotic leaders of Official English and slow growth.

Thus, some Japanese Americans looked upon the Chinese newcomers as a threat to the respect and ethnic harmony that they had achieved and, more broadly, a threat to their American identity. This was not the typical response of their leaders in the professional and business community, who were more likely to see the newcomers as an economic and political resource for the Asian community as a whole. In an interview, a prominent Japanese American businessman dismissed the familiar complaints about the Chinese and looked pragmatically to the future:

> I think the only complaint that I hear from most residents and from native-born Japanese and Chinese is about traffic congestion and the

> rudeness of the immigrants in the supermarket and that they're pushy. Well, you know, they come from a country where there's a billion people. You've got to push your way around—otherwise you're not going to get anyplace. You're going to be sitting in the rear of the bus every time. So I guess they resolved that from a different culture. So I have probably a different attitude from most people. I don't resent anybody, unless they do something to me, and I, you know, have always been a business-oriented person, so I always appreciate population, because population is our business. Without population we're going to have a hell of a time selling things.

Japanese Americans, Chinese Americans, and Asian immigrants have shown the ability to unite behind selected Asian candidates. A large majority of Japanese Americans, regardless of their often critical views of Chinese newcomers and Chinese-language signs, voted for Chinese candidates in the 1988 and 1990 Monterey Park elections, thereby seizing the historical opportunity to expand Asian representation. The majority also cast their votes to defeat Hatch. While the older Nisei left town or continued to keep a low political profile, younger Japanese Americans stressed their Asian American identity by joining with other Asians to form the West San Gabriel Valley Asian Pacific Democratic Club. Like the newly established chapter of LULAC, the Democratic club worked for ethnic power through interethnic alliances around progressive candidates and issues.

With the arrival of Chinese immigrants, Japanese Americans lost their position of dominance in the local Asian community. Unlike Mexican Americans, they lacked the numbers to achieve power and representation as Japanese Americans. As part of an expanding Asian population in a predominantly Latino area, perhaps the best response was to see the dramatic increase in Chinese as a potential resource for Asian American power and to form alliances with Latinos on this basis. The fundamental ambivalence and flexibility of middle-class Japanese and Chinese American as well as Mexican American identities make this a possibility.

Today Monterey Park and the western San Gabriel Valley are a regional point and symbolic center for the development of Asian American politics. Monterey Park is the home of the parents of Michael Woo, a former member of the Los Angeles city council and a candidate for Mayor of Los Angeles in 1992. In 1990, March Fong Eu set up her campaign office in the city during her successful bid for reelection as California's State Treasurer. In 1994, Judy Chu, steeled in the battles of Monterey politics, ran for the California State Assembly.

Compared with the fairly homogeneous population of Mexican

Americans in Monterey Park and the western San Gabriel Valley, Chinese, Japanese, Vietnamese, Filipino, and Korean Americans have a more formidable task of building a common Asian identity. But that problem should not detract from the fact that the new immigration has decisively changed the political rules of the game for Asian Americans. Until recently, they lacked the numbers to exert a direct political influence. Japanese and Chinese Americans coming to Monterey Park after World War II had little choice but to accommodate to the local power structure. Today there are more options for Chinese and Asian power and self-determining ethnic and American identities.[22]

CHINESE IMMIGRANTS: BECOMING CHINESE AND AMERICAN

At a class in a local preschool for children of Chinese immigrants, the teacher asked his pupils, in Chinese, "How many of you are Chinese?" Two out of 20 raised their hands. Their peers objected, "Hey, you are Americans." Bowing to peer pressure, the 2 students decided that they were Americans after all, and lowered their hands. This story was passed around by concerned Taiwanese parents in the San Gabriel Valley in 1991.[23]

The effect of demographic change and diversity on the social identities of established Anglos, Latinos, and Asian Americans is only part of our story. The other concerns immigrants, and the evolution of their own ethnic and American identities through interactions within the very heterogeneous Chinese community and in reaction to nativists and ethnic groups in the established-resident community. Traditionally, research has emphasized the adaptation of newcomers to established residents. Here we emphasize also their interaction with residents and involvement in determining their own American identities.

The Crisis of Chinese Identities

Many established residents and newcomers to Monterey Park and parts of the San Gabriel Valley perceive the region as "so Chinese": a transplanted and self-contained world existing in the heart of suburban Los Angeles, which is, paradoxically, where middle-class people go to get away from the inner city with its Chinatowns and ethnic enclaves. For the monolingual newcomers, the elderly, and the sojourners, Monterey Park is in fact a Chinatown where they can keep their Chinese language and identity intact.

Maintaining an unquestioned identity is more difficult for residents affected by non-Chinese neighbors with very different ideas about space and language, developers who invade their suburban peace, and Americanized children. In his exemplary study of Chinese in Los Angeles, Charles Wong argued that traditional Chinatown identities, formed under the conditions of relative geographic concentration, ethnic homogeneity, continuity, and solidarity, have a taken-for-granted, essential, and unexamined character. In Monterey Park, under conditions of greater geographic dispersion, ethnic heterogeneity, discontinuity, and conflict, ethnic identities take on a more "problematic character and fluidity."[24]

Monterey Park is not a traditional Chinatown where people grow inward in response to exclusion and discrimination. It is a point of entry and outward mobility into ethnically mixed middle-class suburbs, a staging area rather than a place of retreat. Given their geographic convergence, Chinese immigrants from mainland China, Hong Kong, Taiwan, and Southeast Asia have greater opportunity for increased contact with each other, with immigrants from Vietnam, Korea, and elsewhere in Asia, and with established Anglos, Latinos, and Asian Americans. As an expanding part of the local middle and upper classes, moreover, Chinese newcomers have much greater flexibility in negotiating their ethnic and American identities than did the Latinos and Japanese Americans who preceded them.

Monterey Park and the surrounding San Gabriel Valley are historically unique crucibles for the formation of new Chinese, Chinese American, Asian American, and American identities. The possibilities are many and complex, ranging from traditional (the emphasis on being Chinese) to bicultural (being Chinese and American) to multicultural (being at the intersection of different cultures) to assimilated (being American). The options are wide, as are the possibilities for conflict between Chinese of different nations, generations, and perspectives.

Our understanding of these options was limited by the people interviewed and the situations observed. Given our focus on interactions between immigrants and established residents active in local political and civic affairs, the Chinese immigrants we describe are primarily bilingual, middle- or upper-middle-class business and professional people who cross the borders between old-timers and newcomers in their everyday lives.

These seasoned border-crossers consciously took on the role of interpreting what is Chinese and what is American. Many were biculturalists who liked to think they could pick and choose the best aspects of two cultures. A few were fatalistic assimilationists who saw Americanization as a zero-sum game wherein they would inevitably lose their Chineseness. In practice, Chinese, Chinese American, and Asian American identities were not solely determined or chosen, but were fashioned through co-ethnic and interethnic interactions in specific situations.

Co-Ethnic Interpretations of Fitting In

For newcomers with limited English and economic and family ties within the immigrant community, the claims to ethnic and American identity are interpreted through many different agents who mediate and negotiate relations between newcomers and established residents.

There are two major Chinese (Taiwanese) newspapers in Monterey Park, and their reporters are familiar figures to immigrants and established residents at most important public and political events. Their articles both report and editorialize the meaning of events in terms of Chinese interests. The result is sometimes a lesson in becoming American.

The same instructive style was visible in the Chinese articles that appeared in a book written by local residents to commemorate the seventy-fifth anniversary of Monterey Park. The English- and Spanish-language articles tended to convey an upbeat boosterism. Several Anglos who participated in the project were suspicious about what the Chinese had actually written, since not all their articles had been translated. They would be surprised to know that the major Chinese article, "Monterey Park: Looking to the Future," actually contained recommendations on how to be better Americans. The authors urged the Chinese, "who will be the pivotal population of the future, to adjust to the environment and needs of the time; contribute money and hard work; energetically take part in community service, and wash away the bad image of being indifferent about community affairs."[25]

The interpretation of America and American customs also occurs regularly in churches and service organizations. Playing the role of middlemen and -women, leaders told us that they would sometimes intervene to suppress cultural traits that might seem strange in the United States. For example, Dr. Frances Wu, the Director of the Golden Age Manor, an apartment complex for elderly Chinese people, explained that she tells the residents, "Don't follow the Chinese custom of leaving your shoes outside your door." More subtly, new customs were learned through the organization of the facility, which was modeled after American retirement homes. Likewise, former Councilman Kiang told us that he had advised managers of Chinese supermarkets to clean up the throw-away newspapers that clutter their entrances, and retailers to abandon the Chinese custom of displaying wares on racks outside their stores.

Several prominent Chinese businessmen claim that they consciously use civic organizations like the Chamber of Commerce, Kiwanis Club, and Rotary Club to socialize immigrants to American ways. A leader of the predominantly Chinese Monterey Park Kiwanis Club explained his theory of the function of civic clubs: "Service groups instead of kinship offer Americans the basic supports. Chinese always go to their family networks, so they don't regard social groups as important like Americans do. For Americans to take you as one of them, you need to take part in these clubs." His club tried to teach the importance of volunteering and to instill patriotism. The pledge of allegiance, the invocations, and the stress on service, as well as the organization of the meeting itself, were interpreted as a way of acquainting Chinese with American practices. In an interview, he said:

> A lot of old residents have complained about Chinese to me. They said, Chinese hardly ever volunteer for service in the community. They just care about themselves and don't care about the neighborhood. In order to change the image of Chinese in old residents' mind, we need to join social service groups and work together with old residents to pursue the same goal—that is, the well-being of the community.[26]

In theory, the civic clubs sanction accommodation to America as defined by established residents. But, in practice, the process of Americanization through the mediation of established Chinese residents has more complex outcomes. In the case of the service clubs, although the formal business is conducted in accented English, the informal interaction, the making of connections and deals, is conducted in Mandarin or Cantonese. Rather than create networks between established residents and immigrants, a more obvious function of the service clubs is to create solidarity and a sense of being Chinese.

Perhaps in order to become American or Chinese American, the heterogeneous population of immigrants must first become *Chinese,* rather than Taiwanese, mainlanders, and so on. Family ties and a multitude of organizations specific to nationality reinforce particular linguistic, cultural, and regional identities. By contrast, civic organizations, like the Kiwanis Club, foster a Pan-Chinese identity, at least in the arenas where culturally diverse business and professional people come into contact with each other and established residents.

Defining What Is American

In more confrontational and political situations, immigrants have constructed their own dynamic, future-oriented versions of America and American identities in opposition to the more static, past-oriented versions of nativists. For the nativist fringe of the growth-control and Official English movements, America is a tradition, a fixed set of rules for assimilating and containing immigrants. Their warning to immigrants is: "America, adapt to it, or leave it."

In an interview, a Chinese immigrant from Southeast Asia, a doctor trained in Los Angeles, countered with his own slogan: "I think the old-timers have to be educated to be made aware of what America is. It should be written in bold letters: 'We will continue to have immigrants. This is America, and if you don't like it, don't live here.'"

The doctor thus legitimated his own claim to being American as a hard-working immigrant, a participant in the revitalizing cycles of immigration, diversity, and change—precisely the qualities nativists associate with the disintegration of America. Reflecting on the discrimination against Chinese in Southeast Asia, he argued that the greatest danger for America would be to become nationalistic, to hinder ethnic diversity, and stop the process of change:

> I think that the founding fathers must have had the dynamic definition of American in their minds, that America should never cease to grow. When you stop growing and become nationalistic, when you say we have grown and this is how we are going to be, and now we are going to safeguard our borders, push everybody out, treat everybody else differently—that's the beginning of the downfall of every nation.[27]

At the end of the twentieth century, an ever-narrowing nationalism may well be the downfall of all multiethnic nations. The doctor hoped that the United States would be the exception, a place where the newcomers are the true bearers of the American tradition, not the old-timers who want to keep them out.

This definition of America fostered a respect for differences, including the use of a language other than English. In Monterey Park, the American value of diversity was defended in the local fight against "English Only." When immigrant business and professional people formed the Chinese Civil Rights and Education Association in 1989 to oppose restrictions on Chinese business signs, progressive Asian American lawyers came to their defense and provided them with legal weapons. The plan was to take the language battle to the courts and argue that signage restrictions were a violation of freedom of speech and First Amendment rights.

The sign struggle was an interesting example of how Chinese immigrants used the Constitution and legal system to legitimate their claim that a bilingual identity was an American right. It was also an example of the formation and legitimation of a self-determining Chinese American identity through an unlikely alliance between conservative Chinese professional and businesspeople and progressive Asian Americans who had developed their vision of America in the civil rights movement. Thus, a tradition of social justice was extended from the poor and minorities to defend the principle of diversity for affluent newcomers.

That the legal battle was a lesson in Americanism did not escape the observation of a Chinese middleman. At a meeting to consider suing the city over its sign restrictions, he remarked:

> To sue the city is a process of educating Chinese to be Americans. Through this event, people are going to be taught what civil rights are, how they can fight for them in cases of repression. This is an invaluable lesson for Chinese who want to grasp the American spirit. This is what America is about.

In Monterey Park, the Chinese organization did not sue the city, and the council decided not to alter existing signage practices. It was a victory for a more culturally diverse definition of American identity. Elsewhere in the western San Gabriel Valley, Chinese sometimes did and sometimes did not seize upon language to defend this interpretation. In Pomona, for example, Chinese hired their own lawyer to sue the city, and the courts declared sign restrictions unconstitutional. In San Marino, the most affluent suburb in the region, a real estate office's Chinese sign was stolen eight times. When the owner finally gave up and put out an English sign, he received many complaints from his Chinese customers, not because they needed a Chinese sign to find the office, but because they felt that he was giving up Chinese culture. He put the Chinese sign back.

In Arcadia, another affluent suburb, however, Chinese leaders seemed reluctant to confront established residents on the issue of language. They preferred negotiation to litigation. Some immigrants saw the fight to maintain Chinese signs as unnecessarily divisive and culturally and economically backward. A prominent developer, a Chinese immigrant and American citizen, said:

> I think Chinese businessmen are stupid to let old residents make use of the signage issue to attack them. Only in Chinatowns—and I wouldn't want Monterey Park to become one of them—in those tourist hot spots is there a need for Chinese signs, and the women had better bind their feet and the men have their queues. No, I don't want to see this city become a second Chinatown. There is a limited Chinese population. We need Chinese as well as American customers to enlarge our market.

The developer's argument brings us to another way in which Chinese immigrants defended their claim to be true Americans. Chinese developers defended diversity and self-determination against slow-growth restrictions by invoking the American value of free enterprise, the capitalist's right to use and invest his own property. At a public forum in 1987 on the future of Monterey Park, a Chinese developer criticized the slow-growth activists:

> In China, after I built a hotel, the government said I was blocking a view and made me remove one story. Planning limits developers in China. But here it's supposed to be "freedom and justice for all." That's why I prefer the United States to China. But there are people in Monterey Park who want to put restrictions on inalienable property rights. I hadn't expected this in the U.S. It's what they do in China and did to the Jews in Germany.

Another Chinese businessman used a different version of America to legitimate his opposition to local nationalism:

> In Monterey Park there are many people, like Barry Hatch, who care too much about American identity. Look at West Los Angeles [a very white, liberal, and wealthy part of town]. People there don't care that much about American identity. I prefer having an international mind. Your research should go more deeply into the international factors that are affecting people's lives in Monterey Park.

He had a point. The growth of a Pacific Rim economy could favor international, as opposed to more chauvinistic, American identities. Like the developer, some of the new immigrants were part of a growing trans-Pacific professional and entrepreneurial class. In Monterey Park and Los Angeles, their lives and networks spanned and intersected a Pacific Rim economy.[28] International identities became possible through these practical activities and were being presented as alternatives to the more parochial and exclusionary definitions of America and Americans.

Thus, in opposition to resurgent nativism, some of the more affluent newcomers were legitimating their dynamic and self-determining identities on the basis of selected American values (immigration, diversity, First Amendment rights, free enterprise) and the emergence of a more ethnically diverse and globalized society. At least in Monterey Park, they have been fairly successful. There are still Chinese signs on businesses; many Chinese books are in the library; Chinese is increasingly used in city and local election material; and symbols of Chinese culture are present at major public events and festivals.

The Generational Struggle to Maintain Chinese Language and Identity

If immigrant elites were sometimes winning the battle for maintaining, reproducing, and legitimizing a Chinese cultural identity in public places, they could still lose the battle at home. If the history of language loss is any guide to the future, then pressure on the second generation to succeed in American society will undermine the best-laid plans for retaining Chinese, a powerful symbol of ethnic identity.[29]

Immigrants tend to use language retention as the dividing line between Chinese and Chinese American identities. From this perspective, Councilwoman Chu is American or Asian American because she cannot speak Chinese fluently, while Councilman Kiang is clearly Chinese, since he speaks several dialects.

The label "American" may also extend to immigrants who have not encouraged their children to retain Chinese language and culture. For example, in an interview, Mrs. Wu, an immigrant, claimed that Mrs. Peng, another immigrant, was an American because at her house "they speak English and eat hamburgers."

The critic was really self-critical. She had lived in Monterey Park for more than 20 years and deeply regretted the fact that she had not encouraged her children to speak Chinese. Contrary to the fears of conservatives about the assault on English, immigrants bent on mobility for themselves and their children strongly support learning English, but often regret the loss of Chinese.

A conversation overheard by a field worker at a banquet given by the Taiwanese American Citizens League reveals the ongoing generational struggle over retaining elements of Chinese culture:

> *A recent immigrant woman:* I think it is cruel to make children identify with the mother culture. They need to go out and compete with Americans and have the same mentality.
>
> *An elderly male resident of 20 years:* When I first got here, I thought the same way as you do. At that time, I was trying to succeed in this society and hoped that my children would become American as soon as possible. This is the worst thing I have ever done in my lifetime! One of my children finally learned Chinese in his undergraduate career at Stanford. I really feel sorry for my other two children. [Other older immigrants at the table agree].
>
> *Another immigrant:* The longer you live here, the more eager you are to search for your roots.[30]

In an interview, a resident of Monterey Park who emigrated from Taiwan 15 years ago expressed her own ambivalent feelings about being Americanized:

> I know that I am viewed as an outsider and will be viewed this way forever. Especially in this city, all the Orientals seem to bear a shameful label. I found it's almost impossible for me to become an American. I can never talk like them, behave like them, and I am not trying to. As to my children, I don't object to their being Americanized, because they must survive and succeed in American society. They are not immigrants, and they must compete like everybody else for any possible opportunity. Once my elder son who is studying

> engineering at the University of California, San Diego, told me that I can't expect him to be Chinese, because he actually is foreign to anything Chinese. To him, the most urgent thing to do is to make sure people don't take him for a foreigner and treat him in a different way. He hasn't started to appreciate his heritage, and I can't blame him. When children know how to judge things based on a global perspective, they will look at their parents' origins more fairly.[31]

If some children of immigrants are eagerly rejecting their Chineseness, some exclusively English-speaking Chinese are acquiring a global perspective and bemoan their loss of language and culture as the unfortunate cost of repressive Americanization. A successful young Chinese-born American explains how he lost Chinese some 25 years ago in Los Angeles:

> Until I was four and one-half years old, I couldn't speak English. And now I can't speak Chinese. Today the rules have changed, specifically in places like Monterey Park where there's a greater number of Chinese, more pride, less pressure to shed this language shackle and get into the mainstream as quickly as possible. We were the only Chinese family on the block. When I was six or seven years old, my mom was going to adult school to learn English. She said, "I don't want you guys to speak Chinese to me ever again so I can learn English." And that was it.[32]

Indeed, until recently there were few professional rewards for knowing Chinese. A China-born lawyer raised in the United States explained the situation in the public schools two decades ago:

> I took three or four years of French and two years of German and would never have gotten credit for Chinese, so now I can't even speak Chinese. I can't speak Spanish either, because they would not let me take Spanish in high school. They said, Take French—that's relevant to your graduate work. I said, Show me a book that's in French or German, but that, you know, was in the seventies, and that's the way it was then.[33]

Today, in reaction to the new Chinese immigration and the Official English movement, politically active members of the second and third generations may not speak Chinese, but they are advocating bilingualism and language maintenance. The development of a multicultural Pacific Rim society favors this position. However, for immigrants who are not truly transnational in their lives and livelihoods, the pressure for mobility outside the immigrant community does not encourage the maintenance of global and bicultural identities.

Forging Identity in Relation to Other Ethnic and Immigrant Groups

For children of immigrants, mobility is the primary agent of Americanization. For some, the message is: "If you want to be an acceptable American, speak English, don't dress like a foreigner, don't be a freeloader, and distinguish yourself from inferior ethnic groups." Succumbing to these pressures, several of our younger respondents were much less interested in preserving their cultural heritage than fitting in at the highest ranks of the American ethnic and class hierarchies.

One strategy was to identify themselves in the eyes of white Americans as good immigrants, distinct from bad immigrants and low-achieving ethnic Americans. For example, a Taiwanese student complained that refugees pull down the image of Asian immigrants in American eyes:

> You should come to my school [Pasadena City College] to see the huge number of Southeast Asian refugees. Their clothes look so sloppy that I am ashamed to be one of the Orientals. They destroy the good image of Asian immigrants. Sometimes I think, No wonder Americans in my school look down upon Asian students, because those Southeast Asian students have turned P.C.C into a refugee camp.

Similarly, an immigrant from mainland China, a woman who has lived in Monterey Park for five years, remarked that the situation for Chinese is worse in Los Angeles than in some other areas of the country because of the large number of refugees:

> Before we moved to Monterey Park, we had lived in North Carolina for ten years. There, Asian immigrants are well respected, and Americans treat us very kindly. But here, in L.A., Americans are tough on immigrants. They don't pay respect to the achievement of immigrants. Do you know why it is the case? Because we have a lot of Southeast Asian refugees in this area; they are very poor and become a burden on American people. So Americans see us Asian immigrants as the source of trouble.

Another Chinese immigrant invoked a racial stereotype of African Americans to argue for the superiority of Chinese in the ethnic hierarchy: "Blacks have been in this country for more than one hundred years, and they are still in the bottom of the society. They should feel ashamed for this. We Chinese work hard to become successful in much shorter time."[34] There are in fact very few African Americans in Monterey Park or the San Gabriel Valley. Racial and ethnic stereotyping is more likely to be directed against Latinos and, occasionally, at Anglos and Americans in general, who are faulted for not working hard enough and letting the country slip economically and culturally in face of international competition. Ironically, as other nations and ethnic groups rise in the global economy, Americans can fall victim to the very cultural and racial stereotypes that they have sometimes used to explain the situation of "less developed" nations.

Thus, one strategy for acquiring a good identity is to distance oneself from bad immigrants and ethnic groups or even lazy Americans. In these cases, the result is a tendency to explain status in terms of presumed racial and ethnic characteristics rather than social and economic conditions. Those immigrants who take these conditions into account are more open to developing a multiethnic perspective by finding common cause with American ethnic groups in a struggle against shared problems.

We have seen evidence of this in local politics. Exit poll data indicate that although Mexican Americans and Chinese Americans generally favor their own ethnic candidates on the Monterey Park city council, they will vote across ethnic lines for specific candidates and issues. In the elections of 1990 and 1994, for example, the second most favored candidate of Chinese voters, immigrants as well as American-born, was Fred Balderrama, an established Mexican American who had business relations with all ethnic groups. One major Chinese newspaper even identified Balderrama as a "friend of the Chinese."[35]

Similarly, in 1988 and 1992 Mexican Americans gave strong support to Judy Chu, a native-born Chinese American who had stressed her ties to established residents. Moreover, our polls showed that Chinese immigrants and Latino residents tended to line up together on certain issues—favoring bilingual education and rejecting a gambling parlor in Monterey Park.

Nevertheless, many instances of disagreement and conflict between Latinos and Chinese immigrants reinforce divisions. For example, tensions between Asian newcomers and Latino students and tensions between their parents have become more frequent in local high schools. Finding a common identity under these conditions requires political struggle.

In 1992, in reaction to fights at San Gabriel High School, leaders from LULAC and the Chinese PTA brought parents together to exchange views and work out a common strategy to deal with the problem of violence in their school. Rather than blame each other for tensions, they took the problem to the high school, which had evaded its own responsibility. Time will tell whether the struggle around shared problems will lead to shared identities for Chinese and Mexican Americans as people of color confronting Anglo-dominated institutions.

THE RECONSTRUCTION OF ETHNIC AND AMERICAN IDENTITIES

In an ethnically mixed city where at least 51 percent of the population is foreign-born, residents live at the intersection of unstable ethnic boundaries. Their ethnic and American identities are shaped by boundary crossings and by the complicated process of finding a place within a shifting hierarchy of power and privilege. The process is interactive: Chinese immigrants defining themselves in relation to Anglos, Latinos, and established Asian Americans; established residents seeing themselves in relation to newcomers. The process is situational: Latinos and Japanese Americans sometimes bonding with Anglos in opposition to newcomers, but also reacting to Anglo nativism by becoming more ethnic in their political choices; unhyphenated Americans, confronting their minoritization, slowly and reluctantly redefining themselves as Anglos and European Americans; Chinese immigrants, depending on the circumstances, identifying themselves by place of birth, by country of last residence, or as Chinese, Chinese Americans, or just plain Americans.

At this time, in middle-class Monterey Park, the meaning of ethnic and American identity is an open question. In a sense, everyone, including the Anglo, is becoming a hyphenated American. One consequence has been increased division and conflict. However, the preoccupation with difference has also led to the construction of more inclusive and diverse definitions of unity. In the next chapter, we describe that process in situations where residents come together to display their identities as Americans.

Chapter 9
NEGOTIATING A CULTURE OF DIVERSITY

"What's the Chinese Lion's Dance doing in our Cinco de Mayo?"
—Heard during the Cinco de Mayo celebration in Barnes Park, 1989

THE CRISIS of identity in Monterey Park may be extreme, but it is a problem faced generally by Angelinos and other Americans who live in territory internationalized by immigration. One aspect of this crisis is uncertainty about the meaning of ethnicity; another is resisting or asserting the ethnic component of American culture and power.

Nativists use public occasions to contain ethnic and cultural diversity by affirming Anglo or European symbols of America. Ethnic groups seize the moment to assert their positive identities. They want cultural as well as political inclusion, a collective recognition of their distinctive Americanness. Multiculturalists seek ways of linking the differences together in a new pattern of unity. The clash of perspectives can result in an outdated replay of the mythical good old days, a juxtaposition of separate ethnic traditions, or a new interpretation of *e pluribus unum*.

Whatever the outcome, festivals, public events, and public spaces are lively sites for observing the political construction of the culture of diversity. The process involves resistance, accommodation, and change. In Monterey Park, nativists are finding their efforts restricted by their lack of numbers and transformed by the diversity surrounding them. In recent years, the preferred alternative is to mix cultures at national and local holidays, while pledging allegiance to "one nation, indivisible, under God." The barrage of media attention at any sign of ethnic conflict has made residents sensitive to their differences, but also determined to stress the things that hold them together in diversity.

"A STROLL DOWN MEMORY LANE"

Although a numerical minority, Anglos, as the self-appointed bearers of American tradition, continue to exert a strong influence on the definition of historical and patriotic events. Their more nationalist members fight to impose their vision of America in public spaces—City Hall, the library, the parks—and at civic festivals—like the Fourth of July and the Play Days that commemorate the founding of the city. Their vision is of national unity purged of ethnic and foreign references, patriotism defined by loyalty to the Constitution, the Founding Fathers, the Flag, God, the Past, and English. But given the current ethnic composition of the community, that vision can no longer be sustained.

In 1989, the theme for the week-long celebration of the city's founding was "A Stroll Down Memory Lane." That year Councilman Barry Hatch proposed that the city sponsor old-fashioned "block parties." Old-timers say that years ago, on every Fourth of July streets were closed and neighbors brought out tables, chairs, and food and celebrated until it was time to set off fireworks. It is in that real or imagined tradition that Councilman Hatch promoted block parties as a patriotic, small-town build-up to celebrating the founding of the city and the Fourth of July.

Field researcher Jose Calderon attended the block party in Hatch's own neighborhood. The event took place at the small Sierra Vista Park, directly across the street from a large Chinese retirement complex. Although the complex was built and run in the American style, the tiled roof gives it a very Chinese appearance, especially in the eyes of non-Chinese locals. Calderon's notes describe a happening that did not go exactly as Hatch planned it. Few Anglos were present. The people who did attend transformed the Anglo block party into a sneak preview of Cinco de Mayo for Chinese immigrants.

> As the Mark Keppel High School band began to play [the high school is now predominantly Asian], I looked around briefly at who had come to the party. To the right of the little recreation center, there were about four rows of folding chairs filled with some 25 elderly Chinese. About fifteen steps away, directly in front of the serving tables, there was another group of elderly Chinese sitting in the shade of a tree and near a picnic table. Attached to the tree was a banner with a round symbol and Chinese characters on it. I immediately thought, what does that banner represent? Wait until Barry Hatch sees this. To the left of the recreation center some young people, mostly Latinos, were playing baseball as their parents watched. The only Anglo person present in the entire area was the Director of the city's Recreation Department.
>
> When the band finished, David Barron, a Latino and the City Clerk, went to a microphone set up on a table and thanked everyone for coming. He introduced the Monterey Park queen and princesses, who are selected every year to represent the city at public events.

Interestingly, they wished everyone a "Happy Cinco de Mayo." I thought to myself, they are turning this into a Cinco de Mayo event. Someone is confused. I looked around for Barry Hatch, but he was nowhere in sight, although he lives nearby on Orange Avenue.

Next Barron asked me to come up front and talk about the Cinco de Mayo event scheduled for the next day. At the microphone, I presented the agenda for the next day's activities and, seeing the character of the audience, I especially gave a plug to the Chinese Lion Dance. I mentioned that tomorrow will be the first day that the Cinco de Mayo committee has made an effort to involve the Chinese culture by inviting the Chinese Lion dancers to perform. This is part of an effort to pull our communities together. Even as I spoke, I did not know that the majority of people who were there did not understand a word I was saying.

After I was done speaking, I began to pass out leaflets on the Cinco de Mayo event to everyone who was there. When I gave leaflets to the Chinese, they accepted it humbly as though I was doing a wonderful act. Some bowed, shook my hand, smiled, reached out toward me, patted me on the shoulder. But, hard as I tried, it seemed like they didn't really understand what the leaflet was all about. One older Chinese man accidentally took the leaflet upside down and shook his head in approval (while acting like he was reading it). I dared not point out to him that he was looking at it upside down.

When I was done passing out leaflets, Barron announced that everyone could eat in a few minutes, and began to pull out box after box of hot dogs. Last year there had been a big battle over what type of American food should dominate at the Fourth of July. Of course, Barry Hatch's choice was "hot dogs."

As the hot dogs began to cook, an elderly Chinese man walked toward me, grabbed me by the arm, and pointed me in the direction of the picnic table where a number of Chinese were sitting near their banner. I went over there and saw that they had brought boxes of Chinese food. They pulled me to the table and gave me an entire plate full. They circled round, and I kept saying, "Thank you. Thank you." They kept shaking their heads, over and over, as though in appreciation.

I went back to serving hot dogs. The baseball players came and devoured them, while the Chinese mostly ate their own food. Barry Hatch never showed up to attend his lesson in Americanism. Overall, it was a good event—but certainly not what Hatch had dreamed of. Rather than "A Stroll Down Memory Lane," the theme of the block party was a stroll down the lane of tomorrow.[1]

The mere fact that the town is first of all Asian and second Latino turned around an effort at assimilation and containment.

DOING HISTORY

In recent years, coincident with the decline in the Anglo population and the rise of Asian Americans, the Monterey Park Historical Society has enjoyed a renaissance. Its members, predominantly white old-timers, have volunteered and raised funds to revitalize the city's museum of local history.

Located in Garvey Ranch Park, on property once owned by an Irish immigrant who rose from rags to riches as a rancher and land developer in the 1880s, the museum is a careful reconstruction of the good old days: a turn-of-the-century "housekeeping" room with artifacts from a Monterey Park living room, kitchen, and bedroom; a "California Room" devoted to the early Indian and mission history of the region and state.

Here history is constructed and told primarily from a white viewpoint, using the memories and voices of those who are becoming history, but not before leaving proud evidence of their lives in a city that is no longer Anglo. Models of missions and tributes to defeated Indians are acceptable components of that history, along with artifacts of the disappearing white majority, but there are no prominent displays about the Latinos and Asians who have lived in Monterey Park. They will have to carry on the concept of the museum by including their own excluded history.

Anglo solidarity was invoked in 1989 by the celebration of a local heroine and entrepreneur, Laura Scudder. On a warm Sunday afternoon, some 150 mostly white residents crowded into a stuffy room in the museum to view a 60-minute documentary about her life (1881–1959). The event reenacted white history. The message was one of historical discontinuity and continuity.

In spite of the heat, the audience sat through the speeches and watched the documentary with fascination: Laura's childhood in Philadelphia, a desire to become a doctor, thwarted by poverty, her nursing degree, her marriage to Scudder, 20 years older and not very ambitious, their journey to Ukiah, California, where the enterprising Laura operated a restaurant and got a law degree, the move (in 1920) to Monterey Park, the two-acre ranch, the filling station, and then her famous potato chip, peanut butter, and mayonnaise business.

After the film there were testimonials from the Scudder clan and old-timers whose families had known or worked for Laura. One woman began to cry as she talked about her father's getting a franchise to sell Scudder's products. The event was a moving tribute to the city's Anglo past. It spoke to established residents' nostalgia and values—the story of a woman making it in the promised land through hard work and the old-fashioned virtues of integrity and concern for her employees and community. For some old-timers, Scudder was a much needed white hero in a city being bought by immigrants with scant concern for its past.

The celebration also had a more universal message, particularly for women and immigrants. The event was put on mainly by women, who had become increasingly active in local politics. The master of ceremonies was former Councilwoman Louise Davis, and the current councilwomen, Betty Couch and Judy Chu, were principal speakers. Davis spoke for them all when she said: "I admire Laura Scudder as a woman. I can sympathize with her; as a former Mayor and now Treasurer of Monterey Park, I've been out in the old-boys' network too."

The Scudder story was also about the newcomer who comes to Monterey Park to make it. She brought with her solidly middle-class values and some cash; she had brains; and she worked hard. But were her white American values and experience really so different from those of the new Asian immigrants? Maybe some of the non-Anglos in the audience did not think so—the young Latino who got the Scudder award for entrepreneurship, the Asian American Boy Scouts who directed parking, the young Asian American and Latina women who modeled dresses from the 1920s. These immigrants and minorities could understand the old values, and they were the future. Besides, there were no longer enough Anglo kids to receive awards of excellence and help the Anglos perform their history.

Some of the old-timers could not see continuity in the historical change. During the intermission, an elderly white woman with a little red, white, and blue rhinestone flag pinned on her lapel approached a researcher with a challenge: "We are really counting on you to tell our story." She went on to tell her own story in a torrent of fearful words. "One of them"—an Asian—had hit her with a bike in the park, and she had been frightened by hostile arms lurching out from the morning mist (6:30 Tai Chi exercises). "They have to learn to obey our laws. I have friends among their people, but they must obey the law."

Cornering the same researcher at the punch bowl, a local historian who had lived in the community all of his seventy-plus years had a different take on the past and present:

> I feel the area's doing well. What are people complaining about? I have Vietnamese, Chinese, and other neighbors. I love Asian people. Used to play with Japanese kids when I was growing up. They had strawberry patches in the neighborhood. Before the changes in the seventies, I had trouble with my Anglo neighbors. People always in

> trouble with the law. Today my Asian neighbors are quiet and law-abiding. What could be better than that? I'm a historian, and I like to talk about the past. I can see two Monterey Parks. I can see Coyote Canyon in the thirties. People were often robbed there. Kids were hazed by making them ride their bikes through the canyon at night. They would be stopped and stripped. Today Cayote Canyon is congested Monterey Pass Road. I don't know about the future, but I see the past and live in the present. The only problem is that the changes came too fast in Monterey Park. I don't agree with all this nostalgia for the past. It was never like they say it was. Imagine people having nostalgia for the Depression. It was terrible![2]

The members and friends of the Monterey Park Historical Society do a fine job of preserving and promoting the city's past. They have also been challenged and changed by the present. Several years after the Scudder event, the patriot with the little American flag and fearful tales of violent immigrants could be found celebrating the inauguration of Samuel Kiang. As for the Historical Society, Asians and Latinos are now becoming part of the community's history. The elderly white docents of the museum conduct many tours for Asian children, who are the majority in the local schools. Asian and Latino youths have worked in the museum. In the early 1990s, the Historical Society cooperated closely with Timothy Fong, a young Asian American scholar, to collect oral histories. The emphasis was on the white old-timers. However, of the 32 transcribed interviews available in the city's library, 7 were with Chinese immigrants, 3 with Latinos, and 2 with Japanese Americans.

MAKING A CULTURE OF DIVERSITY AT PUBLIC FESTIVALS

Resistance can turn to inclusion, especially when diverse groups consciously come together to negotiate a civic and American culture. This happens during the preparation of public festivals at Barnes Park, itself a visible testimony to demographic and cultural change. The park is a postcard-perfect representation of small-town Middle America: stretches of grass and trees, a baseball diamond, a swimming pool, tennis courts, sandboxes and swings, a covered picnic area built by the local Lions Club, and a band shell, which is the focus of entertainment and patriotic speeches. Designed according to Anglo-American tastes of yesterday, today the park is inhabited primarily by Asians and Latinos. The set remains the same, but the players now bear the faces of the world.

Mornings in the park begin quietly, with Chinese newcomers executing the graceful motions of Tai Chi. By mid-morning, Chinese, Vietnamese, and Latino mothers bring their young and watch them play together. Later in the afternoon the baseball fields are loud with the shouts of teenage Asians, Latinos, and a few whites. Early evening can bring the shrill sounds of the local Chinese opera from an open door of City Hall's community room.

The pace and the traffic pick up on the weekends, when Latino families from poorer areas east and south of the town bring their families for picnics in what is considered a relatively crime-free spot. The park is crowded during patriotic and ethnic festivals, prime time to observe interaction between newcomers and established residents and spectacles of unity and cultural diversity.

In recent years, city officials and grassroots activists have struggled with each other to define the content of yearly festivals. The smallest details become matters of political debate. Is it appropriate to have Mexican American music on the Fourth of July, introduce the Chinese Lion's Dance into Cinco de Mayo, or bring karaoke into a Chinese New Year's celebration? However trivial the answers, they are part of an ongoing reexamination and reconstruction of American culture(s).

Our field notes from the Fourth of July in 1989 show a multiethnic progression over the 1987 celebration reported in the Introduction:

> The regulars, two middle-aged Anglo women and a slightly younger first-generation Chinese American, are selling tickets for food and events. Behind their table, a native-born Japanese American man in his forties is concentrating on not burning hot dogs, the only official Fourth of July food according to some old-timers. This year, because of the multiethnic character of the planning committee, there are also egg rolls donated by a predominantly Asian Kiwanis Club, Mexican sweet bread, and a flat cake decorated with the American flag. Unfortunately, there is no carne asada. It is rumored that the Latino president of the Chamber of Commerce decided not to donate the meat in protest against the city council's decision to raise business taxes.
>
> Given the dearth of volunteers among adults, the food was sold mostly by Asian volunteers from a local high school. They were acutely aware of the symbolic character of the food. As one of our researchers approached the food table, a Chinese girl shouted, "Get your hot dogs here, they're so American." A male competitor retorted: "No, hot dogs are an American cliche. Expand your cultural experiences. Eat an egg roll."
>
> Meanwhile, on stage, an old-timer white band was playing old-timer American tunes. Next, a Chinese girl prodigy in a white dress sat sedately at a grand piano and regaled the audience with a Chopin nocturne. Following her performance, the crowd, predominantly Latinos with a sprinkling of Asians and whites, danced to hot salsa.

> Later as the heat of the day was giving way to shade, family groups spread themselves strategically on the grass in expectation of the fireworks. A young immigrant was lying down on a blanket, chatting to his wife in Chinese, and playing with his tiny child. The man's bare feet extended into the sidewalk toward the circle of Latino teenagers hanging out around their parked car. Into their own rap, they showed no visible signs of established-resident resentment. Everyone seemed comfortable in separate spaces. Two young Asian women drove by, their Chinese and laughter audible from the open windows. They were at home. At least on this Fourth of July, there was a feeling of security among the Latino and Asian families lounging, walking, and picnicking in the park.[3]

Revived by Barry Hatch in the mid-1980s as a patriotic reaction against the tide of diversity, today Fourth of July celebrations in Monterey Park are displays of the city's Latino, Asian, and Anglo-American cultures. Now the event is inevitably a result of negotiation between nationalist and internationalist definitions of American unity. These negotiations have also affected ethnic celebrations like Cinco de Mayo and the Chinese New Year.

In 1989, for the first time, the Cinco de Mayo organizing committee included Chinese and Anglos. Some of the Latino leaders wanted to include a cultural exchange in the event; others favored a more traditional celebration of their Mexican descent. In Monterey Park style, the outcome was a compromise and an improvisation. The nationalist tendency was represented by the keynote speaker. Addressing the audience in Spanish and English, he made a political speech pointing out the lack of Chicano representation in Monterey Park and elsewhere.

The diversity and interethnic unity forces also achieved their ends. They persuaded the organizers to include a Lion's Dance in the festivities, certainly an unusual event in the history of Cinco de Mayo celebrations. Moreover, the day's theme was "Somos Una Familia" ("We Are a Family," or "One Family"), which could be understood narrowly to mean all Mexican Americans or broadly to mean all races and ethnicities. Reactions to the Lion's Dance ranged from enthusiasm to "What are Chinos doing in our Cinco de Mayo?"

The tension between ethnic, interethnic, and patriotic themes has also been apparent in the yearly Chinese New Year's celebration held by the multiethnic Monterey Park Chamber of Commerce. The balance of themes is essentially a political decision determined by the leadership. In 1989 the President was a first-generation Chinese American. She wanted to deliver a message of patriotism focusing on Chinese contributions to America. The festivities began predictably, with some four hundred guests standing for the pledge of allegiance and newcomers fumbling with the unfamiliar words. A group of mainly white, Latino, and black high school kids sang a sentimental version of "This Is My Country." To add nativism to Americanism, the main address was given by Councilman Hatch. He began by talking nostalgically about his two years as a missionary in Hong Kong and how much he loved the people and their family values. Next came the Americanism theme: "But we are one country, one constitution, one people"; then the anti-Chinese theme; jokingly: "All the Chinese I ever meet here are developers and politicians."

However, the Chinese presence outweighed xenophobia. The setting was a vast, Hong Kong–style Chinese restaurant, and the diners were about 80 percent Chinese. The event coincided with a commemoration of the bicentennial of the arrival of the first Chinese immigrant to the United States. Local, county, and state officials offered verbal and written testimonies to Chinese contributions. Children performed a Taiwanese folk dance. The room was filled with the sound of Chinese dialects and a pride that comes with success. This was not the old Chamber of Commerce. Toward the end of the evening, a young Anglo man mounted the stage and proceeded to crack jokes and sing popular Hong Kong songs in fluent Mandarin.

In 1990, with the lessening of anti-immigrant sentiment, the entertainment for the Chamber of Commerce Chinese New Year was almost entirely Chinese. In 1991, however, under the leadership of Fred Balderrama and Marie Purvis, the scene took on an uneasy multiethnic character. The Chinese magic show ended with the disappearance of the Chinese magician and the appearance of his Anglo assistant. Equally interesting was the choice of the master of ceremonies, Christopher Nance, an African American and the wisecracking weatherman for KNBC–Channel 4 Television. Bouncing about the stage, he singled out a couple in the audience as "the only black family in Monterey Park" and made jokes about the aphrodisiac effects of chewing the ginseng gum that had been placed on the banquet tables. At this juncture, some Chinese began to find reasons to leave the party, but the majority stayed to laugh at Nance's jokes, sing "Happy Birthday" to Balderrama's 72-year-old mother, and listen to city officials belting out "The Tennessee Waltz" and the Beatles' "When I'm 64" in karaoke style.

OFFICIAL VERSIONS OF DIVERSITY

Although it may often verge on absurdity or be perfunctory, some gesture of cultural diversity has become obligatory in all public events. As the city council became more ethnically diverse, cultural diversity was institutionalized in mayoral inauguration ceremonies. Every nine months on a rotating basis, the new Mayor gets to orchestrate his or her interpretation of patriotism, community service, and diversity.

For her inaugurations of 1991 and 1994, Mayor Chu attracted a large Chinese audience to listen to a message of diversity and bridge-building backed up by an ethnically balanced array of political and institutional representatives, entertainment, and food.

In 1991, Mayor Couch attracted a mostly elderly and Anglo audience. Although the food included luscious mounds of Chinese noodles and egg rolls, her theme was the Anglo past and values that Laura Scudder would have praised. Couch's friend, Linda Organ, put on a slide show about the life of a girl from Little Rock, Arkansas: her family's move to San Diego, her graduation from high school, marriage, children, her business skills, and community service in the Boys and Girls Club, the Parks and Recreation Commission, and RAMP. It was a story about a conservative American grassroots activist whose service extended beyond the family to the community. Couch's presentation concluded with testimonies from a group of predominantly white former city officials and a reminder to the audience, "Remember the city's past."

The message changed again in 1992 with the inauguration of Samuel Kiang. His ceremonies in the city council opened with the rousing sounds of a multiethnic Salvation Army Band playing "Home on the Range" and "The Battle Hymn of the Republic" to a standing-room-only and largely Chinese audience. Pushed toward the exit by the crowd, a white man in his thirties remarked to a white researcher, "I came to see the future of Monterey Park. Now that I've seen it, I'm leaving."

The message for the many newcomers and established residents who stayed was found in the refrain of the "Happy New Year Song," written by Susanna Cheung for Kiang's swearing-in ceremony: "While the world is ever changing so fast, we have to improve ourselves, to understand our role and ability, to share our culture and the pride of being here. Whether you're born here or just immigrated, California [is] the land of hope and golden opportunity."

In contrast to Couch's emphasis on the Anglo past, Kiang's eyes were on the Chinese future of Monterey Park. Representatives from the Chinese Consolidated Benevolent Association, the Chinese American Association of Southern California, three Chinese newspapers, writers' and cultural foundations, the Chinese American Political Action Committee, and other organizations lined up to offer gifts and praise Kiang, sometimes in Chinese. The occasion even brought together old enemies. Official representatives from Taiwan and the People's Republic of China found themselves sitting together in the front row to honor the immigrant Mayor of America's first suburban Chinatown.

TOWARD A CULTURE OF DIVERSITY

Although the pressure to be American without "foreign" influence is increasing in California, in places like Monterey Park, where the world has already imploded, an Anglo or Eurocentric American identity is giving way to greater openness.

The transformation happens unconsciously and on an incremental basis through compromise and accommodation in the pragmatic process of getting things done. It is also undertaken consciously at public events and festivals where diversity and patriotism come together, using a formula that varies with the ethnicity and politics of those who plan the events.

Whatever the variations on the themes of patriotism and diversity, newcomers and new majorities have succeeded in questioning the exclusive identification of the nation with Anglo/European culture. The ambivalent cultural symbols of unity and difference reflect the same dilemmas of diversity identified in local politics: the drive for respect and empowerment on an ethnic basis and the search for a community that transcends ethnicity. The results may be small and seemingly trivial, but in an era of virulent nationalism and ethnic genocide, these local experiments in multiculturalism are advances to be celebrated.

Chapter 10
THE PRACTICE AND POLITICS OF DIVERSITY

"Pride in the Past, Faith in the Future."

—*Motto in Monterey Park City Hall*

TO COMMEMORATE Monterey Park's 75th birthday in 1991, the Anniversary Committee agreed on a motto. "Pride in the Past, Faith in the Future" was suggested by Chairperson Louise Davis, a resident of the city for over 35 years, City Treasurer, and twice Mayor. Davis was not sure whether she had heard the phrase before or invented it.[1] Nobody was sure, but the motto, now emblazoned on the front wall of the council chambers, seemed appropriate for a city in transition.

New words signify new social relationships—in this case, greater accommodation between old-timers and newcomers as the bearers of the city's past and future. For old-timers, particularly Anglos, the accommodation is to a future made by people who will look different and have pride in their own Latino and Asian pasts. For newcomers accommodation means learning how to use and improve the tools of citizenship forged by city pioneers, many of whom happened to be white.

Like the official motto, the language of public life is also symbolic of a changing civic identity. Five years after the city was torn by the controversy over Official English, a group of volunteers working with the approval of the city council produced a commemorative book written in English, Spanish, and Chinese. David T. Lau, Chairperson of the 75th Anniversary Book Committee, naturalized citizen, established resident, and elected member of a local Board of Education, described the publication as "an historical journal, reference book, and tour guide"; "the city's most valuable asset," he wrote, was "our cultural diversity."[2]

The work of the various anniversary committees was an example of cooperation under conditions of great ethnic and cultural diversity. Citizens, often opposed to each other on many issues, collectively adopted a new motto and celebrated their city—its past, its future, and also its immigrant and ethnically diverse present. The accomplishment showed how far Latinos, Asians, and Anglos, immigrant and native-born, had come in recognizing each other as part of the same community after the initial shock of finding themselves neighbors.

THE EMERGENCE OF THE POLITICS OF DIVERSITY

In Monterey Park, people are beginning to use fashionable words like "diversity" and "multiculturalism." By this they mean not so much an abstract appreciation of separateness and difference as a concrete sense of interconnections and collective assets. Divisions were crossed and differences used in the process of getting things done. The job, whether producing a book or electing a candidate, required struggle and negotiation.

The result has been an emerging practice of diversity: a movement toward greater empowerment of immigrants, ethnic groups, and women, their gradual incorporation into a local political system that had once been the exclusive province of white males, and the formation of complex and changing alliances on issues of representation and community development.

The process developed unevenly. By the mid-1970s, the demographic and economic changes associated with immigration were destabilizing local politics, undermining the already frail old-boy network of control, challenging patterns of ethnic and gender accommodation, and unleashing new political actors: women, ethnic groups, immigrants pressing for representation and empowerment; established residents protesting against developers, newcomers, and their supporters in city government; progressives pushing for greater multiculturalism and diversity in civic life.

The politics of the 1980s were dominated by the reaction of established residents against rapid demographic, economic, and cultural change: an unstable mix of antideveloper and antigovernment populism and anti-immigrant and anti-Chinese nativism. The particular line-up of established-resident/immigrant, class, and ethnic forces exacerbated the nativist and racial components of the conflict. The connections between the white leaders of the immigrant- and growth-control movements put a nativist stamp on what was also a class-based protest against rapid and uncontrolled development: the message that Chinese newcomers as a racial and ethnic group were responsible for the city's many problems. In reaction, newcomers and established residents fought harder for immigrant and ethnic rights, and developers took advantage of the situation to dismiss growth control as racist.

By 1990, a realignment of political forces signaled the decline of nativism and the emergence of a more accommodating politics of diversity. Two factors were key: the break-up of the alliance between the Anglo leaders of the controlled-growth and Official English movements and the rise of multiethnic leadership in the struggle to control the course of local development. Multiculturalism was also emerging in public events and festivals whenever diverse ethnic and immigrant groups came together to challenge strictly Anglo/European symbols of American identity.

Ethnic and immigrant boundaries were frequently respected, crossed, and redrawn in neighborhoods and civic organizations. This also happened, but less predictably, in the contentious realm of politics whenever residents backed away from nationalism in its nativist or ethnic expressions and started looking for interethnic allies in the fight for representation, accountable local government, and control over land use.

The reconstruction of local politics and culture on the basis of greater ethnic diversity was a matter of negotiating, making interethnic alliances, and compromising. However, the alliances tended to be situational and unstable, based less on ideology than on political pragmatism. The stability of the political process depended less on the continuity of particular alliances than on the practice of making alliances.

Stability was precarious, a flair-up of nativism and ethnic conflict always a possibility. As the political process evolved, divisions of birth and ethnicity did not so much break down and disappear as become more fluid, sometimes retreating, sometimes aggressively reappearing, depending on the situation and balance of political forces. Divisions retreated when diverse residents united to elect Judy Chu (1988, 1992) and Samuel Kiang (1990) and to defeat Barry Hatch (1990). They resurfaced in 1991, when newcomers and established residents accused each other of discrimination during the controversy over affirmative action. They broke down and reformed in 1993 when Latino and Chinese American residents joined to protest a card parlor, while a small group of Anglos associated with the controlled-growth and nativist movements made common cause with its Taiwanese developer.

With all the fluctuations, the political and cultural trends were clear. There were new political actors and perspectives. Women, organizing at the grassroots and moving from backstage supporters to elected leaders, have generally played a mediating role in local politics. Asians and Latinos may not have much political power in state and national politics, but they are certainly exerting influence in Monterey Park and the surrounding San Gabriel Valley. At least in this corner of the nation, the days of uncontested Anglo power were over in both the political and the cultural arena. The ethnic component of class had changed, and with it the taken-for-granted identification of Anglos with class power.

THE SOCIAL AND POLITICAL CONDITIONS FOR ACCOMMODATION

The movement away from nativism to ethnic politics and the emergence of unstable, fluctuating interethnic alliances and loyalties were responses to specific historical, social, and political conditions. These conditions in Monterey Park and the San Gabriel Valley were generally favorable to new forms of political and cultural accommodation between ethnic groups and immigrants and established residents.

The arrival of newcomers changed the ethnic composition of the class structure at all levels, Chinese replacing Anglos as the dominant business class, and Asians and Latinos becoming the most numerous sectors of the middle and working classes. The effect was to increase ethnic diversity and ethnic consciousness. Everyone was becoming a member of an ethnic group, including whites, who reluctantly started calling themselves "Anglos" rather than unqualified "Americans." The changing ethnic balance challenged both immigrants and established residents to reexamine their own identities and patterns of accommodation.

Over time, emerging ethnic divisions cut across newcomer/established-resident lines and ethnicity became a major force in politics, touching every issue of power. However, the rising importance of ethnicity did not preclude interethnic cooperation. This was facilitated by the ambiguous, fluid, and ambivalent character of ethnicity; the middle-class status of the participants and the class character of development problems; and political leadership and participation.

The Ambiguous Salience of Ethnicity

In every city election, we found evidence of ethnic voting, yet ethnic identities were inconsistent and situational when it came to taking sides and making political choices. For example, council members Chu and Kiang were sometimes allied as Chinese or Asian Americans and just as often divided as Chinese American and Chinese immigrant politicians. Likewise, Asian voters sometimes voted as Chinese immigrants, Japanese Americans, Asian Americans, or native-born Americans, depending on the candidate choices and issues.

Moreover, native-born and long-established immigrants were often ambivalent about their rising ethnic consciousness. The new immigration and increased diversity had made them acutely aware of their ethnicity, but not necessarily more comfortable with a label that set them apart. Pressure to fit into a middle-class suburban lifestyle and to be established residents and Americans was often stronger than the desire to be Japanese, Mexican, Chinese, or Anglo. This flexibility in deciding when and to what degree one is ethnic is a suburban luxury, not always granted to poorer groups in the inner city, whose ethnicity is more strongly imposed by agents of economic and ethnic domination.

Crossing ethnic boundaries was also facilitated by the heterogeneity of conventionally labeled ethnic groups, the ethnic fragmentation of the region, and the integration of neighborhoods and civic groups. To win something under these conditions, political leaders had to widen their appeal and make ethnic alliances even in the struggle to gain ethnic representation. Some politicians were more successful than others in this endeavor. As a U.S.-born Asian American with a Chinese and interethnic network of support, Chu was a master of interethnic politics. Immigrant candidates with a stronger ethnic identity rooted in the immigrant community suffered politically for "being too Chinese," in the words of one long-established immigrant, but they too were learning to define ethnicity more flexibly in their bids for political support.

Thus, in multiethnic, middle-class Monterey Park, ethnicity was a salient political force, but unstable in meaning and equally in its situational application. Ethnicity was less a fixed attribute or tradition that people could always take for granted and organize around than a resource that they could mine and shape for political advantage. It could be a resource for organizing and empowering Latinos and Asians, who have been singled out for discrimination on the basis of their ethnicity. It could also be personal weapon for putting down opponents as racist, nationalist, or nativist.[3]

The Unspoken Salience of Class

Compared with ethnicity, class was not a central part of local spoken and unspoken discourse. Yet it was as salient as ethnicity in affecting political change and less ambiguous in the sense that it was determined by the structure of property ownership and less fluid and open to choice.

Two factors that initially inflamed and ultimately weakened polarization between newcomers and established residents were the large size of the immigration and the class resources of the immigrants. The newcomers, along with established immigrants, had numbers, class, and potential political power on their side. Contrary to the local stereotypes, all immigrants were not rich, but many did have the international connections and the economic and educational "capital" to enter the ranks of the local middle and upper-middle classes. The class status of immigrants, particularly of those who entered civic affairs and local politics, placed them in a position to broker and negotiate accommodation on a more equal and multicultural basis without succumbing to established-resident definitions of good Asian Americans. They had to be taken into account.

Another factor in accommodation was the generally middle-class status of established residents. The presence of newcomers altered the composition of the population and the course of development, but it also revitalized the local economy and did not threaten the property values and jobs of established residents.

The class conditions for accommodation have been much less favorable in poorer Los Angeles communities where immigrants and established residents were markedly unequal or equally poor. It was no accident that the "riots" of 1992 took place in South Central and Central Los Angeles, where the established residents were working-class African Americans and the newcomers were middle-class Korean shopkeepers and working-class Latinos. Monterey Park had one major precondition for accommodation—a level of economic prosperity and equality between newcomers and established residents.

The high level of homeownership in Monterey Park among Latinos, Anglos, and Asians also created the possibility of a common struggle against property managers and profiteers who threatened the quality of suburban life. In a city actively organized to oppose big developers and big government in collusion with development, class issues could sometimes transcend divisions between ethnic groups and between newcomers and established residents.

Political Involvement and Leadership

Economic conditions did not dictate accommodation to diversity. Accommodation was achieved through leadership and political struggle on the foundation of economic conditions.

The small size of Monterey Park and the possibility of intervening in the city council and commissions made democratic participation possible. Residents could and did affect decisions and hold their representatives accountable. Many were involved in grassroots political organizations that informed, organized, and regularly intervened in local political life: Democratic clubs, neighborhood associations, and single-issue organizations like RAMP and CHAMP. Long-established residents relied on the electoral process; those disenfranchised by their noncitizen status took direct action. Influence is not so easily exerted through the massive juridical units of the City and County of Los Angeles. The vast region would have to be broken down into coordinated regional and neighborhood councils for newcomers and established residents to approach the political opportunities available in Monterey Park.

Other factors favorable to accommodation were leadership and the role of women in facilitating interethnic cooperation. Monterey Park produced leaders open to building alliances. An interethnic group of political progressives, including both old-timers and more recent residents, were catalysts for the process of accommodation. They believed in ethnic representation and interethnic alliances and provided the political space for this to happen.

One significant accomplishment behind the move away from nativism toward political diversity was the increased participation of ethnic leaders in the struggle for control over development, weakening its identification with white leadership and xenophobia. Councilwoman Chu and her interethnic supporters facilitated this change by championing both ethnic harmony and growth control. Over time, Chinese and Latino residents have demanded the right to define problems of development. This was strikingly visible in the struggle against the gambling club.

The increased involvement of minorities and immigrants in fights over land use laid the foundation for a sophisticated political alternative to the reduction of development problems to immigrants (nativism), developers (the official position of RAMP), or the alleged racism of residents who wanted more control over change (the developer position). Leaders and residents began to understand the interconnectedness of ethnic and class issues and sort them out in political practice. One method was to avoid organizing exclusively around ethnicity (thereby denying class differences within ethnic groups) or class (thereby ignoring ethnic inequalities), but instead to mobilize interethnic support against the power of the state to impose an unwanted parole office, the power of the developer to profit from unwanted residential and commercial growth, or the power of the nativist and nationalist to impose one ethnic standard on a culturally diverse population.

This process took progressive leadership and the ability of residents who occupied the political center to compromise and work together across ethnic and immigrant barriers to find solutions to shared problems of class and ethnic domination.

THE MEANING OF DIVERSITY

The major implications of these findings concern the possibility of political diversity and multiculturalism in a society that is becoming global in its economic and demographic structure. In Monterey Park, nativism and ethnic conflict were not the inevitable outcomes of the immigration of Asian people and capital. Under conditions of relative class equality, a level of democracy based on ethnic and cultural diversity was achieved at the grassroots through the formation of interethnic alliances. In electing a candidate, putting on a cultural performance, or just saying "no" to a developer and "yes" to a safe neighborhood, what counted in the end was not the racist or antiracist beliefs of individuals, but the collective, pragmatic practice of cooperation in civic organizations, neighborhoods, and political arenas.

The case of Monterey Park also clarifies the often contradictory and competing meanings of diversity. Our baptism into local politics taught us that diversity based on ethnicity and immigration favored accommodation when it was connective—that is, associated with the formation of interethnic alliances favoring the empowerment and inclusion of underrepresented populations. Connective diversity differs from what can be called "establishment" and "competitive" diversity, which perpetuate domination and division.[4]

Establishment diversity expresses an ideology of control propagated by dominant institutions, such as corporations, schools, the media, and government. They perpetuate existing patterns of control by hiding the reality of power behind a benign façade of cultural differences. The tactic is to celebrate local ethnic cultures as quaint customs and pleasant decorations that can be safely packaged like commodities, all equally good and desirable, depending on the tastes of consumers.

In Monterey Park, the obligatory display of Latino, Chinese, and European food and music at public ceremonies and festivals looks suspiciously like the mainstream management of diversity in that conflict and power are played down. However, this is not always the case. Establishment harmony is mandated from the top without regard for fundamental inequalities. In Monterey Park, the depoliticized display of cultural differences is often the negotiated result of resident participation and compromise. Such grassroots practices can be cultural expressions of ethnic empowerment.

Locally, the arrival of ethnic politics and the habit of organizing on an ethnic basis have generated competitive diversity. Here power is at least privately acknowledged, but as a zero-sum game in which ethnic groups struggle against each other for a share of a shrinking pie. As we have seen, this nationalistic approach to diversity, while understandable given the history of racial and ethnic discrimination, can pit Chinese against Latinos, and Anglos against everyone else. The approach ignores power and class differences that cut across the permeable lines of ethnicity. It fails to make connections between ethnicity and class, or assumes that they are identical.

The dilemma of diversity is to legitimate the continual expression and creation of ethnic and other differences while making connections that transcend them. This connective diversity takes place in Monterey Park whenever people from different ethnic backgrounds work on common projects. It takes place on an everyday level when residents with different memories of home and place begin to feel accountable to the place where they now live, and to its people. This pragmatic process of making connections between people in neighborhoods, civic organizations, and local politics may be our only hope if diversity is be more than an ornament to the status quo or a polite word for ethnic conflict.

Making ethnic connections is not an impossible task. Our findings point to the fluidity of American and ethnic identities constructed at the porous borders between residents on the basis of situationally defined political and class interests. Ethnicity is not traditional or primordial, nor is it a voluntary construction.[5] In America, it counts as basis for identity and political organizing. The issue is how it counts and how it is constructed as a means of empowerment, whether it facilitates connections, alliances, and community or sets up barriers.

The theoretical and political points about making connections and refusing to essentialize concepts like ethnicity apply also to the concepts of immigrant and immigration. In our research, we have refused to enter the debate about the costs and debits of immigration, thereby separating and disconnecting immigrants from the society in which they live. Try as they may, national governments cannot stop people from crossing penetrable borders that have lost their relevance in an interconnected world. Whatever the direction of future policies, immigrants have already changed the ethnic and economic character of border cities like Los Angeles and Miami and become an integral part of economic life. Given the situation, the sensible approach is to take newcomers and established residents as part of the same society, look at their interactions, and learn under what conditions they can cooperate with each other and negotiate their shared problems.

From our research, one policy recommendation forcefully emerges. The politics of resistance—singling out for exclusion and control immigrants who have established lives in a community—will not work. The result in Monterey Park was division and conflict. The only viable alternative is a politics of incorporation and inclusion, encouraging social and political participation, education, language skills: the tools for citizenship and equality in a society of immigrants.

AFTERWORD 1994

Time and change continually overtake and contradict a slow writer quick to generalize a pattern from a dramatic moment. In 1993, after Chu's reelection and the fight against the gambling club, there was a temptation to conclude that interethnic alliances had become the dominant pattern in Monterey Park. The events of 1994 seemed to challenge this interpretation.

Chu ran a tough, interethnic, precinct-pounding race against a Latina incumbent in the Democratic primary for California State Assembly

District 49, an area including Monterey Park and several neighboring cities. She lost and has returned to being Mayor of Monterey Park. Kiang ran for reelection and lost, as did two naturalized Chinese American residents who had been active at the grassroots—Peter Chan and Mitchell Ing. Incumbents Fred Balderrama and Marie Purvis won, along with the politically untested Francisco Alonso, who had run unsuccessfully for city council in 1992.

Chu's defeat in the Democratic primary was not a surprise. It was a first try in a predominantly Latino district with few registered Chinese American voters. Chu gained visibility, newly registered voters, and multiethnic support—assests that will serve her well next time around. In the Monterey Park elections, however, Chinese candidates not only failed to win a majority in city council, they lost one of their two seats.

The interpretation favored by the winners and their supporters was that the best candidates had won. Balderrama had strong Latino support, Chinese connections, and endorsements from big names in the California Democratic Party; Purvis was the mainstay of old-timer whites. Alonso seemed sensible and was favored by voters suspicious of big money because he ran the lowest-budget campaign with no visible ties to "special interests."[6]

The interpretation favored by the losers and their supporters was that there had been a backlash of conservative white voters and Latinos against Kiang and the other Chinese candidates. Although this argument ignores the issue of candidate qualifications, events had in fact reopened divisions between native-born and immigrant Americans and between Chinese Americans and Latinos.

In an act welcomed by few Latino and Chinese residents, the Los Angeles Archdiocese announced the formation of a evangelizing center for Chinese and the replacement of a popular, Spanish-speaking priest with two Chinese-speaking priests at Monterey Park's primarily Latino St. Thomas Aquinas Catholic Church. After protests and demands for consultation from both Chinese and Mexican Americans, a compromise was reached, but the effect of the Church's intervention was to feed Latino fears of Chinese privilege and takeover.

Second, the media made divisive interventions into local affairs. By emphasizing the possibility of a Chinese American majority on city council, the conservative *Citizen's Voice* deliberately and the more mainstream *Los Angeles Times* (with its message of establishment diversity) inadvertently contributed to takeover hysteria.[7] Third, developer money may have intervened. An intimidating, official-looking pamphlet in Chinese and English was sent to all Monterey Park voters, warning against the illegal use of absentee ballots. Given the high use of absentee ballots by Chinese-speaking voters and the suspicion among some established residents that the practice was shady, the electoral effect could have been to drive non-Chinese voters to the polls and to keep recent Chinese voters away. The anonymous pamphlet was traced to the BCTC Development Corporation, the Taiwanese firm behind the proposed gambling facility for Monterey Park.[8] Interestingly, the three Chinese candidates who lost the election had strongly opposed the card club, while the three Anglo and Latino candidates who won were more open to exploring the idea.

Finally, the actions of the Chinese candidates themselves may have reinforced the divisions of ethnicity and nativity and precluded interethnic support, a point not raised by the losers. Kiang's enthusiasm for the rights of newcomers and for mass demonstrations definitely turned off the support of old-timers. RAMP, for example, sent out a pamphlet opposing all the Chinese American candidates, and particularly deploring Kiang's "SCORN for Democracy, and [his] willingness to resort to RACISM to gain his purpose."[9] Old-timers expressed their opposition through the one channel that more than adequately represented their diminishing voices—the ballot.

Given the abundant signs of divisions within the complex Chinese community, the Chinese American candidates should not have counted on a level of Chinese support so strong and unified that it would result in the election of two out of the three Chinese American candidates who were, in effect, running against each other. They were more "Chinese" than the Chinese American voters in their miscalculation of ethnic support.

Whatever the reasons—nativism, ethnic tensions, the candidates' political records—the1994 election was a setback for Chinese American and Asian representation in an Asian city. But in the larger sweep of Monterey Park history and in this period of transition, vacillations are the norm. The 1994 election, like the others we have studied, confirms the overall vitality and complexity of the politics of diversity. Greater ethnic representation is clearly a local trend. Latinos made gains this time, but Chinese immigrants and Chinese Americans are increasingly involved in local politics through electoral and extraelectoral channels.

In the near future, as the influence of aging old-timers wanes and as more Asians become citizens and vote, there will be an Asian—probably a Chinese—majority on the Monterey Park city council. When that happens, the celebration or the fear of Asian power will be short-lived and will give way to inter-Asian competition based on national origins (Taiwanese, Vietnamese, mainland Chinese, etc.), generation, and class. The complexity of the Chinese and Asian population and the issues that citizens face, and the level of grassroots involvement, mean that a unified front of Asian old boys is unlikely to replace the Anglo old boys and return local politics to the earlier days of ethnic and gender domination.

However, at regional and national levels, Asian Americans, Latinos, and other Americans will have to practice the art of interethnic politics to stem the rising nativist and conservative tide in California and the nation as a whole.

In Monterey Park the trend has been toward the incorporation of newcomers and ethnic groups into mainstream and grassroots politics, an ongoing struggle. The actors in the fight over language rights, immigration, and development in the 1980s are not silent in the mid-1990s. Barry Hatch left his home town in defeat and disgust, but he has not given up the fight for his vision of America. In 1994, he ran as a write-in candidate for the House of Representatives in the nearby, whiter, and more conservative Congressional District 28. He and his rebel allies in S.O.S. (Save Our State) backed California's Proposition 187, which threatens to deprive undocumented immigrants of public social services, nonemergency health care, and public education.[10] The Monterey Park city council passed a resolution opposing 187, and, in a state that passed the proposition by a margin of 59 to 41, the multiethnic voters of Monterey Park opposed it by 53 to 47 percent. The story of Monterey Park tells us that inclusion, citizenship, and empowerment are the weapons against the politics of exclusion.

Notes

INTRODUCTION

1. The beating of Rodney King, an African American, by Anglo policemen, the wide circulation of a videotape of that beating, and the initial acquittal of the policemen on brutality charges sparked the Los Angeles uprising. Pleading for peace on the third day of civil unrest, May Day, 1992, King asked Angelinos the simple and direct question that appears in the epigraph. Quoted in "Understanding the Riots," *Los Angeles Times,* July 22, 1992.

King's question was still relevant in November 1994, when the primarily Anglo voting population of Los Angeles approved California's Proposition 187, making undocumented immigrants ineligible for public social services, nonemergency health care, and attendance at public schools.

2. Jose Calderon is Assistant Professor of Sociology and Chicano Studies, Pitzer College. Mary Pardo is a Professor of Chicana/o Studies, California State University at Northridge. Leland Saito is Assistant Professor of Ethnic and Urban Studies, University of California, San Diego. Linda Shaw is Assistant Professor of Sociology, Syracuse University. Yen-Fen Tseng is Assistant Professor of Sociology, Tunghai University, Taiwan.

3. Team members have produced the following works related to the Monterey Park research. Jose Z. Calderon is the author of: "Situational Identity of Suburban Mexican American Politicians in a Multi-Ethnic Community," in Roberto M. De Anda, ed., *Contemporary Chicanos: Explorations in Culture, Politics, and Society* (Boston: Allyn and Bacon, 1995, forthcoming); (with John Horton) "Language Struggles in a Changing California Community," in James Crawford, ed., *Language Loyalties: A Source Book on the Official English Controversy* (Chicago: University of Chicago Press, 1992), pp. 186–94; "Hispanic and Latino: The Viability of Categories for Panethnic Unity," *Latin American Perspectives* 19 (Fall 1992): 37–44; "Mexican American Politics in a Multi-Ethnic Community: The Case of Monterey Park, 1985–1990" (Ph.D. diss., University of California, Los Angeles, 1991); "Latinos and Ethnic Conflict in Suburbia: The Case of Monterey Park," *Latino Studies Journal* 2 (May 1990): 23–32; "How the English Only Initiative Passed in California," in Mary Romero and Cordelia Candelaria, eds., *Estudios Chicanos and the Politics of Community* (Ann Arbor, Mich.: National Association of Chicano Studies, 1988), pp. 132–43.

Mary Pardo has written: "Doing It for the Kids: Mexican American Community Activists, Border Feminists?" in Myra Marx Ferree and Patricia Yancey Martin, eds., *Feminist Organizations: Harvest of the New Women's Movement* (Philadelphia: Temple University Press, 1995), pp. 356–71; "Creating Community: Mexican American Women in Eastside Los Angeles," *Aztlan* 20 (1991); "Identity and Resistance: Mexican American Women and Grassroots Activism in Two Los Angeles Communities" (Ph.D. diss., University of California, Los Angeles, 1990); "Mexican American Women Grassroots Community Activists: Mothers of East Los Angeles," *Frontiers* 11 (1990): 1–7.

Works by Leland T. Saito are: "Contrasting Patterns of Adaptation: Japanese Americans and Chinese Immigrants in Monterey Park," in Linda Revilla, Gail Nomura, Shawn Wong, and Shirley Hune, eds., *Bearing Dreams, Shaping Visions: Asian Pacific American Perspectives* (Pullman, Wash.: Washington State University Press, 1993), pp. 33–43; "Asian Americans and Latinos in San Gabriel Valley, California: Ethnic Political Cooperation and Redistricting, 1990–92," *Amerasia Journal* 19 (1993): 55–68; "Japanese Americans and the New Chinese Immigrants: The Politics of Adaptation," *California Sociologist* 12 (1989): 195–211; (with John Horton) "The New Chinese Immigration and the Rise of Asian American Politics in Monterey Park, California," in Paul Ong, Edna Bonacich, and Lucie Cheng, eds., *The New Asian Immigration in Los Angeles and Global Restructuring* (Philadelphia: Temple University Press, 1994), pp. 233–63; "Politics in a New Demographic Era: Asian Americans in Monterey Park, California" (Ph.D. diss., University of California, Los Angeles, 1992).

Yen-Fen Tseng is the author of: "Suburban Ethnic Economy: Chinese Business Communities in Los Angeles" (Ph.D. diss., University of California, Los Angeles, 1994); (with Roger Waldinger) "Divergent Diasporas: The Chinese Communities of New York and Los Angeles Compared," *Revue Européenne des Migrations Internationales* 8 (1992): 91–114; "The Chinese Ethnic Economy: San Gabriel Valley, Los Angeles County," *Journal of Urban Affairs* 16 (1994): 169–89. "'Little Taipei' and Beyond: The Development of Taiwanese Immigrant Businesses in Los Angeles," *International Migration Review* (forthcoming, 1995).

4. These unpublished data are available for consultation in our UCLA project files.

5. For a discussion of "critical tales," particularly in anthropology, see John Van Maanen, *Tales of the Field* (Chicago: University of Chicago Press, 1988); and Louise Lamphere, ed., *Structuring Diversity: Ethnographic Perspectives on the New Immigration* (Chicago: University of Chicago Press, 1992), pp. 14–18. For a recent sociological attempt to link ethnography and larger economic and political systems, see Michael Burawoy et al., *Ethnography Unbound: Power and Resistance in the Modern Metropolis* (Berkeley: University of California Press, 1991). Two outstanding examples of "critical ethnography" and models for our own work are Paul Willis, *Learning to Labor* (New York: Columbia University Press, 1981); Jonathan Rieder, *Canarsie: The Jews and Italians of Brooklyn Against Liberalism* (Cambridge: Harvard University Press, 1985).

6. Robert L. Bach, *Changing Relations: Newcomers and Established Residents in U.S. Communities,* a report to the Ford Foundation by the National Board of the Changing Relations Project (New York: Ford Foundation, April 1993), p. 11. In addition to Bach, the members of the National Board were Rudolfo de la Garza, Karen Ito, Louise Lamphere, and Niara Sudarkasa. Publications related to this project include Lamphere, *Structuring Diversity;* Louise Lamphere, Alex Stepick, and Guillermo Grenier, eds., *Newcomers in the Workplace: Immigrants and the Restructuring of the U.S. Economy* (Philadelphia: Temple University Press,

1994); Judith Goode and Jo Anne Schneider, *Reshaping Ethnic and Racial Relations in Philadelphia: Immigrants in a Divided City* (Philadelphia: Temple University Press, 1994). A film on the six sites of the Changing Relations Project, *America Becoming,* was directed by Charles Burnett, produced by Dai Sil Kim-Gibson, and distributed in 1990.

CHAPTER 1

1. The phrase "first suburban Chinatown" has been used by both journalists and social scientists. See Mark Arax, "Nation's First Suburban Chinatown," *Los Angeles Times,* April 6, 1987; Timothy P. Fong, *The First Suburban Chinatown: The Remaking of Monterey Park, California* (Philadelphia: Temple University Press, 1994).

2. The story of the postwar migration of minorities to Monterey Park has been told by Fong, *First Suburban Chinatown,* pp. 17–34.

3. Eugene Turner and James P. Allen, *An Atlas of Population Patterns in Metropolitan Los Angeles and Orange Counties 1990* (Department of Geography, California State University, Northridge, 1991). For a discussion of the relatively neglected topic of suburban patterns of ethnic transition, see Richard D. Alba and John R. Logan, "Variations on Two Themes: Racial and Ethnic Patterns in the Attainment of Suburban Residence," *Demography* 28 (1991): 431–53; Nancy A. Denton and Douglas S. Massey, "Patterns of Neighborhood Transition in a Multiethnic World: U.S. Metropolitan Areas, 1970–1980," *Demography* 23 (1991): 41–63.

4. Recognizing that population labels are geographically situated, ever-changing, and politically contested constructions, unless otherwise indicated we employ terms current in Los Angeles: Asian American or Asian Pacific American; Anglo or white (specifically, non-Hispanic whites of European or Middle Eastern origin); Latino or Hispanic (people of Mexican, Central American, Puerto Rican, or Latin American origin, regardless of their racial background), and African Americans. The usage varies with context, but the general trend seems to favor terms referring to national or regional origin rather than race. Thus, in the future, we might expect Euro-American and Middle Eastern American to replace "white." Since the histories and backgrounds of groups contained in the general labels are so diverse, whenever possible we identify specific groups, such as Mexican Americans, Taiwanese, and Vietnamese. In any case, the ethnic labels can never be taken for granted. The major task of our research is to explain them in the context of Monterey Park.

5. The cover of *Time* magazine, April 9, 1990, featured a rainbow-colored flag and the heading: "America's Changing Colors. What will the U.S. be like when whites are no longer the majority?" The question may be premature, since in 1990 the major racial group in the United States still traced its ancestry to Europe. Nevertheless, about 75 percent of the 700,000 immigrants allowed into the United States annually are likely to come from outside Europe. Thus, an ethnic and racial transformation is occurring, and it has already taken place in Los Angeles and in Monterey Park.

6. Paul Ong, Edna Bonacich, and Lucie Cheng, eds., *The New Asian Immigration in Los Angeles and Global Restructuring* (Philadelphia: Temple University

Press, 1994), offers a global perspective on Asian immigration. As authors who contributed to the collection, we participated in a series of discussions devoted to developing a world economic perspective on Asian immigration.

7. For a discussion of the sometimes conflicting objectives behind the Immigration Act of 1965, see Paul Ong and John M. Liu, "U.S. Immigration Policies and Asian Migration," in Ong, Bonacich, and Cheng, *New Asian Immigration,* pp. 45–73.

8. Paul Ong and Suzanne J. Hee, "The Growth of the Asian Pacific American Population: Twenty Million in 2020," in *The State of Asian Pacific America: Policy Issues to the Year 2020* (Los Angeles: LEAP [Leadership Education for Asian Pacifics] Asian Pacific American Public Policy Institute, and UCLA Asian American Studies Center, 1993), p. 11.

9. John M. Liu and Lucie Cheng, "Pacific Rim Development and the Duality of Post-1965 Asian Immigration to the United States," in Ong, Bonacich, and Cheng, *New Asian Immigration,* pp. 74–99.

10. Paul Ong and Tania Azores, "Asian Americans in Los Angeles: Diversity and Divisions," ibid., p. 100.

11. Maps 2 and 3 were made available by the Urban Research Sector of Los Angeles County from their immigration series maps prepared by Manuel Moreno-Evans and Iannis Pissimissis.

12. PUMS data have been collected for Los Angeles County since the 1960 census, but only in 1990 were they reported by subsamples. The PUMS file contains individual weights for each person, which, when applied to the individual records, expand the sample to a total population. Weighted calculations were used in this report. I am indebted to Manuel Moreno-Evans for helping with the running and analysis of the PUMS data. His own work assessing the fiscal costs and contributions of immigrants in Los Angeles County is at the forefront of research countering the oversimplifications of the highly politicized debate on immigration: *Impact of Undocumented Persons and Other Immigrants on Costs, Revenues and Services in Los Angeles County* (Los Angeles County: Internal Services Department, 1992), a report prepared for the Los Angeles County Board of Supervisors; "The Impact of Immigration in Los Angeles County: Lessons from the Los Angeles Research," paper presented at the California Immigration 1994 Conference, Sacramento, April 29, 1994; "Effects of Immigration on Los Angeles County: Fiscal and Demographic Trends," paper presented at the Seventh Annual Demographic Workshop, University of Southern California, Los Angeles, May 9, 1994.

13. Robert Warren, Director, Statistics Division, Immigration and Naturalization Service, "Estimates of the Unauthorized Immigrant Population Residing in the United States, by Country of Origin and State of Resident: October 1992" (Washington, D.C.: INS Statistics Division, 1994).

14. Mexicans began arriving in larger numbers in the Southwest after 1910. See Alejandro Portes and Robert L. Bach, *Latin Journey: Cuban and Mexican Immigrants in the United States* (Berkeley: University of California Press, 1985), pp. 76–77.

15. Two informative sources on the history of Asian Americans are: Sucheng Chan, *Asian Americans: An Interpretive History* (Boston: Twayne, 1991);

and Ronald Takaki, *Strangers from a Different Shore: A History of Asian Americans* (New York: Penguin, 1990).

16. The PUMS data provide no information on immigrants' port of departure. Nevertheless, we know from history and observation that many China-born immigrants who fled the Communist Revolution came to the region via Taiwan and Hong Kong.

17. These remarks are based on anecdotal evidence taken from interviews with Chinese immigrants and from the research of Yen-Fen Tseng, a Taiwanese immigrant who was part of our Monterey Park research team.

18. The influence of Taiwanese in the local Chinese immigrant community has even been mentioned in the English-language press. The *Los Angeles Times* ran a story about Joseph Jinn, a popular anchor of the Chinese-language news show on cable station KCSI (Los Angeles), who complained that he was fired in January 1993 for making critical remarks about the relatively small and low-key reception for Taiwanese Premier Chan Lien in Los Angeles. Jinn's point was that the large Chinese community is very diverse in background and political ideology, but that the major Chinese media, including KCSI, have a tendency to discourage views that are not friendly to the Taiwanese government. See Robert Scheer, "They Don't Think They Need to Change: One Person's Story About Chinese in America," *Los Angeles Times,* February 14, 1994. One might add that it is increasingly difficult to characterize the Taiwanese government as hard-line Kuomintang. In recent years, more native-born Taiwanese have entered the political arena. For example, Premier Chan Lien was born in Taiwan, not in mainland China.

19. For a history of nativism in the labor movement, see Alexander Saxton, *The Indispensable Enemy: Labor and the Anti-Chinese Movement in California* (Berkeley: University of California Press, 1971).

20. See Fong, *First Suburban Chinatown,* pp. 26–34, for a brief, informative historical discussion of Chinese immigration to the United States and Monterey Park.

21. For a study of the "invisible" Asian Americans—the working poor, the unemployed, and those on welfare, see Paul Ong, Project Director, *Beyond Asian American Poverty: Community Economic Development Policies and Strategies* (Los Angeles: LEAP Asian Pacific American Public Policy Institute, 1993).

22. Asians and Chinese Americans are already making their mark at the University of California, Los Angeles. Asians constituted 41.8 percent of the incoming freshman class of 1994, followed by non-Latino whites, 27.7 percent; Latinos, 18.9 percent; African Americans, 6.9 percent; American Indians, 1 percent; and 0.7 percent "other" and "unknown." Chinese Americans were the largest group of Asian freshmen (40.5 percent) and constituted 16.9 percent of the total freshman class. Data on admissions provided by Don Nakanishi, Chair of the Asian American Studies Center, University of California, Los Angeles.

23. The suburban Chinese economy of Monterey Park conforms to the general definition of ethnic economy developed by Ivan Light. See Ivan Light and Stavros Karageorgis, "The Ethnic Economy," in Neil Smelser and Richard Swedberg, eds., *Handbook of Economic Sociology* (Princeton: Princeton University Press, 1994), p. 647.

24. Sources for Frederic Hsieh include an interview with Hsieh by Timothy P.

Fong for the Monterey Park Oral History Project, sponsored by the Monterey Park Historical Heritage Commission, April 25, 1990, p. 7; Fong, *First Suburban Chinatown,* pp. 29–31; interview with Frederic Hsieh by John Horton, 1989.

25. City of Monterey Park, California, *Comprehensive Annual Financial Report, June 30, 1989,* and *Comprehensive Annual Financial Report, June 30, 1991.*

26. Liangwen Kuo, a member of our research team, conducted the survey of Chinese supermarkets in July and August 1989.

27. U.S. Bureau of the Census, *Survey of Minority-Owned Business Enterprises 1987,* MB87-1/3 (Washington, D.C.: U.S. Department of Commerce, 1992), table 1, as quoted by Yen-Fen Tseng, "Suburban Ethnic Economy: Chinese Business Communities in Los Angeles" (Ph.D. diss., University of California, Los Angeles, 1994), p. 24. My interpretation of the Chinese ethnic economy in Los Angeles and the San Gabriel Valley relies heavily on Tseng's pioneering research.

28. Tseng, "Suburban Ethnic Economy," p. 4.

29. The 1983 figure was calculated for our research team by Liangwen Kuo and does not include an unknown number of unlisted businesses. The 1992 data were calculated from the Chinese Business Directory (Asia Media System, 1992), and reported in Roger Waldinger and Yen-Fen Tseng, "Divergent Diasporas: The Chinese Communities of New York and Los Angeles Compared," *Revue Européenne des Migrations Internationales* 8 (1992): 99.

30. Waldinger and Tseng, "Divergent Diasporas," p. 104.

31. Tseng, "Suburban Ethnic Economy," pp. 154–63. See also Tseng, "The Chinese Ethnic Economy: San Gabriel Valley, Los Angeles County," *Journal of Urban Affairs* 16 (1994): 169–89; "'Little Taipei' and Beyond: The Development of Taiwanese Immigrant Businesses in Los Angeles," *International Migration Review* (forthcoming, 1995). For a discussion of the impact of immigrant economies in New York, see Louis Winnick, *New People in Old Neighborhoods: The Role of New Immigrants in Rejuvenating New York's Communities* (New York: Russell Sage Foundation, 1990). For a comment on the positive impact of the Chinese ethnic economy of Monterey Park and the San Gabriel Valley on recessionary Los Angeles, see Seth Mydans, "Asian Investors Create a Pocket of Prosperity," *New York Times,* October 17, 1994.

32. Traditionally, theorists of ethnic minorities in the United States have tended to see ethnic economies as barriers to assimilation into the mainstream. See, for example, Milton M. Gordon, *Assimilation in American Life: The Role of Race, Religion, and National Origins* (New York: Oxford University Press, 1964). More recently, theorists have pointed out that many groups, such as Cubans and Asians, are achieving mobility into the mainsteam through ethnic economies and ethnic politics. For a strong statement of this argument, see Alejandro Portes and Rubén G. Rumbaut, *Immigrant America: A Portrait* (Berkeley: University of California Press, 1990).

33. For an ethnographic study of unintended neighbors sharing "problematic communities," see Brett Williams, "Owning Places and Buying Time: Claims, Culture, and Stalled Gentrification," *Urban Life* 14 (1985): 251–73.

CHAPTER 2

1. The long-time resident whose view of community life appears in the epigraph to this chapter was quoted by Henry Chu, "Film on Monterey Park

Conflict Previewed," *Los Angeles Times,* October 25, 1990, San Gabriel Section. Her statement was made during an interview after the discussion of *American Becoming,* a film commissioned by the National Changing Relations Project and directed by Charles Burnett. It was based on ethnographic research on relations between immigrants and established residents in Monterey Park, Houston, Miami, Philadelphia, Chicago, and Garden City, Kansas.

2. Anonymous informant interviewed by Yen-Fen Tseng, 1989.

3. I borrow the term "problematic community" from Brett Williams, "Owning Places and Buying Time: Claims, Culture, and Stalled Gentrification," *Urban Life* 14 (1985): 251–73. Her description of the clashing perceptions of newcomers and established residents in a community is relevant to the sentiments in Monterey Park.

The sociological concept of community as interdependencies formed by established residents in residential areas and the potential structurally based conflict between these residents, their community, and newcomers was used and developed by Norbert Elias and John L. Scotson, *The Established and the Outsiders: A Sociological Inquiry Into Community Problems* (London: Frank Cass, 1965).

4. The accomplishments were well documented in the city's entry for a second "All-America Award" in 1992.

5. Beth Ryan, director of Langley Senior Citizen Center, interviewed by John Horton, 1994.

6. Conversation with Dr. Frances Wu, director of Golden Age Village, at Langley Senior Center, Monterey Park, 1989, reported by John Horton. According to *Asian Week,* August 27, 1993, p. 21, a poll conducted in the California "Bay area" by the Volunteerism Project, Independent Sector, showed that Asians had a relatively low rate of volunteerism: 36 percent, compared with Hispanics at 45 percent, blacks at 39 percent, and whites at 53 percent.

7. Virginia Chavez, director of the Monterey Park Community Office, interviewed by John Horton, 1992.

8. Jim Roberts, the director of LAMP, interviewed by John Horton, September 1992.

9. Dr. Frances Wu, interviewed by John Horton, 1989. See also Chih-Yin Lew-Ting, "Health Perceptions of Aging and Self-Care of Chinese Elderly Residing in Retirement Homes—A Comparative Study" (Ph.D. diss., University of California, Los Angeles, 1992).

10. John Horton, field notes, 1989.

11. Candidate statements of David M. Barron, Official Ballots for General Municipal Elections, April 12, 1988, and April 10, 1990, City of Monterey Park.

12. These and subsequent field notes of Jose Calderon were taken during the winter of 1989.

13. The survey results were compiled by Jose Calderon from data provided by the research team. The field notes were taken by Calderon, John Horton, and Yen-Fen Tseng.

14. Mary Pardo incorporated her research on the parole office fight into a comparative study of Latina grassroots activism in middle-class and multiethnic Monterey Park and working-class and Latino East Los Angeles: "Identity and

Resistance: Mexican American Women and Grassroots Activism in Two Los Angeles Communities" (Ph.D. diss., University of California, Los Angeles, 1990).

CHAPTER 3

1. Mary Pardo, field notes, 1989.

2. Clarence Y. H. Lo, *Small Property Versus Big Government: The Social Origins of the Property Tax Revolt* (Berkeley: University of California Press, 1990), p. 38.

3. H. Russell Paine, ed., *The History of Monterey Park: A Bicentennial Report* (Monterey Park: n.p., April 1976).

4. Office of the City Manager, *Monterey Park: Its History and City Government* (City of Monterey Park, April 1988), pp. 3–4.

5. Ed Salzman, "Mayors Move to Power in California City Halls," *Los Angeles Times,* July 23, 1989.

6. Local businessman interviewed by John Horton, 1989.

7. Ibid.

8. Member of the Kaffee Klatch interviewed by John Horton, 1989.

9. Hal Fiebelkorn, "The Kaffee Klatch," *Citizen's Voice,* April 1993, p. 7.

10. Local Republican leader interviewed by John Horton, 1989. See also Don T. Nakanishi, "The Next Swing Vote? Asian Pacific Americans and California Politics," in Bryan O. Jackson and Michael B. Preston, eds., *Racial and Ethnic Politics in California* (Berkeley: Institute of Governmental Studies Press, 1991), pp. 41–46.

11. Former Monterey Park city councilman interviewed by John Horton, 1992.

12. Ibid.

13. Former member of the Monterey Park Democratic Club interviewed by Linda Shaw, 1989.

14. For a perceptive ethnographic account of responses of white Democrats to ethnic change in their community, see Jonathan Rieder, *Canarsie: The Jews and Italians of Brooklyn Against Liberalism* (Cambridge: Harvard University Press, 1985).

15. Member of the United Democratic Club interviewed by John Horton, 1990.

16. *News Digest,* June 3–9, 1987, p. 19.

17. Howard Winant has argued that while "racial conflict is the archetype of discord in North America," in the current period racial discourse is "decentered and lacking overall coherence": "Postmodern Racial Politics in the United States: Difference and Inequality," *Socialist Review* 20 (January–March 1990): 121–47.

18. Member of the Monterey Park Lions Club interviewed by John Horton, 1989.

19. Louise Davis, interviewed by Linda Shaw, Monterey Park, 1989.

20. Ibid.

21. I owe this interpretation to Mary Pardo, who studied the politicization of women in middle-class Monterey Park and working-class East Los Angeles.

See Mary Pardo, "Identity and Resistance: Mexican American Women and Grassroots Activism in Two Los Angeles Communities" (Ph.D. diss., University of California, Los Angeles, 1990); "Doing It for the Kids: Latina Activism, Border Feminism?" in Myra Marx Ferree and Patricia Yancey Martin, eds., *Feminist Organizations: Harvest of the New Women's Movement* (Philadelphia: Temple University Press, forthcoming, 1995).

22. For an important attempt to define class and ethnicity in a community setting, see Richard H. Thompson, "Ethnicity Versus Class: An Analysis of Conflict in a North American Chinese Community," *Ethnicity* 6 (1979): 306–26.

23. For an ethnographic account of the changing meaning and formation of racial and ethnic identities, see Philip Kasinitz, *Caribbean New York: Black Immigrants and the Politics of Race* (Ithaca and London: Cornell University Press, 1992). For an influential historical theory of race, see Michael Omi and Howard Winant, *Racial Formation in the United States From the 1960s to the 1990s* (New York and London: Routledge, 1994).

24. This emphasis on the construction of ethnicity contrasts sharply with the position of theorists who have stressed the primordial meaning of ethnicity. See, for example, Clifford Goertz, "The Integrative Revolution: Primordial Sentiments and Civic Politics in New States," in *The Interpretation of Cultures* (New York: Basic Books, 1973), pp. 255–310.

25. Our stress on both the analytical independence of newcomer/established-resident struggles and their practical dependence on race and class applies to all struggles, of course. The particular emphasis depends on the social strand and historical moment examined. At one point in time, nativism may dominate; at another, class or ethnicity. This contextual approach does not so much avoid the question of causality as examine it through patterns of determination over time.

CHAPTER 4

1. Rubin and Hsieh made their statements at a panel on economic development held at Monterey Park's second annual Harmony Week, October 26, 1991. Given the range of opinions regarding growth and language control in Monterey Park, an explanation needs to be made of the terminology used to describe the movements discussed in this chapter and elsewhere in the text. My usage depends on viewpoint and context. The more positive term, "Official English," has been favored by the supporters of language legislation. Opponents have favored "English Only" to stress the xeonophobic overtones of the movement. The labels associated with growth control have been more varied. Pro-growth forces have preferred the label "no growth" to emphasize the parochial character of the movement. In Monterey Park, "slow growth" has been a fairly accurate description of the movement's early activist goals. However, slow-growth leaders have increasingly preferred the more neutral terms "growth control" and "managed growth." The latter also suggests negotiation and compromise on the part of growth-control leaders who have joined local governments facing recession and the pressure for growth and revenue.

When speaking for myself rather than for an informant, I use the more neutral "Official English" and "growth control," in recognition of the ideological complexity of these movements. I sometimes use "English Only" and "slow growth" to emphasize the historical association of these movements with immigration and backlash in Monterey Park.

I have benefited from discussions with David R. Diaz concerning the terminology of the growth-control movement. See his informative work, "The Illusionary Grail 'Quality of Life': The Growth Control Movement in Southern California" (Ph.D. diss., University of California, Los Angeles, 1994). For the terminology of language politics, see James Crawford, ed., *Language Loyalties: A Source Book on the Official English Controversy* (Chicago: University of Chicago Press, 1992).

2. *Monterey Park Living* (official newsletter of the City of Monterey Park), June–August 1985, p. 4.

3. Jay Mathews, "Asian-Americans in Ascendancy," *Washington Post*, November 29, 1983.

4. In the early 1980s, the media portraits of immigrant and multiethnic Los Angeles and Monterey Park were glowingly optimistic. See, for example, Kurt Andersen, "The New Ellis Island: Immigrants from All Over Change the Beat, Bop and Character of Los Angeles," *Time*, June 13, 1983, pp. 18–25. By 1989, the portrait had grown darker. In 1989, KCBS included Monterey Park in its documentary on racism in Los Angeles: *Screams of Hatred, Tears of Despair*.

5. City of Monterey Park Sample Ballot and Voter Information Pamphlet, April 8, 1986.

6. Mike Ward, "Monterey Park's New Council Calls a Halt to Building," *Los Angeles Times*, May 1, 1986.

7. Chris Houseman, the fourth Anglo on the Monterey Park city council in 1986, abstained from the vote and later strongly opposed the measure. The fifth councilman, G. Monty Manibog, a Filipino American and a lawyer, was strongly opposed from the start.

8. Text of resolution reprinted in Mike Ward, "Both Sides in Recall Charge 'Racism,'" *Los Angeles Times*, June 7, 1987.

9. Council member interviewed by Mary Pardo, Monterey Park, 1989.

10. Lloyd de Llamas, interviewed by Timothy Fong, Monterey Park, October 23, 1986, as quoted in Timothy Patrick Fong, "The Unique Convergence: A Community Study of Monterey Park, California" (Ph.D. diss., University of California, Berkeley, 1992), p. 310.

11. Gary T. Hunt (consultant to the Monterey Park Community Relations Commission), "Community Relations and Neighborhood Improvement Survey," Monterey Park, March 1986.

12. Mary Pardo, field notes, 1989.

13. Old-time Monterey Park resident interviewed by Jerry Kimery, 1989.

14. Japanese American resident intereviewed by Leland Saito, Monterey Park, 1989.

15. Conversation heard by John Horton during a campaign walk, Monterey Park, 1990.

16. Anglo resident interviewed by Mary Pardo, Monterey Park, 1989.

17. Jose Calderon, field notes, 1989.

18. See John R. Logan and Harvey L. Molotch, *Urban Fortunes: The Politi-*

cal Economy of Place (Berkeley: University of California Press, 1987). The authors generally support the interpretation that the struggle over land use and development is a form of class conflict. The book contains an excellent bibliography on the politics of growth. See also Diaz, "The Illusionary Grail."

19. Mike Davis, *City of Quartz: Excavating the Future in Los Angeles* (London and New York: Verso, 1990), pp. 156, 213, n. 6.

20. For a sympathetic account of RAMP and slow-growth politics in Monterey Park, see Nicholas Lemann, "Growing Pains," *The Atlantic* 261 (January 1988): 57–62. The complex history of Monterey Park's growth-control movement is documented in Timothy P. Fong, *The First Suburban Chinatown: The Remaking of Monterey Park, California* (Philadelphia: Temple University Press, 1994).

21. Irv Gilman, "A Divided City," in "Letters," *Monterey Park Progress,* June 20, 1984, as quoted by Fong, "The Unique Convergence," p. 307.

22. See, for example, Harry C. Boyte and Frank Riessman, eds., *The New Populism: The Politics of Empowerment* (Philadelphia: Temple University Press, 1986). For a well-documented account of the populist movement initially behind Proposition 13 in California, see Clarence Y. H. Lo, *Small Property Versus Big Government: The Social Origins of the Property Tax Revolt* (Berkeley: University of California Press, 1990). Lo convincingly shows a connection between the local homeowners' associations, the tax revolt of the 1970s, and the slow-growth revolt of the 1980s. He argues that the grassroots base of the taxpayers' revolt was progressive, but ultimately the movement was coopted by the upper classes. In the end, Prop. 13 produced a phenomenal tax break for big business.

23. Davis, *City of Quartz,* p. 159. Others have stressed the reactionary and exclusionary class and racial tendencies of the new populist movements. See, for example, Carl Boggs, "The New Populism and the Limits of Structural Reform," *Theory and Society* 12 (1983): 343–63.

24. Frederic Hsieh, statement made in a forum on development, Monterey Park, 1987, field notes, John Horton.

25. Joseph Rubin, interviewed by John Horton, Monterey Park, 1989.

26. In a flyer that appeared during the April 1992 city council elections, Ruth and Irv Willner, long-time Democratic activists and 33-year residents of Monterey Park, attacked RAMP's support of Atlantic Square on the following grounds (emphasis in the original):

> 1) We need shopping 2) we need retail sales taxes–All true, but the cost to obtain the shopping and to garner the sales tax needs to be weighed. *The CRA* [the Community Redevelopment Authority] *issued $14M in bonds and agreed to pay interest and amortization in the amount of $1M/yr which can never be recouped by the anticipated sales tax increase of $250,000/yr.* No amount of boasting can hide the fact that Atlantic Square is both ill advised use of CRA funds (your property tax money) and an unconscionable under the table subsidy ($17M) of a private developer. . . . *RAMP's* anti-development fever gave way to full *support for subsidizing an Anglo Developer* while commending North Atlantic [another large development] which is being fully paid by the Asian Developer.

27. Terri Yachen Peng, translation from Chinese, *Reflections 1916–1991:*

Monterey Park's Past, Present, and Future (Monterey Park, Calif.: Monterey Park 75th Anniversary Committee, Historical Society of Monterey Park, and the City of Monterey Park, 1991), p. 124.

28. Frank Arcuri, "English on Signs," in "Letters," *Monterey Park Progress,* June 20, 1984, as quoted by Fong, "The Unique Convergence," pp. 313–14.

29. The following article was particularly useful in helping me place the racial discourse in Monterey Park within a wider political context: Howard Winant, "Postmodern Racial Politics in the United States: Difference and Inequality," *Socialist Review* 20 (January–March 1990): 121–47.

30. For an analysis of the leadership and supporters of Official English see James Crawford, *Hold Your Tongue: Bilingualism and the Politics of "English Only"* (Chicago: University of Chicago Press, 1992), pp. 175–202.

31. Transcription of the minutes of "Oral Communications," Monterey Park city council meeting, October 27, 1986.

32. Barry Hatch, interviewed by John Horton, Monterey Park, 1989.

33. Jamie B. Draper and Martha Jimenez, "A Chronology of the Official English Movement," in Crawford, *Language Loyalties,* pp. 89–94.

34. Crawford, *Hold Your Tongue,* p. 175.

35. Carol Schmid, "The English Only Movement: Social Bases of Support and Opposition Among Anglos and Latinos," in Crawford, *Language Loyalties,* pp. 202–9.

36. These precinct data were provided by Bryan O. Jackson, who wrote extensively about ethnic politics. See, for example, "Racial and Ethnic Voting Cleavages in Los Angeles Politics," in Byran O. Jackson and Michael B. Preston, eds., *Racial and Ethnic Politics in California* (Berkeley, Calif.: IGS Press, 1991), pp. 193–218.

37. For the neoconservative political tendency see Nathan Glazer, *Affirmative Discrimination: Ethnic Inequality and Public Policy* (Cambridge, Mass.: Harvard University Press, 1987); Norman Podhoretz, *Breaking Ranks: A Political Memoir* (New York: Harper & Row, 1979); Irving Kristol, *Reflections of a Neoconservative: Looking Back, Looking Ahead* (New York: Basic Books, 1983); Arthur Meier Schlesinger, Jr., *The Disuniting of America* (New York: Norton, 1992).

38. Anonymous informant interviewed by John Horton, Monterey Park, 1989.

39. In taking this position, we are agreeing with other urban social scientists who have stressed the contradictory tendencies within populist movements, which may develop in either a progressive or a reactionary direction through political struggle: Joe R. Feagin and Stella M. Capek, "Grassroots Movements in a Class Perspective," *Research in Political Sociology* 5 (1991): 27–53; Mark E. Kann, "The New Populism and the New Marxism: A Response to Carl Boggs," *Theory and Society* 12 (1983): 365–73; Allan David Heskin, *The Struggle for Community* (Boulder, Colo.: Westview Press, 1991).

CHAPTER 5

1. Monterey Park business leader interviewed by John Horton, 1989.
2. Jose Zapata Calderon, "Mexican American Politics in a Multi-Ethnic

Community: The Case of Monterey Park, 1985–1990" (Ph.D. diss., University of California, Los Angeles, 1991), p. 126.

3. Examining ABC's official financial disclosure statement, Timothy Fong calculated that "90 percent of their contributions came from developer-associated individuals and companies." See Timothy Fong, "The Unique Convergence: Monterey Park," *California Sociologist* 12 (Summer 1989): 181.

4. Mike Ward, "Reforms Urged in Monterey Park After Recall Fails," *Los Angeles Times,* June 18, 1987.

5. Alfred H. Song, "The Asian-American in Politics," in Yung-Hwan Jo, ed., *Political Participation of Asian Americans: Problems and Strategies* (Chicago: Pacific/Asian American Mental Health Research Center, 1980), p. 16. For a discussion of rising Asian politics in Monterey Park, see Leland T. Saito and John Horton, "The New Chinese Immigration and the Rise of Asian American Politics in Monterey Park, California," in Paul Ong, Edna Bonacich, and Lucie Cheng, eds., *The New Asian Immigration in Los Angeles and Global Restructuring* (Philadelphia: Temple University Press, 1994), pp. 233–63.

6. For a detailed description and analysis of emerging ethnic and interethnic politics among Latinos in Monterey Park, see Calderon, "Mexican American Politics"; Jose Calderon, "Latinos and Ethnic Conflict in Suburbia: The Case of Monterey Park," *Latino Studies Journal* 2 (May 1990): 23–32.

7. Mike Davis, *City of Quartz: Excavating the Future in Los Angeles* (London and New York: Verso, 1990), p. 141.

8. Calderon, "Mexican American Politics," pp. 139–40.

9. The self-administered questionnaire consisted of 15 items, including candidate choice, sex, ethnicity, age, income, education, place of birth, and length of residence. There were no questions about opinions. Asians were deliberately oversampled in order to tap and examine the diversity of that population. In the end, we collected 1,390 usable questionnaires, representing 17 percent of the 8,148 residents who voted. The voter turnout was fairly high for a city election: 36.3 percent of the 22,436 registered voters.

10. Ward, "Reforms Urged in Monterey Park."

11. The Asian Pacific American Voter Registration Project and the Southwest Voter Research Institute arrived at these figures by using an ethnic name dictionary. This method is not totally accurate, since non-Asian women can acquire Asian names by marriage, names like Lee can be Anglo, Korean, or Chinese, and people with "Latino" names may actually be Filipino. Over time, however, corrections have been made based on precinct walks. Given the demographic composition of Monterey Park, we calculated the Anglo percentage as the percentage which had not been identified as Asian or Latino.

12. Don T. Nakanishi, "The Next Swing Vote? Asian Pacific Americans and California Politics," in Bryan O. Jackson and Michael B. Preston, eds., *Racial and Ethnic Politics in California* (Berkeley: Institute of Governmental Studies Press, University of California, 1991), p. 43.

CHAPTER 6

1. In Monterey Park, mayors are not elected; council members become mayors for nine months on a rotating basis. With the increased politicization of

the city council, the mayoral inauguration has become a royal occasion, a potlatch with sometimes lavish displays of multiethnic entertainment, food, and endorsements.

2. Barry L. Hatch, Mayor Pro Tem, letter dated July 28, 1988.

3. Mary Pardo, field notes, 1989.

4. Chinese American informant interviewed by Mary Pardo, Monterey Park, 1989.

5. John Horton, field notes, 1989.

6. Given the highly competitive character of education and professional jobs in Taiwan, Hong Kong, and other areas of Asia, some parents believe that their children will have a better chance of success and mobility in the American system. Moreover, those who stay in the United States and become citizens can send for their relatives under family unification laws. However, separation is hard on parents and the children, who may live alone or with other relatives. Hence, the need for programs to address the needs of "orphaned" immigrant children.

7. Marc Cooper, "Monterey Park Fights Back," *LA Weekly,* May 19–25, 1989, p. 32.

8. RAMP member interviewed by John Horton, Monterey Park, 1989.

9. Ibid.

10. Research team field notes, 1989.

11. Research team field notes, 1989.

12. Prominent Republican woman interviewed by John Horton, 1989.

13. Ibid.

14. John Horton, field notes, 1989.

15. Anonymous informant interviewed by Yen-Fen Tseng, Monterey Park, 1989.

16. *The Record,* a campaign newsletter paid for by the Residents' Association of Monterey Park. PAC: Monterey Park Residents for Responsible Growth, April 1990. Emphasis in original.

17. As mentioned elsewhere, Chinese have a much better record of fundraising than other established residents, but some locals are catching on to the pattern. Collecting $24,000, with ample representation from business interests, Balderrama was the second-biggest spender. By contrast, Hatch, opposed in principle to the spiraling of campaign costs, reported a total of $950.00, of which $600.00 came from personal loans and $350.00 from the Monterey Park Republican Club, three local residents, and one person from Texas listed as "retired." Although Hatch had close ties to national organizations like U.S. English, he did not command the dollars of local professional and business people. The other three candidates, Purvis, Barron, and Reichenberger, reported from $11,000 to $19,000, closer to Balderrama's funds but far short of Kiang's.

18. *The Record.*

19. The 1990 exit poll was initiated and carried out entirely by our research team without input from local groups. In 1988, we had participated in a poll designed by the Asian Pacific American Voters Registration Project with technical assistance from the Southwest Voters Research Institute. Having learned about polling from them, we designed our own questionnaire and printed it in English and Chinese. In addition to repeating most of the questions of the 1988

poll, we added more questions on the ethnic origins and language of voters and on their attitudes on several issues (bilingualism and pesticide spraying). The poll was conducted in all precincts during the busy morning and evening hours. The multiethnic UCLA pollsters were instructed to approach every third voter. We collected 974 usable questionnaires.

20. These data on voters who voted in the 1990 Monterey Park municipal election were provided by Political Data, Inc., P.O. Box 1706, Burbank, Calif., May 1993. The data are limited in two respects. First, they refer only to persons registered in 1993 who voted in 1990, thereby excluding persons who voted in 1990 but were not registered in 1993. Second, the method of identifying ethnicity by name is only approximate. Nevertheless, a comparison with the profile of self-identified ethnic voters in the poll suggests that it is roughly accurate. See note 11 to chapter 5 for further discussion.

21. "The Process of Empowerment," editorial, *Los Angeles Times,* June 11, 1993.

22. "Anglo Vote Carried Riordan to Victory," *Los Angeles Times,* June 10, 1993.

23. The data on the exit poll presented in this chapter were analyzed by Yen-Fen Tseng, a member of our UCLA research team. She ran six log-linear models of six candidate choices by controlling for the seven independent variables at the same time.

24. Conversation reported by Yen-Fen Tseng, 1990.

25. For discussions of Asian American, Anglo, and Latino views on language issues, see the following articles in James Crawford, ed., *Language Loyalties: A Source Book on the Official English Controversy* (Chicago: University of Chicago Press, 1992): Max Castro, "On the Curious Question of Language in Miami," pp. 178–86; John Horton and Jose Calderon, "Language Struggles in a Changing California Community," pp. 186–94; Camilo Perez-Bustillo, "What Happens When English Only Comes to Town? A Case Study of Lowell, Massachusetts," pp. 194–201; Carol Schmid, "The English Only Movement: Social Bases of Support and Opposition Among Anglos and Latinos," pp. 202–9.

CHAPTER 7

1. Irene Chang, "New Council Majority Takes a Softer Line on Growth," *Los Angeles Times,* San Gabriel Section, November 18, 1990.

2. Er-Lee Wang, "Has Judy Chu Changed Direction?" *Chinese Daily News,* July 22, 1991. Translated by Terri Yachen Peng.

3. See the detailed coverage of Irene Chang: "Low Employee Morale Cost Lewis His Job," *Los Angeles Times,* San Gabriel Section, July 25, 1991; "Embattled Chu Airs Bilingual Hiring Plan," July 28, 1991; "Lewis Did Not Reveal Unfavorable Report," August 1, 1991; "Chu Backs Off from Bilingual Hiring Plan," August 1, 1991.

For coverage in *Asian Week,* the major Asian American newspaper, see Howard Hong, "Chinese Split Signals Power Play in Monterey Park," August 2, 1991, p. 1; Edward Cheng, "Councilwoman Judy Chu Draws Ire of Chinese American Community," August 2, 1991, p. B1; Howard Hong, "Monterey Park Councilman Sam Kiang Fires Back, Responds to Asian Week Analysis," August

9, 1991, p. B1; Ronald W. Wong, "Monterey Park: A Melting Pot Boils Over Once Again," August 16, 1991, p. B1.

4. All quotations in this section are taken from the field notes of John Horton, made in July 1991 during the city council sessions devoted to a public discussion of Lewis's firing and Kiang's proposal to implement the hiring of bilingual dispatchers.

5. For a discussion of the historical roots of Chinese separatism in America, see Peter Kwong, *Chinatown, New York: Labor and Politics, 1930–1950* (New York: Monthly Review Press, 1979), p. 148. Today, in suburban Los Angeles, the structural basis for separatism and Chinese nationalism is fear of discrimination and the existence of a local ethnic economy with strong links to Chinese in Taiwan, Hong Kong, and elsewhere.

6. Samuel Kiang, interviewed by John Horton, June 1992.

7. Ibid.

8. *Citizen's Voice,* January–March 1992, p. 3. The newspaper is published by Frank J. Arcuri, an activist in the Official English movement and three-time candidate for city council.

9. James Rainey, "Minorities Poised for Gains at Ballot Box," *Los Angeles Times,* April 14, 1992.

10. Tina Griego, "Replanting Bell Gardens," *Los Angeles Times,* March 24, 1992. For an analysis of ethnic and class conflict between Latinos and Anglos in southeast Los Angeles, see Mike Davis, "The Empty Quarter," in David Reid, ed., *Sex, Death and God in L.A.* (New York: Pantheon Books, 1992), pp. 54–71. As in Monterey Park, ethnic conflict in Bell Gardens was intertwined with the local class struggle over the control and use of land. However, in working-class Bell Gardens, the rebels were renters, not homeowners. In middle-class Monterey Park, white slow-growth rebels fought for their single-family dwellings against Chinese-financed high-density land uses. In Bell Gardens, Latino rebels opposed the white council's approval of low-density and, by implication, unaffordable housing for the unwanted immigrant hordes.

11. Rainey, "Minorities Poised for Gains."

12. Edmund Newton and Berkeley Hudson, "Ethnic Diversity Is an Election Winner," *Los Angeles Times,* San Gabriel Section, April 16, 1992.

13. Irene Chang, "Council Victors Stressed Community Ties," *Los Angeles Times,* April 16, 1992. Unfortunately, Bonnie Wai did not grant us an interview and the opportunity to understand the election more fully from her viewpoint.

14. Ibid.

15. City of Monterey Park voter information pamphlet, General Municipal Election, April 14, 1992, p. 5.

16. Monterey Park General Municipal Election of April 10, 1990, Office of the City Clerk.

17. Campaign disclosure statements, January 1, 1992, through March 28, 1992, Office of the City Clerk, Monterey Park. George Pla, a political consultant working in the San Gabriel region, estimated that some candidates (primarily the Chinese) were spending between fifteen and twenty dollars per vote, compared with an average of three dollars in neighboring San Gabriel cities. Irene Chang,

"Fund-Raisers Target Asian-Americans," the *Los Angeles Times,* San Gabriel edition, March 12, 1992.

18. Rita Valenzuela, a long-established Mexican American resident and an active member of the city's Arts and Cultural Commission, ran a low-key, low-financed campaign that depended on support from her family and a cross-section of established residents. Her electoral strategy was to target Mexican American voters in the southern part of town.

19. *The Record,* paid for by the Residents' Association of Monterey Park, April 1992.

20. Newton and Hudson, "Ethnic Diversity Is an Election Winner"; Mike Ward, "Ethnic Diversity Is an Election Winner," *Los Angeles Times,* San Gabriel edition, April 16, 1992.

21. James Rainey, "Latinos Make Gains in Council Election," *Los Angeles Times,* April 15, 1992; Tina Griego, "Bell Gardens Recall Vote Tests Latino Power," *Los Angeles Times,* December 8, 1991.

22. Mark Kendall, "Asians Elected for the First Time in Two Valley Cities," *San Gabriel Valley Tribune,* April 16, 1992.

23. Chang, "Council Victors Stressed Community Ties."

24. Lucia Su, "Chinese People Did Go to Polls," Letters to the Editor, *Los Angeles Times,* San Gabriel Section, April 26, 1992.

25. These calculations were based on information provided by Political Data, Inc., Burbank, Calif. They refer to voters who were registered in 1993 and voted in the 1992 municipal elections. They are approximate because they omit people who voted in 1992, but were not living in the same precinct in 1993.

26. According to California law, if BCTC had decided to go ahead with the card club, it would have had to file public notice, then within 30 days collect 3,466 valid signatures, or 15 percent of the city's registered voters, in order to call a special election on the issue. Renee Tawa, "Developer Drops Plan to Build Card Casino," *Los Angeles Times,* San Gabriel Valley edition, March 11, 1993. Unlike Nevada-style "casinos," California card clubs allow only so-called games of skill, such as poker, and players gamble against each other, rather than against the house.

27. Tawa, "Developer Drops Plan to Build Card Casino."

28. In 1981, city residents had no heart for gambling, and developers, in their frenzy for speculative building, had no heart for slow-growth advocates. A week before the municipal election of 1982, candidates Gilman, Couch, and Sonya Gerlach, their comrade in no-growth and pro-casino revolt, were proclaimed the "poker-slate" by a "hit piece" financed by pro-growth interests. They lost the election to David Almada, Lily Chen, and Rudy Peralta, who, in turn, lost their reelection campaign in 1986 when RAMP hit them with the "pro-developer" label. For a discussion of Monterey Park politics during this period see Timothy P. Fong, *The First Suburban Chinatown: The Remaking of Monterey Park, California* (Philadelphia: Temple University Press, 1994), pp. 90–95.

29. Before 1980, the only card club in Los Angeles County was in Gardena, a city with a large Japanese American population. In the 1980s clubs were established in the poorer and increasingly Latino southern part of the county in Bell,

the City of Commerce, Huntington Park, and Bell Gardens. The largest and most competitive facility was and still is the Bicycle Club in Bell Gardens. In 1992, voters in Los Angeles County approved clubs in two cities, bringing the total to seven, all located south of Monterey Park. In 1993, four more facilities were being planned or proposed, and BCTC Development Corporation was studying the possibility of a fifth club in Monterey Park. See Sandra Sutphen, Ronald M. Grant, and Barbara Ball, "Upping the Ante: Gambling as a Revenue Source for Local Government," *Southeastern Political Review* 22 (1994): 77–96; Ken Ellingwood, "Card Clubs Come Up Losers with Voters," *Los Angeles Times,* June 10, 1993.

30. J. Richard Myers, Vice President of the BCTC Development Corporation, letter to the Monterey Park city council, February 23, 1993.

31. Phyllis Rabins, statement made publicly during the city council meeting of February 22, 1993.

32. John Horton, field notes taken at council meeting, February 22, 1993.

33. Undated editorial (1991) from the *Monterey Park Progress.*

34. The city council resolution of February 22, 1993, thus affirmed an existing municipal code prohibiting gambling within Monterey Park. Kiang wanted to strengthen the resolution with the words "take all steps necessary to keep gambling establishments illegal." On the advice of the City Attorney, four council members added the words "all legal steps." In the end, Kiang alone voted against his own amended resolution and vowed that residents would have to vote him out of office to change his resolve on the issue of gambling.

35. Tawa, "Developer Drops Plan to Build Card Casino."

36. Card parlor referendums were defeated in Pico Rivera, Bellflower, and West Hollywood (Los Angeles County) and in Cypress and Stanton (Orange County). Political scientists who have studied the effect of gambling on crime and revenues in Los Angeles County have argued that the two major bases of opposition were fear of crime and fear of giving cities any more money: See Sutphen, Grant, and Ball, "Upping the Ante." Underlying both was the drive of ordinary citizens to have greater control over their lived environment, a matter complicated by the racial and class composition of the cities involved.

37. See Mary Pardo, "Identity and Resistance: Mexican American Women and Grassroots Activism in Two Los Angeles Communities" (Ph.D. diss., University of California, Los Angeles, 1990). Pardo compares working-class Latina activists in Boyle Heights, an ethnically homogeneous part of Los Angeles, with women in ethnically mixed and middle-class Monterey Park.

38. Lucia Su, statement made publicly during the city council meeting of February 22, 1993.

39. *Reflections, 1916–1991: Monterey Park's Past, Present, and Future* (Monterey Park, Calif.: Monterey Park 75th Anniversary Committee, Historical Society of Monterey Park, and the City of Monterey Park, 1991), p. 124. Translation from Chinese by Terri Yachen Peng.

40. Leland T. Saito and John Horton, "The New Chinese Immigration and the Rise of Asian American Politics in Monterey Park, California" in Paul Ong, Edna Bonacich, and Lucie Cheng, eds., *The New Asian Immigration in Los Angeles and Global Restructuring* (Philadelphia: Temple University Press, 1994), p. 384.

CHAPTER 8

1. Between 1989 and 1994, 92 formal interviews were conducted with 34 Anglos, 12 Japanese Americans, 6 American-born Chinese, 26 Chinese American immigrants, and 14 Mexican Americans. The method used in this chapter was to look for important trends within and between ethnic and immigrant groups, then illustrate these trends with quotations from the lives of the persons interviewed. None of them are identified by name.

This chapter relies heavily on data collected by different members of the team. Several have published their own analyses of identity. See Jose Z. Calderon, "Situational Identity of Suburban Mexican American Politicians in a Multi-Ethnic Community," in Roberto M. De Anda, ed., *Contemporary Chicanos: Explorations in Culture, Politics, and Society* (Boston: Allyn and Bacon, forthcoming); Mary Pardo, "Doing It for the Kids: Latina Activism, Border Feminism?" in Myra Marx Ferree and Patricia Yancey Martin, eds., *Feminist Organizations: Harvest of the New Women's Movement* (Philadelphia: Temple University Press, forthcoming, 1995); Leland T. Saito, "Contrasting Patterns of Adaptation: Japanese Americans and Chinese Immigrants in Monterey Park," in Linda Revilla, Gail Nomura, Shawn Wong, and Shirley Hune, eds., *Bearing Dreams, Shaping Visions: Asian Pacific American Perspectives* (Pullman, Wash.: Washington State University Press, 1993), pp. 33–43; Leland T. Saito, "Japanese Americans and the New Chinese Immigrants: The Politics of Adaptation," *California Sociologist* 12 (1989): 195–211.

2. Here we are describing a visible tendency among Anglo Americans in Monterey Park. Everyone is aware of it, but it is expressed most clearly by older and more conservative whites. Republicans or Democrats, liberals or reactionaries, these residents were conservative in the sense that they identified themselves first and foremost as Americans—core, unhyphenated Americans, the exemplars and conservators of national values. They were the leaders and rank-and-file of the slow-growth and nativist movements—people who resisted change, but who were themselves changed by doing the practical work of living in a multiethnic community.

3. See, for example, Charles Hirschman, "America's Melting Pot Reconsidered," *Annual Review of Sociology* 9 (1983): 397–423.

4. William L. Yancey, Eugene P. Ericksen, and Richard N. Juliani, "Emergent Ethnicity: A Review and Reformulation," *American Sociological Review* 41 (1976): 391–403; Michael Omi and Howard Winant, *Racial Formation in the United States From the 1960s to the 1990s* (New York: Routledge, 1994).

5. Nathan Glazer and Daniel Patrick Moynihan, *Beyond the Melting Pot: The Negroes, Puerto Ricans, Jews, Italians and Irish of New York City* (Cambridge, Mass.: MIT Press, 1963); Michael Novak, *The Rise of the Unmeltable Ethnics: Politics and Culture in the Seventies* (New York: Macmillan, 1973).

6. Stephen Steinberg, *The Ethnic Myth: Race, Ethnicity, and Class in America* (Boston: Beacon Press, 1981).

7. Micaela di Leonardo, *The Varieties of Ethnic Experience: Kinship, Class, and Gender Among California Italian-Americans* (Ithaca: Cornell University Press, 1984), p. 103.

8. Other social scientists have noted the "symbolic" and voluntary charac-

ter of white ethnicity; see Herbert J. Gans, "Symbolic Ethnicity: The Future of Ethnic Groups and Cultures in America," *Ethnic and Racial Studies* 2 (1979): 1–20; Mary C. Waters, *Ethnic Options: Choosing Identities in America* (Berkeley: University of California Press, 1990).

9. I am arguing less for the disappearance of ethnicity among white Americans than the transformation of their unhyphenated American identity into new ethnic categories such as "Anglo" and, increasingly, "European American." The position has also been taken by Richard D. Alba, *Ethnic Identity: The Transformation of White America* (New Haven: Yale University Press, 1990).

10. Anonymous informant interviewed by Jose Calderon, Monterey Park, 1989. All quotations in this section, unless otherwise identified, are taken from interviews conducted by Calderon.

11. Anonymous informant interviewed by John Horton, Monterey Park, 1989.

12. Jose Z. Calderon, "Mexican American Politics in a Multi-Ethnic Community: The Case of Monterey Park, 1985–1990" (Ph.D. diss., University of California, Los Angeles, 1991), p. 84.

13. Anonymous informant interviewed by Mary Pardo, Monterey Park, 1989.

14. Anonymous informant interviewed by Mary Pardo, Monterey Park, 1989.

15. Anonymous informant interviewed by John Horton, Monterey Park, 1989.

16. Anonymous informant interviewed by Mary Pardo, Monterey Park, 1989.

17. Anonymous informant interviewed by Mary Pardo, Monterey Park, 1989.

18. Calderon, "Mexican American Politics," pp. 151–52.

19. Anonymous informant interviewed by Leland Saito, Monterey Park, 1989. Unless otherwise indicated, all quotations in this section come from Saito's interviews.

20. See Saito, "Patterns of Adaptation"; Saito, "Japanese Americans and the New Chinese Immigrants"; Yuji Ichioka, *The Issei: The World of First Generation Japanese Immigrants, 1885–1924* (New York: Free Press, 1988); Harry Kitano, *Japanese Americans: The Evolution of a Subculture* (Englewood Cliff, N.J.: Prentice-Hall, 1969); Ronald Takaki, *Strangers from a Different Shore: A History of Asian Americans* (New York: Penguin, 1990).

21. Leland T. Saito, "Politics in a New Demographic Era: Asian Americans in Monterey Park, California" (Ph.D. diss., University of California, Los Angeles, 1992), p. 96.

22. For a discussion of the favorable and unfavorable conditions for the construction of Asian American politics and identities see: Leland T. Saito and John Horton, "The New Chinese Immigration and the Rise of Asian American Politics in Monterey Park, California," in Paul Ong, Edna Bonacich, and Lucie Cheng, eds., *The New Asian Immigration in Los Angeles and Global Restructuring* (Philadelphia: Temple University Press, 1994), pp. 233–63; Yen Le Espiritu,

Asian American Panethnicity: Bridging Institutions and Identities (Philadelphia: Temple University Press, 1992).

23. Story reported by Yen-Fen Tseng, 1991.

24. Charles Choy Wong, "Ethnicity, Work, and Community: The Case of Chinese in Los Angeles" (Ph.D. diss., University of California, Los Angeles, 1979), pp. 259–60, 297–300. See also Charles Choy Wong, "Monterey Park: A Community in Transition," in Gail M. Nomura, Russell Endo, Stephen H. Sumida, and Russell Leong, eds., *Frontiers of Asian American Studies* (Pullman: Washington State University Press, 1989), pp. 113–26.

25. Terri Yachen Peng, translation from Chinese, "Monterey Park, Looking to the Future," in *Reflections, 1916–1991: Monterey Park's Past, Present, and Future* (Monterey Park, Calif.: Monterey Park 75th Anniversary Committee, Historical Society of Monterey Park, and the City of Monterey Park, 1991), p. 124.

26. Anonymous informant interviewed by Yen-Fen Tseng, 1989.

27. Anonymous informant interviewed by John Horton, 1990.

28. For a discussion of the immigration of highly educated people in the context of the world economy, see Paul Ong, Lucie Cheng, and Leslie Evans, "Migration of Highly Educated Asians and Global Dynamics," *Asian and Pacific Migration* 1 (1992): 543–67.

29. The major finding is that the shift from bilingualism to monolingualism is more rapid in the United States than in any other country. See Stanley Lieberson, Guy Dalto, and Mary Ellen Johnston, "The Course of Mother-Tongue Diversity in Nations," *American Journal of Sociology* 81 (1975): 34–61; Stanley Lieberson, *Language Diversity and Language Contact* (Stanford, Calif.: Stanford University Press, 1981). For a defense of the benefits of bilingualism in the current period of U.S. history, see Alejandro Portes and Rubén G. Rumbaut, *Immigrant America: A Portrait* (Berkeley: University of California Press, 1990), pp. 180–221.

30. Field notes by Yen-Fen Tseng, 1990.

31. Anonymous informant interviewed by Yen-Fen Tseng, 1989.

32. Anonymous informant interviewed by John Horton, 1989.

33. Anonymous informant interviewed by John Horton, 1989.

34. Anonymous informants interviewed by Yen-Fen Tseng, 1989.

35. "Balderrama a Friend of the Chinese," *World Journal*, April 11, 1990.

CHAPTER 9

1. Jose Calderon, field notes taken during Play Days (an annual festival celebrating the founding of Monterey Park), May 1989.

2. John Horton, field notes, 1989.

3. John Horton, field notes, Fourth of July celebration, 1989.

CHAPTER 10

1. John Horton, conversation with Louise Davis, June 1994.

2. David T. Lau, "Introduction," in *Reflections, 1916–1991: Monterey Park's Past, Present, and Future* (Monterey Park, Calif.: Monterey Park 75th Anniversary Committee, Historical Society of Monterey Park, and the City of Mon-

terey Park, 1991), p. 3. In addition to Lau, the book was edited by David Barron, City Clerk; Russ Paine of the Monterey Park Historical Society; and Timothy Fong, who served on the Committee while living in Monterey Park and doing research on the city.

3. I am indebted to Linda Shaw, always the ethnographer, for suggesting that ethnicity functioned as a resource in Monterey Park politics.

4. The discussion of types of diversity was inspired by remarks made by Korbena Mercer at a panel on "Constructing Identity" during a conference entitled "Act of Commitment/Arts of Change," sponsored by the Los Angeles Festival, Pasadena, Calif., January 15, 1994. In talking about identity in multiethnic societies, Mercer distinguished between "corporate," "competitive," and "connective multiculturalism." I have adapted these insightful concepts, developed in the field of art, to my discussion of the politics of diversity.

5. Immanuel Wallerstein has observed that if we wish to understand the cultural forms of politico-economic struggles, "we cannot afford to take 'traditions' at their face value, in particular we cannot afford to assume that 'traditions' are in fact traditional." He meant that cultural and ethnic formations are the changing outcomes of the way groups have been incorporated into the capitalist world system. See Immanuel Wallerstein, *Historical Capitalism* (London: Verso, 1983), p. 76. For an ethnographic view of the construction of identities in an ethnically mixed and multicultural world, see Renato Rosaldo, *Culture and Truth: The Remaking of Social Analysis* (Boston: Beacon, 1989), pp. 196–217.

6. My interpretations are based on knowledge of Monterey Park politics and interviews with some of the activists and candidates involved in the 1994 election.

7. "City Council to Have Chinese Majority? Would Be First in America," *Citizen's Voice,* March 1994, p. 1; Duke Helfand and Richard Winton, "Local Elections Decide Range of Offices, Issues," *Los Angeles Times,* April 4, 1994.

8. Acting Secretary of State Tony Miller, News Release, "Anonymous Monterey Park Mailing Blasted," April 5, 1994; Hector Gonzalez, "'Intimidating' Election Mailer Linked to Firm That Lost Bid to Build Casino," *Star News,* April 7, 1994.

9. *The Record,* sponsored by the Residents' Association of Monterey Park, April 1994.

10. Barry Hatch's past and recent political activities were featured in Ed Liebowitz, "Master Race Theater: To Understand the Push for 187, Watch How Some of Its Backers Deport Themselves," *LA Weekly,* October 14–20, 1994, pp. 26–33.

Index

ABC: interethnic politics and, 121; municipal elections of 1988 and, 110
ABC (A Better Cityhood), 101, 104–6, 251n.3
absentee ballots, 165–66, 235–36
accommodation: meaning of diversity in, 232–34; socio-political conditions for, 229–32
affirmative action: newcomer-established resident confrontation over, 151–60; newcomer-established resident cooperation regarding, 38–40
African Americans: absence of, in Monterey Park, 11; Chinese immigrants' stereotyping of, 212–13
age levels, among newcomers and established residents, 20
Ai Hoa supermarket, 30
alienation, established residents' perceptions of, 84–88
Almada, David, 80–82, 100, 104, 138, 177, 196
Alonso, Francisco, 235
Alpha Beta Market, 30
American Becoming, 245n.1
American identity: ambiguity of ethnicity in face of, 229–30; Chinese immigrant ethnicity and, 203–14; definition of, 206–209; ethnicity and, 185–214; of "hyphenated" Americans, 190–203; of "unhyphenated" Americans, 186–90
Americanism. *See also* nativism; ethnicity and, 185–214; flag ordinance and, 104; as Hatch's campaign theme, 126–29; Monterey Park politics and, 81–83; Official English movement and, 95–97
Americans for Border Control, 96
Anglos: Asian American politics and, 107–8; candidate choices among, 143–44; card club dispute and, 176–84; on City Council, 60, 123–24; decline in political power of, 140–41, 228; Democratic Party politics and, 66–69; disenchantment with Hatch, 130–35; ethnicity and identity crisis among, 186–90, 257n.2, 258n.9; growth-control movement and, 70, 81; history of Monterey Park and, 218–20; interethnic and cross-ethnic alliances, 116, 145–47, 150; multiethnic empowerment at expense of, 140–41; observations of, 5; Official English movement supported by, 98; opposition to Kiang among, 159; perceived racial discrimination against, 84–88; progressive multiculturalism among, 71; statistics concerning, 19–20; suspicion of Chu among, 133–34; voting patterns among, 114, 116, 120–21, 141–43, 171
anti-immigrant movement: capitalist/progressive alliance against, 101–4; card club dispute and, 178–79; City Council structure and, 123–24; defeat of Hatch and, 124–25, 134–35; ethnic politics and, 106–9; growth control politics and, 91–93, 100; municipal elections of 1988, 110–11; Official English movement and, 94–97, 100
Arcadia, 208
architecture in Monterey Park, 13
Arcuri, Frank, 81–82, 94, 96–97, 111, 113, 162, 168, 174, 254n.8
Asian Americans. *See also specific Asian groups, e.g.,* Japanese Americans; American identity of, 197–203; card club proposal, attitudes regarding, 176–78, 180–82; Chu's campaign and, 164–66; in civic organizations, 65–66; class restructuring among, 33–34; Democratic Party politics and, 67–69; ethnic and cross-ethnic politics, 106–8, 115–16; ethnic diversity among, 21; ethnic-interethnic dialectic among, 158–60, 162–63; global context of immigration, 13–

Asian Americans (*cont.*)
18; growth control movement and, 70; history of Monterey Park and, 220; identity crisis among, 202–3; immigration patterns among, 11–14, 18–19; in Monterey Park Sports Club, 43–45; observations of, 5; "old-boy" network attitudes regarding, 63–64; political empowerment of, 118–19, 162–166, 228; progressive multiculturalism among, 71; racism regarding, 84–88; Republican Party embrace of, 134; socioeconomic profiles, 24–27; stereotypes of, 24–26; terminology regarding, 241n.4; undocumented immigrant estimates, 18–19; voting patterns, 114–16
Asian Americans for a Better Community, 162–63
Asian Pacific American Voter Registration Project, 11, 112, 114, 251n.9, 252n.19
Asian Youth Project, 129–30
assimilation: by Chinese immigrants, 203–14; co-ethnic interpretations of, 205–6; definitions of newcomers and established residents and, 19–20; empowerment not linked with, 194–97; ethnic economy and, 32–33, 244n.32; ethnicity and, 185–214; by Japanese Americans, 118–19, 198–203; in Mexican Americans, 191–97
Atlantic Square Mall, 92–93, 249n.26

Bach, Robert L., 8
Balderrama, Fred, 110, 113; Asian support for, 115, 117, 213; candidate choice and ethnicity, 142–44, 147; card club proposal and, 175, 180; Latino support for, 119–20, 252n.17; festivals under, 223; growth control movement and, 137, 139–40; immigrants defended by, 151–60; reelection of, 235
ballroom dancing, ethnic separateness and, 41–42
banks, Chinese ethnic economy and, 29
Barnes Park: culturally diverse festivals in, 220–23; traditional celebrations in, 4, 64
Barron, David, 43–44, 136, 138, 216–17, 142–44, 147, 252n.17
BCTC Development Corporation, 174–77, 180, 236, 255n.26, 256n.29
Bell Gardens, 160–61, 254n.10, 256n.29
Berman, Howard, 108
bilingualism. *See also* English proficiency ***and*** Official English movement; established residents-newcomer confrontation over, 151–60; ethnicity balanced with interethnic currents in support of, 145–47, 171, 183–84; generational differences in Chinese ethnicity and, 209–11, 259n.29; in candidate forums, 163; Official English movement and, 94
block parties, cultural diversity promoted through, 216–18
Bradshaw, James, 62
Briglio, Cam, 103, 110, 113, 117, 119–20
Brown, George Jr., 67

cable television, 243n.18
Calderon, Charles, 108, 167
Calderon, Jose: on affirmative action, 154–55; on block parties, 216–18; card club dispute, 177–78; community building efforts, 37–38, 42, 102–9; Mexican American sense of ethnicity and, 192, 196–97
Californians for Population Stability, 96
capitalism, alliance with progressives for civil rights, 101–4
card club proposal, 174–82, 235–36, 255nn.26–29, 256nn.34–36; emergence of diversity and, 228; Los Angeles budget crisis, 175
Casperson, John, 162
Census reports, ethnic diversity of Chinese immigrants masked by, 22
Central American immigrants, undocumented immigrant estimates, 18–19. *See also* Latinos
Central Daily News, 117
Chamber of Commerce of Monterey Park: Chinese immigrant assimilation through, 205–6, 223; ethnic group membership in, 65; "old-boy" network and, 62–63
CHAMP (Citizens for Harmony in Monterey Park): interethnic politics and, 121–22; municipal elections of 1988 and, 110; progressive-capitalist alliance in, 101–4
Chan Lien, 243n.18
Chan, Peter, 47, 235

Changing Relations Project, 7–8, 245n.1
Chau, Chester, 169
Chen, Lily Lee, 68, 74, 153; defeated as incumbent, 82, 100; elected mayor of Monterey Park, 80–81, 102, 107, 138; Official English movement politics and, 94, 97
Cheung, Susanna, 224
Child Task Force, 38
China TV, 162
Chinatown Service Center, 84
Chinese American Association of Southern California, 162, 224
Chinese American Political Action Committee, 224
Chinese American Political Alliance, 162–63
Chinese American Professional Society, 162
Chinese Americans: ambivalence regarding identity of, 185–86; attitude toward Chinese immigrants among, 27; candidate choice and ethnicity among, 142–44; card club dispute and, 174–84; City Council structure and, 123–24; defeat of Hatch and, 126–29; empowerment patterns and, 140–41; ethnicity crossed with interethnic currents among, 145–47, 234–37; Official English movement supported by, 98; racism against, 199–200; voting patterns, 114–16, 141–42, 170–72
Chinese Civil Rights and Education Association, 207
Chinese Consolidated Benevolent Association, 224
Chinese Daily News/World Journal, 30, 117, 152–53, 163
Chinese Evangelical Free Church, 177
Chinese Exclusion Act of 1882, 23
Chinese immigrants. *See also* Taiwanese immigrants; age levels among, 20; American identity defined by, 206–9; backlash against, 235–37; characteristics of, 15–21; Chinese Americans' isolation from, 37–38; Chu's 1992 campaign and, 164–66; civic organizations, involvement in, 65–66; community vision of, 36–58; established residents' confrontation with, 151–60; ethnic economy of, 28–33; ethnicity and identity crisis among, 186, 203–14; generational differences in, 209–11; geographic diversity among, 21–22, 243n.16; geographic shift of, in Monterey Park region, 21, 24; growth control politics and, 91–93, 100; history of, 23–24; interethnic alliances and ethnicity for, 107–8, 163, 212–13; language proficiency among, 209–11; migration and settlement patterns, 11–12, 15–18; municipal elections of 1988 and, 113–14; political empowerment of, 116–17, 155–56, 161–63; primacy of ethnic representation for, 116–17; Russell Avenue Neighborhood Watch Association and, 48–52; senior citizen care among, 40–41; separatism among, 158–60, 254n.5; settlement patterns, 15–18; socioeconomic profile, 25–27, 116–17
Chinese Lion Dance, 217, 221
Chinese New Year, cultural diversity at, 222–23
Chinese Parent-Teacher Association, 37, 213
Chinese Political Action Committee, 155, 162–63
Chinese-language television, 243n.18
Christmas in April, 38
Chu, Judy, 68, 74; Anglo support for, 120–21; as Chinese immigrants' representative, 116–17, 151–60; calculation of ethnic votes by, 161; California State Assembly campaign of, 202; card club dispute and, 179–80, 183; councilwomen's relations with, 129–30; diversity, commitment to, 224, 228; election campaign of 1994, 234–35; election to City Council, 101, 109–11, 113, 124–25, 138, 150; erosion of support for, 156–58; ethnic and cross-ethnic voting patterns and, 115–16, 156–60; firing of Mark Lewis by, 152; history of Monterey Park and, 219; Japanese American support for, 118–19; Latino support for, 119–20, 194; Mexican American support for, 213; municipal election of 1990 and, 136–37; municipal election of 1992 and, 162, 164–74; Official English movement and, 97–99; RAMP alliance with, 131–33
Cinco de Mayo festivals, 216–17, 222

Citizen Advisory Board: parole office dispute, 52
citizenship, ideology of, newcomers vs. established residents, 76–78
Citizen's Voice, 81–82, 97, 160, 174, 235
City Council of Monterey Park: Asian majority predicted for, 236–37; community service record of members, 56–57; comparison of 1988 and 1990 council membership, 123–24; contentiousness of, 4, 59–60; ethnic changes in, 59, 81–83, 168–69; multiethnic community building and, 51–52; Official English movement politics and, 94–99; political structure of, 59–62; Resolution 9004 rescinded by, 103–4; women on, 129–30
City Manager government, structure of, 59–62
city programs, newcomer and established resident cooperation regarding, 37–40
civic organizations: Asian American politics and, 107–8; Chinese immigrant assimilation through, 65, 205–6; interethnic alliances and, 183–84; Mexican American assimilation in, 194; "old-boy" network and, 62–63; political functions of, 5–6, 65–66
civil rights: alliance with progressives for, 101–4; immigration patterns and, 13–14
class: among Asian immigrants, 14–15, 24; card club dispute and, 178–84, 256n.36; in civic organizations, 65–66; electoral politics and, 254n.10; ethnicity and, 230–31; growth control politics and, 82–83, 88–93, 195–97, 249n.18; Monterey Park politics and, 75; native-born vs. immigrant residents, 26–27; progressive-capitalist alliance and, 102–4
Club Amistad, 41
Club Bella Vista, 41
coalition politics, emergence of, in Monterey Park, 4–5
commercial property, "old-boy" network and, 63
community, defined, 36–37, 245n.3; grassroots organization and, 35–58; multiethnic community building case studies, 40–57; process of building, 57–58
Community Concern Committee, 177
Community Design Advisory Committee, 89–90
Community Volunteer Office (Monterey Park), 38–40
Concerned Citizen Organization, parole office dispute, 52
Congress of Racial Equality, 11
Couch, Betty, 74, 109–11, 113, 116–20, 129–30, 149; card club dispute and, 176; cultural diversity under, 224; declines reelection bid, 162, 166; endorsement of Chu, 167; as established residents' representative, 151–60; history of Monterey Park and, 219
Couch, Harry, 175–76
Cousins, Norman, 97–99
Coyote Canyon, 220
Cronkite, Walter, 97
cross-ethnic interaction. *See also* interethnic alliances; in voting patterns, 115–16, 119–21; Russell Avenue Neighborhood Watch Association and, 49–52
Cuban immigrants, ethnic economy of, 244n.32
cultural norms of behavior, grassroots community building and, 51–52

Davis, Louise: card club dispute, 176; endorsement of Chu, 80; grassroots organization for, 72–73; history of Monterey Park and, 219, 226; municipal election of 1992, 162, 167–69
Davis, Mike, 89, 91
Dearfield Plaza, development of, 29
de Llamas, Lloyd, 80, 84
Democratic Party: Monterey Park politics and, 66–69; Official English movement and, 98–99
development. *See* economic development
Di Leonardo, Micaela, 188
Diederich, Evelyn, 176–78
Diho supermarket, 29–30
diversity: American identity and, 207–9; defined, 8–9; dilemmas of, 149–84; meaning of, 232–34; negotiating culture for, 215–25; official versions of, 223–24; politics of, 147–48, 226–37

earthquakes, community building through, 47–48
Eastside Optimist Club, 107, 110
economic aid, Asian immigration and, 14

economic development. *See also* growth control movement *and* real estate development; card clubs seen as spur for, 175–76; Chinese ethnic economy and, 32–33; Chinese immigrants linked with, 81; established residents-newcomer confrontation over, 151–60; ethnic diversity regarding, 166–67; growth control and, 79, 82–83, 90–93; interethnic alliances for, 159–60, 168–69; Monterey Park politics and, 69–71; municipal elections of 1988 and, 110–11; political break linked with, 63–66; recall of Official English leaders and, 104–6; role of leadership in, 232
economic zones, in Monterey Park, 13
educational levels: among immigrant residents, 26, 243n.22; ethnicity in electoral politics and, 145–46, 162; voting patterns and, 114–15
electoral politics: Anglo voting patterns, 120–21; candidates and issues, 109–11, 167–68; card club dispute, 174–82; Chinese immigrant empowerment through, 116–17, 161–63, 169–71; economic development issue and, 166–67; ethnic tensions at polls, 111–13; ethnicity and candidate choice, 113–14, 142–47; fund raising for, ethnic patterns in, 136–37, 252n.17; interethnic alliances and, 144–47, 163, 168–69, 171–74; Japanese-American voting patterns, 117–19; Latino voting patterns, 119–20; municipal elections of 1988, 109–21; municipal elections of 1990, 135–47; municipal elections of 1992, 160–74; negotiated development and, 168–69; regional trends in, 169; voting patterns, 114–16
Eng, Mike, 102, 132
English language proficiency: among newcomers and established residents, 19–20, 77; community participation and, 55–56; ethnic-interethnic dialectic and, 159; generational differences in Chinese ethnicity and, 209–11, 259n.29
English Only movement. *See* Official English movement
entrepreneurship, among Chinese immigrants, 28–33
established residents. *See also* native-born residents; ambivalence regarding ethnicity among, 99–100, 229–30, 250n.39; Chu's 1992 campaign and, 164–66; class consciousness of, 230–31; confrontation with immigrant power, 151–60; ethnicity and identity crisis among, 190–203; growth control politics and, 81–93; Japanese American voting patterns and, 118–19; newcomers, polarization with, 152–53; "old-boy" network and, 62–66; parole dispute and, 53–56; relations with city government, 59–62
ethnic economy, dominance of Chinese in, 12–13, 28–33
ethnic empowerment: assimilation not linked with, 194–97; focus on, 7; Monterey Park politics and, 75–76, 101–22; interethnic alliances and, 140–41; municipal elections of 1992 and, 161
ethnicity. *See also* interethnic alliances; accommodation and, 229–30; assimilation and, 185–214; candidate choice and, 114–15, 142–44; card club dispute and, 174–84; economic development issues and, 166–67; "hyphenated" Americans and, 190–203; in Monterey Park Sports Club, 44–46; interethnic currents balanced with, 144–47, 158–60; labeling of, 3–4, 241n.4; Mexican American sense of, 191–97; Monterey Park politics and, 71–74, 75–76, 106–9, 111–13, 247n.24; nativism and, 123–48; Official English movement, 97–99; primacy of, for Chinese, 116–17; Russell Avenue Neighborhood Watch Association and, 47–49; senior citizens' maintenance of, 40–42; "unhyphenated" Americans and, 186–90; voting patterns and, 114–15, 121–22, 142–44
ethnography: Monterey Park research using, 6–7; research on interethnic alliances and, 125–35
Eu, March Fong, 124, 202
European immigrants, settlement patterns of, 14–15. *See also* Anglos
exit polls: municipal elections of 1988, 112–13; municipal elections of 1990, 138–39, 252n.19; municipal elections of 1992, 170–71; voting patterns, 114–15

family reunification policy, immigrant settlement patterns and, 15, 18, 252n.6

Federation for American Immigration Reform (FAIR), 96
festivals: culture of diversity at, 220–23; managed diversity in, 233–34; newcomer-established resident cooperation regarding, 38
Fiebelkorn, Hal, 64–65, 72
flag ordinances, 104
Fong, Timothy, ix, 220
Ford Foundation, 7
foreign policy: Asian immigration and, 14
Fourth of July celebrations, cultural diversity at, 221–23
fund raising, ethnic patterns in, 136–37, 162, 165–66, 252n.17, 254n.17
Furutani, Warren, 132–33

gambling: card club proposal, 28–29, 174–82, 255n.26; crime linked with, 256n.36; interethnic alliances regarding, 180–82; Monterey Park resistance to, 57, 255n.28
Gardena, 255n.29
gender power, Monterey Park politics and, 74
generational differences: Chinese immigrant ethnicity and, 209–11; interethnic alliances and, 159, 163
George Washington monument, interethnic alliance against, 126–29
Gilman, Irv, 90, 174–75
Glazer, Nathan, 99
gold mining, Chinese immigration and, 23–24
Golden Age Association, 41
Golden Age Village and Manor, 41, 205
Gonzales, Arnold (Rev.), 178
grassroots organization: card club dispute and, 177–82; community building through, 35–58; defeat of Hatch and, 126–29; growth control politics and, 90–93, 249n.22; Monterey Park politics and, 57, 72–74; women's role as, 53–56
growth control movement: alliance with Hatch undermined, 130–33; American identity crisis and, 207–9; Anglo support for, 120–21; anti-Chinese sentiments and, 91–93; card club dispute and, 175–82, 255n.28; Chinese ethnic empowerment and, 32–33, 116–17; City Council role in, 123–24, 129–30; class politics and, 75; established residents-newcomer confrontation over, 83–88, 151–60; ethnicity balanced with interethnic currents regarding, 106–9, 145–50, 166–67; history of, 88–93; interethnic alliances and dialectic on, 102–4, 145–47, 159–60; Japanese Americans and, 118–19; Latinos and, 119–20; municipal elections of 1988 and, 110–11, 113–14; municipal election of 1990 and, 136–40; Official English movement and, 104–6; political endorsements and, 69–70, 137–38; role of leadership, 232; terminology of, 247n.1

Harmony Week, 5, 38, 149, 158
Hatch, Barry, 43; Congressional campaign of, 237; councilwomen united against, 129–30; electoral defeat of, 124–26, 135–37, 139–40, 202; ethnicity balanced with interethnic currents against, 106–9, 142–47, 228; Fourth of July celebrations revived by, 222; fund-raising by, 252n.17; grassroots opposition to, 126–29; growth control movement and, 81, 130–33; moves from Monterey Park, 156; municipal elections of 1988 and, 113; Official English movement and, 94–97, 99; opposition to affirmative action and bilingualism, 154–55; recall campaign against, 104–6; Republican Party and, 133–34; rescinding of Resolution 9004 and, 103; "Stroll Down Memory Lane" celebration, 216–18
Hayakawa, S. I., 94
Hispanic Round Table, 104, 109, 196
history in Monterey Park, culture of diversity and, 218–20
Hoa Binh supermarket, 30
Homecoming Day celebrations, 134–35
homeowners' associations, growth control politics and, 91
Hong Kong: Chinese immigrants from, 22, 26–27, 243n.16
Hong Kong Supermarket, 30
Houseman, Chris, 81, 129, 177, 248n.7
Hsieh, Frederic, 63–64, 79, 247n.1; entrepreneurship of, 28–30; on growth control politics, 91–92

Ige, George, 67, 80, 107
immigrants. *See also specific groups, e.g.,* Chinese immigrants; class resources of, 230–31; community participation by, 54–56; community vision of, 35–36; established residents' polarization toward, 153–55; global context of migration, 13–18; pessimism regarding, 3, 239n.1; politics of control regarding, 7–8; socioeconomic profiles, 24–27; undocumented immigrant estimates, 18–19
Immigration and Naturalization Act of 1965, 13–14, 19, 24
Immigration and Naturalization Service (INS): Taiwan immigration patterns reported by, 22–23; undocumented immigrant estimates, 18–19
income levels: ethnic differences in, 13; ethnicity in electoral politics and, 13, 145–46; in Monterey Park electoral candidates, 162; of native-born vs. immigrant residents, 25–26; voting patterns and, 114–15
Ing, Gloria, 180–81
Ing, Mitchell, 180–81, 235
integration in Monterey Park, 11, 13
interethnic alliances: American identity crisis and, 202–3; card club controversy and, 180–84; Chinese immigrants' ethnicity and, 212–13; culturally diverse festivals and, 222–23; defeat of Hatch and, 124–26; ethnicity balanced with, 144–47, 158–60; growth control movement and, 166–69; Latinos and, 194–97; Monterey Park politics and, 101–22; municipal elections of 1990 and, 137–40; municipal elections of 1992 and, 169–74; nativism and, 123–40; politics and, 137–38, 149–50; progressive-capitalist elements in, 101–4
International Daily News, 30, 163
international trade, Chinese ethnic economy and, 31–33
Irvine, Rod, 62
Italian Americans, 188

Japanese American Club, 41
Japanese Americans: American identity of, 197–203; attitude toward Chinese immigrants among, 27, 199–203; card club controversy and, 180–82; Democratic Party politics and, 66–69; ethnicity balanced with interethnic currents among, 107–8, 144–45; growth control movement and, 117–19; migration of, to Monterey Park, 10; newcomers and established residents, estimates of, 19–20; Official English movement supported by, 98; racism perceived by, 85; socioeconomic profile, 25–26; voting patterns among, 114–16, 142–44, 171, 173–74
Jewish Americans: ethnicity and, 188; party politics and, 66–69
Jinn, Joseph, 243n.18

"Kaffee Klatch," demise of "old-boy" network and, 64–66
karaoke, at Monterey Park festivals, 221, 223
Kiang, Samuel, 57, 68, 125; on assimilation, 205; calculation of ethnic votes by, 161; card club proposal and, 174–83; as Chinese immigrants' representative, 142–44, 151–60; confrontation with Chu, 150; cultural diversity under, 224, 228; erosion of support for, 156–58; ethnic-interethnic dialectic and, 144–47, 158–60; loses reelection campaign in 1994, 235; municipal election of 1990 and, 136–40, 252n.17; municipal election of 1992 and, 162–63, 167–68, 170–71; Official English movement and, 98
King, Rodney, 239n.1
Koreans, immigrant settlement patterns, 15
Kristol, Irving, 99
KSCI TV, 163
Kuomintang, 22–23

Langley Senior Citizen Center: community building through, 38–43, 58, 80; Latino presence in, 194; volunteerism at, 73
language. *See* bilingualism; English proficiency; Official English movement
Latinos. *See also* Mexican Americans; age levels among, 20; America-first attitudes among, 191–97; attitude toward Chinese immigrants among, 27; candidate choice and ethnicity among, 143–44; card club dispute and, 174–84, 255n.29; Chinese entrepreneurs' employment of, 30; Chinese immigrants'

Latinos (*cont.*)
stereotyping of, 212–13; Chinese takeover of Church feared by, 235; defeat of Hatch and, 127–29; electoral politics and, 66–69, 106–9, 160–63; ethnicity and identity crisis among, 190–97; growth control movement and, 70, 195–97; history of Monterey Park and, 220; immigrant settlement patterns, 10, 14–18; in Monterey Park Sports Club, 43–47; interethnic alliances with Chinese among, 145–47, 213; newcomers and established residents, estimates of, 5, 19–20; Official English movement and, 98, 104–6; opposition to Kiang among, 159; political empowerment of, 66–69, 106–9, 160–63, 228; progressive multiculturalism among, 71; racism against, 84–88; Republican Party and, 134; Russell Avenue Neighborhood Watch Association and, 48–49; socioeconomic profile of, 26–27; terminology regarding, 241n.4; undocumented immigrant estimates, 18–19; voting patterns among, 114–16, 119–20, 141–42, 171
Lau, David T., 226, 259n.2
Lau, James H. K., 177
League of United Latin American Citizens, 5. *See* LULAC
League of Women Voters, 162
Lewis, Gershon, 67
Lewis, Mark, 62, 151–60, 179
Lions Manor, 41, 64, 112
Literacy for All in Monterey Park (LAMP), 38–40
literacy programs, community spirit developed by, 39–40
Little Taipei Lions Club, 37, 65
Lo, Clarence, 60
local government, Chinese ethnic economy and, 32–33
Los Angeles, Chinese businesses in, 31; pessimistic images of, 3–4
Los Angeles County: budget crisis in, 175–76; gambling referendums in, 180, 256n.36
Los Angeles County Democratic Central Committee, 69
Los Angeles County Human Relations Commission, 129, 199
Los Angeles Times, 169–71, 235, 243n.18
LULAC (West San Gabriel Valley League of United Latin American Citizens), 102, 109, 131–33, 196–97, 213
Luna, Dora, 178–79

Mandarin Realty, 29
Manibog, G. Monty, 80, 107, 110, 248n.7
Martin, Tina, 181
Martinez, Diane, 108, 177
Martinez, Matthew, 67, 108, 167
mayor's office: cultural diversity through, 223–24; Monterey Park political structure and, 61–62, 123, 251n.1
media: Chinese ethnic economy and, 30; Chinese press in Monterey Park, 152–53; Chinese-language television, 243n.18; co-ethnic interpretations of assimilation in, 205–6; images of Monterey Park in, 4, 80–81, 248n.4
Mercer, Korbena, 260n.4
Mexican American Legal Defense Educational Fund (MALDEF), 161
Mexican Americans. *See also* Latinos; alliances with Chinese immigrants, 213; anti-Chinese sentiments among, 194–95; as established Monterey Park residents, 19–20; ethnic politics and, 108–9; ethnicity and identity crisis among, 191–97; Monterey Park Sports Club and, 43–44; political endorsements by, 138; Republican Party embrace of, 134; voting patterns among, 119–20
minority rights: politics of, 71–72; progressive-capitalist alliance for, 102–4
mobility. *See* assimilation
mobilization of fear, in parole office dispute, 53
Molina, Gloria, 108, 177, 181
Monterey Park: "All-America City" designation, 80–83, 101; card club proposal in, 174–82; Democratic Party politics in, 66–69; history of diversity in, 227–28; history of ethnic transformation, 10–34; immigrant settlement patterns in, 15–18; impact of Chinese ethnic economy on, 32–33; as "Little Taipei," 10, 30, 37; migration of Chinese businesses from, 32; municipal elections of 1988, 109–21; municipal elections of 1992, 160–74; "old-boy" network in, 62–66; parole office dispute, 52–57;

politics of diversity in, 150; 75th anniversary celebration, 226
Monterey Park Boys and Girls Club, 176, 224
Monterey Park Community Relations Commission, 67, 84, 149
Monterey Park Democratic Club, 66–69, 102, 131–33, 138, 162
Monterey Park General Employees' Association, 151
Monterey Park Historical Society, 5, 35, 73, 218–20
Monterey Park Kiwanis Club, 62, 65, 205–6
Monterey Park Lions Club, 62, 64–65, 72, 108
Monterey Park Planning Commission, 129
Monterey Park Progress, 90, 94
Monterey Park Republican Club, 69, 252n.17
Monterey Park Senior Citizen Club, 41
Monterey Park Sports Club, 43–46; community building through, 43–46, 57; Latino presence in, 194; newcomer and established residents cooperation regarding, 38
Monterey Park Taxpayers Association, 89
multiculturalism: City Council structure and, 124; city councilwomen's support for, 130; empowerment through, 140–41; focus on, 7; festivals in Monterey Park, 221–23; history of diversity in Monterey Park and, 227–28; interethnic alliances and, 215; Langley Senior Center case study, 40–43; Monterey Park Sports Club case study, 43–46; Official English movement and, 94; parole office fight case study, 52–57; politics of diversity and, 71–74, 106–9, 138–39, 147–48, 227–28; Russell Avenue Neighborhood Watch Association case study, 47–52
Myers, J. Richard, 175–76

Nance, Christopher, 223
National Municipal League, 80
nationalism, multiethnicity and, 207–9
native-born residents. *See also* Anglos *and* established residents; community vision of, 35; defined, 8; definition of, 19–20; lack of contact with newcomers among, 37; "old-boy" network of Monterey Park and, 62–66; Russell Avenue Neighborhood Watch Association and, 47–52; social profile of, 18–24; socioeconomic profiles, 24–27; stereotyping of Chinese immigrants by, 20–21
nativism. *See also* Americanism *and* American identity; crisis and, 208–9; Chinese Exclusion Act, 23; cultural diversity of festivals and, 223; emergence of diversity and, 147–48, 215, 228, 232–34; growth control politics and, 81–83; interethnic politics and, 123–48, 163; Japanese American attitudes toward, 201–2; Monterey Park politics and, 69–70, 76; municipal elections of 1988 and, 111, 113; newcomers' impact on, 156; Official English movement and, 93–99; progressive-capitalist alliance against, 101–4; Republican Party rejection of, 134
neighborhood associations, community building through, 5, 37
neoconservatism, Official English movement and, 99
networking. *See* "old-boy" networks; interethnic alliances
New York City, Chinese immigration to, 22–23, 31–32
newcomers. *See also* established residents; class consciousness of, 230–31; community building process and, 58; defined, 8, 19–20; established residents' attitudes toward, 37, 84–88, 152–53; growth control politics and, 79, 90–93; "hyphenated" American identity of, 190–203; political development of, 66–69, 76–77, 156, 245n.25; parole dispute and, 54–56; social profile of, 18–24
"Night Stalker" incident, 47
NIMBY ideology: growth control politics and, 71, 92; interethnic alliances and, 181–82; political endorsements and, 138

Official English movement, 43, 68; American identity crisis and, 189–90, 194–95, 207–9; Anglo politics and, 81–83; capitalist/progressive alliance against, 101–4; City Council structure and, 123–24; interethnic politics and, 93–99, 121–22;

Official English movement (*cont.*)
Latino opposition to, 120; leadership of, 95–97, 104–6, 129; municipal elections of 1988 and, 110; terminology of, 247n.1
"old-boy" network, demise of, in Monterey Park, 62–66
Olympic Restaurant, 64
Omni Bank, 29
Orange County, gambling referendums in, 180, 256n.36
Organ, Dr. Stan, 44
Organ, Linda, 224
Organization of Chinese Americans, 163

Pa, Abel, 152
Pacific Rim: Asian immigration and, 14; Chinese ethnic economy and, 31–32
Paris Restaurant, 64
parole office dispute, community building through, 52–57
Parra, Jim, 47
People for the American Way, 133–34
People's Republic of China, Chinese immigrants from, 22
Peralta, Rudy, 80–82, 100, 177, 196
Pla, George, 254n.17
pluralistic problem-solving, community building and, 42–43
Podhoretz, Norman, 99
Police, brutality of, 239n.1
Police Reserves, 30, 38
political clubs. *See also specific political clubs;* alliances among, 131–33; Asian American politics and, 107–8; campaigns and, 66–69
Political Data, Inc., 253n.20, 255n.25
politics in Monterey Park. *See also* electoral politics; card club dispute, 174–82; city government structure and, 59–62; class structure and, 75; demise of "old-boy" network, 62–66; Democratic Party legacy in, 66–69; diversity's impact on, 226–37; ethnicity as force in, 75–76, 106–9, 121–22; gender-based power, 74; growth control movement, 69–71; history of diversity in, 227–28; ideology of incorporation and inclusion in, 234; impact of immigrants on, 59–78; interethnic endorsements, 137–38; municipal elections of 1988, 109–21; municipal elections of 1990 and, 135–47; nativists and, 69–70; newcomers incorporated into, 76–77, 155–56; progressive multiculturalists, 71; transition of power in, 77–78, 231–32; women and, 72–74
populism, growth control politics and, 70, 81–82, 90–91, 249n.22
poverty levels, of native-born vs. immigrant residents, 25–26. *See also* income levels
"problematic" community: defined, 36, 245n.3
professional immigrants: Chinese immigrants as, 24; role of, in ethnic economy, 30; visa allocations of, 14–15
Progressive Movement, Monterey Park politics and, 60–61
progressive multiculturalism: alliance against racism and, 101–4; Monterey Park politics and, 69, 71; recall of Official English leaders and, 104–6
property ownership, class politics and, 75. *See also* economic development; real estate development
Proposition 13, 88–89, 249n.22
Proposition 63, 95, 103–4
Proposition 187, 237, 239n.1
Proposition A, 89
Proposition K, 89
Proposition L, 89
Proposition S, 139–40, 145–47, 171
Proposition U, 89
Public Use Microdata Samples (PUMS), 18, 242n.12, 243n.16
Purvis, Marie: card club dispute, 180; ethnic support for, 142–44, 147; as established residents' representative, 151–60; festivals under, 223; fundraising by, 252n.17; municipal elections of 1988, 111; municipal elections of 1990, 136; Proposition S and, 139–40; reelection of, 235; women and, 74

Quang Hoa supermarket, 30

Rabins, Phyllis, 181
racism: capitalist/progressive alliance against, 101–4; card club dispute and, 178–82, 256n.36; growth control movement and, 70–71, 84–88, 91–93, 100, 195–97, 249n.23; Japanese Ameri-

cans and, 197–203; newcomers vs. established residents and, 77–78; Official English movement and, 95–100, 104–6; politics of diversity and, 157–58
RAMP (Residents Association of Monterey Park): card club dispute and, 150, 174, 176–78; criticism of Kiang by, 236; endorsement of Chu, 167–68, 173; endorsements by, 137–38; Hatch/growth control alliance undermined, 129–33; growth control politics and, 89, 91–92, 249n.26; interethnic politics and, 106–9, 122; Japanese American voting patterns and, 118–19; Latino connections with, 119–20, 195–96; municipal elections of 1988, 109–11, 113; municipal elections of 1990 and, 136–37; Official English movement and, 104–5
real estate development, 32–33; Chinese entrepreneurship and, 28–29; growth control movement and, 88–93; "old-boy" network and, 63–64
Record, The, 167–68
Reichenberger, Patricia: candidate choice and ethnicity, 142–47; growth control movement and, 81, 129; municipal elections of 1990, 135–37, 252n.17; Resolution 9004 and, 103–6
Republican Party: Chinese affiliation with, 114–15, 141–42; Hatch as liability for, 133–34, 138; Latinos and, 67; Official English movement and, 98; "old-boy" network of Monterey Park and, 62–66
research methodology, 5–9, 239n.3; Public Use Microdata Samples (PUMS), 18, 242n.12; regarding ethnicity and American identity, 257n.1; terminology regarding ethnic groups, 241n.4
Residential Design Review Board, 163
Residents Against Gambling in Monterey Park, 181
Resolution 9004, 83, 94–95, 100–104
restaurants: Chinese ethnic economy and, 29; growth-control politics and, 92–93; patterns of patronization by established residents among, 64–66
Riordan, Richard, 141
riots in Los Angeles, 239n.1
Ristic, George, 109–11, 113, 116–18
Rotary Club, 62, 64, 205–6
Rubin, Joseph, 79, 91–92, 247n.1
Russell Avenue Neighborhood Watch Association: community building through, 46–52, 58; potluck dinner for revitalized organization, 47–49
Ryan, Beth, 42–43

safety concerns, as mobilizing community force, 53
San Gabriel Valley: as regional Chinese business center, 31; Chinese immigrant ethnicity in, 204–8; immigrant settlement patterns in, 15–18; Mexican immigration to, 20; regional political trends in, 160, 169; suburban ethnic economy of, 28–30; Taiwan immigration patterns in, 22–23
San Marino, 208
Schlesinger, Arthur, 99
Schoff, Norman F., 179
Scudder, Laura, 218–19, 224
senior citizen organizations, 37, 41–43
Sequoia Park Homeowners' Association, 89
settlement patterns, of Asian immigrants, 15–18
signage issue, American identity crisis and, 207–9
Sister City programs, 80, 104
slow-growth movement. *See* growth control
Smith, Kevin, 102–4
smuggling rings, undocumented immigrant estimates, 18–19
socioeconomic characteristics, native-born vs. immigrant residents, 24–26, 141–42. *See also* educational and income levels
Song, Alfred H., 67, 107
Soroptimist International of Monterey Park, 73, 110, 162
S.O.S. (Save Our State), 237
Soto, Mary, 181
Southeast Asian countries, profile of immigrants from, 26–27
Southern California Chinese Radio Broadcasting Company, 152
Southwest Voter Registration Education Project, 108–9, 113–14, 251n.11, 252n.19

Southwest Voter Registration Institute, 113–14, 251n.11, 252n.19
stereotyping: of Asian immigrants, 24–26; by Chinese immigrants, 212–13; of Chinese by established residents, 21, 47, 85–88
"Stroll Down Memory Lane" celebration, 215–18
Su, Lucia, 177
Suarez, Omero (Dr.), 124
supermarkets: Chinese ethnic economy and, 29–30

Taiwanese American Citizens League, 162–63
Taiwanese immigrants: mainland Chinese among, 22–24, 243n.16; cultural behavior patterns in, 51; ethnic economy of, 31–33; ethnicity among, 186; influence of, in Monterey Park, 22–23, 243n.18; socioeconomic profile of, 5, 25–27
Tan, Steven, 104
Tanton, John, 94, 96
taxpayers' revolt: Chinese ethnic economy and, 33; city politics and, 60–61; growth control movement and, 88–89
Tom, Betty Gin, 181
Torres, Art, 190

undocumented immigrants, estimates of, 18–19
United Democratic Club (UDC), 5, 68, 73, 131–33, 138, 162
United Neighborhood Organizations (UNO), 177–79
United States, ethnic transformation of, 13, 241n.5
University of California, Los Angeles, Asians as freshmen, 243n.22
USA Today, 80

Valenzuela, Rita, 74, 167–70, 172–73, 180, 255n.18
Van de Kamp, John, 124
Van Maanen, John, 7
Vidal, Gore, 97
Vietnamese immigrants: age levels among, 20; Chinese entrepreneurs' employment of, 30; classification as newcomers, 19–20; multiculturalism among, 86–87; as percentage of San Gabriel immigrant population, 21–22; Russell Avenue Neighborhood Watch Association and, 49; socioeconomic profile of, 25
volunteerism: Chinese immigrant assimilation through, 206; in Monterey Park Sports Club, 43–44; multiethnicity and, 80; newcomer-established resident cooperation regarding, 38–40; political importance of, 65–66, 73–74; rates of, by ethnic groups, 245n.6
voter registration and turnout patterns: Anglo voters, 120–21; by ethnic group, 114; candidate choice and ethnicity, 142–44; ethnic and cross-ethnic trends, 115–16, 229–30; ethnic voter profiles, 141–42; ethnicity balanced with interethnic currents, 144–47; Japanese American voters, 117–19; Latino voters, 119–20; multiethnic empowerment through, 140–41, 253n.20; municipal elections of 1988 and, 114, 251n.11; municipal elections of 1990 and, 139–40; municipal elections of 1992 and, 170–71; primacy of ethnicity for Chinese and, 116–17
Voting Rights Act, 190

Wai, Bonnie, 163, 166–67, 170
Wallerstein, Immanuel, 260n.5
Waxman, Henry, 108
West San Gabriel Valley Asian Pacific Democratic Club, 5, 68, 102, 108, 126, 131, 138, 158, 202
Willner, Irv, 181, 249n.26
Willner, Ruth, 68, 102, 138, 177, 181, 249n.26
women: card club controversy and, 181–82, 256n.37; City Council structure and, 123–24, 129–30; defeat of Hatch and, 126–30; emergence of diversity and, 5, 72–74, 228; as grassroots organizers, 53–56; history of Monterey Park and, 219–20; support for Chu among, 166
Wong, Charles, ix, 204
Woo, Michael, 141, 202
World Journal, 30

Wu, Frances (Dr.), 205
Wu, Victoria, 111, 117

xenophobia: cultural diversity of festivals and, 223; Monterey Park politics and, 124–25; Official English movement and, 95–97, 100; progressive-capitalist alliance against, 103

Yee, Cindy, 181
youth organizations, 37